A TRANSATLANTIC HISTORY OF HAITIAN VODOU

A TRANSATLANTIC HISTORY OF HAITIAN VODOU

Rasin Figuier, Rasin Bwa Kayiman,
and the Rada and Gede Rites

Benjamin Hebblethwaite

University Press of Mississippi / Jackson

The University Press of Mississippi is the scholarly publishing agency of
the Mississippi Institutions of Higher Learning: Alcorn State University,
Delta State University, Jackson State University, Mississippi State University,
Mississippi University for Women, Mississippi Valley State University,
University of Mississippi, and University of Southern Mississippi.

www.upress.state.ms.us

The University Press of Mississippi is a member
of the Association of University Presses.

Copyright © 2021 by University Press of Mississippi
All rights reserved
Manufactured in the United States of America

First printing 2021
∞

The lyrics of Rasin Figuier and Rasin Bwa Kayiman appear with the permission of
Jean Altidor and Mass Konpa Productions.

The painting *Migration des Dieux* is reprinted with the permission of
Edouard Duval-Carrié.

The maps are included courtesy of Joe Aufmuth, Geospatial Consultant at University
of Florida's George A. Smathers Libraries.

Library of Congress Cataloging-in-Publication Data

Names: Hebblethwaite, Benjamin, author.
Title: A transatlantic history of Haitian Vodou: Rasin Figuier, Rasin Bwa Kayiman,
and the Rada and Gede Rites / Benjamin Hebblethwaite.
Description: Jackson: University Press of Mississippi, 2021. | Includes
bibliographical references and index.
Identifiers: LCCN 2021022939 (print) | LCCN 2021022940 (ebook) |
ISBN 978-1-4968-3560-4 (hardback) | ISBN 978-1-4968-3561-1 (paperback) |
ISBN 978-1-4968-3562-8 (epub) | ISBN 978-1-4968-3563-5 (epub) |
ISBN 978-1-4968-3564-2 (pdf) | ISBN 978-1-4968-3565-9 (pdf)
Subjects: LCSH: Vodou music—Haiti—History and criticism. | Vodou music—
Social aspects—Haiti. | Rasin Bwa Kayiman (Musical group) | Rasin Figuier
(Musical group) | Vodou—Haiti—Rites and ceremonies. | Vodou—Haiti. | Rada
(Vodou rite) | Vodou—Haiti—Rituals. | Hueda (African people)—Rites and
ceremonies. | Haiti—Religious life and customs. | Haiti—Social life and customs. |
Benin—History. | Allada (Benin)—History. | Abomey (Benin)—History. |
BISAC: SOCIAL SCIENCE / Ethnic Studies / Caribbean & Latin American
Studies | RELIGION / History
Classification: LCC ML3197 .H42 2021 (print) | LCC ML3197 (ebook) |
DDC 782.3/9675—dc23
LC record available at https://lccn.loc.gov/2021022939
LC ebook record available at https://lccn.loc.gov/2021022940

British Library Cataloging-in-Publication Data available

CONTENTS

Foreword vii

Acknowledgments ix

Introduction: Rada and Gede in Transatlantic History 3

Chapter 1: The African Political Roots of Haitian Vodou:
    The Aja-Fon and Gedevi-Yoruba Kingdoms and the Slave Trade 45

Chapter 2: The African Spiritual Roots of Haitian Vodou:
    The Religious Cultures of the Aja-Fon and Gedevi-Yoruba 91

Chapter 3: The Rada Rite in Haiti: Rasin Figuier's *Vodou Lakay* 134

Chapter 4: The Gede Rite in Haiti: Rasin Bwa Kayiman's *Guede* 184

Chapter 5: Chains and Rainbows over the Atlantic 232

Notes 241

Discography and Bibliography 249

Index 261

FOREWORD

I've always been interested in the effects of the transatlantic slave trade on the understanding and perceptions that Haitian Vodouists have of the Vodou spirits, the *lwa* or gods they venerate. I've always wondered if the attributes of the different *lwas* are exactly the same on either side of the Atlantic. Some anthropologists have delved into the matter, but there is no real go-to text that elucidates the ways that the transatlantic slave trade impacted how those Vodou spirits are perceived or how they are different from those on the African side, mainly in the Bight of Benin. It is evident that the slave traders had no interest in collecting such information, as their activity was simply to gather enslaved people for work in the New World plantation system, and, as their lifespan was certainly short in view of the treatment they received there, those extremely important facts were irrelevant for their purposes. The only types of information they sought were the places of origin of the enslaved people and, of utmost importance, whether the enslaved people were from a region considered to be docile or not. Such places were the kingdoms established in the Benin region such as the kingdom of Dahomey and the kingdom of Allada. These were small states with a militaristic penchant, and they excelled in delivering their war captives as enslaved people for the insatiable plantation system in the Americas.

In Haiti, the core group of the displaced cosmogony accompanying the enslaved people was hence from that region in West Africa composed mainly of Fon citizens of all ilk and a good number of warriors who proved not so docile in the aftermath. As in most religions, there is a hierarchy in the world of Vodou deities, and one of the most important is depicted on the cover of this book. Danbala is akin to god, and his major attribute is that of crossing worlds and being the guardian of all crossroads. The journey to the Americas was fraught with dangers, and he was the one called upon to guarantee a safe passage. One would think that the god of the sea, Agwe, would be the one invoked on that journey, but Agwe, here represented by the small boat with a bull's head, was also dependent on Danbala's whim to achieve that crossing. In the boat, he is carrying the palm tree that will ultimately represent the Haitian people.
—Edouard Duval-Carrié

ACKNOWLEDGMENTS

The National Endowment for the Humanities Collaborative Research Award (RZ-51441-12) funded teams from the University of Florida and Duke University to collect and analyze resources for "The Archive of Haitian Religion and Culture" (www.dloc.com/vodou). Thanks are owed to Lydia Medici and Mary Macklem at the NEH for their help administering the grant. The University of Florida's Laurie Taylor, Sophia Acord, and Beth De Farber helped throughout the project, as did Laurent Dubois, Jacques Pierre, Eric Barstow, Claire Payton, and Deborah Jenson at Duke University.

I thank my friend and colleague Jean Altidor, proprietor of Mass Konpa Records in Miami, for his support of this book. Jean's dedication as a producer and publisher of Haitian music and films laid the foundation for this study of Rasin Figuier and Rasin Bwa Kayiman.

Thanks are due to Edouard Duval-Carrié for authorizing the reprinting of his painting *Migration des Dieux* on the cover and for the original text he composed about it.

University of Florida students and faculty Tahiri Jean-Baptiste, Myrlande Denis, Megan Raitano, Alexandra Cenatus, Andrew Tarter, and Richard Freeman made valuable contributions to the task of transcribing and translating the lyrics of Rasin Figuier and Rasin Bwa Kayiman in chapters 3 and 4.

The NEH grant supported fieldwork in Haiti, south Florida, and Cuba between 2012 and 2017, providing teams from the University of Florida and Duke with opportunities to visit Vodou temples and ceremonies in Port-au-Prince, Gonaïves, Léogâne, Miami, and Santiago de Cuba. We thank oungan Michelet Tibosse Alisma at Société Linto Roi Trois Mystères in Miami, sèvitè Roger Bien-Aimé at Lakou Souvenance, sèvitè Prophète and sèvitè Marie-Carme Delvas at Lakou Soukri, sèvitè Dorsainville Estimé at Lakou Nan Badjo, oungan Ati Max Beauvoir at Le Peristyle de Mariani, sèvitè Bonapat at Jenndantor des Gonaïves, and manbo Micla at Société Makaya in Miami. We also thank the members of Société Halouba and Société Tipa Tipa for welcoming us at their ceremonies.

Our fieldwork in Gonaïves, Haiti, and in Miami was possible thanks to the generosity of oungan Michelet Tibosse Alisma, our guide and host on several journeys. He and his leadership team, including manbo Marie Alisma, oungan Emmanuel, and oungan Marcus Saint-Pierre, were exceptional hosts and teachers.

Departed friend, photographer, and anthropology librarian Richard Freeman ה״ע, who traveled to Miami, Haiti, and Cuba working on the NEH grant, may peace be upon him.

I thank Akíntúndé Akínyẹmí, Celucien Joseph, David Geggus, Silke Jansen, Michel Weber, Grete Viddal, Terry Rey, Patrick Bellegarde-Smith, Mariana Past, James Essegbey, Kelsey Bona, Stephan Kory, W. Gabriel Selassie I, Kiran Jayaram, Martin Tsang, Crystal Felima, Sean MacDonald, Kole Odutola, David Tezil, Robin Wright, Nick André, Lois Wilcken, Tracey Weldon-Stewart, Stephanye Hunter, and Meredith Babb for helping me at various stages of this project.

I am indebted to geospatial consultant Joe Aufmuth at the University of Florida's George A. Smathers Libraries for the volume's maps. Paul Losch and Richard Phillips at UF's Latin American and Caribbean Collection unfailingly supplied me with books and articles, and Amey Owen and Megan Meissner at the University of Florida's College of Liberal Arts and Sciences' Media Services kindly took photographs of Rasin Figuier's and Bwa Kayiman's album covers.

Craig Gill, Lisa McMurtray, Jordan Nettles, Laura Strong, and Pete Halverson at the University Press of Mississippi shared generously of their talents throughout the publication process. I am deeply grateful for Norman Ware's beautiful copy editing and meticulous attention to accuracy.

I gratefully acknowledge the contributions of my friends and informants Welele Doubout, Jean-Eddy Dieujuste, Jean-Sebastien Duvilaire, Jerry and Yvrose Gilles, Bozanfè Bon Houngan, manbo Sally Ann Glassman, and Marc Kenson Theus.

I thank my hermano Kevin Meehan and the peer reviewers for their labor of love improving and enriching the manuscript. I own the book's shortcomings.

I am thankful for the love and support of my parents, John and Meg Hebblethwaite. To my wife, Julie Rhee, and my daughters Chloe and Ellie, I give thanks for the love that has nourished my journey throughout this project.

A note on the text: In the spelling of Aja and Fon words from Aja, Fon, English, French, Dutch, and German sources, I strove as much as possible to use simplified and unaccented spellings for ease of reading. In many instances, this deviates from the standard orthography of contemporary Aja and Fon.

A TRANSATLANTIC HISTORY OF
HAITIAN VODOU

INTRODUCTION

Rada and Gede in Transatlantic History

INTRODUCTION

The religions of Vodun in Dahomey and Vodou in Saint-Domingue were inextricably interwoven with the powers of colonialism and slavery. The French colonial regime in Saint-Domingue tried to demolish African religions, while the practitioners of Vodou preserved and transformed them. In Dahomey, royal Vodun religious traditions sanctified the kingdom's militarism and slave raiding. Dahomey's royal family smashed the opposition that rallied in Vodun houses and sold enemies off. In Saint-Domingue, like-minded Africans and Creoles regrouped under a new Vodou to resist slavery, forge Haitian independence, and keep traditions on the scale of continents. While the French colonists undermined the biological family with slavery, Vodouists advanced a spiritual family, produced education through initiation, prepared medicine and poison, and constructed a strong culture of resistance in apocalyptic conditions. Vodun and Vodou, like the Christianity of the Europeans, were multipolar transatlantic traditions under which enslavers and liberators gathered to empower opposing projects.

An examination of the European slave trade with African kingdoms is critical if we hope to understand the historical and cultural roots of Haitian Vodou. Reviewing the politics, economics, and religious cultures of the Aja, Fon, and Gedevi peoples assists in understanding the story of important founding ethnic and linguistic groups in Saint-Domingue. In the context of Haitian studies, the politics and cultures of the people who were enslaved in the Bight of Benin and who preserved Vodou in the Caribbean are still submerged in deep waters, and require a multidisciplinary "Vodou hermeneutical methodology" if we hope to understand the origin and structure of the religion in Saint-Domingue and, later, Haiti.

The determination of enslaved people preserved service to the spirits in Saint-Domingue's merciless slave society. Across the Americas, the colonists and enslavers trampled on the faith of Vodouists and practitioners of African traditional religions, but in Saint-Domingue the servants of the spirits resisted and made their mark in the war for Haitian independence. Today, the Rada and Gede Rites of Haitian Vodou are prominent ritual traditions in this religion, which counts perhaps a million adherents worldwide. The Rada and Gede Rites are building blocks of the Sèvis Ginen (Ginen Service) system, which incorporates twenty-one rites, each the expression of unique African religious traditions. The Sèvis Ginen traditions are a kind of Vodou "school" where the *oungan ason* and *manbo ason* (male or female priests of the shaker[1]) teach, initiate, guide, and worship. Sèvis Ginen is one of several streams in Vodou, but it is the most studied, offering significant sources for this project.

My historical study in chapter 1 stretches between 1500 CE and the declaration of Haitian independence in 1804. The period examined in chapter 2's study of religion in the Bight of Benin stretches between 1700 and the present day. Chapters 3 and 4 focus on the meanings of Haitian Vodou songs by major Haitian *rasin* (roots) groups: Chapter 3 examines all the lyrics on Rasin Figuier's Rada album, *Vodou Lakay* (2004), and Chapter 4 examines all the lyrics on Rasin Bwa Kayiman's Gede album, *Guede* (2004).

Founded in 1697, French Saint-Domingue's slave society produced more sugar and coffee than anywhere else. After years of gruesome violence, General Jean-Jacques Dessalines and the "indigenous army" declared independence on January 1, 1804, establishing Haiti as one of the few nations to be founded by a coalition of formerly enslaved people, free Blacks, and free people of mixed race. The Haitian breakthrough was won after thirteen years of armed conflict that annihilated half of the population, mostly among the formerly enslaved.

Haitian Vodou is connected to African history and religion. Several studies have demonstrated Kongo influences in Haitian Vodou, including those by John Janzen (1982), Luc de Heusch (2000), and Christina Frances Mobley (2015). John K. Thornton (1998) sheds light on the African-controlled slave trade while tracing African cultural influences on both sides of the Atlantic. Pierre Verger (1957, 1999) illuminates connections in the direction of West Africa and Brazil, providing a blueprint for work on transatlantic religions.

In the Bight of Benin area that I focus on, Melville Herskovits (1937), and Melville Herskovits and Frances Herskovits (1938), write separately on Haiti and Dahomey, providing a basis for comparison. Guérin Montilus (1985) studies the connections between the kingdom of Allada and Haitian Vodou based on fieldwork in Haiti and Allada, Benin, illustrating a path-finding contribution in transatlantic research. Leslie Gerald Desmangles (2006) rightly calls for deeper study of "Dahomian" religion in order to inform the understanding of Haitian Vodou. Finally, documentary filmmaker Norluck Dorange (2009) investigates Haitian connections to Benin, including discussing the ways in which the African slave trade with Europeans impacted Haitians.

Notwithstanding these pioneering works, writings examining the history of the Bight of Benin and Saint-Domingue in the transatlantic period have mostly blossomed as separate fields of study. To wrestle with this disciplinary divide, and in the process to make discoveries about the links between these twin regions, I have dedicated the first half of this book to unraveling central features of Aja-Fon and Gedevi-Yoruba history and religion and the second half to interpreting the Rada and Gede Rites using a dialectical hermeneutical method that ping-pongs between Africa and the Caribbean.

Study of the Aja-Fon and Gedevi-Yoruba societies and religions during the transatlantic period has helped answer questions I had on Haitian Vodou. Research on Haitian Vodou hitherto has underutilized African and Africanist sources. Too few specialists are familiar with the powerful Dahomian kings in spite of the incalculable impact these slave sellers had on the lives of the mostly Vodunist captives whom they sold to European slave buyers, who quickly dispatched them on ships to destinations like Saint-Domingue.

Unconsciousness about the past is an inevitability of historical writing. Unconsciousness about the African component of the transatlantic slave trading system is an impediment, however, to understanding the multiracial slave trading system and its impact on Africans taken to Saint-Domingue. The traders and armies of the Aja-Fon and Yoruba kingdoms, among others, sold to Europeans the people who would lay the foundations of colonial Vodou. Scholars must examine kingdoms like Hueda, Allada, and Dahomey where Vodun was the state religion and where slave trading was the principal source of state revenue. Royal power, royal Vodun, and slave trading were interlocked systems like royal power, royal Catholicism, and slave trading in Europe. Of course, the slave trading in the United States, Jamaica, and other English colonies reflected Protestantism.

The Dahomian monarchy organized its religion around the veneration of the royal family's ancestors while it patronized the nonroyal communities that worshiped the national vodun spirits. Since Vodun specialists were the main sources of popular inspiration, the activities of influential vodunon (Vodun priests) and bokanto (diviners) were closely monitored by the royal administration (Bay 1998). The Dahomian elite developed a complex bureaucratic and military regime that was designed to supply the European slave traders with large numbers of captives. Although a small African elite drew immense profits from the slave trade, the flow of global commerce undercut local economic production, and stagnation set in as the slave trade syphoned off a regional workforce (Monroe 2014, 26).

The African political and economic elite became dependent on escalating European economic influences. Along the coast, imported commodities became status symbols. The limited, new material wealth that appeared in the region provoked competition and fighting between neighboring polities. Coastal populations had to manage contacts with Europeans' money, influence, and military and naval forces (Monroe 2014, 26). The capture and creation of enslaved people became the raw economic engine for members of the African elite to seize political and material advantages. Likewise, the purchase and enslavement of Africans became the economic engine of the European elite who controlled, primed, and profited from the trade in the colonies, where enslaved people worked to death producing commodities for European consumers.

SLAVE TRADING IN DAHOMEY

The victims of the slave trade, vulnerable practitioners of popular Vodun but also allies and members of the royal family who had fallen out of favor, were captured, held in stockades, transported, and sold by a powerful but small coterie of African slave traders. They received licenses from the kings of Dahomey, Allada, and Hueda, depending on the historical period. The armies of those kingdoms provided security and services for the slave traders. Their slave trading system persisted for three centuries.

The people they sold off to Saint-Domingue combined forces to end the dehumanization of slavery, defeat the French army and administration, and create Haiti, the first Black republic of the Americas. Africans and African Caribbean people used Vodun and Vodou to take, make, and keep power (Lando 2016, 29). Vodunists used Vodun to support or attack social, political, or economic projects in the kingdom of Dahomey. Vodouists in Saint-Domingue used Vodou along with the Haitian Creole language to transform the French slave colony into independent Haiti. Haitian Creole, Vodou religion, and the dream of a "sliver of land" provided the former enslaved people with a cohesive culture of resistance that led to the defeat of French and Catholic colonialism (Trouillot, Past, and Hebblethwaite 2021, 54). Vodun and Vodou are still used to take and keep power in Africa and the Caribbean, even if Christianity, Islam, and consumerism have profoundly curtailed their influence. Vodun and Vodou—like any religion connected to political power, or alienated from it—can embolden enslavers and liberators.

The religions of the African and European elites stood in a warped mirror-like relationship, the reflections asymmetrically bent for Europe's benefit. The African slave raiders and traders fed a massive European shipping operation centered on extracting enslaved people. The European slave traders, shippers, investors, and pro-slavery ideologues were linked to Christian Europe and its colonies.[2] Europeans maintained a toehold on the Aja coast in trading forts that the Aja and Aja-Fon kings authorized. The problem of African slave traders selling other captured Africans to Europeans is a historical reality that haunts the Atlantic world. It is so abhorrent a topic that it is rarely discussed in historical writing about Haitians or African Americans. Ibram X. Kendi's celebrated *Stamped from the Beginning: The Definitive History of Racist Ideas in America* (2016), for example, undertakes no discussion of the African-controlled side of the slave trade. Yet the disposableness of enslaved people in kingdoms like Dahomey, and the kingdom's use of enslavement to carry out ethnic or ideological cleansing, reflect underlying problems that are impossible for a project like this one to overlook. To begin to understand the history of Haitian Vodou, one must examine the African-controlled supply side of the system of slavery without losing sight of the role that European powers had in fueling the involvement of African middlemen.

In Saint-Domingue, enslaved Africans were in a hellish French and Catholic colony. While freedom fighters abolished slavery in 1793 and drove out the last of the white French citizens at the dawn of Haitian independence in 1804, no former enslaved person or free African could thwart the kingdom of Dahomey's slave trade. Europeans deported enslaved people on a one-way trip across the Atlantic. As a bestial culmination to the epochal tragedy, the French—who had drained the region's population—began a military occupation of the coast in 1872 and conquered the entire kingdom in the Second Franco-Dahomian War of 1894, usurping it as a French protectorate and then colony from 1904 until 1958.

There are no eyewitness accounts of slave markets in the Aja-Yoruba region during the early period of contact with Europeans (Akinjogbin 1967). Prior to European colonialism, slavery was nevertheless widespread because it was the only way to accumulate wealth, since land ownership was not possible (Thornton 1998). Criminals, debtors, and outcasts could become slaves. The types of slavery escalated rapidly once the European market materialized (Rodney 1966). European trading posts on the African coast imported commodities and luxury goods, fomenting acquisitiveness. Traders encouraged the purchase of weapons, which tore inter-African alliances asunder. The price of imported goods was set in human beings. Europeans only accepted enslaved people for the goods they offered to kings. Slave raiding by African state armies and private armed groups reflected an expanding enslaver industry that was responding to structural and contractual agreements (Monroe 2014, 27).

Although there were enslaved people in Dahomey, especially captives, criminals, and debtors, most people who were sold to Europeans had once been free or feudal citizens. The fate of enslaved people vis-à-vis their African captors was primarily related to the demands of European slave traders. Captives who were too weak, too old, or unwanted by European slave merchants were enslaved in Africa, ritually murdered, or, in rare cases, freed for a fee. In the noncapitalist economies of the region, the novelty of imported luxury goods accelerated competition, introducing the local elite to status symbols that magnified social and political claims while promoting long-distance trade (Monroe 2014, 27).

The peer polity competition for commodities turned the distribution of power on its head (Monroe 2014, 27). The shift of power wrought by the slave trade and the influx of commodities is encapsulated in the rise of the Aja Agasuvi family and its political spawn, the kingdom of Dahomey. The Dahomians' enslavement of the Gedevi-Yoruba people (circa 1625–1724) followed by their conquest of the Aja towns of Allada in 1724 and Hueda in 1727, and the enslavement of the survivors, were military and political events in Africa that ultimately thundered through Saint-Domingue, since so many of the victims of those conflicts were disembarked in the colony as enslaved people. Similarly, Nago-Yoruba raids on Dahomian towns and Dahomian raids on Nago-Yoruba towns likewise rumble across Saint-Domingue's history (circa 1650–1791).

The wealthy and socially stable members of the elite were able to create multicultural societies in towns like Abomey, Allada, Hueda, Badagry, and others. The culture in those towns reflected coexistence among diverse religious traditions. While enjoying multiculturalism among established groups, the economically dominant classes, especially kings, armies, and the commercial and trading elite, organized the deportation of millions of vulnerable Africans over several centuries. Those enslaved Africans practiced religions that venerated family ancestors and the national vodun spirits. To understand how it happened, the politics and religions of those kingdoms are examined in chapters 1 and 2.

AN OVERVIEW OF THE SITUATION IN SAINT-DOMINGUE, 1650–1803

The late seventeenth and eighteenth centuries are the most pertinent to understanding the implantation of African deportees and their cultures. This period of Saint-Domingue's history is characterized as a preindustrial and agrocommercial slave society (de Cauna 2009, 46). The transatlantic conflicts between France and the colony, and the racism and merciless exploitation of the enslaved inside the colony, created a powder keg (Casimir 2009, xi). Enslaved people suffered from poor nutrition and harsh labor conditions. Low fertility and a short life expectancy created a permanent demand for the importation of enslaved Africans (Geggus 2009, 11).

This section examines the conditions of African captives and free people in the French colony in order to provide a sketch of the world that incubated Vodou. According to some estimates, in 1687 the population of Saint-Domingue included 4,411 free whites and 3,358 Black enslaved people. In 1715, there were 6,668 free whites and 35,451 Black enslaved people. The Black enslaved population was 79,545 in 1730. In 1779, there were 32,650 free whites and 249,098 Black enslaved people (Popkin 2012, 12). On the eve of the insurrection of August 1791, there were at least 500,000 Black enslaved people, 30,000 free whites, and 28,000 free people of color. According to surviving records, 685,000 enslaved Africans were imported into Saint-Domingue between 1700 and the uprisings of 1791 (Dubois and Garrigus 2006, 13).

The slave colony of Saint-Domingue underwent explosive growth. Between 1700 and 1725, 2,000 men, women, and children were deported from Africa to Saint-Domingue annually. From 1725 until 1750, there were 4,000 captives disembarking annually. Between 1751 and 1775, the number of deportees doubled to 8,000 annually. From 1776 until 1789, the number expanded even more with 22,000 in 1777 and 48,000 in 1790, massive increases that in part set the stage for the uprisings (Dubois and Garrigus 2006, 12–13). Between 1784 and 1790, two-fifths of all African enslaved people brought to the Americas were disembarked in Saint-Domingue (Geggus 2009, 7). The thousands of African enslaved people, many of whom were soldiers captured in war, arrived in Cap-Français—today, Cap-Haïtien—and fanned out to the very plantations that would burn in 1791.

One-sixth of all enslaved people sent to Saint-Domingue—probably more than 114,000 people—perished on the fleets of French slave ships destined for that colony due to disease or mistreatment (Popkin 2012, 13). After sale, the surviving *bosal* (African-born) enslaved people were dispersed around the colony to be "seasoned" in the ways of "plantation culture." Today, the remains of over 8,500 plantations are scattered around Haiti (de Cauna 2009, 22). African captives had to eke out an existence and cope with the colonists' efforts to maximize their productivity.

Cap-Français was the biggest city in Saint-Domingue and one of the busiest ports in the Atlantic trading area (Popkin 2012, 10). Although Port-au-Prince became the administrative capital of Saint-Domingue in 1752, it was far more modest in size. The northern town was the main port for importing African enslaved people and exporting the agricultural products they produced. In the built landscape, the enslaved people would have seen churches, houses, garrisons, mills, workshops, paved roads and bridges, fortifications, farmhouses, barns, sheds, stables, coach houses, distilleries, market gardens, lime kilns, tile factories, tanneries, brickworks, potteries, smithies, timber operations, artisanal workshops for metalworkers, slave dormitories, and huts (de Cauna 2009, 22).

The main agricultural products cultivated by the captives in Saint-Domingue were tobacco, sugar, coffee, indigo, and hardwoods (de Cauna 2009, 22). The captives were organized into *ateliers* (work crews), which undertook the heaviest labor. *Petit ateliers* broke children into plantation work. Enslaved women cleared, hoed, planted, weeded, and harvested fields. In the lowlands, one in four men held skilled positions such as processing sugar or coffee, or working as tradesmen, carpenters, or coachmen. Men were eight times more likely than women to receive a position that did not involve the toil of laboring the fields. On the highland coffee plantations, where production was less complex, only one in eleven enslaved people held a position of importance (Geggus 1993, 84). Enslaved people too old or sick to work in the fields guarded plantation animals or storehouses (Popkin 2012, 14).

The Code Noir (Black Code) of 1685 gave the French slave trade a "legal" framework, but it did little to protect enslaved people in French colonies. Living conditions on the plantations were horrible. Although some captives lived in wattle and daub huts of African design, the French enslavers preferred lodging them in larger dormitory buildings with less privacy and more supervision (Popkin 2012, 16–17). Malnutrition was chronic in the colony and meat a rare luxury. The small, private plots that enslaved people received to cultivate their own food did not meet their caloric needs. Barbaric physical punishment included whipping, branding, and the cutting of noses, ears, and hamstrings. Slave owners threw rebellious enslaved people into dungeons that they built on the plantation. While some European colonies in the Caribbean became places where enslaved people would slowly bear children of their own, in Saint-Domingue conditions were too abject, and replacement enslaved labor was in constant demand (Casimir 2009, xiii).

The seasoning that the newly arrived Africans received was hastened by the acquisition of Creole, or *kreyòl*. Reflecting African, European, Taíno Native Caribbean, and universal linguistic elements, the *kreyòl* language fused the linguistic and cultural currents that arrived in the colony. Free or enslaved people born in the colony were called *kreyòl*. Creole enslaved people grew up in the slave society and were desired for their familiarity with island culture. Enslaved people born in Africa (*bosal*) formed half of Saint-Domingue's population on the eve of the uprising of 1791. Apart from the enslaved *kreyòl* and *bosal* populations, the *mawon* (maroon, or escaped ex-slave) population had fled from the plantations and formed groups in remote regions. Other runaways melted into the cities, pretending to be freedmen seeking day labor (Popkin 2012, 17–19).

The social categories of the European population reflected economic status. The *petits blancs* (little whites) were poor and sought opportunities, most having recently arrived in the colony. Although the *petits blancs* shared more in common with enslaved people than with wealthy whites, white legislators implemented racist laws to separate whites from Blacks and people of color. Many of them hoped to become wealthy like the *grands blancs* (big whites). One such "big white" enumerated what he had lost after the Haitian revolution: "a sugar plantation with 352 slaves, a coffee plantation with 46 slaves, a stud farm with 48 mares and 148 mules, and a lime-making establishment with 25 slaves" (Popkin 2012, 21). Some *grands blancs* lived in the colony, while others were absentee owners who hired *gérants* (managers) to run their properties while they resided in France. The managers dreamed of establishing a foothold in slave society, and absentee employers blamed them for skimming revenue. The white population included planters, managers, police officers, soldiers, urban merchants, and tradesmen, in addition to the military governors and civil intendants who were sent from France to administer the colony. The Saint-Domingue-born whites despised the French-born administrators.

In the decade before the insurrections, the white population encountered several changes in the colonial system that disposed them to independence. In 1784–1785, decrees and new laws attempted to limit the abuse of captives and to punish perpetrators (Geggus 2009, 13). Slave owners had to keep records of the clothing and food they supplied, and slaves were now able to complain of mistreatment. When the French authorities dissolved the appeals court in Cap-Français and moved it to Port-au-Prince, dissatisfaction increased. To their liking, however, the whites got a taste of financial independence when parts of the *exclusif* trade law were lifted. The "exclusive" mandated that trade could only be conducted between France and Saint-Domingue. The new rules allowed colonists to buy and sell directly with the newly independent United States (Popkin 2012, 25–26).

During the eighteenth century, free people of color grew in number and influence compared to other communities of color in the Caribbean. Enslaved people looked to free people of color as a source of hope, dreaming of manumission from the occasional success stories. Free people of color originated through the sexual relationships French colonists had with women of color, whether Black or mixed race. White women were reluctant to settle in Saint-Domingue, and French men sought relationships with the women of color they found in the colony. The free people of color who descended from those relationships typically inherited property, including enslaved people, from their white fathers. They tended to stay in the colony and accepted business risks and difficult working conditions that the whites avoided, ensuring economic success over Europeans in many instances (Popkin 2012, 23). Their successes made whites jealous, while the racism of the whites infuriated free people of color.

Free men of color worked as *maréchaussé* (rural police) who hunted *mawon* runaways, a line of work that illustrates how they served as a wedge between the free white minority and the captive Black majority. People of color operated small businesses, served in the colonial army, and labored as artisans and tradespeople; the most successful became wealthy buying land and developing coffee and indigo plantations. Not much is known about free women of color in the society, but many historians note their sexual desirability among white men. Free women of color were sometimes entrusted with managing properties for white men with whom they may or may not have been sexually involved. Some of these free women of color established financially successful enterprises, encouraging their children to marry white men or men of color. Free people of color became as numerous as whites. They resented the racist laws and regulations that assailed their rights and dignity. In October 1790, free man of color Vincent Ogé and his followers took up arms to demand rights for people of color, but not the abolition of slavery. The French colonial army captured, tortured, and executed Ogé with twenty of his followers in early 1791 (Popkin 2012, 23, 30).

SUGAR, COFFEE, AND INDIGO PLANTATIONS

Europeans of the eighteenth century developed a predilection for sugar, one that has not yet abated. The dependency on sugary foods, beverages, and alcoholic spirits fueled France's transatlantic slave trade like nothing else. In 1789, there were more than 730 sugar plantations around Saint-Domingue (Popkin 2012, 13). Those sugar plantations and the alcohol distilleries they supplied represented 40 percent of the capital invested in the colony (de Cauna 2009, 24). On the northern plains of Saint-Domingue, the biggest sugar plantations were three hundred acres in size, confining enslaved workforces that ranged between fifty and six hundred men, women, and children (Geggus 1993, 75).[3]

As a result of the wealth they generated, plantations were the focus of innovations in efficiency and technology and were the sites with the best buildings, both domestic and industrial. A sugar plantation included lodging for a nurse, domestic servants, a cook, and guests. Chicken coops; dove cages; storehouses; a forge; a workshop for coopers, carters, masons, and wheelwrights; a corral for horses and mules; a well and water troughs; and a bell tower for calling enslaved people to assembly were typical on plantations. A wrought-iron gate that opened to a tree-lined avenue leading to the "big house" was a source of pride among wealthy colonists. Some plantations had aqueducts that carried water one hundred yards or more in order to propel the sugarcane mill in the mill house (de Cauna 2009, 27).

On many sugar plantations, the planter, bookkeeper, plantation manager, and sometimes a surgeon were the few white people present. Plantation labor was divided between fieldworkers and domestic workers. Enslaved female

Creoles were preferred for domestic work (Geggus 1993, 84). The *commandeur* (slave driver) was a ranked enslaved person who used a whip to direct the work in the fields in exchange for better food and living conditions. A ranked slave also directed the work of domestic enslaved people (Dubois and Garrigus 2006, 13, 15). Clearing fields for planting, harvesting, crushing cane, boiling its juice, and refining it into crystalized sugar were excruciating tasks.

The sugarcane industry boomed in the early part of the 1700s as African deportees were arriving in large numbers to work. Over time, particular African ethnic groups were preferred by slave buyers for given crops. Slave buyers for the sugar plantations preferred captives from the ethnic groups from the region of the Bight of Benin, meaning that captives from the ethnic groups that practiced prototypical forms of the Rada and Gede Rites were the most prevalent on the plains.

The central West African enslaved people whom sugar plantation slave buyers did not select were sold to those buying for coffee plantations (Geggus 1993, 80).[4] The spirit-based religious traditions of the Kongo, such as the Petwo-Kongo Rite, exerted more influence in mountainous coffee areas of Saint-Domingue. However, these ethnic differences were mere tendencies given that the Kongo ethnic group was a majority on sugar plantations *and* coffee plantations from the 1770s to the 1790s.

The prominence of enslaved people from West Africa in the early period of the colony probably explains the primacy of the Rada Rite in Haitian society today. Not only were Aja-Fon captives an early component of the colony, but also many captives from the towns of Allada and Hueda arrived in Saint-Domingue after the Dahomian invasions in the 1720s. In addition to this layered Aja-Fon influence, there were enslaved people from every part of Africa in Saint-Domingue, and this reality underlies the balanced pan-African syncretism that one encounters in the Sèvis Ginen system. The "comprehensive compendium of religious ideas" that Vodouists borrowed from Aja, Fon, Ewe, Yoruba, Ibo, Angolan, and Kongo people is the most important expression of syncretism in Vodou (Bellegarde-Smith 2004, 24–25).

Working on sugarcane plantations entailed dealing with a tropical lowland ecology and its diseases. In Saint-Domingue, lifestyles were split between the plains and the mountains. The older sugar plantations were in the plains, and the newer coffee plantations were in the mountains. There was a higher density of the enslaved population on the plains, allowing for more mingling (Geggus 1993, 73, 78). The mingling among different Africans on the plains accounts for the syncretic nature of the Sèvis Ginen traditions that are still situated on Haiti's plains today, especially around Léogâne and Port-au-Prince. Sèvis Ginen's prominence in the capital reflects the syncretic tradition's historical roots in the Department of the West (in contrast with Gonaïves, for example).[5]

Coffee cultivation was the second major agrocommercial development in eighteenth-century Saint-Domingue. Jesuits introduced coffee bushes in 1725 on their plantation at Terrier-Rouge. Coffee bushes were planted in the mountains near Dondon in 1738, an elevation that yielded denser beans. Coffee plantations began to spread into the mountain ranges of the south, since bushes thrived on steep slopes (Popkin 2012, 13). Production grew from seven million pounds of coffee in 1755 to seventy-seven million pounds in 1789, ultimately surpassing sugar with 60 percent of cultivated land. There were three thousand coffee plantations by 1789 (de Cauna 2009, 32).

Plantation owners had much of the land on the plains under cultivation by the first decades of the 1700s. Available land was situated in the mountains, precisely where coffee thrives. The embrace of coffee by Europeans meant cash for cultivators. Along with working-class whites, free people of color sought opportunities in coffee cultivation. The coffee sector was controlled by the descendants of free people of color into the contemporary period (Vieux-Chauvet 2009).[6]

Coffee plantations produced less wealth and were less desirable than sugar plantations, although they required less infrastructure. The availability of stone led to the construction of buildings for washing, drying, and crushing coffee beans (de Cauna 2009, 41). Coffee plantations included the owner's or manager's "big house," with a separate kitchen and bread oven topped with a chimney. The enslaved people dwelled in stone buildings and picked coffee berries, which they carried to the plantation's decorticating mill. As the coffee plantations were in more remote parts of the island, the industry led to road-building projects.

The coffee highlands had a cooler climate and lower humidity level than the lowlands, factors that impacted diseases and access to services. Coffee plantations attracted less capital investment and were smaller in scale. The enslaved population was less dense, giving fewer opportunities to mingle.[7] Between 1767 and 1792, the enslaved coffee plantation workforce was composed of 45 percent men, 34 percent women, and 21 percent children, shifting to 36 percent men, 36 percent women, and 28 percent children in the years 1796–1797 (Geggus 1993, 76–79). Because the coffee industry grew most rapidly in the late 1700s, most enslaved people working on the plantations were recent arrivals (Geggus 2009, 8). Coffee plantations had more African-born than Creole enslaved people.

The cultivation of indigo began in 1676 in the northern plain among French refugees who had been driven out of Samaná by the Spanish. In 1789, there were three thousand small-scale indigo plantations in Saint-Domingue, accounting for 22 percent of cultivated land just before the uprising of 1791 (de Cauna 2009, 24). Indigo was cultivated for the plant's blue dye, an important coloring additive in textiles and an antecedent of denim (Popkin 2012, 13). The *gwo ble/gros bleu* indigo dye was used to color the clothing of enslaved people. In Haitian Vodou, the farmer spirit, Azaka Mede, wears blue denim, a trace of blue indigo's colonial importance.[8]

Saint-Domingue was a slave society in which forced labor was the central feature of every aspect of life (Popkin 2012, 14). The agrocommercial slave society was designed to make French businessmen wealthy through the production of agricultural products for metropolitan French citizens. The French forced Black Africans and Creoles of color into an economic system that obliterated their rights, freedoms, and humanity. It stole their labor and lives in order to maximize the production of commodities like sugar, alcohol, coffee, indigo, and tobacco. Enslaved people had to struggle for survival, for dignity, for memory, and for empowerment in this agrocommercial slave society. The African captives' struggle for memory and power resonated in the Vodou religion. Saint-Domingue's African founders laid Vodou's foundations, and the new religion expanded to absorb the many spirit-based traditions of the African deportees who arrived on Hispaniola in increasing waves until the 1790s. The next section touches on basic Vodou concepts, introducing the building blocks of the tradition.

THE CORE FEATURES OF THE CREOLE RELIGION, HAITIAN VODOU

The Haitian Vodou vocabulary reflects the fundamentals of the religion's ceremonies and beliefs. In a Vodou community, the *sèvitè* (servants, worshippers) pray (*lapriyè*) as they *sèvi Bondye* and *sèvi lwa* (serve God and serve spirits). They *bat tanbou* (beat drums) and *chante* (sing) from memory and with conviction in the *ounfò* (temple). They *danse* and *djayi* (dance and gyrate) at the *peristil* (dance floor) while circling, counterclockwise, the *potomitan* (center post). The *oungan* (priest) and *manbo* (priestess) *souke ason* (shake the rattle) in order to *rele lwa yo* (call the spirits). The term *oungan* is from the Fon word *hungán* (chief of the vodun), and the term *manbo* is from the Fon word *nāgbō* (priestess).[9] Related to the word *oungan*, the *ounsi* (*oun-* "spirit" + *-si* "wife") is the initiated spouse of the spirits (Desmangles 2006, 40).

Vodouists perform cycles of salutation in ceremonies to *salye lwa yo* (greet the spirits) and honor them in a formal order called *règleman*. Vodouists *montre* (teach) the tradition using Vodou's own style of oral pedagogy, which culminates in the *kanzo* initiation (Michel 1995). Even if initiation formalizes a relationship, *aprann* (learning) is a lifelong journey for Vodouists, since the revelations of the spirits continue through life in the form of possessions, dreams, or songs. Inspiration is open, not closed in Vodou. Vodouists serve the spirits by making offerings, *bay manje* (offering food), *jete dlo* (pouring libations), or *sakrifye bèt* (sacrificing animals). In exchange, they receive *pwoteksyon* (protection) from the *lwa*.

An intimate devotion in Vodou is when the *lwa desann* (the spirit comes down) in order to *monte* (mount) the *chwal* (horse, spirit's vessel) and *danse* or *pale nan tèt li* (dance or speak in her or his head). Vodouists *bati badji* (build altar rooms), and they *trase vèvè* (trace spirit designs) on the ground in order to serve as symbolic adorations and spiritual portals. Vodouists *kreye* (create) ritual objects like *boutèy* (bottles), *drapo* (flags), and *pakèt* (membership packets). These terms fit succinctly into Vodou's theological system, examined below.

VODUN AND VODOU THEOLOGY

The Vodou cosmos is split on two axes, the horizontal sea-axis and the vertical sky-axis. Ancestors and the spirits reside under the horizontal ocean surface. The intersection of the vertical sky-axis with the horizontal sea-axis is a meeting point between the physical and spiritual (Wilcken and Augustin 1992, 21).

Vodou is rooted in African theology and ceremonialism (Herskovits 1937, 141). Vodun means "spirit" in Fon, one of the main languages of the Aja ethnic group (Lando 2016, 42). Vodou is the "family of the spirits" in Haiti and Dahomey (Desmangles 2006, 40). The sources of the Vodun religion evolved over many centuries in ethnic groups and nations that include the Aja, Mina, Fon, Gedevi, Yoruba, Mahi, Gen, and Ewe peoples living in southern Togo, Benin, Nigeria, Ghana, Côte d'Ivoire, Liberia, and Sierra Leone (Lando 2016, 42). These ethnic groups speak languages that share a degree of mutual intelligibility and cultural commonalities.

Space and the cosmos; objects like the earth, rivers, and storms; geological formations like waterfalls and mountains; and trees and forests are aspects of the spiritual universe. Within that spiritual universe, the ancestors, spirits, and priests are the means for humankind to approach a distant supreme being. Vodun and Vodou practitioners discover and learn from divine manifestations that are expressed in nature and beings. The holiness of nature and beings causes a profusion of "spirit objects" and a "marking" of sacred space (Lando 2016, 51). Spirits like Legba or Ogou are elevated great ancestors. Those great ancestors are in turn linked to revered practitioners forming a relationship that benefits spirit and priest (Brown 2001).

In the Vodun of Benin, the *ayì vodún* are earth spirits and include Gede, Sakpata, Kúxòsú, Dan, and others (Segurola and Rassinoux 2000, 470). The *ako vodún* are spirits of the clan, tribe, or family.

The *atínmévódún* are spirits that dwell in trees like Loko. Some trees are also sacred in Haitian Vodou, but their role as a food source excludes any harm to a person who eats their fruit (Tarter 2015, 97). In Haiti, tree-cutting taboos of *pye repozwa* (spirit resting trees) have protected many trees, especially the *mapou* (*Ceiba pentanahan* L.) (Tarter 2015, 99). Sacred trees are usually so big and old that community members find them at birth, experiencing an "arboreal timelessness" (Tarter 2015, 101).

The *hennou-vodún* are of the nuclear family. The *jì vodún* are from the sky and include Lisa, Mawu, Jī, and Xebyoso. The *nùkánme vodún* are of the forest like Fa, and the *tò vodún* are of a city or a nation, for example tò Legba (Segurola and Rassinoux 2000, 470).

Vodou spirits in Haiti are ancestral deities that have become "life principles" through a process of abstraction over multiple generations (Wilcken and Augustin 1992, 22). They reflect parts of nature like the serpent in Danbala and the rainbow in Ayida, trees in Loko and Gran Bwa, or the ocean in Agwe and Lasirèn. Spirits in Vodun or Vodou are the concentration of properties. They can stem from nations, like the Yoruba spirit Ogou, or be restricted to villages or familial settings. The spirits or *lwa* reflect "exemplarity" in that they are models of transcendent notions, the totality of which is "the God of the collective subconscious of the Haitian Vodouist" (Beauvoir 2008b, 55; my translation). The 401 spirits identified in Haitian Vodou are facets of God's "diamond," each uniquely reflecting the light of God (Beauvoir 2008a, 30).

Lapriyè Ginen or *Lapriyè Dyò* is a liturgical text chanted before ceremonies. The term *Ginen* is related to "Guinea" and is also found in *lakòt Ginen*, which once designated a stretch of the West African slave coast (Beauvoir 2008a). There is also *pitit Ginen* (child of Africa or child of the ancestors), or the expression *nèg Ginen* (African conscious person).[10] The expression *Ginen yo* (the Ginen) refers to the ancestors and the Vodou spirits. Ginen is where the ancestors gather after traveling under the waters after death (Beauvoir 2008a, 13). The souls of the ancestors permanently mingle in Ginen but can be called back by Vodou priests through mortuary rituals. "Sèvis Ginen" is rooted in the African traditions of the Bight of Benin, even though it ultimately absorbed traditions from a wider ethnogeographic area, including the Kongo.

Vodou is grounded in the Lakou, the extended family homestead and burial site where "God placed humankind" (Beauvoir 2008b, 42). The Lakou reflects the residual African village and is considered a prototypical residential setup (Michel 2006, 44). Vodouists live temporally in cycles that mirror the sun, the moon, the earth, rains, seasons, and the self on its journey from birth to death (Beauvoir 2008b, 43). Nothing is greater than God, and everything depends upon Her, including the Vodou spirits who are Her creations (Daly 1974; Beauvoir 2008b, 51).

God's properties are mediated through the spirits, who are variously called *lwa*, *djab*, *gad*, *pwen*, *mistè*, *oricha*, and *zany*. Abstract and universal ideas are transformed into sacred beings who connect people to ideas that are essential for happiness and survival. The spirits connect people to notions of "exemplarity" (Beauvoir 2008b, 53).

The spirits are the emanations of great ancestors and their descendants who were taken into slavery. Although ethnic origins are still remembered, the *lwa* are primarily associated with concepts like healing, love, nature, plant medicine, defense and war, protection, leadership, motherhood, fatherhood, childhood, priesthood, drums, and rites of passage like birth, initiation, and death. The founders of Haitian Sèvis Ginen gathered the 401 *lwa*—the 401 examples—and the 21 Rites they fit within, and built a religious culture that preserves diverse African traditions and gives spiritual meaning to people (Beauvoir 2008b, 56).

In addition to the Lakou, Vodouists contact the *lwa* by making a small *ogatwa* (altar) in a private room, under a tree, beside a spring, or in the courtyard of their home. Some Vodouists who live in towns in Haiti's lowlands seek contact with the *lwa* in an *ounfò* (temple). The temple is a strictly hierarchical environment with a *manbo* or an *oungan* who mediates the spirit world as a shaman-priest, organizes ceremonies, initiates adepts, and handles matters as various as childbirth, mental illness, and burial (Beauvoir 2008b, 68). Such a wide range of occupations points to a tradition with a clear sense of values.

VODOU'S VALUES, BELIEFS, AND PRACTICES

Vodouists put the values of truth, liberty, and justice into action in order to win Haitian independence, and these values remain central today (Beauvoir 2008a, 68). In terms of the value of *truth*, the Vodouist respects and venerates God and the "sacred Forces" that she (or he) sent called Yehwé, Houn, Lwa, or Vodou. Several of these terms are found in contemporary Fon, for example *Yɛhwè* (spirit), *Houn* (spirit) and *Vodun* (spirit) (Segurola and Rassinoux 2000, 527, 239, 469). A sacred light guides the Vodouist's thoughtfulness and love for others, keeping her or him from beastliness. The Vodouist does not tempt forces that transcend her or him. The Vodouist conforms to the attitudes and acts of the model ancestors (Beauvoir 2008a, 68–69).

With respect to *liberty*, Vodou is nonapostolic and thus has no single prophetic figure and no select group of founders or leaders who make centralized decisions (Beauvoir 2008a, 70). Each *oungan* and *manbo* leads his or her respective community. Vodou is not lacking in national structures, which include the Konfederasyon Nasyonal Vodou Ayisyen,[11] defending Vodou from its enemies in Haiti and abroad.

Part of the Vodouists' liberty is the "emotional participation" in individual and collective communion with the holy by means of ceremonies and rituals, songs, dances, and listening to sacred music; through possession and dreams;

and in a comportment that is religious. The Vodouist places value on mutual respect and reciprocity, and consequently involvement in pogroms and autos-da-fé that are inspired by the "fallacious and cruel pretext that he [or she] received from God the mission of going to convert the nations" is forbidden. The one who kills in God's name reduces God to the status of a nonuniversal and vulgar idol propitiated with human sacrifices (Beauvoir 2008a, 70).

Central to Vodou liberty is the practice of spirit possession in the context of community worship. Possession involves the *lwa* crossing through the spiritual-physical surface to displace the spirit of the living worshipper, becoming the animating force for a brief time. Because conscious cognition has been displaced, the person who is possessed cannot recall the experience. Possession is a "collective remembering" that summons ancestral wisdom and traditions into the present (Wilcken and Augustin 1992, 22).

The values rooted in *justice* include altruism, solidarity, hospitality, collaboration, and sharing. Justice is expressed in the fight against slavery, racism, and colonialism. Vodouists struggle against prejudice and exclusion, and they value reciprocity. If Vodouists detect similar values in an ethical, moral, aesthetic, philosophical, or logical system, they engage with them respectfully. The Vodouist values deference and circumspection (Beauvoir 2008a, 71–72).

VODOU IN THE SEVENTEENTH AND EIGHTEENTH CENTURIES

It is difficult to reconstruct the history of a religion that was besmirched by colonizers and enslavers in many early records. For Vodou in Saint-Domingue and Haiti, caution is needed, since European authors hostile to Black culture generated many historical reports.

French slave owners in the Americas were supposed to baptize enslaved people as Catholics, according to a police decree of 1664 issued by the Marquis de Tracy (Métraux 1972, 33). The Code Noir legislated that only Catholicism was acceptable. Judaism and "reformed religion" (i.e., Protestantism) were banned, and no mention of African religion was made except to render illegal its "public exercise." Europeans did not consider African religions to be worthy of respect, instead treating them like types of "superstition" or "sorcery" (Ramsey 2011, 24). One of the first mentions of African religion was a 1727 record of enslaved people who were accused of working as "sorcerers" and executed by their owners (Ramsey 2011, 32). The execution for "sorcery" may indicate that the practice of African religion contained elements of resistance.

Between 1740 and 1750, maroonage became more common than before. By conservative accounts, there were three thousand maroons in Saint-Domingue in 1751 (Beauvoir-Dominique 2019, 28). In 1752, the colonial record offers riveting accounts of waves of poisonings. The maroon Vodou priest and herbalist François Makandal was allegedly killing off French colonists and livestock with poisons he skillfully prepared and distributed through a large network of collaborators (Beauvoir-Dominique 2019, 29). He ran away from his owner, Lenormand de Mézy, and traveled armed, refusing to acknowledge that he was property (Casimir 2009, xii). He was accused of killing six thousand people and was eventually arrested and executed in 1758. The Conseil Supérieur du Cap issued a decree that accused him of "profanations," constructing "magical packets," and providing "evil spells to the Blacks." His name, Makandal, reflects a Kikongo word for "charms," a notion the word still refers to in Haitian Creole (Ramsey 2011, 34).[12] After Makandal's execution, the colony was changed forever. Expressions of African culture were suspected of stoking revolt (Beauvoir-Dominique 2019, 29).

In 1758, the Conseil Supérieur du Cap prohibited "the superstitious assemblies and ceremonies that certain Slaves are accustomed to holding at the death of one of them." The prohibition points to the presence of religious mortuary rites, here perhaps a reference to Gede culture. The same edict also banned the acquisition of charms called "Garde Corps and Macandals" and prohibited enslaved people from beating drums at night (Ramsey 2011, 35). The reference to the generic term *macandals* is striking given that "François Makandal" had been executed in the same year.

It was feared among colonial authorities and colonists that enslaved people were progressing from "superstitions," "*garde-corps*," and "fetishes" to more powerful practices such as "profanation, sacrilege, and poisoning," the last notion being a revolutionary political construct as the objective was to kill whites for the crime of slavery (Ramsey 2011, 35). In the same year of 1758, a planter was sentenced to pay a fine for allowing "an assembly of Blacks" and a "Calenda," a reference to a religious dance performed at night. Again, in 1772, the police in Port-au-Prince banned nighttime Calenda dances altogether.

In 1786, a decision by the Conseil Supérieur du Cap reiterated the ban on assemblies and "*magnétisme*"[13] among people of African descent. The town of Marmelade was becoming a "theater" for gatherings at night in which "magicians" orchestrated forms of "contagion" at their *bila* (Ramsey 2011, 38). The *bila* is a table or tent employed to honor the spirits in the Kongo Rite, and the word appears in the call-and-response formula that introduces songs for Kongo spirits:

> Afoutayi!—*Yi!*
> Bila bila—Kongo!
> Lè bounda fache, kote l chita?
> —Atè!

Afoutayi!—*Yi!*
Bila bila—Kongo!
When an ass is angry, where does it sit?
—*On the ground!* (Hebblethwaite et al. 2012, 219)

The Conseil Supérieur du Cap convicted three men in 1786 for creating *garde-corps* (protective amulets), *fonda* (magic sacks) with *manman-bila* (magic stones) inside of them, and *mayombo* (protective sticks) (Ramsey 2011, 39).[14] As interesting as these mentions are in the historical record, they ultimately offer only a meager idea of Vodou.

MOREAU DE SAINT-MÉRY'S 1797 ACCOUNT OF VODOU IN SAINT-DOMINGUE

An early source on Vodou is the enslaver Médéric Louis Élie Moreau de Saint-Méry's influential descriptions relating his observations of the 1780s. His text provides intimations that much remains the same in urban Haitian Vodou over the past two centuries. Moreau de Saint-Méry's report is required reading, in spite of his prejudices. A slave owner and aggressive defender of slavery, he provides a list of African populations in the colony (Popkin 2012, 33). For each nation, he gives a set of characteristics that they were known for. The two main groups, the Aradas and Yoruba, appear in his list, in addition to other important West African groups like the "Popos," the "Fons," the "Fidas/Foëdas" (Huedans), and the "Dahomets" (Dahomians).[15] The term "Aradas" was "almost generic" for describing captives from the Aja region in general, but Moreau de Saint-Méry points out that the "true Aradas" were distinguished from others who claimed the origin (1797, 27). His remark suggests that the "Aradas" from Allada had a pedigree in the colony.

Moreau de Saint-Méry claims that "Vaudoux" is "an institution where superstition and bizarre practices have a major part" (1797, 46). Although belittling, the term "institution" suggests some scale. He describes the Arada population as the most zealous practitioners and maintainers of "the principles and rules," suggesting that practitioners from the kingdoms of Allada and Hueda were recognizable and followed the disciplined code they are still known for. "Vaudoux" is an "all-powerful and supernatural being," a "nonvenomous serpent" under whose "auspices" those who profess the religion assemble. The powers of Vaudoux, including knowledge of the past, present, and future, belong to the "serpent" and are only mediated via a "high priest or high priestess chosen by the worshippers." In the Fon language, vodun is a spirit being. The "serpent" is likely a depiction of one of the communities dedicated to the python spirit Dan. The serpent-centered description of Vaudoux suggests the successful transplantation of a congregation dedicated to Dangbe (related to Dan, O'Dan, and Danbala) from the town of Hueda, where it is still present. Moreau de Saint-Méry also noticed gender parity, and that worshippers selected their own spiritual leader.

His descriptions imply that Vodou was established as a systematic religion organized around priests and initiates. Vodou leadership described as *grand prêtre* (high priest), *roi* (king), or *papa* (father) in the case of men, and *grande prêtresse* (high priestess), *reine* (queen), or *maman* (mother) in the case of women, reflects current structures, especially the idea of spiritual kinship in which the initiating priest assumes the title of *papa* or *maman* for the initiates. The priests claim to be "inspired by God." The authenticity of their inspiration is demonstrated by the engagement of the adepts. The priests are the leaders for life of "great Vaudoux families," another reference to spiritual kinship (Moreau de Saint-Méry 1797, 46–47). Vodou's connection to African Vodun monarchies is reflected in terms like *roi* or *reine*, terms more associated with *rara* than Vodou today.[16]

In a passage that explores initiation, the priests determine if "the serpent" accepts a candidate into the "society." Priests prescribe obligations and receive donations and gifts on behalf of the spirit. The observation that the serpent spirit presides over initiation is still reflected in Haitian Vodou today, in which candidates for initiation *kouche sou Danbala* (sleep on Danbala's empowerment). Danbala *reklame* (claims) initiation by *kenbe* (holding) the candidate in a mild sickness until the initiation is undertaken (Richman 2005, 130).

The term *société* referring to a community of Vodouists is still common today in, for example, Société Tipa Tipa and Société Jenndantor des Gonaïves in Haiti or Société Linto Roi Trois Mystères, Société Makaya, or Société Halouba in Miami (Hebblethwaite 2015b, 5). The reference to the "serpent," the "candidate," "obligations," and "donations" points to the *kanzo* initiation, the expectations that issue from it, and the required financial contributions. Resisting the obligations of initiation is to risk misfortune; thus, for Moreau de Saint-Méry, the religion reflects "a system of domination."

Priests preside over "assemblies" in which the habits (*usages*) on display reflect a mixture of African and Creole "variants," an observation that probably references Vodou-Catholic syncretistic features. An example of European-influenced hybridity in Vaudoux includes the "scarf" and "rich belt" that the *prêtresse* wears (1797, 46). Moreau de Saint-Méry notices the bright silk scarfs that are tied to worshippers to represent which spirit has possessed the "horse."

Meetings for Vaudoux services in their "primitive purity," the colonial author writes, only take place under the cloak of secrecy.[17] The initiates wore "sandals," whereas barefooted worship is more typical of Vodou. They tied a significant number of red scarves around their bodies, but not more than the priest wore. A blue cord dignified the priest's appearance. During the ceremony, the *roi* and *reine* stood by a kind of "altar" upon which a chest for the serpent was placed so that each "affiliate" (*affilé*) could see it from behind bars. After ensuring privacy, the ceremony began with the "worship" of the snake, enjoinders to remain faithful to its cult, and signs of submission to the spirit. The "oath of the secret [was] renewed," and a period of religious "delirium" ensued, likely possession. The priests, taking a paternal tone, praised "the happiness that is the province of whoever is dedicated to the Vaudoux." They exhorted the initiates "to have confidence in him" and to "provide proof of it" by taking the spirit's advice.

At that point in the ceremony, the congregants implored the Vaudoux according to "seniority in the sect" (Moreau de Saint-Méry 1797, 47). Most of the supplicants asked the *lwa* to "guide the spirit of their masters"; others asked for money or the power to attract someone, to discipline an unfaithful lover, or to receive a quick healing, a prolonged life, eternal love, or other demands. At each invocation, the priest withdrew trembling, finally placing the chest with the python on the ground. After straddling it, the *reine* entered the "convulsive state" of possession in which "the oracle speaks from her mouth." The spirit "flattered," "promised happiness," "lambasted," "reproached," and "dictated laws with no appeal." The spirit took questions and gave answers, while congregants promised to obey the instructions.

After the Vaudoux spoke, donations were dropped into a hat in order to keep amounts discreet. The donations paid for the "gatherings," helped "members," or advanced the society, demonstrating altruism in Vodou. An oath of secrecy was sealed with goat's blood smeared on lips, a ritual still found in some circles of Haitian Vodou (48). After the oath, the "dance of Vaudoux" began at the ceremony. The *roi* Vaudoux "trace[d]" a large circle with a blackening substance and positioned within the circle those people who wished to become initiated. This "tracing" calls to mind the *trase vèvè* of Vodou ceremonies.[18]

The initiates held a "packet composed of herbs, horse hairs, [and] pieces of horn," probably a reference to the *pakèt inisyasyon*, a bottle constructed to represent membership within the congregation (48). The *pakèt* are important in the career of the *oungan* and *manbo* as they represent their initiates. The *pakèt* "constitutes the initiate's double," and its placement on the altar represents obligations and protections (Saint-Lot 2003, 122).[19]

The priest tapped the candidate lightly with a wooden paddle and struck up "an African song that is chorally repeated by those who surround the circle" (Moreau de Saint-Méry 1797, 49). The recipient of the packet trembled and danced, ridden by the spirit (*monter* Vaudoux). The possessed dancer remained inside the traced circle, and the "Roi Vaudoux" expelled the spirit with a light tap on the head with the paddle. The candidate swore an oath and thus belonged to the congregation.

After the initiatory sequence had ended, the *roi* touched the serpent box and began trembling, a state that he transferred to the *reine*, who sent it on to the worshippers in circular order. The *reine* collected "charms" from the snake box in the course of her possession. The ceremony was intensified with alcohol. Dizzy spells, swooning, furor, and trembling pervaded the dancing. Worshippers tore their clothing, and others bit the flesh of their horse (49).

Vaudoux owes its origins to the cult of the serpent in "Juida" (that is, Hueda), "who say it originates in the kingdom of Allada" (49). The "truth" of Vaudoux is the "magnetism" that carries people to "the loss of the senses." So powerful is it that "Whites" discovered peeking at the ceremonies and "touched" by a worshipper found themselves "dancing" and paying the "Reine Vaudoux" to put an end to the "punishment" of possession (50). The police, who "have sworn war on Vaudoux," do not fall under its spell. The initiate who neglects the obligations of the congregation is threatened with spiritual punishment, and therefore Vaudoux is "dangerous."

The proponents of Vaudoux "dance in public to the sound of drums and handclapping," and they offer a meal exclusively of poultry. The handclapping was to "escape from the vigilance of the magistrates" and to ensure the success of its "shadowy mutterings." Vodouists expressed themselves in public spaces in the colony and sought opportunities to influence public opinion through a charitable meal.

A Black man of Spanish colonial origin from Petit-Goâve introduced in 1768 a dance that was analogous to but more precipitous than the one in Vaudoux. In this rite, gunpowder is added to the communal white rum. The Don Pèdre could kill a worshipper, and it electrified spectators who experienced catharsis in the communal "crisis." The Don Pèdre was forbidden.

The mention of the Don Pèdre tradition points to a multipolar congregational Vodou.[20] Don Pèdre (or Dom Pedro) was probably born in the Kongo, as Ferrand de Baudière, a judge in Petit Goâve, suggests in a 1769 letter. De Baudière wrote that Don Pèdre and his "accomplices" "incited" enslaved people to "rebellion" and to be "independent of their masters," and was therefore "killed in a hunt" (Geggus 2014, 24–25). Don Pèdre is linked to the fiery Petwo Rite, which also originates in the Petwo region of the Kongo.[21] Moreau de Saint-Méry (1797) thus mentions two different communities and shows that the structural and organizational attributes of today's temple Vodou were well rooted in the 1780s.

THE BWA KAYIMAN CEREMONIES AND ROMAINE-LA-PROPHÉTESSE

The Bwa Kayiman ceremonies of August 14 and 21, 1791, sanctified the slave insurrection that exploded on August 22–23 and fanned a revolutionary struggle fueling thirteen years of conflict. Today, Bwa Kayiman is linked to Haiti's "national essence," transcending classes and categories (Beauvoir-Dominique 2019, 15). The ceremonies took place on the plantation of Lenormand de Mézy and included oungan Boukman and manbo Cécile Fatiman's sacrifice of a black pig, the reading of its entrails, and the plucking of its hair for talismans (Beauvoir-Dominique 2019, 39–40). Today, celebrations and sacrifices for the Vodou spirit Èzili Dantò take place on August 14 and 15 annually. This Petwo manifestation of Èzili is known for plunging her dagger into a pig in her possession performance. At Bwa Kayiman, the pig's blood was collected for consecrating the insurrectionists in a blood ritual, the most serious of pacts in Dahomian culture (Rouget 2001). The fighters took sips of the blood to seal their secrecy.

Antoine Dalmas published an account of Bois Caïman in 1814 based on his notes from 1793–1794 (Hebblethwaite et al. 2012, 48; Ramsey 2011, 42). *Lapriyè Boukman* (Boukman's Prayer) was published in Hérard Dumesle's 1824 *Voyage in the North of Haiti*. In the prayer attributed to the *oungan*, Boukman Dutty, the fighters are encouraged to "[t]hrow down the portrait of the god of the whites who is thirsty for the tears in our eyes" (cited in Kadish and Jenson 2015, 226).

Vodou helped to mobilize resistance and encourage a revolutionary mentality, giving people "the conviction to fight" and providing valuable strategic and military information through its networks (Trouillot, Past, and Hebblethwaite 2021, 54; Geggus 1991, 48). Leaders of the Haitian liberation movement were commonly priests—oungan Boukman, manbo Cécile Fatiman, and bòkò Makandal are famous examples (Bellegarde-Smith 2006, 101).

Between 1791 and 1793, the revolutionary Romaine-la-Prophétesse drew on Catholic and Kongo religious traditions in his recruitment of loyal fighters, who carried out several attacks on French holdings (Rey 1998, 343). Of Hispanic origin, his race is uncertain. He claimed to be the "godchild of the Virgin," and he received messages from "his Holy Godmother" to massacre whites (Métraux 1972, 47). He ruled the town of Léogâne for several months. During his rule, the mayor called him a "hermaphroditic tiger," a reference to his transgender sensibilities. Romaine-la-Prophétesse asserted that the abolition of slavery was a divine mission, demanded total personal freedom, and inspired his followers with militaristic Kongolese Marianism (Rey 2017, 51–52, 72).

In 1796, the colonial administrator Léger-Félicité Sonthonax banned *le Vaudou* and the dance associated with it. Penalties of one to three months of imprisonment and fines were imposed for perpetrators. Sonthonax called for the arrest of a "witch" named "Maman Dio"[22] because she was "terrifying the weak minded" with "fanaticism" and "disorder" (Ramsey 2011, 47–48). In the year 1800, Toussaint Louverture likewise banned *le Vaudoux*, and dances and assemblies at night. In 1800, Louverture's ally, Jean-Jacques Dessalines, killed fifty members of a Vodou secret society (Métraux 1972, 49).

The killing likely was the end result of a temporary political dispute, since Dessalines is honored in Vodou today. The Nago temple Nan Badjo near Gonaïves displays the painted words "Anperè Desalin" on its outer wall, linking Dessalines to the war spirit Ogou, who is the focus of their devotions.

HAITIAN VODOU IN THE NINETEENTH CENTURY

After 1804, Haiti's leaders treated the ancestral traditions with hostility. They were driven by the fear that Vodou communities stood as parallel powers "detrimental to tranquility," as Henri Christophe's 1805 ban put it (Ramsey 2011, 51). Banning Vodou matched European norms of intolerance. President Jean-Pierre Boyer outlawed *le Vaudoux* as a class of "spells" in his 1835 Code Pénal (Ramsey 2011, 55). In 1864, laws were tightened under the pro-Catholic president Fabre Nicolas Geffrard. He signed a concordat with the Catholic Church in 1860, signaling an escalation in difficulties for Vodou communities.

Article 405 of President Boyer's 1835 law stated that "makers of *ouangas*, *caprelatas*, *vaudoux*, *donpèdre*, *macandals*, and other *sortilèges*" were forbidden from doing so, and Article 406 banned "fortune-telling, divination, fortune-telling dreams, [and] reading cards," while Article 407 banned "instruments, utensils, and costumes" that were employed "in the acts referred to in the two preceding articles" (Ramsey 2011, 58–59). These were classified as "minor offenses" and punishable accordingly, unlike the death penalty imposed in Barbados.

During the rule of President and Emperor Faustin Soulouque (1847–1859), Vodou culture flourished. Soulouque consulted with *manbo* to protect the National Palace by removing a "hidden charm" that was hurting Haitian presidents. After his coronation as emperor in 1849, he organized a ceremony in his dead mother's memory at the Catholic church of her hometown, Petit-Goâve, and at midnight he sacrificed a lamb over her grave (Métraux 1972, 51).

Nineteenth-century politicians often suspected the poor of "sorcery." The elite's demonization of Vodou was accompanied by the "barbarization" of Black culture. The *affaire de Bizoton* in 1864 in which a group of Vodouists was accused of cannibalism, tortured to confession, judged, and executed was exploited by authors like Spenser St. John (1884) and used to impugn Vodou and Haiti. President Geffrard condemned Vaudoux, claiming that it represented "slavery and barbarity" (Ramsey 2011, 76, 86). Geffrard's claims were inflammatory but faded in the face of popular support for Vodou.

Bishop François-Marie Kersuzan of Cap-Haïtien launched a campaign against Vodou in the 1890s. Dancers who engaged in "savage orgies" could not become a "working people." The bishop preached in favor of a "crusade" against

Vodou. In 1896, he founded the newspaper *La Croix* to increase pressure on Vodou. The publication of a list of "bocors," the locations of sanctuaries, and the identities of their patrons led to "raids, arrests, the destruction of temples, and the widespread [...] burning of drums" (Ramsey 2011, 96, 108).

Kersuzan's pogrom fell apart after he ordered the removal of the statue of Saint-Jacques (otherwise Ogou in Vodou) from the sanctuary in Plaine-du-Nord. He faced gunfire as he removed it, and he then decided to shutter *La Croix*. Haitians defended their ancestral traditions and rejected claims of savagery that were heaped on the scapegoat of Vodou. The attacks gave rise to authors who argued that Vodou was opposed to "witchcraft" and "sorcery" (Ramsey 2011, 115–17). The town of Plaine-du-Nord remains a destination for pilgrims who seek the aid of Papa Ogou.

The Haitian intellectuals Anténor Firmin, Duverneau Trouillot, and Hannibal Price opposed the maligning of Vodou. Their publications mark a turning point in Vodou's intellectual history. Firmin suggested that people of African descent do not suffer from "religious fanaticism and dogmatism" but prefer "rationalist and positivist conceptions." Indifferent to "external aspects of religious worship," African descendants are better disposed to "the emancipation of reason" (Firmin 2004, 340–43). The "fetishistic stage" of African religion is superior because it leads to rational analyses of the universe and suffers less the entrenchment of dogmatism and fanaticism found in European religious traditions.

Trouillot's (1885) book was an early Vodou ethnography, providing a list of spirits and their characteristics, plus descriptions of ceremonies (Ramsey 2011, 98). Price (1900) criticized the misinformed publications of foreign observers, especially Spencer St. John (1884). He argued that "*le vaudou*" was no "obstacle to the civilization of this country." However, Trouillot and Price believed that "*le vaudou*" was in decline and that too many con artists were taking advantage of the gullible. They echoed sentiments that viewed Vodou as threatened by "laws of evolution," enlightenment thinking, scientific reasoning, and conversion to Christianity. Bishop Kersuzan's anti-Vodou "crusade" a decade later claimed, however, that Vodou was an ascendant threat (Ramsey 2011, 99).

HAITIAN VODOU IN THE TWENTIETH AND TWENTY-FIRST CENTURIES

Three major events impacted Vodou in the twentieth century. The first was the US occupation of Haiti between 1915 and 1934. The second was the anti-Vodou pogrom led by Protestants during the US occupation, and by the Catholic Church and the Haitian state in the 1940s. The third was the rescinding of anti-Vodou laws that came with the new Haitian constitution after Jean-Claude Duvalier fled in 1986.

In the context of the First World War, President Woodrow Wilson and members of the US government ordered the occupation of Haiti in order to collect debts; to control the political and economic system, especially revenue at customs; and to staunch German claims on the nation. In 1916, US marines in Haiti received an English translation of the Haitian "rural code." Emphasis was placed on the enforcement of laws that prohibited "vagrancy, poisoning to produce a deathlike state, and *les sortilèges.*" The laws of the "rural code" state that dances that "foster in the people a spirit of fetishism and superstition, will be considered sorceries." Although written by Haitian lawmakers of the nineteenth century, they were not enforced until the marines applied them literally in order to conscript people to work on chain gangs. It became clear to the marines that the *caco* resistance fighters came from the peasantry, where Vodou was strongest and where struggle was seen in religious terms (Nicholls 1996, 149).

The US occupiers prohibited "voodoo" in order to "uplift" Haiti's "reputation," and there are reports of marines massacring Vodouists (Ramsey 2011, 128–29, 140–44). The religion was viewed as an anathema to eviscerate. Priests and worshippers were arrested, sacred trees cut down, shrines shuttered, and drums, *govi*, and *pakèt* confiscated as souvenirs or burned (Ramsey 2011, 147, 162). The forced enlistment of Vodouists in chain labor gangs, and the abandonment of customary law in favor of nineteenth-century articles of law, fomented a crisis. The oppression from whites produced a backlash from Haitian researchers like Jean Price-Mars (1954), Jacques Roumain (1943), and Milo Marcelin (1950). The Black nationalist political forces that thrust François Duvalier into power in 1957 were responses in opposition to the US occupation and the anti-Vodou campaigns of the 1930s and 1940s, among other resentments.

The US occupation hastened the flow of Protestants into Haiti. Baptists, Episcopalians, and Seventh-day Adventists spread across the country carrying religious prejudices and colonialist attitudes. Missionaries charged that the Catholic Church was "contaminated" with Vodou influence (Ramsey 2011, 198). Catholics and Vodouists had to convert to their "purer" religion. In 1921–1922, the Baptist missionary Ton Evans delighted at the burning of paraphernalia turned in by Vodou priests who had converted. Wesleyan Methodist pastor H. Ormonde McConnell celebrated the incineration of Vodou material culture during his conversion campaigns of 1933. The attacks of the Protestant missionaries motivated Catholics to prepare their own anti-Vodou campaign.

The last marines left Haiti in 1934, and the standing president at the time, Sténio Vincent, was a militant Catholic and Francophile. In 1935, his government banned *pratiques superstitieuses.*[23] These prohibitions emboldened the enemies of Vodou, foremost the white Roman Catholic churchmen. In 1940, Catholic leaders began preaching again against mixing Vodou practices with Catholic ones. The *curé* (priest) of Hinche told Bishop Paul Robert about the *rejete* movement that had purged itself of Vodou. In June 1940, an "antisuperstition oath" became a prerequisite for receiving a card that authorized communion, burial, and marriage (Ramsey 2011, 195–96). Services were denied to people who had not obtained the card.

The anti-Vodou campaign reached a climax in 1941 when the *curés*, the *rejete* horde that knew the local shrines, members of the Garde d'Haïti, and sheriffs descended on homesteads, temples (*houmforts*), and shrines to destroy drums, *ason*, *govi*, bottles, and objects on altars. Items were piled into sacks on donkeys and taken away for burning as people sang Christian hymns. *Bwa sèvi* or *pye repozwa* spirit trees were exorcised or chopped down. The church published pamphlets about forbidden "superstitious" objects and the rationalizations for its pogrom. The mobilization of the rural police was the only reason the destruction did not encounter greater opposition (Ramsey 2011, 201–2, 206).

Although President Élie Lescot had endorsed the *campagne antisuperstitieuse* in 1941 and authorized the deployment of civil and military forces, by 1942 the campaign had become unpopular. On February 22, 1942, during a mass at the chapel of Saint-Michel-de-l'Atalaye in Port-au-Prince, gunshots rang out. As the Haitian vicar of the Cathedral of Port-au-Prince, Rémy Augustin, was launching the antisuperstition missions' campaign in the capital, two hundred shots were fired into the air inside and outside the chapel, traumatizing the congregants and the Catholic churchmen. The next day, a letter appeared in *Haïti-Journal* to condemn the pogroms. Anger and resentment was spilling over. The Protestants and Catholics believed that their violence would rid Haiti of "the indelible mark of our inferiority, of our original fall," but the gunshots provided notice that killing would begin if agitation continued (Ramsey 2011, 207–9).

In spite of Vodou's co-option by President François Duvalier (1957–1971) and his son and successor Jean-Claude Duvalier (1971–1987), both enforced prohibitions against *les pratiques superstitieuses*, using the law as a means of control and licensure (Ramsey 2011, 252). Anti-Vodou legislation was repealed in the 1987 Haitian constitution, meaning that the religion was illegal from 1664 until 1987, or about 323 years.

CONTINUITIES AND ADAPTIONS IN HAITIAN VODOU

Continuities and adaptions can be found in Vodou in the contemporary period. Ritual change took place in some Vodou communities in the twentieth century as a result of the crumbling rural economy, demographic and ecological pressures, and the seizure of peasant lands by outsiders. The rise of urban wage labor and the momentum of migration patterns drew rural residents to cities. Urban dwellers tend to orient toward individual consumerism, a magnet for rural residents that diminishes familial traditions (Richman 2005, 116).[24]

Vodou practices in lowland villages like Ti Rivyè changed in the twentieth century. They increased the emphasis on money for ritual, adopted and adapted practices found in urban congregations, professionalized leadership, and included novel rituals imported from urban temples.[25] An assortment of new traditions from the towns and cities of Haiti were represented as peasant practices and given the blessing of the ancestors in villages like Ti Rivyè (Richman 2005, 116).

There is a "domestic" type of Vodou associated with the Lakou (extended family homestead) in rural areas and linked to descent groups. There is also a "temple" variety of Vodou associated with congregations built on "fictive kinship ties" and tending to include costly rituals and a division between ritualists and the audience. Lakou family compounds are gradually disappearing, because inalienable familial land has been carved up and subdivided (Métraux 1972, 60–61). Migration weakens kinship ties; therefore, as members of a rural descent group settle in towns and cities, attachment to a surrogate "spiritual family" in a congregation helps fill social breaches. Domestic Vodou traditions have not been lost but embedded in urban congregations through urban migration (Richman 2005, 117).

Rural Vodou centers on the inheritors (*eritaj*, *lafanmi*) of the religious traditions and the land (*tè eritaj*, *lakou*) where their ancestors once lived. People maintain inheritances in four lines mediated via grandparents. The first inheritor is the original owner of a family's property, and the descendants share property rights and the spirits (familial, local, and national) passed down by the ancestors. These pantheons are unique to each ancestral inheritor, reflecting family traditions of African origin. The *eritaj* encapsulates a wealth of historical and cultural knowledge. Inheritors gather to feed family spirits on the Lakou's *demanbre* (inalienable family land), where a shrine is kept (Richman 2005, 117–18). In consuming the food, the spirit links the living with the ancestral inheritors and the land inheritance.

Haiti has experienced rapid population growth and accompanying ecological challenges. The "degradation" of forests by "wood fuel–driven deforestation" leads to erosion, warming, and drought (Ghilardi, Tarter, and Bailis 2018). Centralized government services, health care, employment, education, electricity, and technology attract rural Haitians to the cities. Urban Vodou has absorbed ideas from the migrants and boomeranged urban Vodou back to the countryside or abroad.

Temple Vodou of the plains changed to accommodate societal shifts. In Ti Rivyè near Léogâne, new "ritual intermediaries" and new "rites of passage" were introduced to adapt to the evolving situation of the Haitian people (Richman 2005, 118–19). A new class of ritual intermediaries claimed their authority on the basis of the long and costly initiation they received from a well-known *oungan* initiator at a temple away from their home village. The rise of this new class of *oungan ason* (priest of the sacred rattle) trained in Sèvis Ginen was accompanied by a shift in communication with the spirits. Rather than direct oracular interventions as described in Moreau de Saint-Méry (1797), a priest summoned the *lwa* from behind a white sheet via a sacred jar (*govi*).[26] Priests no longer spoke directly to spirits, and the spirits no longer spoke to people (Richman 2005, 120).

Familial descent groups attached to the Lakou viewed this professional class of priests as lacking prestige for having *purchased* rather than *inherited* the religion (Richman 2005, 121). In Ti Rivyè, some of the *oungan ason* proposed costly new rituals like the *maryaj lwa* (marriage to a spirit) in which a Vodouist marries a spirit who provides protection in return for service. Initiated in the ten-day *kanzo* initiation, the new Sèvis Ginen priest may take the prestigious *kanzo* ritual from the urban temple back to the countryside. The initiated Sèvis Ginen priests solidified the urban traditions by linking them to their own kinship lines, the family's inherited land, and locally prominent spirits (Richman 2005, 121). Oungan Michelet Alisma's Société Linto Roi Trois Mystères also fuses the mythology and structure of Sèvis Ginen with the traditions inherited through his family and the diverse traditions that emanate from Gonaïves.

The *oungan ason* who received the prestigious *kanzo* ritual and knew how to implement its services emerged as the most authoritative practitioners in Ti Rivyè. Priests who paid for the *ason* of the *kanzo* initiation enjoyed prestige and mobility. The process empowered charismatic priests to work full-time as leaders of temples. Oungan Nelson Marcenat in Bèl Rivyè expressed skepticism about the *oungan ason*'s "purchased" traditions compared to his "inherited Ginen" ones. In 2008, this sixty-five-year-old *oungan* had given a dozen *kanzo* initiations, a smaller number than urban priests.

Even if the *kanzo* initiation is associated with Sèvis Ginen in Haiti, it is not the only tradition to practice it. The *kanzo*, the *lave tèt*, or the *deka* are practiced in the diverse schools of Haitian Vodou. Vodun and Vodou are initiatory religions. The term *ká yíyi* in the Fon language means "receive the calabash," referring to a Vodun initiation ceremony in which a symbolic calabash is given along the lines of taking the *ason* calabash shaker in Haiti (Brand 2000b, 55). The Haitian Creole expression *kanzo* ("receive" + "fire"), from the Fon language, reflects a rite in the Haitian Vodou initiation ceremony in which the candidate takes a hot object (a dumpling or flame) to symbolize a new spiritual birth (Segurola and Rassinoux 2000, 546). It is not surprising that the *kanzo* initiation ritual was introduced in Ti Rivyè, since the production of initiates is the central function of a Sèvis Ginen priest. The priest must offer a significant experience in a competitive religious arena. A larger neoliberal dynamic produces local and regional displacements, the erosion of family networks, a rise in sex work, and intense competition, trends that set the stage for the Gede songs in chapter 4.

Born in Gonaïves, oungan Alisma resides in Miami, where he leads Société Linto Roi Trois Mystères. He was raised in the traditions of his family and in the temples of Gonaïves. In L'Artibonite, Sèvis Ginen and the *kanzo* are not yet established; instead, the *lave tèt* and *deka* initiations are practiced. The priests around Gonaïves refer to themselves as *sèvitè*, and their initiation takes a couple of days.

Called to the priestly vocation at age seven, oungan Alisma received a familial foundation. However, he wanted to refine his knowledge in the prestigious *kanzo* "school." The Sèvis Ginen *kanzo* initiation he received was a kind of doctorate in Vodou initiations. He had already been connected to the world of spirits since childhood. His guardian spirit had been healing people through him since his youth. Later as a teenager he traveled to Léogâne, where he completed his *kanzo*. In his early twenties, he spent some time in Togo, studying Vodun with a priest in that country. By 2018, oungan Alisma had initiated several dozen people in the *kanzo* initiation at Société Linto Roi in Miami.

I visited oungan Alisma in Gonaïves in 2014, and he showed me the temple he was building in order to introduce Sèvis Ginen's *kanzo* tradition to the city of his birth. He owns a hotel in the town and travels between Miami and Gonaïves on a regular basis. Oungan Alisma and oungan Misdor in Ti Rivyè illustrate the importance of travel to Sèvis Ginen initiation centers and *kanzo*'s subsequent diffusion from those sites. Each person who completes the rank of *oungan ason* or *manbo ason* can initiate others, but only dynamic priests lead. There are often second-, third-, and fourth-ranked priests working under a leader and proprietor. Oungan Alisma shows his hospitality in his willingness to share his culture with tourists, students, and candidates for initiation.

In Ti Rivyè, oungan Misdor (1892–1967) was charismatic, introducing locally several Sèvis Ginen traditions he had acquired in urban temples. He was so successful that he attracted regional and foreign guests, including researchers like Odette Mennesson-Rigaud, Harold Courlander, and Alfred Métraux. He introduced into the village Sèvis Ginen mortuary rites of passage, the *wete mò nan dlo* (retrieving the dead from the water) (Richman 2005, 122–24). The Sèvis Ginen mortuary rites are now added on top of a wake, a traditional Catholic service, burial, final prayer, a nine-day period of mourning, and a banquet. The *voye* (sending) ritual occurs shortly after death as the *oungan* sends the soul under the water to Ginen, briefly channeling the dead's faint voice. One year later, the soul is called from the water in an elaborate reclamation ritual. At that time, the reclaimed soul speaks to the living family members through the priest. A clay pot (*boule zen/boule wazen*) is consecrated for the ancestor, who can be contacted on the priest's altar (Deren 1953, 46–53; Richman 2005, 126).

In 1937, oungan Misdor was the only *oungan ason* capable of conducting the ritual. Prior to him, it was unknown. Its introduction suggests that the *oungan ason* had "laundered the changes in ritual practice" (Richman 2005, 28). This characterization goes a step too far, with a term like "laundered." Prestigious institutions with talented leaders are able to transform themselves. The formality, discipline, pageantry, and status of the Sèvis Ginen traditions are attractive.

Although the traditions of Sèvis Ginen may have been new in Ti Rivyè in the 1930s, they can be seen as formalizing looser preexisting structures. As the best-known tradition in the Department of the West, aspects of Sèvis Ginen's culture were likely known before oungan Misdor promoted them personally (Welele Doubout, personal correspondence, March 10, 2018). As Port-au-Prince draws Haitians for visits, the city also serves as a revolving door for the cultural dissemination of traditions like Sèvis Ginen.

In Ti Rivyè, oungan Misdor was the head of an all-male group of *oungan* that initiates females to serve as *ounsi* (initiates) who serve in ritual roles in ceremonies. The women complete a ten-day *kanzo* initiation in which they receive spiritual training and membership. The costly ritual imbues recipients with secret knowledge, protection, and inclusion as assistants or "horses" for spirit possession.

Membership was codified in the ritual clothing worn by women at ceremonies. Oungan Misdor did not produce *manbo ason* who could share his leadership. He viewed men taking the *ason* and women receiving the spirits. Possession performance from the female *ounsi* took place in ritual worship with dancing, drumming, and singing, and lacked the oracular dimension (Richman 2005, 129). Possession performances in oungan Misdor's community were not necessarily reflective of other communities in Haiti and its diaspora, where spirits do speak. I have seen Ogou possess a *manbo* and speak to Vodouists at Société Makaya in Miami, and Simbi possess an *oungan* and speak to his followers at Société Linto Roi Trois Mystères. As Welele Doubout explained: "[T]he spirits still speak. The spirits are happy to speak with their servants. Nothing has changed in the power that the *lwa* have in their mystical dimension, but they adapt themselves in each instant."[27]

I agree that the *lwa* are not big talkers in ceremonies, where they prefer to act out lessons, receive greetings, or show affection to their servants. Nevertheless, spirit possession and communication with the *lwa* is common in the context of consulting and in ceremonies for the great *lwa*.

I noticed a comparable scenario at a Gede service I attended at sèvitè Bonapat's Société Jenndantor des Gonaïves in Gonaïves. The gender division was similar to Karen Richman's description in Ti Rivyè (2005). Sèvitè Bonapat's two dozen all-female initiates wore black-and-purple dresses in honor of Gede, with the exception of an older *manbo*, dressed in white with a black scarf tied around her head. Unlike his initiates, sèvitè Bonapat dressed casually in jeans and a T-shirt. A major difference, however, was the prominence of sèvitè Bonapat, who maintained control over danced ritual.

When the drumming stopped, the *manbo* led prayers and hymns around the altar, however, illustrating female leadership in a male-led temple. Unlike the Sèvis Ginen system in which male and female priests frequently replace one another in ritual without regard to gender, sèvitè Bonapat led the danced ritual. There were counterclockwise circular features to the ceremony but also a back-and-forth movement characteristic of danced worship in Lakou Souvenance. Sèvis Ginen's greetings of the "stations" in the cycles of salutation were absent.

Several *ounsi* were possessed, and none of them spoke but instead quivered, kneeled with eyes fluttering, and held candles whose flames licked their chins and brows. The peak of the ceremony was sèvitè Bonapat's ten-minute possession performance in which he fed the *lwa* liquor and soft drinks through a hole in the dirt floor of the temple and caressed his chest with the candle's flame. He carried the most impressive possession. This is also the case in Sèvis Ginen, in which the great spirits ride the priests.

The gender exclusion of oungan Misdor's system may reflect an "invented" feature of his implementation of Sèvis Ginen in Ti Rivyè (Richman 2005). Sèvis Ginen does tend to be gender inclusive in cities like Miami. A candidate for initiation can work with either a *manbo* or an *oungan*. In a typical case in Miami, the main initiator collaborates with other priests and priestesses to assist with the arduous initiation.

Oungan Misdor's or sèvitè Bonapat's gender divisions differed from the way priests operate in Miami. Oungan Alisma operates his North Miami temple with the help of several male priests, but there are just as many *manbo* among them, including manbo Marie, oungan Alisma's wife.

Manbo Micla leads Société Makaya in Miami in coordination with several priests. There is no doubt about her authority, as female and male priests integrate into the cycles of salutation in her services. I have also attended ceremonies at Société Halouba in Miami, and, not knowing the community well, I could not tell if men or women were in charge. In all three of them, male and female priests from all three temples, in addition to priests from other congregations, took turns leading cycles of salutation in a type of relay. For example, oungan Alisma might lead the cycle for Legba, manbo Marie for Marasa, oungan Emmanuel for Loko, manbo Micla for Ayizan, and so on. Over the course of a Sèvis Ginen ceremony, the priest who completes a cycle of salutation shakes the *ason* in the direction of another priest seated in the audience to designate him or her for the next cycle. As there are as many as twenty-one cycles in a ceremony, it is common for several priests of both genders to take a turn leading one of the cycles of salutation.

Another way in which Sèvis Ginen in Miami differs from the description of the situation in Ti Rivyè pertains to gender and initiation. In Sèvis Ginen temples in Miami, initiators and candidates for initiation are both male and female, even if there is a tendency for more women to initiate.

There are perhaps tendencies in gender representation: male priests tend to become male spirits, and female priests tend to become female spirits. However, they are not blanket gender roles. Vodouists tend to recognize gender and sexual diversity. Men and women are priests; men and women are *ounsi*. Male spirits possess female priests: manbo Micla was the male Ogou's horse at a ceremony at Société Makaya. Female spirits possess male priests: Èzili Freda possessed oungan Alexis Stephan, and later, at the same ceremony, Ogou danced in his head, illustrating the unimportance of the horse's gender (Courlander 1973, 55).

Given the expenses surrounding the *kanzo* initiation and the collaboration between allied congregations, the *kanzo* ceremonies bring *oungan* and *manbo* from several temples together to take part in fastidious preparations. Days leading up to the *antre kanzo* (entering ceremony), days of seclusion (*kouche*), and a closing ceremony called the *leve kanzo* (lifting of the *kanzo*) are so demanding that a team of priests is needed. Oungan Alisma explained that the *kanzo* was the most difficult part of being a Vodou priest.

Temple Vodou transmitted common knowledge that has persisted in the face of slavery, colonialism, and occupation. The core features of the priesthood, the temple, ceremonies and services, the initiation, and the traditions and their rites are maintained in Haiti and its diaspora. The confederation of various African traditions in Sèvis Ginen is reflected in the motto "21 Nanchon Ginen" (21 Nations of Ginen). This school of Vodou has been successful at expanding the practice from Léogâne and Port-au-Prince to the towns and villages to which initiates return. Oungan Max Beauvoir's published collections of Vodou texts (2008a, 2008b) represent the culmination of Sèvis Ginen's sophistication in this generation, wedding mastery of Vodou's sacred language, Creole, with the highest expertise in the technicalities of preserving sacred songs.

THE LIMITATION OF THE BIGHT OF BENIN AND GAPS IN HAITIAN VODOU STUDIES

Captured Africans from regions where Vodun was practiced have managed to preserve major African traditions within Haitian Vodou. The traditions are as diverse as the regions from which enslaved people were taken. In addition to the ones from the Bight of Benin like Rit Rada, Rit Gede, Rit Danwonmen, Rit Nago, and Rit Ibo, for example, those from the Kongo and western Central Africa like Rit Kongo Fran, Rit Kongo Savann, Rit Makaya, and Rit Petwo Fran, among others, are active (Beauvoir 2008a, 187–96). I focus narrowly on the history and culture of the Aja-Fon and Gedevi-Yoruba founders of Vodou in Saint-Domingue for two reasons: their centrality in Haiti and the paucity of work on them.

The heavy emphasis on Saint-Domingue and Haiti in studies on Vodou (and Haitian studies in general) has produced textured knowledge on the Caribbean. Work on Kongo influences in Haiti from John Janzen (1982), Luc de Heusch (2000), and Christina Frances Mobley (2015) illustrates the potential of Africa-centered research for understanding the Caribbean. The nations of the Bight of Benin, however, have not been adequately studied even though they are a significant source of Vodou's traditions. This book benefits from the contributions of Haitianist scholars of Vodou, but it breaks away from the heavy emphasis on Saint-Domingue and Haiti by building the case that a deeper understanding of West African political, economic, and religious systems helps account for the foundation of Haitian Vodou and Haiti itself.

There are few mentions of Dahomian kings like Dako, Wegbadja, Akaba, Agaja, Tegbesu, or Kpengla in publications about Haitian Vodou. Scarce research exists on Dahomey and the Bight of Benin from a Haitian point of view. Where Dahomey is mentioned, little attention is paid to the slave-trading system of the royal family and its impact on the people sent to Saint-Domingue. Studies like Roumain (1943), Marcelin (1949), Deren (1953), Métraux (1972), Laguerre (1980), Brown (2001), McAlister (2002), Richman (2005), and Smith (2010) have advanced knowledge on aspects of Vodou, but few have yet parsed the historical sources of Haitian culture in the Bight of Benin. Zora Neale Hurston's (2018) retelling of Oluale Kossola's account of capture by the Dahomians has emerged as a significant exception.

A few authors have hinted at the potential for research focused on African kingdoms in the task of grappling with Vodou's historical and political roots. Rachel Beauvoir-Dominique and Didier Dominique describe King Agaja in positive terms:

> KADJA MENSOU, KADJA DOSOU, or AGADJA was a great conquering king of Dahomey between 1708 and 1732 [*sic*]. He created an army of female Amazons (Mazonn) who had as a motto that they would not strike the enemy until they saw the whites of their eyes. They also say, those women used to cut off their left breasts so they would not be obstructed when they drew their warm saber. (Beauvoir-Dominique and Dominique 2003, 69; authors' capitalization, my translation)

Maya Deren mentions "Kadja Bossu" and connects the king to the spirit "Bossu" (Bosou) (1953, 137). She relates a legend purporting that "[i]n his kingdom there was no Vodu" and that "women bore goats and goats gave birth to men." Recent publications begin to address the problems that underlie the study of Haitian Vodou's history. As Mimerose Beaubrun writes, the Fon were a people "from the region of Dahomey who vanquished the Gedevis (or Gedes) and then took them prisoner" (2013, 237–38). There are counternarratives about Dahomian kings, too. Dyeri Jil and Ivwoz S. Jil, for example, suggest that in spite of King Agaja's putative opposition to slavery, he was "obliged" to sell people in order to buy the modern weapons needed to keep power (2009, 106).

I will instead adopt John Thornton's argument that the African elite sold enslaved people to Europeans on a voluntary basis and not through "weapons whitemail" (1998), a case that is made in chapter 1. The focus on Haitian Vodou through the study of African history and culture reflects a methodological approach, a topic explored next.

THE THEORIES AND METHODOLOGIES THAT SHAPE VODOU HERMENEUTICS

The linguistic, literary, religious studies, historical, comparative, mythological, ethnomusicological, and cultural analyses in this volume reflect this book's methodology of "Vodou hermeneutics." The theory and practice of Vodou textual hermeneutics is rooted in explanatory methodologies in the humanities and social sciences. Analyzing Vodou songs with diverse scholarly methods serves an informed public culture and nourishes the quest for mutual recognition and consensus between scholars and Vodouists (Ernst 2011, 20–22).

The use of resources from multiple disciplines seeks diverse perspectives and a fair-minded understanding of the religion of other people (Ernst 2011, 20–22). Vodou culture and texts reflect historical and material relationships. Ideological, political, racial, and gender dynamics are conscious, semiconscious, or unconscious in texts. Vodou hermeneutics assumes that texts and interpreters have discernable, hidden, and unconscious ideological motivations (Mosala 1989, 5–9). The plethora of methods seeks to discover history and explicate material struggles by adopting diverse tools of analysis and interpretation.

Social scientific methodologies reconstruct the societies, systems, and cultural practices of Vodun and Vodou. Materialist orientation examines the modes of economic production and the competing and clashing social classes within them. Dahomian, Alladan, Huedan, and Gedevi, as well as Saint-Dominguan and international modes of production and social formation shape the historical discussion on Haitian Vodou (Mosala 1989, 103). As adherents of one of the founding cultures of the African Atlantic world, Vodouists were closely connected to the modes of economic production, supporting or disputing social structure and strongly shaping ideology.

The Vodou hermeneutical methodology of this book seeks to critically interrogate the history, culture, and ideologies of the creators and practitioners of Vodun and Vodou. Examining the social structures, languages, and cultures of Haitian Vodou's sources is the backbone of a transatlantic empirical orientation. The social scientific approach interprets by means of texts the interactions of civilizations, social classes, economic policies, and social determinants. Social scientific research helps me reconstruct the interactions of people in the Aja-Fon and Gedevi-Yoruba areas. The identification of African place-names and ethnic groups connected to Haiti in history books and maps—and their reproduction in Joe Aufmuth's maps in this volume—illustrate the centrality of cartography and ethnography in this project.

Linguistic methodologies connect Vodun and Vodou through comparative etymological analyses. Phonological and semantic comparison of the names and attributes of spirits, ethnolinguistic groups, toponyms, flora and fauna, and the extended Vodun and Vodou lexical fields represents a corpus of evidence about African cultural transfer in the Caribbean. In addition to an analysis of hundreds of words, the methodology of language documentation is reflected in the Haitian Creole transcriptions and English translations of the songs.

The Vodou hermeneutics developed in this volume borrows from literary critical analyses in order to understand the genre, structure, style, language, meanings, and poetics of songs. Literary critical approaches consider the functions, intertextual features, and historical context of songs. The notions of unwritten history and the unconsciousness of texts are literary critical notions reflected in my study of West African politics and religion between 1600 and 1800 in chapters 1 and 2 (Eagleton 1978, 89). The unconscious aspect of Vodou songs can be retrieved partially through multidisciplinary, historical, social scientific, and comparative methodologies.

Formalist analysis focused on structure draws from exegetical approaches to the Qur'an. For example, Carl W. Ernst's study of the "symmetrical or ring structure" (2011, 49) of passages that include lines that mirror each other, is helpful for the discernment of similar structures in Vodou songs. "Ring composition" in the Qur'an looks at how tensions at the center of a passage are resolved with affirmations that "ring in" conflict at the beginning or ending edges of a passage (Ernst 2011, 67). Resolving tension through ring structure is also a feature of Vodou songs.

Methodologies in ethnomusicology are reflected in my study of the physical and verbal behaviors of music, its symbolic dimensions, and the place of songs as cultural history (Merriam 1964, 32). A central concern of ethnomusicology is the discovery of the role that music plays in humanity's cultures of the past and present (Nettl 1964, 242). I borrow from ethnomusicology the focus on the products of musicians as social groups, the content of their song texts, and the religious and social functions of Vodun and Vodou music. The ethnomusicological approach treats Vodou songs as symbolic systems that shed light on cognitive, behavioral, aural, and historical constructions (Howard 2014, 9).

Studies on West African ethnomusicology and Vodun provided guidance on the form of spirit-based religion in the region from which Haitian ancestors were taken. Gilbert Rouget (1990) compares music and trance worldwide, including in Aja-Fon culture, while in a later work Rouget (2001) examines music in Aja-Fon Vodun initiation, yielding valuable connections. My book does not, however, offer music notation in the manner of Lois Wilcken and Frisner Augustin (1992) or Georges Vilson (2013), instead focusing on the transcription, translation, and interpretation of songs.

Vodou hermeneutics is founded on pioneering works in the documentation of Haitian songs. The path was beaten by Milo Marcelin (1949), Michel Laguerre (1980), Gage Averill (1997), Elizabeth McAlister (2002), and Max Beauvoir (2008a, 2008b). Each of them studies songs, in the process building a corpus of texts and text-analytic practices for Haitian studies. Averill (1997) examines the intersections of political power with the lyrics of *konpa* pop music, whereas McAlister (2002) studies the songs and culture of *rara* festival bands. They illustrate the use of multiple methodologies including participant observation, interviews, research on the historical and political context, and the documentation and interpretation of songs presented bilingually in Haitian Creole and English.

Historical methodology entailed poring over contemporary histories and period narratives in order to get an idea about the African kingdoms, peoples, cultures, and economic activities under examination. The study of Alladan, Huedan, Gedevi, and Dahomian polities, the wax and wane of their political and military power, their slave trade, and their religious cultures aims to contextualize the experience and world view of the enslaved people who founded the Rada Rite and the Gede Rite.

The historical account of the agents of political and religious power in West Africa helps to explicate the genesis and historical layers of Vodou songs. While bearing their part of Caribbean culture, Vodou songs and mythology reflect the deep well of African cultures, norms, and politics. Songs encase historical and mythological memory. Vodou hermeneutics is centuries removed from the historical origins of the songs and therefore tries to approach the songs by reconstructing the sources and conditions that gave rise to them. The accounts of slave traders and diplomats like William Snelgrave ([1734] 1971), Robert Norris ([1789] 1968), Archibald Dalzel ([1793] 1967), and others are flawed but unavoidable perspectives on the Aja kingdoms.

Research on the Aja-Fon and Gedevi-Yoruba region builds on I. A. Akinjogbin's (1967) and Maurice Ahanhanzo Glélé's (1974) historical studies, Edna Bay's (1998) research on Dahomian royalty, Robin Law's (1997, 2004) portraits of the kingdoms of Allada and Hueda, and John Thornton's (1998) macroscopic examination of slavery in the African Atlantic world. Chapter 1 differs from accounts by Africanist historians because it dialectically reads for the ways that the slave trade in African kingdoms impacted Saint-Domingue and Haiti. This involves detailing the targets of African military conquests and slave raiding while examining the mechanisms in African kingdoms for turning people into commodities for the European slave market.

The focus on religion in the Aja-Fon and Gedevi-Yoruba region in chapter 2 brings together comparative approaches in religious studies, anthropology, and history. Early sources for Vodun in Dahomey, Allada, and Hueda include the biased but unavoidable Sir Richard Francis Burton (1893) and Auguste Le Hérissé (1911). Serious research on Vodun abounds in the later twentieth century with Pierre Verger (1957), who collects and interprets Vodun and Orisha songs, and Roger Brand (2000a, 2000b), who studies the Fon Vodun lexicon and translates source texts into French. Gilbert Rouget (1990, 2001) carries out anthropological fieldwork and takes photographs that chronicle initiation in Dahomey in the 1960s. Basilio Segurola and Jean Rassinoux's dictionary of the Fon language (2000) facilitates the discovery of transatlantic etymological relationships.

The comparative methodology used in this book identifies African, Haitian, and Haitian diaspora cultural features (Bastide 2003, xxxi). The main resources for intra-Haitian comparison are Beauvoir's magisterial song collections (2008a, 2008b). Both collections mark Vodou's journey from oral literature to scripture, giving access to a broad array of the religion's sacred literature. They provide a basis for an exegetical methodology that compares source texts within a tradition in order to build an interpretation based on relevant contextual data. Other resources in Haitian Vodou songs enabled me to pursue comparative readings, especially Roumain (1943), Marcelin (1949), and Laguerre (1980). Important publications on Vodou include Herskovits (1937), Deren (1953), Métraux (1972), Courlander (1973), Brown (2001), Michel (1995), McAlister (2002), Beauvoir-Dominique and Dominique (2003), Richman (2005), Bellegarde-Smith and Michel (2006), Jil and Jil (2009), Smith (2010), LaMenfo (2011), and Beaubrun (2013), among others.

Vodou hermeneutics relies on the analysis of mythology. Myths reflect a spectrum of stories stretching from entertaining tales to religious stories taken as the foundation of spiritual and temporal authority (Campbell 1959, 3). Mythology in the Aja-Fon and the Gedevi-Yoruba cultures serves as an agent of socialization, education, and psychological "easement" in the form of entertainment (Ifie and Adelugbo 1998, iv). Mystics, seers, poets, theologians, and kings assert the authority of sacred myths. Written or memorized liturgies, songs, and stories concretize their significance. Myths are "energy-releasing, life-motivating, and directing agents" (Campbell 1959, 4). Although people may agree about the nature of the world, their myths drive them apart as political systems exploit them for horrific objectives. Myths serve as a foundation for life in providing a schema for discovering meaning, and as a sign of death in their inspiration of fanaticism and violence.

Myths about creation, governance, the foundation of society, and feats of heroism are topics germane to the "gods" (Ifie and Adelugbo 1998, 22). This mythology of the gods or spirits is rooted in the themes of family, being and nonbeing, armies, palaces and kingdoms, original heroes, farming grounds, fishing waters and the sea, mountains, springs, trees, and fire. Myths of death and the afterlife are centered on "communality with the dead" (Ifie and Adelugbo 1998, 24–26).

Three theories inform the historical treatment of myths. Diffusionary analysis examines how myths diffused around the Bight of Benin and thereafter to Haiti during the slave trade. Likewise, variations in myths and the breadth of their geographical dispersion raise stakes for theories of a single source, called "monogenesis," versus theories of spontaneous multiple generation, called "polygenesis" (Ifie and Adelugbo 1998, 18).

The methodologies employed in this volume are grounded in a Creolist approach to Haitian studies in the sense that I give two complete collections of *rasin* songs in Haitian Creole and English. The corpus and the interpretations seek to illustrate aspects of Haitian civilization that merit enfranchisement: the Creole language and the Vodou religion.

As important as reading and writing, this book depended on participant observation. Our contacts and friendships, our fluency in Haitian Creole, our active participation in formal and informal activities, the recording of our observations on video, the taking of field notes, and our attention to tacit and explicit information are hallmarks of the approach that we embraced (DeWalt and DeWalt 2011, 5). Funding from the National Endowment for the Humanities to build the Archive of Haitian Religion and Culture provided dozens of University of Florida and Duke University faculty members and students, including myself, with opportunities to travel to Haiti and locations in the Haitian diaspora like Miami and Cuba to record ceremonies and interviews.

On our voyages, senior Vodou priests and priestesses escorted us, facilitated meetings, and helped us obtain consent to attend and film ceremonies. After a ceremony or interview, we gave a small love offering of cash as a token of our appreciation. We remained respectful and mindful of the people we met, because our efforts were guided by respect for Haiti's Creole and Vodou cultures. The biggest blessing of the fieldwork was the chance to meet insightful informants who were generous in their correspondence. Welele Doubout and Jean-Eddy Dieujuste answered dozens of questions over the years. Experts like Jistis Liben, and Dyeri Jil and Ivwoz S. Jil, offered insightful responses. Oungan Michelet Alisma, oungan Max Beauvoir, oungan Emmanuel, oungan Marcus, manbo Marie, manbo Micla, manbo Maria van Daalen, oungan Bozanfè, manbo Vye Zo Komande LaMenfo, and manbo Sally Ann Glassman gave generously of their knowledge as I navigated the Vodou tradition as an academic researcher.

MY PERSONAL STAKE IN THIS PROJECT

There are two complementary efforts dedicated to decolonization demonstrated in my modest body of writing and teaching: the defense and documentation of Haitian Creole and Vodou. The inclusion of Haitian Creole song lyrics here illustrates my ongoing effort to document and celebrate the language and culture of Haiti. I am fighting for the idea that Creole speakers and Vodouists deserve the same rights and protections as the speakers of other languages and the practitioners of other religions. Creole and Vodou, in my view, reflect features of greatness and authenticity.

Lastly, this project aims to fill in gaps left by our earlier book, *Vodou Songs in Haitian Creole and English*. Several people have asked about obtaining recorded music and in-depth interpretations of the songs. The compact discs this book is based upon are available to the public. As a music lover, my goal in writing a book that examines the historical and religious roots of Rasin Figuier and Rasin Bwa Kayiman's songs has been to gain the opportunity to focus on recordings and songs that I consider among the finest treasures of Haiti's intangible culture.

CONCLUSION: CHAINS AND RAINBOWS OVER THE ATLANTIC

The captives shackled into the hulls of boats in the Middle Passage projected Vodou's rainbow culture, grounding this tragedy in hope. The history of the kings of Dahomey, the structure of their state and economy, and their alliances with European slave traders are central problems addressed next, in chapter 1. The impact of the political, social, economic, and religious policies of Dahomey, Allada, and Hueda on the people dragged away to Saint-Domingue is a submerged part of Haitian history.

I focus on historical narratives to discover the communities and nations identified by historians as profiting from or falling prey to the slave trade. The history of profiteering and victimization informs the story of Haitian Vodou's

Rada Rite and Gede Rite, among other rites, since their founders in Saint-Domingue were enslaved in the region of the Bight of Benin.

Chapter 2 examines religion in the kingdoms of Allada, Hueda, and Dahomey, straddling the Atlantic to explore a part of Haitian Vodou's heterogeneous African sources. Since Dahomian society has been studied for three centuries, chapter 2 mines a wide range of literature on its religion and culture.

The second half of the book examines the structure, history, and traditions of two major Haitian Sèvis Ginen rites that originate in those African kingdoms. The Rada Rite (from "Allada") is one of the core rites of the "21 Nanchon Ginen" (21 Nations of Ginen) and the focus of chapter 3. The Rada Rite has the largest recorded pantheon among the Vodou rites and also involves the best-known spirits, including Ountò, Legba, Marasa, Loko, Ayizan, Danbala Wèdo and Ayida Wèdo, Sobo and Badè, Èzili, Agwe, and others (Beauvoir 2008a, 187–96). Chapter 3 explores the history and structure of the Rada Rite. The heart of the chapter focuses on songs for Rada spirits recorded on Racine (Rasin) Figuier's compact disc *Vodou Lakay* (Vodou at Home; 2004). I wanted the songs examined in the book to be accessible and of the highest audio quality. I treated the songs as sacred literature, as do Haitian Vodouists. When asked about spirits, Vodouists cite songs for evidence, "suggesting that they are the 'holy word' of *vodun* theology and an important device in stabilizing the details of belief" (Herskovits 1937, 314). I hold to this methodology and have utilized a large corpus of Vodou songs to inform discussions.

Chapter 4 analyzes the Gede Rite and its spirits. While Rada originates in ethnic Aja communities that settled around the towns of Allada and Hueda near the Atlantic coast, the Gede Rite comes from the Gedevi-Yoruba communities that once claimed the Abomey plateau in the northern hinterland. The Aja invaders who founded the kingdom of Dahomey around 1625 conquered, integrated, and enslaved a significant number of Gedevi people. Aja practitioners of the Alladan or Huedan Rada traditions and the Gedevi-Yoruba practitioners of the Abomeyan Gede traditions were swept up by the hundreds of thousands and traded as enslaved people for objects by members of the ruling enslaver classes of the Aja kingdom of Dahomey and the Yoruba kingdom of Oyo, among others. Before falling to the Dahomians, the Alladans and Huedans ran their own vast slave trade.

Gede takes center stage each November in Haiti, a time when people remember their dearly departed and pay homage to Gede spirits. Images of death such as crosses, skulls, and cemeteries are backdrops for pelvic thrusting, phallic symbols, and the rubbing of the genitals with rum soaked in twenty-one types of hot peppers. Gede's patronage covers birth, childhood, sex, and death. Gede heals or harms—in equal measures, Gede saves the living from annihilation and carries them over death's precipice. Chapter 4 examines the history and structure of the Gede Rite. The heart of the chapter is the study of the songs for the Gede spirits recorded on Rasin Bwa Kayiman's compact disc *Guede* (2004). The original recordings, the bilingual presentation of the songs, and the interpretations strive to understand this world religion and culture.

Moreau de Saint-Méry's description of Vodou (1797) provides evidence for continuity from the colonial through the neocolonial historical periods. Vodou was practiced in towns and plantations, and emerged in each setting with local features and adaptions linked to the needs of priests and worshippers. Vodou ritual and tradition may be dynamic and changing, but there is profound consistency in the transmission. Old traditions are kept unchanged in some places. Traditions are replaced or upgraded with complementary but distinct Vodou traditions in others. The importation of traditions may take a particular form, like gender exclusion in the case of Ti Rivyè's male-only priesthood versus the gender inclusivity of many temples in Port-au-Prince and Miami. There are communities that initiate homosexuals and others that do not. Each *oungan* or *manbo* implements the tradition in a manner that adheres to the one received from her or his initiators and their main spirits.

Sèvis Ginen is a systematic religion. The "21 Nations of Ginen" that assemble within it reflect a structure that balances uniformity with heterogeneity. The ceremonies in the twenty-one rites are built on a common core of cycles of salutation and ritual greetings at the "stations" of the temple, in addition to a multitude of rite-specific and cycle-specific traditions.

Although adaptions are important to Sèvis Ginen's dynamism, its rigidity indicates its solid foundation and the dependability of the religion's transmitters. The next chapter explores Aja-Fon and Gedevi-Yoruba politics and history in order to lay a foundation for examining the emergence of Haitian Vodou.

Chapter 1

THE AFRICAN POLITICAL ROOTS OF HAITIAN VODOU

The Aja-Fon and Gedevi-Yoruba Kingdoms and the Slave Trade

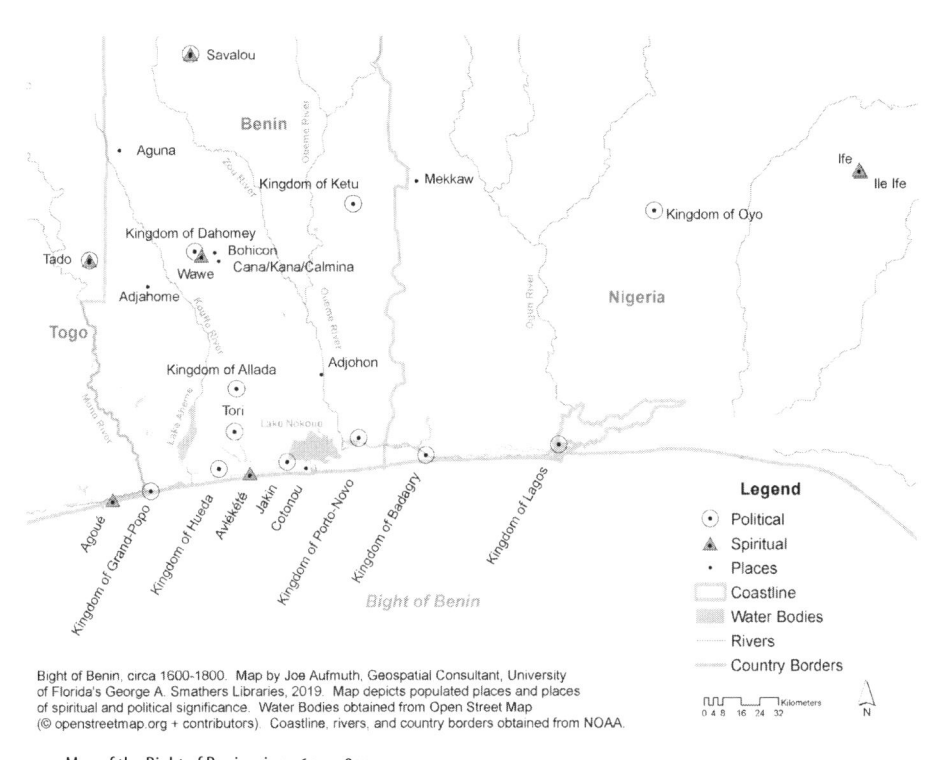

Map of the Bight of Benin, circa 1600–1800.

INTRODUCTION

The Rada and Gede Rites originate in the Aja-Fon (or Aja for short) and Gedevi-Yoruba (or Gedevi for short) regions of West Africa, which form a "commonwealth" with some degree of shared linguistic intelligibility

(Akinjogbin 1967). The history and culture of the Aja and Gedevi peoples require attention if we hope to understand the origins of the Rada and Gede Rites in Haitian Vodou. Vodunists were both victims and organizers of the African leg of the slave trade. To understand how Vodou appeared in Saint-Domingue, one must study the relationship of Vodun to royal power. Why did royal Aja authorities order the capture of African people, including vulnerable Aja people, for the racist economic project of foreigners from Europe? Where do Vodun and Vodou fit into the transatlantic slave trade?

To approach Haitian Vodou, I examine the history and culture of its early sources, the people from the Aja and Yoruba kingdoms and their service to vodun or orisha spirits. More than 685,000 enslaved people were transported to Saint-Domingue from West Africa and western Central Africa in the eighteenth century (Ramsey 2011, 29). Early in the colony's "sugar boom" period between 1697 and 1720, Arada (Aja) and Nago (Yoruba) captives from the Bight of Benin made up the dominant imported groups (Ramsey 2011, 29). They were the "founders" of core aspects of Vodou tradition. Rada and Gede were well established when enslaved people from western Central Africa began to outnumber them after the 1720s (Geggus 1991, 36).

The earlier arrival of captives from the Bight of Benin gave them the advantage of time, linguistic knowledge, and adjustment. Other factors that favored their traditions were linked to the habits of slave buyers. Sugarcane planters preferred purchasing enslaved people from the Bight of Benin, while coffee planters purchased the western Central Africans that the sugar planters had turned down (Geggus 1993, 81). Since Saint-Domingue's sugarcane plantations were situated near the settled plains and towns, the practitioners of the Rada and Gede Rites would have had greater access to the towns and cities after independence. The settled plains surrounding the capital of Port-au-Prince in the Department of the West remain the stronghold for the "Rada-centric" Sèvis Ginen traditions.

THE UNCONSCIOUS PAST

Dahomian kings were authoritarian rulers and slave traders who expanded the kingdom to ensure their own security while capturing people for a lucrative market. In my study of the kingdoms that profited from slave deportations, I examine who raided and who got raided, what justifications were made, and when and where it occurred. Studying slave trading informs the history of Haitian Vodou, since its practitioners got caught up in that system. The deportees reconstituted traditions like Rada, Gede, and Nago as self-standing systems with linkages to each other. To understand how they were reconstituted into systematic rites in Saint-Domingue and Haiti, it helps to study the political, cultural, and religious systems that were mobilized to facilitate the slave trade.

I examine the slave trade in the interior of African kingdoms and study the state, army, and rogue militia groups that controlled it. African armies raided and traded the people they enslaved. Residents of small towns like Cetre-Crue (in present-day Benin) sold residents of rival villages into slavery. Entrepreneurial slave raiders and traders were active (Snelgrave 1971, 186). The slave trade pervaded the Aja economy. The Aja slave trade supplied labor to the agricultural sector, and the sale of slaves to foreigners enriched the owners, the royal family, and licensed traders (Savary 1975, 34). As Saint-Domingue was a slave society, so, too, were the coastal kingdoms of the Bight of Benin. However, their relationship with the Europeans was asymmetrical, as demonstrated by the unidirectional flow of enslaved people out of Africa. Books on Saint-Domingue, Haiti, and Haitian Vodou give the impression that the only meaningful discussion of the island's history involves events that took place on the island itself. Historians of Haiti have generally not written on the history of West Africa in spite of its centrality to Haitian studies.

AFRICAN SLAVERY

Cornerstone works on kingdoms like Allada, Hueda, and Dahomey confirm the arguments outlined in John Thornton's *Africa and Africans in the Making of the Atlantic World, 1400–1800* (1998). He demonstrates that slavery was widespread among the African elite when European traders first arrived in the 1400s. Aja and Gedevi histories suggest, however, that in diverting the African slave trade, European slave traders vastly increased its size and violence. The kingdom of Dahomey presents an example of the rapid magnification of violence and slave raiding after contact with Europeans.

In bureaucratic terms, the European slave trade mirrored the Atlantic African one in its administration to maximize profit to the state. A European slave trader obtained a license from a European state official and eventually negotiated the purchase of African enslaved people with an African state official, often a king. Europeans visited kings and officials, negotiated with them, provided presents, and paid customs. Over the decades and centuries, Europeans sought to stabilize prices, ensure access to enslaved people, and eliminate competition via exclusive treaties that they negotiated, mostly unsuccessfully, with African states (Thornton 1998, 54–56, 65).

The participation of the African elite in the slave trade was voluntary. Financial and political motivations were more significant than coercion from Europeans. African states that allowed the slave trade did not experience significant disruptions in that trade, suggesting its established status. The African elite participated voluntarily in the slave trade because it was a structural feature of most African states. The transatlantic slave trade was an expansive outgrowth of the internal slave trade on the African continent (Thornton 1998, 73–74, 120).

The practice of slavery was ubiquitous in Atlantic Africa because it was one of the only means of producing private wealth. The African elite lived in societies in which the transfer of the ownership of people was the legal basis for wealth. Under European law, private land ownership was the precondition for slavery and wealth production. Slavery was the equivalent of the landlord-tenant relationship in the African context, since land in African states was not owned privately but corporately (Thornton 1998, 74, 95).

Because the African elite accumulated substantial wealth in the form of enslaved people, they could sell large numbers of them to Europeans. As land could not be owned, enslaved people provided the primary means of holding private wealth and enhancing economic gains. African slave owners could use the king's land and pay rent on it, but they could not claim ownership over it. The king could remove a land user at will and freely reassign that land to another rent producer. In the absence of private property, legal systems in African states ensured that small cultivators could farm for long tenures (Thornton 1998, 76, 82, 84). The products of the land were owned, not the actual land, hence the centrality of slavery in Africa before European slave buyers arrived.

The African elite's slave ownership represented potential human capital for European buyers. In owning enslaved people, African entrepreneurs controlled the production of wealth. Enslaved people were put to the service of building administrations and armies. Amassing agriculturalist and military slaves, as was done by the Kongo kings in the town of Mbanza in the 1400s, increased centralized power. Intelligent enslaved people who were owned by kings could become wealthy and powerful, too, a fact that points to a different type of slavery than the one practiced in the Caribbean (Thornton 1998, 85, 91, 93).

Marriage was another African institution in which elite men could employ wives as a labor force for agriculture, weaving, pottery, and manufacturing. Marriage to several wives indicated status and the assemblage of a loyal workforce (Thornton 1998, 86). The participation of Africans in the Atlantic slave trade was tied to legal systems that turned free people into enslaved people. Judicial enslavement entailed the capture of an entire extended family. The military enslavement of "aliens" was the most important source of such people. They were captured through land conquest or raiding. Snatching people had advantages over taking land, since new territories had to be administered, requiring time and effort. Captured enslaved people were marched home and put to work, a strategy typical of the ministates on the Atlantic coast. Armies representing Oyo, Dahomey, Songhay, and Jolof captured territory and enslaved survivors who toiled domestically, serving to centralize the state, accrue power to kings, and bring revenue to their sellers (Thornton 1998, 99–111).

European technology and armies may have occasionally assisted African armies to capture people, but they were not decisive factors in the Atlantic slave trade. European weapons had slow rates of fire and were designed for opponents in armor. African warfare was close range, and thus the slow and bulky firearms were inefficient. In the Kongo, slave raiding was conducted by the Portuguese army between 1580 and 1622, with African armies supporting the Europeans. The growth of mass African armies led to the expansion of human exports from 9,500 enslaved people annually in 1600 to 36,000 annually in 1700. African armies adopted methods of musket warfare, but that never allowed Europeans to engage in weapons embargoes against African states because no Europeans maintained a monopoly on weapons trading (Thornton 1998, 114, 118, 123).

EARLY CONTACT BETWEEN THE AJA AND FRENCH SLAVE TRADERS

Prior to the arrival of European traders, the mining of iron and the extraction of clay were conducted in the Bight of Benin. After 1400, the northern Sahelian states' demand for iron reached the Aja region. Commodities in coastal markets included salt, salted fish, meat and wild game, textiles, basketry, calabashes, wooden and ceramic bowls, coral, produce, and medicinal plants. Several thousand people visited the markets that were held every four days in Apa, Savi, and Jakin (Monroe 2014, 38–41).

French slave traders began doing business on the coast of West Africa in the seventeenth century and expanded their trade to western Central Africa and southern East Africa in the eighteenth century. This book's focus is on the Aja and Yoruba regions, an area including parts of present-day Ghana, Togo, Benin, and Nigeria, where the Vodun religion remains anchored. In 1700, the Aja and Yoruba regions stretched along the coast from the Niger River in the east to the Mono River in the west, and plunged two hundred miles inland (Akinjogbin 1967, 10). The peoples of the region shared compatible cultures by virtue of related languages as well as long-standing contacts, treaties, and military conflicts. The state and society were organized around important towns and leading families. At the head of these societies, an absolute monarch was served through the work of his subjects.

THE AJA AND YORUBA REGIONS AND THE TERM "AJA"

The Yoruba people controlled the central and eastern regions of the area under discussion, whereas the Aja controlled the west (Akinjogbin 1967, 11). "Aja" is more or less synonymous with "Fon," designating both a people and a language. Today, linguists group languages like Aja, Fon, and Ewe under the term "Gbe" (Bay 1998, 41). This chapter will follow the story of the Aja, who migrated to the Abomey plateau, founded the Dahomian kingdom, subjugated and intermarried with the local Gedevi-Yoruba, and ultimately generated the Fon language, today the largest linguistic group in Benin (Brand 1975, 15). The salience of the Rada and Gede Rites in Haitian Vodou suggests, however, that many Aja and Gedevi were sold into slavery. The question is, how?

The Yoruba kingdoms included Benin (Ibini), Ife, Oyo, and others. Some of the Aja kingdoms included Allada, Hueda, Popo, Jakin, and Dahomey. The polities of Dahomey, Hueda, Allada, Gedevi-Yoruba, and Oyo are my focus, because their armies and mercenaries sold to the French many of the enslaved people who arrived in Saint-Domingue.

The word "Aja" or "Adja" still refers to the ethnic group. In the theology of the Haitian *manbo* Aunt Tansia, a Vodouist becomes "Adja" when he or she accepts the "Ginen order," avoiding malicious acts for personal gain. A person chosen by the spirits merits confidence; she possesses "Je" (clairvoyance) and is "Adja" (Beaubrun 2013, 95, 187). The "Adja initiate" has attained the highest spiritual degree. In these Caribbean uses, the ethnonym "Aja" points to an excellent practitioner and a model citizen. Grann Adja, as we will see, is also a female, glass-eating Rada spirit.

EARLY YORUBA CONQUESTS OF AJA TERRITORIES

Territorial claims exacerbated tensions between the Aja and Yoruba people. Oral records suggest that when the Aja came into closer contact with the Yoruba in the 1300s, they formed Yoruba-like kingdoms and absorbed elements of Yoruba culture and language, a process that continues. The Yoruba armies expanded westward into Aja territories, causing the displacement of Aja populations further to the west. The large Yoruba population had far-reaching influence (Akinjogbin 1967, 11, 13). Travelers in the Aja and Yoruba region noted that the lingua franca was "Alkomysh," spoken by the "Olukumi," a term used to refer to the Yoruba people in the once Aja-controlled region (Akinjogbin 1967, 13).

The Yoruba people who took Aja lands included the Igede Yoruba subgroup. The Gedevi people settled and grew numerous on the Abomey plateau between 1400 and 1600. These Gedevi people established the Gede Rite as one of the building blocks of Sèvis Ginen and Haitian identity. The story of how the Gedevi got to Saint-Domingue is at the heart of "submerged" precolonial African history.

THE IMPETUS FOR FOUNDING THE KINGDOM OF DAHOMEY

The European slave trade produced the crisis behind the rapid formation of the kingdom of Dahomey. The rise of Dahomey meant the disappearance or submission of the Gedevi people on the Abomey plateau. Prior to the arrival of Europeans, slave trading was not a significant part of the Aja and Yoruba regions. No early visitors witnessed a slave market in the area (Akinjogbin 1967, 18). This does not mean that slavery was not practiced, but it suggests that the form and scale were completely different from what emerged after contact with Europeans. Aja people in kingdoms like Hueda, Allada, and Jakin were the first to encounter the Portuguese, who were looking for gold, pepper, and enslaved people in the 1460s. The French (first arrived in 1530), English (1553), and Dutch (1595) slave traders came soon after (Akinjogbin 1967, 21).

The construction of a Dutch factory in Aja territory in 1595 set off a crisis. The Europeans fought for dominance and terrorized coastal communities, including burning homes and canoes in retaliation for resistance. The Dutch fomented divisions as they groomed African strongmen to supply them with enslaved people. African slave-trading partners sought the economic advantages and products offered by the European traders. Imported goods, guns, ammunition, gunpowder, currency in cowries, gold, alcohol, cloth, and luxury goods like music boxes, mirrors, and beads were offered for enslaved people.

The incursions and settlements of the Yoruba people had pushed the Aja people into towns like Allada and Hueda on the Atlantic coast twenty years before the arrival of the Dutch in 1595 (Akinjogbin 1967, 21). Although the Aja and Yoruba waged war periodically, many Yoruba people in the Aja region had settled there before the transatlantic period (Merlo and Vidaud 1984, 281). The Yoruba king Oduduwa controlled an area between the Oueme and Volta Rivers in the twelfth century, and Yoruba population movements into the coastal Aja region followed countless Yoruba military expeditions. The Ayizo near Allada paid annual tributes to the Yoruba capital of Oyo, illustrating Yoruba influence in Aja areas. One of the Ayizo's main vodun was Aida, a spirit known as Ayida Wèdo in Haitian Vodou's Rada Rite. The Ayizo in Allada absorbed Aja and Huedan people, a process helped along by a shared culture. The absorptiveness of Alladan culture gave the city a "mystical suzerainty" (Merlo and Vidaud 1984, 283).

In the memories of the Aja of the 1590s, the Gedevi-Yoruba areas of the Abomey plateau were once their lands, a fount of resentment soon to be mobilized for political purposes and slave trading. After contact was made with the European slave traders, a new way of thinking was emerging among the Aja.

THE ORIGIN OF AJA POWER IN TADO AND THE AGASUVI RULING FAMILY

Tado is the Aja people's legendary town of origin. Oral traditions hold that the Aja of Dahomey came from Tado, a place in contemporary Togo. In the 1960s, the ritual language used for prayers and offerings in honor of the kings of Abomey was in "ancient Aja," a language only known by priests and associated with Tado (Glélé 1974, 36).[1] The Aja people settled territory along the coast, east of Tado. Leading Aja families migrated to Allada when they failed to take the throne in Tado (Glélé 1974, 37). The Tado migrants in Allada became the ruling group within a few generations.

In the royal myth of Allada, Tado's Princess Aligbonon mated with a mysterious leopard while traveling through a forest and gave birth to Agasu, the half-leopard founder of the "clan of Agasuvi" (Bay 1998, 48). Half-beast, no woman would marry Agasu, so Aligbonon brought in a "young aunt" from her native village of Yakaki (Merlo and Vidaud 1984, 279). Their descendants grew numerous and aspired to take power. This founding spirit-king of the Dahomian dynasty is preserved in Haitian Vodou's Rada Rite as Agasou, protector of Dahomian culture in Haiti (Jil and Jil 2009, 104).

As a center for trading enslaved people and imported goods, Allada was the leading power in the region in the seventeenth century. The Dahomians were rising to power as the supplier of captives for Allada's trade (Monroe 2014, 13). The Agasuvi ruling family in Dahomey kept the title of Alladahonu, foreshadowing their claims to the ancestral coastal town. The royal line in the kingdom of Dahomey descended from Princess Aligbonon; thus, the dynasty was "matriarchal" even if only males ruled (Bay 1998, 56). As will become clear, women were an important part of Dahomian institutions, including administration, religion, farming, and the military.

KING KOKPON, CALLED ADJAHOUTO

Kokpon, also named Adjahouto, was one of the more successful descendants of Agasu (Segurola and Rassinoux 2000, 35). In Tado, Adjahouto killed his brother, the king, in a succession struggle, resulting in his flight to Allada, where he founded a dynasty with fourteen recorded descendants (Law 1997, 46). Fearing revenge attacks, Adjahouto fled with the skulls of two serpents that protected his ancestors. He took the skulls of his female ancestors, since skull veneration was a facet of Aja and Huedan religion, including the reburial of skulls (Merlo and Vidaud 1984, 279). Aja kings took on "strong names" related to major events in their reigns. The title "Adja + houto" means "Aja killer," a reference to the violence Kokpon unleashed in his quest for power (Law 1997, 29).

ROYAL AND RELIGIOUS INSTITUTIONS IN THE KINGDOMS OF ALLADA AND DAHOMEY

The foreigner François d'Elbée in 1670 observed that the vodun spirits of the king of Allada reflected state traditions. D'Elbée noted that everyone served spirits at their domiciles. In the king's practice, spirits were fed from ritually murdered victims in the palace gardens. The scavenger birds that gathered to feast on the remains figured into the royal mythology (Law 1997, 81). As Alladan migrants founded the kingdom of Dahomey, their use of ritual murder may have originated on the coast.

The cult of the king's ancestors was an important feature of Allada. Since Dahomey issued from Alladan migrants, many of the same ancestors were venerated. The annual ceremonies for the deceased kings included ritual murders in both kingdoms (Law 1997, 82). The funeral of a deceased king necessitated ritual murders. In the case of King Kpengla's death in 1789, 1,500 people were ritually murdered. While carried out on a smaller scale in Allada, the king's practice was a model for Dahomey (Law 1997, 82). The larger scale of the custom, the greater number of ritual murders, and the more frequent public appearances of the king reflected the increased centralization of royal power in Dahomey (Law 1997, 82, 84). This centralization would be put to the service of Dahomey's slave trade.

THE EMERGENCE OF THE KINGDOM OF DAHOMEY

After the death of Adjahouto in Allada, a succession struggle scattered his three sons. One held the throne in Allada; the second, Te-Agbalin, migrated to Adjachè; and the third, Dogbagri, migrated to the Abomey plateau (Merlo and Vidaud 1984, 280). Dogbagri and his supporters settled on Gedevi land at Wawe near Abomey (Akinjogbin 1967, 21). Succession conflicts partly drove the members of the Aja Agasuvi clan to settle the Abomey plateau. As members of the ruling family failed to take control of the monarchy, they sought new territory. At first, Allada would emerge as Hueda and Dahomey's nominal overlord (Law 1997, 27).

Dogbagri's son and successor, Dako ("Dakodonu" or "Aho"), seized land from the local Gedevi to found the kingdom of Dahomey (Merlo and Vidaud 1984, 289). Dogbagri's death in 1625 marked the start of Dako's reign. At the time, the Gedevi people were organized in a confederation of chiefdoms that authorized Dako's settlement in Wawe (Monroe 2011, 769). Dako's takeover has been called the "infection" of a small horde of outlaws who used force, fear, and deception to seize territory (Le Hérissé 1911, 273). The Gedevi "miniscule chiefdoms" were autonomous and fought among themselves over the control of land, a position of disunity that the Aja migrants seized upon.

The succession struggles in Allada were connected to the crisis of European coastal incursions. Europeans traded in firepower and commodities, and their naval technology made coastlines vulnerable. Conflict erupted among the African elite around new consumer goods and the lucrative opportunities triggered by trading enslaved people. The high-stakes violence opened up divisive wounds. European pressure on coastal residents caused many to seek refuge in the hinterland.

KING DAKO AND MOTIVATIONS FOR THE DAHOMIAN SLAVE TRADE

During King Dako's rule (1625–1650), he was known as "the palm tree planter" for his expansion of the trade in palm oil (Akinjogbin 1967, 21; Argyle 1966, 7). For the Aja and Fon people, as well as for Haitians, the palm tree is an important religious and economic symbol.[2]

The Gedevi people populated the Abomey plateau when the Agasuvi clan started migrating there in the early 1620s. They let the coastal migrants settle some land in their region, but soon newcomers demanded even more. An Igede chief named Ouo was Dako's first victim. He became suspicious and resisted the Agasuvis (Argyle 1966, 7). Chiefs and judges who attempted to thwart them were killed. Dako attacked the town of Calmina near Abomey, a place called "the capital of the deceased" due to the ritual focus on death among the Gedevi (Norris 1968, xiv).

After taking Calmina, Dako set his sights on Abomey, where King Dan ruled. Dako allied himself with the enemies of Dan and murdered him after his refusal to cede more land (Foà 1895, 5). At the time, Dan's land was called Danzume ("the forest of Dan"), but after his murder it was called Danxome ("in the stomach of Dan"), a reference to Dako's construction of a palace on top of Dan's entrails, the perfect symbol of the subversion of Gedevi rights (Bay 1998, 50; Monroe 2011, 769).

Usurpations fueled Dahomey's expansion and increase in wealth. At the time of Dako's death in 1650, the small kingdom had grown to a radius of just five miles from its point of origin (Argyle 1966, 8). The greatest motivating factors instigating its growth were the social upheavals and political disturbances incited by early Dutch activities on the coast. The struggle between Dako and his brother, Te-Agbalin, in Adjachè, involved a dispute over banning the Dutch trading post. The memory of that conflict was so strong that King Agaja, Dako's descendant, only targeted Dutch traders when he attacked the coast in 1724, 1727, and 1737 (Akinjogbin 1967, 23).

THE ABSOLUTE MONARCH

One of the altered traditions after Dahomey was the shift from the authority of "blood descent" to the authority of "might" (Akinjogbin 1967, 25). The Aja, who were received as refugees on the Abomey plateau, killed their hosts and took the region by force. The new political regime focused on the king's divine authority as central decider of the state. The Dahomians' murder and sale of Gedevi families reflect the kingdom's early calibration toward the European slavery economy.

Dahomian kings constantly acquired and disposed of royal wives and dependents, an expense and lifestyle that encouraged predation (Bay 1998, 103). The slave trader Robert Norris (1968, 156–57) argued that slave raiding resulted in the execution or sale of male captives, leaving more women than men. This increased the number of wives for elite men in the polygamous society, which in turn increased absolutist male behavior, distancing fathers from their offspring. Common men could have two or three wives, while leaders and the king had dozens or hundreds. Troublesome wives were sold to the slave trade. According to Norris (1968, 158), some children were removed from their mother's care and sent to villages where their parents could not find them. The king's motive was to ensure that no family ties could compromise his absolute power.[3]

While some enslaved people received no pay while others did, the entire population, including the king's ministers, was at the service of the king as "slaves." The individual, not the family, pledged allegiance to the king of Dahomey. Dahomey emerged as a cosmopolitan polity because allegiance to the kingdom was distinct from ethnicity or family status (Akinjogbin 1967, 26). Citizens included Portuguese people of mixed race and at least one Englishman. The king was the "absolute master of the life, liberty, and property of every person in his dominions" (Norris 1968, 157). The citizen's enslavement was symbolized in many ways, including required full-body prostration whenever one met the king.

THE DAHOMIAN WINDOW OF INFLUENCE IN HAITIAN STUDIES

After Dako founded the kingdom of Dahomey in 1625, slave raiding expanded over the decades that followed. With respect to the transmission of Vodun across the Atlantic, questions remain around how French slave traders were able to gain access to the populations that planted the Gede and Rada Rites in Saint-Domingue and Haiti. What is the *African* history of Haitian Vodou's founders? My goal is to understand the circumstances in which these population groups were enslaved. To grasp the culture that these people brought to Saint-Domingue, one must examine activities of the kingdoms of Dahomey, Allada, and Hueda, among others. They shed light on the people and organizations that put into motion the regional system of slavery.

The narratives of Dako (1625–1650) through Kpengla (1775–1789) are important in Vodou's transatlantic history. The transmission of Vodun to Saint-Domingue as Vodou was a major collective historical process. These kings cast long shadows across Haitian and Atlantic history. Hundreds of African kingdoms worked with Europeans to deport people into the slave trade, but Dahomey is best known. As rulers at the center of the state, religion, and slave trade, these are key figures in Haitian history:

1. *Dako* (1625–1650)
2. Dako's son, *Wegbadja* (also spelled Huegaja) (1650–1680)
3. Wegbadja's son, *Akaba* (1680–1708)
4. Akaba's brother, *Agaja* (1708–1740)
5. Agaja's son, *Tegbesu* (1740–1775)
6. Tegbesu's brother, *Kpengla* (1775–1789)
7. Kpengla's son, *Agonglo* (1789–1797) (Glélé 1974, 91)

The relevance of Dahomey ceases for this study in 1793, since slavery was abolished in Saint-Domingue on that date and was never successfully reinstituted. Nevertheless, the Dahomian kings' slave trade continued well into the nineteenth century (Burton 1893). The First and Second Franco-Dahomian Wars led to the kingdom's capitulation in 1894 and the reduction of the nation to the status of "French protectorate."

THE KINGDOM OF ALLADA'S SLAVE TRADING WITH THE FRENCH

Before the arrival of French slave traders, officials insisted that all trading with Europeans be confined to Allada and that all Aja people could access it.

Europeans were barred from constructing forts, but they could build factories and offices (Akinjogbin 1967, 26). By the mid-1600s, Aja kings were keener to trade with Europeans, and in 1658 King Toxonu even sent an embassy to Philip IV of Spain to assert Allada's prerogatives.

There was an increase in slave trading in the 1660s. The French West India Company carried out reconnaissance voyages along the coast of West Africa in 1666. Two ships were sent in 1669 to build a French factory in Allada. In January 1670, François d'Elbée and his envoy reached Allada and met with King Tezifon (Akinjogbin 1967, 29). King Tezifon also sent an Aja embassy to France in 1670, and Louis XIV received his ambassador, Matteo Lopez (Akinjogbin 1967, 28–29; Smith 1989, 21).

D'Elbée's trade negotiator, chevalier Dubourg, offered to build a factory in Allada in 1670 and to send four ships per year to collect enslaved people for the French colonies. Tezifon's line of negotiation was that Allada did not have enough enslaved people to fill French ships. The government of Allada wanted to secure the French trade rather than cede it to a competitor. The French offered presents to influential people and increased the price of enslaved people, while "Tezifon allowed himself to be persuaded" (Akinjogbin 1967, 29).

On January 8 1670, after a few days of negotiation, Tezifon proclaimed that the French could trade with Allada, receiving a house as the Dutch had (Akinjogbin 1967, 29). Although Saint-Domingue became a French colony in 1697, planters received enslaved people from Africa and Spanish Hispaniola before that date (Chisholm 1911).[4] The slave quota necessitated raiding. Allada's increased slave raiding frustrated the king of Dahomey. In 1671, Allada's army fought Dahomian troops who barred the passage of Alladan raiders (Akinjogbin 1967, 31). King Wegbadja of Dahomey wanted control of the slave trade, not its abolition. Wegbadja had in fact killed numerous chiefs in neighboring regions to eliminate their toll taxes (Argyle 1966, 8).

DEVELOPMENTS IN DAHOMEY IN THE LATE 1600s

One of the successful projects of the Aja Agasuvi migrants among the Gedevi was the trade in European fabrics composed of cotton and fiber, a product unknown in the region, where bark cloth was prevalent (Argyle 1966, 9). The Aja Agasuvi settlement in Allada served as an advantageous pipeline for bringing imported European goods to the Abomey branch of the Aja network.

During the reign of Wegbadja, the custom of prostrating before the king was established, a sign of the monarchy's growing absolutism. Prostration before a priest in the religions of West Africa, and the *oungan* or *manbo* in Haitian Vodou, is a customary, ego-effacing ritual linked to the royal-religious cultures of the region. Prostration before Wegbadja was a symbolic submission, becoming an obligatory gesture when addressing the king. King Wegbadja established capital punishment for murder, attempted murder, theft, and rape, while revenge killing was banned. The property of the deceased was returned to the king, who owned everything and everyone in the kingdom, with most then given back to the successor kin leader (Argyle 1966, 11).

THE ANNUAL CUSTOMS AND THE FUNCTIONS OF RITUAL MURDER

The kings of Dahomey took ritual murder further than other regional kings. As war and slave raiding were routine, a certain number of war captives were reserved for the ritual murders of the Annual Customs (Argyle 1966, 82). The Annual Customs of Allada and Abomey included the ritual murder of human victims by sword or club to feed the king's ancestors with blood (Norris 1968, 101). It was the most sacred of rituals in the kingdom of Dahomey, and the king "did not forget to solemnize" on such occasions (Dalzel 1967, 197). A priest placed his hands on a sacrificial victim's head and spoke for a few moments, finally ordering decapitation. Dahomian citizens examined the slaughter "with the least emotion" (Norris 1968, 101).

Wegbadja rekindled Allada's tradition in Abomey (Argyle 1966, 12). A witness speaking to slave trader Robert Norris (1968, 87) described the event as a time "when the king waters the graves of his ancestors with the blood of many human victims." In addition to Dahomian leaders, dignitaries from European forts attended, hence slave trader William Snelgrave's eyewitness reports. Presents and taxes were paid to the king commensurate with the giver's station. Dahomians who pleased the king received "a large cotton cloth manufactured in the Eyo [Oyo] country" (Norris 1968, 86). During the Annual Customs, embassies from distant nations visited Abomey, and the sale of enslaved people was negotiated (Bay 1998, 65). Young men could pay the sum of 20,000 cowries to receive a wife from within the king's residence, but he had to take the woman given (Norris 1968, 88). During Tegbesu's reign, soldiers paraded as hundreds of the "king's women" walked in public accompanied by armed guards. There was a "general dance" with drumming and "war songs" (Norris 1968, 103–5). Visitors from neighboring kingdoms, including North Africans who "speak and write Arabic," paid tribute to the king (Norris 1968, 103).

Ritual murder was a feature of royal religion in Dahomey throughout the period surveyed here. The execution of war captives and criminals was customary in the Aja region. King Kpengla in the late eighteenth century explained King Wegbadja's (and his own) motives for killing them: "What else could he have done with them? Was he to let them remain in his country, to cut the throats of his subjects?" (Argyle 1966, 81). As the enslavement economy expanded, more captives were sold to the slave trade, although a group was always reserved for execution at the Annual Customs. King Kpengla explained that the executions added "grandeur" to the royalty. Although the killings at the Annual Customs were public, killing was the exclusive purview of the king.

Dahomians were not likely cannibals, although they were accused of it and played on the fear it caused others. The kingdom's food supply was good, and the people would have had no use for human flesh. They probably did want their enemies to believe that they were cannibals, and the flight of Hueda's army in 1727, to be discussed below, may reflect that fear. African commoners believed that Dahomian and European elites were cannibals (Bay 1998, 66).

SLAYING CAPTIVES, SELLING CAPTIVES

The slave trade did not supplant the Dahomian practice of slaying captives. European advocates of the transatlantic slave trade like Snelgrave (1971) and Norris (1968) argued that the abolishment of slavery would increase mass executions. Robin Law (2004) points out that this argument was common in eighteenth-century writings that favored the slave trade. If there were no lucrative external slave trade and no agro-industrial world to which it connected, no rapacious demand for enslaved people would fuel inter-African violence and raiding.

The victors of precolonial conquest in West Africa initially executed the conquered elite, but they modified this policy after the European slave trade started to boom. Capturing the vulnerable became profitable, and the Dahomian army became a major supplier. Selling people generated more money than killing them, a situation that led to the transfer of "persons of some rank" into the colonial slave trade (Norris 1968, 160). The slave trade never replaced Dahomey's use of ritual murder, so captives were separated for different ends.

During royal funerals, "body attendants" were murdered. Prior to their execution, victims were given significant titles. Individuals from all classes of society were ritually murdered after the death of the king, reinforcing the idea that the Dahomian king was associated with the entire society (Argyle 1966, 113).

THE ABSENCE OF RITUAL MURDER IN HAITI

Ritual murder did not carry over to Haitian Vodou for straightforward reasons. The practice was intended to appease the ancestors of the living Dahomian king and not the national vodun. Ritual murder added symbolic power to the royal family's ancestral cult. Agbe and Aizan, as we will see, were the only vodun that received ritual murders. In nonroyal congregations, animal and plant offerings were made. The ritual murder of humans was the king's activity.

The type of victim denoted the sacrificer's social class. A poor person could offer corn, beans, and a chicken, whereas a person of means could offer a bull. The king in turn sacrificed the costliest of beings, people (Argyle 1966, 118). What does ritually murdering or "sacrificing" human beings to the king's ancestors suggest about them? Since royal ancestors received the costliest of sacrifices, the implication is that they were the supreme divinities in Dahomey. The cult of ritual murder practiced by the Dahomian kings never crossed the Atlantic because it was exclusively a feature of royal culture in the Bight of Benin.

SIGNS OF ABSOLUTE AUTHORITY AT THE ANNUAL CUSTOMS AND IN THE NESUHWE CULT

The king's absolute authority was symbolized at the Annual Customs in the ritual of the *so-sin* (horse-tie). The chiefs gave up their horses to the king and submitted payment for their return. Horses were precious, and riding one was a privilege; thus, this specific form of annual tax reinforced the power of the king. The Annual Customs were otherwise a major event for Dahomians. Disputes were settled, money from the sale of captives and animals was distributed, soldiers and officers were promoted, and military processions took place, including the elite female Amazonian troops who served as royal guards (Argyle 1966, 114–16).

The Nesuhwe cult involved the veneration of the royal family's ancestors by members of the royal family. Dahomian royalty was prevented from being initiated in nonroyal congregations. No prince or princess could become the vodunsi (spouse of the spirit) of "any great public pantheon," except for the king's grandchildren (Argyle 1966, 110–11). Families of commoners could form alliances with the Agasuvi royal cult. People who depended on the king were more likely to associate with the cult's public rites. Members of the royal family could patronize nonroyal public ceremonies, but they could not be initiated in those communities, just as nonroyals could not be initiated in the royal cult. The kings and their ancestors were on a pedestal that emphasized their prestige and projected their power.

THE UPHEAVALS OF AFRICAN SOCIETIES IN CONTACT WITH EUROPEAN TRADERS

The turmoil unleashed in West African coastal communities as a result of the European slave trade heightened the stakes of involvement versus isolation.

A fateful development under King Wegbadja was an expansion in the trade in firearms, ammunition, and gunpowder. Such weapons were tangible signs of the violence, mass enslavements, deportations, and upheavals that were plaguing the region. The slave trade in the Aja and Yoruba region lasted from 1650 to the 1860s. The monarchies of the coastal kingdoms of Hueda, Allada, and Grand-Popo competed to control it. In Allada, the king's slaves had to be purchased by European traders before the slaves of other traders (Law 1997, 95).

Hueda and Allada resembled one another in ethnic, linguistic, and cultural terms. Both were dynamic commercial centers with cultures more mercantile than militaristic, perhaps a reason they both employed mercenaries from the Gold Coast in their battles. Their thriving economies were not prepared for the invasion of the disciplined Dahomian fighters. The French, Dutch, English, Brandenburgers, and Portuguese competed for enslaved people, pitting the traders in Hueda and Allada against one another (Law 1997, 97, 115).

The concentration of European slave traders along the coast mobilized a struggle for control of the slave trade that exacerbated regional rivalries by concentrating profits in small groups, at the expense of peripheral populations who were dragged into enslavement. As the decades marched along, the tides of power shifted, reversing the fate of groups. The slave trade unraveled the traditional system of father-son kingdoms bound by treaties. European slave traders cultivated a lawlessness in which stealing people became common. The agrarian people of the Tori kingdom, for instance, took up the practice in the 1680s (Akinjogbin 1967, 33–34).

An important dynamic in the contact with Europeans was the introduction of crops like maize, sweet potatoes, cassava, papaya, pineapples, and tobacco from the Americas. Plantains came from Asia, coconuts from East Africa, and oranges and lemons from the Mediterranean. This contributed to population growth, since the increased diversity in subsistence crops and imported goods accelerated economic growth, population growth, and political centralization, developments that would also feed the slave trade (Monroe 2014, 42).

THE NUMBERS OF ENSLAVED PEOPLE DEPORTED TO THE AMERICAS AND THE MANNER IN WHICH THEY WERE SENT

In the decade of the 1640s, roughly ten thousand people were deported from the Aja coast. The first known English slave purchases in Allada were transacted in 1652. In 1664, the English sent seven ships to purchase four thousand enslaved people, although the Dutch prevented them from doing so. In 1670, the Dutch purchased three thousand enslaved people in Allada, while the

French purchased one thousand. Total deportations from Allada were around five thousand people annually in the 1680s and over ten thousand annually in the 1690s, 1700s, and 1710s (Law 1997, 88, 91). By King Agaja's reign in the first half of the 1700s, 150,000 Africans were deported each decade (Bay 1998, 47).

Hueda's slave trade boomed between 1704 and 1727, a period coinciding with the recognition of Saint-Domingue as a French colony in 1697 (Argyle 1966, 15). During this period, between eighteen thousand and twenty-one thousand enslaved people were exported annually. By 1850, the Slave Coast had exported about two million people in total (Bay 1998, 47). One of the main functions of the Dahomian army was to capture men, women, and children. Captives were sold to foreign traders or kept as domestic enslaved people (Argyle 1966, 81). By the 1680s, Dahomey was known as the source of many of the enslaved people sold in Hueda and Allada (Law 1997, 110).

The captives traveled from Dahomey to the coast chained in coffles (Bay 1998, 43). Their enslavers paid tolls in towns on the way. The kingdom of Allada controlled the roads to the coast. Allada and Hueda were the main towns where Gbe- (Aja, Fon, etc.), Yoruba-, and Hausa-speaking slave traders sent enslaved people to French, Dutch, English, or Portuguese forts and ships. Near the coast, enslaved people were locked in stockades until enough were gathered to fill a cargo. Sellers would strip them of clothing and examine them physically. Diseased enslaved people or those over thirty-five were sold into the local trade (Bay 1998, 42, 47).

THE AFRICAN SIDE OF THE SLAVE TRADE

To understand where Haitian Vodou came from, one must ask who was selling enslaved people, who was targeted, and why they were targeted. The income from the slave trade was distributed to the political elite. Distributing wealth from the slave trade among the elite gave prestige to the kings of Hueda, Allada, and Abomey, and it purchased their complicity (Law 1997, 102).

Dahomey took control of Allada and Hueda through its invasions of 1724 and 1727. Private merchants sold enslaved people under the supervision of a state official (Monroe 2014, 18). The mix of people involved in transactions for the ship *Dahomet* in 1773 reflects a typical scenario. Transacting over the 422 enslaved people on board the ship were forty-one private African slave traders, three slave traders representing African states, plus one English, six French, and two Portuguese slave traders. Out of the 422 enslaved people, private African traders sold 184, state officials sold 23, private English traders sold 121, private French traders sold 112, and private Portuguese traders sold 5. The enslaved people sold by European traders had been purchased from

Africans and imprisoned in stockades in the forts until European boats arrived. Ships like *Swallow* in 1791–1792, in comparison, were nearly entirely filled by enslaved people sold by thirty-eight African traders, with three English traders selling 13 out of 142 enslaved people on board (Peukert 1978, 124). African private traders dominated the coastal slave trade. The king's officers oversaw the trade and taxed each sale. African slave traders and royalty became wealthy.

The majority of captives were prisoners of war. Others became enslaved via an annual tribute paid to a powerful kingdom (Law 1997, 104). Some people were born enslaved within a given kingdom and remained in bondage throughout their life. Others became enslaved as punishment for misdemeanors, political activism, theft, adultery, business indiscretions, or debts owed to creditors (Law 1997, 104; Snelgrave 1971, 3, 158; Norris 1968, 99). Others were randomly kidnapped and spirited away.

Paussie was a successful but careless female trader from Hueda (Dalzel 1967, 208–9). Residing in the French fort in Hueda, she acquired seventy enslaved people and other wealth. The governor at the French fort of Grigwhee, Monseigneur Olivier, employed her to sell fine coral to Oyo buyers, who prized it greatly. The king of Oyo intercepted the coral and demanded to know why King Kpengla of Dahomey had failed to include coral in his recent tribute. Kpengla had Paussie and her husband, also a trader, arrested. He sold her husband as a slave and had her hacked into pieces.

Snelgrave (1971, 159) claims that populations in the interior sold their own children, whereas people on the coast did not, except when faced with "Want and Famine." King Kpengla denied that Dahomians sold their own children and family members. Governor Lionel Abson of the English fort told him about discussions in Great Britain regarding the immorality of the slave trade, of parliamentary enquiries, and of abolitionist pamphlets. King Kpengla's response offers insight into his understanding of slavery:

> What hurts me most is that some of your [European] people have maliciousiy represented us in books, which never die, alleging, that we sell our wives and children for the sake of procuring a few kegs of brandy. No; we are shamefully belied; and I hope you will contradict, from my mouth, the scandalous stories that have been propagated, and tell posterity that we have been abused. We do, indeed, sell to white men a part of our prisoners, and we have a right to do so. (Dalzel 1967, 219)

European observers claimed that the king of Hueda received women and children every year from families, and that he would sell them to complete cargos (Bay 1998, 48).

King Agaja's wife, Adonon, convinced the monarch to send troops to capture and enslave the residents of Oueme Jigbe in revenge for the murder of Adonon's son (Bay 1998, 76). King Tegbesu quelled his anger by selling people who infuriated him (Dalzel 1967, 145–46). After a fire damaged the Dahomey palace, his wives blamed each other for "carelessness." Unable to determine who was responsible, Tegbesu sold nineteen wives who resided in the charred residence.

As the Europeans set up warehouses along the coast, they sought influence in local power, illustrated by their involvement in the installation of King Agbangla in Hueda in 1671 and King Aisan in 1703 (Akinjogbin 1967, 35). The enslaved people sold to French colonies were taken from several places. Slave trader Erick Tilleman, commenting in the 1690s, estimated that they came from eighty miles away in the interior. Oluale Kossola ("Cudjoe Lewis") tells of his capture by the Dahomian army when it raided his hometown of Takon, situated to the north of Porto-Novo, and forced him to march to Hueda (Hurston 2018). Baquaqua describes his capture in the town of Tchamba (in modern Togo) and two sales before being purchased by a white man (Law 2004, 105, 139). Before their embarkation onto European boats, family members could redeem victims of slave raiding, but this was rare, since the poor were targeted.

After transiting Abomey and Savi, enslaved people arrived in Hueda on foot. Their custody in Hueda varied depending on the demand, the ships anchored, and the weather. Baquaqua was in Hueda for a single night, whereas Kossola was kept in stockades for three weeks. In the stockade there was no toilet, no mobility, and starvation rations (Law 2004, 140). After the deprivations of incarceration, slave owners took care to present enslaved people in the best light by shaving their beards and heads, oiling their skin, and dressing them in attractive clothes. At the sales point, the ship's surgeon examined teeth to estimate age, faces to check for stubble, and genitals to look for venereal diseases (Law 2004, 140). The men, women, and children were naked, and the men had their hands tied behind their backs (140).[5] Europeans branded enslaved people "the same as they would the heads of barrels or any other inanimate goods or merchandize," Baquaqua explained, after they purchased them from African traders (Law 2004, 142). Enslaved people received a hearty meal prior to embarkation. As the enslaved people stepped onto the ships, Dahomians stripped them of their rags. Enslaved people sold in Hueda were shackled in pairs on skinny canoes and taken out to the European galleons. Drowning was common on those choppy, shark-filled seas (Law 2004, 144). Diseases like smallpox and fevers ravaged enslaved people and seamen alike (Norris 1968). Of three hundred enslaved people Norris held on a ship in Hueda's sea road in 1770, seventy showed signs of smallpox. Norris had them "inoculated," and of those, fifty were inoculated a second time. After the dry harmattan winds began blowing, all but one slave recovered.

THE GROWTH OF DAHOMEY BETWEEN 1680 AND 1708

The instability caused by Aja slave raiding provoked several reprisal attacks from the Yoruba Oyo cavalry on the town of Allada, including one attack that left severe damage in the 1680s. The instability arising from the erosion of social order caused many Aja families to join the descendants of Doku on the Abomey plateau. By 1680, the addition of eighteen towns and villages to Dahomey's fold points to an influx of Aja fighting power. By 1708, Dahomey included forty towns (Akinjogbin 1967, 36–37). The annexations targeted Aja and Yoruba towns around the Abomey plateau. The 1697 Treaty of Rijswijk resulted in "transatlantic pressure" on African kings to supply slave labor for Saint-Domingue. The enstoolment of Agaja in Dahomey in the early 1700s would, like clockwork, intensify coordinated expansion of the slave trade.

AGAJA BECOMES KING OF DAHOMEY

One of Agaja's names was "Dosu," a word that occurs in Haitian culture as *dosou*, referring to a child born after twins (Bay 1998, 78). King Agaja projected immense influence in Dahomian and Haitian history primarily through his organization of massive deportations of local populations. Little is known of his upbringing. Houffon was the king of Hueda in the south when Agaja became the king of Dahomey in roughly 1708. Under Houffon's rule, Hueda became a major port in the slave trade. Hueda's dominance in this trade and collaboration with European traders made the Alladans envious, especially since the Huedans were violating Allada's primacy. Paternalistic politics held that a "son-state" should display deference to a "father-state" (Akinjogbin 1967, 32, 45). As the reign of Akaba, Agaja's father, ended in the early 1700s, European slave traders treated Hueda like a neutral international port.

As enslaved people left the region's ports, guns and gunpowder poured in. Arms were the main imports desired by African kings in the turbulent decades that opened the 1700s (Snelgrave 1971, 21, 169). Battles between the Aja kingdoms of Hueda, Allada, and Dahomey were common in the early 1700s, and pressure from the European demand for enslaved people exacerbated strife.

Dahomey had strong centralization with a disciplined administration, army, and spy service called the Agbadjigbeto (Akinjogbin 1967, 48, 63). The ruling elite preferred a military ethos to an agrarian one. King Adandozan (1797–1818) reminisced that "our fathers . . . cultivated not with hoes but with guns; the kings of Dahomey cultivate only war" (Law 2004, 87). Free men were soldiers first and farmers second, while women, enslaved people, and children bore the brunt of farm labor (Law 2004, 87). In the early 1700s, the Dahomian kingdom was preparing for a regional shake-up.

KING AGAJA'S CONQUESTS OF ALLADA AND HUEDA

King Agaja led several wars against the towns neighboring Dahomey between 1708 and 1724. He led a campaign against the Oueme people and took the towns Didouma and Povey (Akinjogbin 1967, 63). By 1717, Dahomey had attracted the Europeans, impressed by how Agaja had enlarged his wealth through conquest and slave trading. The visitor Bulfinch Lambe estimated that Agaja had two thousand wives, some of whom served as administrators, palace guards, and soldiers (Bay 1998, 51). Dahomian women farmed, trained, and fought, using a short-handled club in both battle and planting (Bay 1998, 68).

King Agaja and the Dahomians were engrossed in the slave trade. Agaja was frustrated by the toll roads to the coast, since they syphoned his kingdom's profits (Glélé 1974, 40). He desired direct trade with Europeans, and he wanted to stop the trading of captured Dahomians. Attacking Allada on a pretext in 1724, the Dahomian army burned down the royal palace, killed the king, and enslaved eight thousand residents, securing a crushing victory (Akinjogbin 1967, 65; Bay 1998, 57). Toussaint Louverture, one of the architects of Haitian independence, was a descendent of Gaou Guinou, a member of the Allada royalty whom Agaja sold into slavery after 1724.

Agaja's army then conquered Hueda on the coast in 1727, resulting in eleven thousand captives and five thousand people killed or executed (Glélé 1974, 40). During the attack on Hueda, the king and his fighters managed to escape. On the eve of the conquest, King Agaja performed "religious ceremonies" in Allada (Law 1997, 119). Three weeks after the conquest, the heads of four thousand beheaded Huedans were displayed in stacks in Abomey during the king's Annual Customs (Snelgrave 1971, 31).

The significance of the vast number of captives for Saint-Domingue's history cannot be underestimated. Agaja raided the strategic ethnic Aja towns of Allada and Hueda and sold off thousands of residents to the European slave trade. Prevailing over any sympathy for fellow Aja people were several issues: the taxes levied by the Allada and Hueda governments, the towns' positions as international Aja commercial hubs, and their trade in Dahomian enslaved people. Unprecedented violence, wealth, weaponry, and alcoholic intoxicants dissolved traditional political and ethnic relationships. Loyalty to the Dahomian king superseded loyalty to Aja ethnicity, language, or father-son political legacies.

The Dahomian conquest of Allada and Hueda are pivotal in Haitian history, especially in the context of the Rada Rite. The residents of Allada and Hueda were the keepers of the prototypical systems that emerged in the Rada Rite in Saint-Domingue and Haiti. Given the large number of captives sold from Allada in 1724 and Hueda in 1727, it is certain that many people taken from these towns carried with them the traditions of the region and contributed their knowledge to the creation of the Rada Rite. The proximity of the two coastal Aja towns had facilitated the fusion of their cultures prior to contact with Europeans, while the Dahomian invasion and enslavement of their residents ensured their coupling in Saint-Domingue.

King Agaja tolerated the free exercise of religion and incorporated elements of the conquered traditions into Dahomian culture by means of intermarriage (Norris 1968, 2). After the conquest, Agaja invited exiles to resettle in their former homes rather than fight for independence. Trading enslaved people with Europeans had produced this revolution. Agaja's conquest of Hueda and Allada brought these regions into his monarchy, and they remained secure as long as local rulers paid an annual tribute to Oyo. After the conquest of 1727, the Oyos looked to Hueda as an inexhaustible source of wealth, and, in the decades that followed, they increased the amounts demanded (Norris 1968, 16). Tensions between the Aja and the Yoruba over tributes generated wars, which became another engine for slave raiding.

RELICS IN ABOMEY, ALLADA, AND HUEDA

The religion of the monarchy was the most important institution in Dahomey. Its practice conferred upon the monarchy continuity, power, and a sense of awe. In the royal religious system, family relics were charged with symbolic meaning. The display of human skulls and bones was a typical feature of royal religious practices throughout the region. Agaja and Tegbesu decorated the royal palace in Abomey with human skulls. In addition to freshly decapitated heads, skulls were placed in front of doorways and entrances. Royal accoutrements included flagpoles with skulls atop, skulls on posts, skulls in baskets, skulls fitted into the royal stool, polished skulls for drinking, and other "material allegories of conquest and the total submission of enemies" (Monroe 2014, 151; citing Forbes 1966, 2).

The courtyard of the Lord of Jakin, ruler of that coastal city, included the official's "Fetiche," designed like "a large Hay-cock, and covered over with Thatch. On the top of this was placed a dead Man's Scull, before which Offerings were made for the Duke's [i.e., the African lord's] Health and Preservation" (Snelgrave 1971, 143). The relics are a link to the protector ancestor spirits, but they are also a symbol of dominance over the dead. The domestic altar of oungan Nelson Marcenat in Haiti that I saw in 2008, like others, included a skull and bones, showing how relics form an ongoing feature of the transatlantic religion.

Ritualizing with relics was also a feature of Aja and Gedevi religions. In Haitian Vodou, such ritualization is manifested as bones and skulls displayed on altars to represent the Gede spirits and the familial dead. So prevalent are relics that undertakers at the Grand Cimetière (Great Cemetery) of Port-au-Prince sell the bones of people whose families can only afford a six-month "entombment" (Smith 2010, 83, 97).

AGAJA'S CONQUESTS AND TRADE IN ENSLAVED PEOPLE

Several conditions enabled Agaja's invasion of Hueda in 1727. Hueda is an ethnonym, referring to the town's founding population (Lando 2016, 74). Agaja ordered the invasion of Allada and Hueda in order to control the trade in enslaved people and goods, an interpretation of events that relies on slave traders like Snelgrave (1971) and Norris (1968) (Akinjogbin 1967, 72). With his victories in Allada and Hueda, Agaja's main goal, according to I. A. Akinjogbin (1967, 77), was the elimination of a system that no longer provided "security and justice," not only to control the slave trade. Akinjogbin wishfully suggests that one of Dahomey's founding principles was opposition to slavery (77–78). Nevertheless, after Dahomey's conquest of Allada, the Portuguese director, Francisco Pereyra Mendes, wrote in 1724 that enslaved people were abundant, a situation dependent on the immediate aftermath of Allada's conquest.

Before attacking Hueda, Agaja had sent an ambassador to the king requesting "an open Traffick to the Sea side, and offering to pay him his usual Customs on *Negroes* exported" (Snelgrave 1971, 5). After the Huedan king's refusal, Agaja decided to attack, and after his victory, residents linked to the old regime were executed or sold into slavery. Agaja assured the Europeans responsible for the trading forts in Hueda that "he would make the Trade flourish" (18). Agaja sent "a great many slaves" to the town of Jakin for Snelgrave to inspect for purchase shortly after the trader's visit to Abomey (66). The Dahomian army plundered and destroyed Jakin in the early 1730s as punishment for the town's alliance with Dahomian defectors (149–50).

Although Agaja allowed a few officials to trade enslaved people, he monopolized the trade, including enlisting his wives for administrative work between the coast and Abomey. Sometimes, the king gave enslaved people to wealthy Dahomians as a reward for their loyalty; slaves could also be purchased from the interior or obtained for military service. Palace authorities and military chiefs sold enslaved people taken in war for compensation (Bay 1998, 104–6). Nonroyal Dahomians could not enslave other Dahomians, however, except via judicial channels. If those condemned of "theft, adultery, or the imputed crime of witchcraft" avoided execution, they were sold (Norris 1968, 160). The "domestics, relations and friends" of the condemned were killed or "sold for slaves" (10). These practices, if true, caused "considerable loss to the state" (10).

One oral account of Agaja's 1727 conquest of Hueda describes how Na Geze, Agaja's daughter and the wife of Huedan King Houffon, told the enemy (her father) how to ford a lagoon that separated the opponents and where to decant water over Hueda's gunpowder, paving the way for the Dahomian victory (Merlo and Vidaud 1984, 291).[6] Learning that King Houffon had removed the flintlocks from weapons sold to Agaja, Na Geze smuggled the missing parts back to her father (Bay 1998, 60). In his flight, Houffon left the thirty-three skulls of his ancestors with a close friend, who handed them over to the Dahomians (Merlo and Vidaud 1984, 291). Agaja struck favorable trading deals with Europeans at the coastal forts and faced no resistance from European guns (Bay 1998, 59).

Once the flurry of slave selling tapered off in Allada, Agaja placed restrictions on the trade. Dahomians sold six hundred out of approximately eleven thousand captives to the slave trader Snelgrave, and enslaved people sold subsequently were more expensive. When asked for more enslaved people, Agaja said that they were occupied working his own lands. Aja citizens who sold residents of Allada and Hueda without authorization were arrested and executed. Between 1726 and 1730, African and European slave traders opposed Agaja's restrictive policy (Akinjogbin 1967, 72, 79–81).

Many Huedan refugees, including King Houffon, fled and settled to the east or west of Hueda near lagoons and in Porto-Novo and Badagry. King Houffon founded the kingdom of Hueda-Henji at Mitogbodji in the west (Law 1997, 51–52). From there, the remnants of Hueda harassed the Dahomian occupiers for many years. The Huedan struggle continued until King Houffon's death in 1733, after which his son submitted to Agaja's rule, allowing several hundred former residents to resettle in Hueda (Law 2004, 59). A 1776 map of Hueda shows that the square in front of the Dahomian administrator's residence was the center of public religious activity. Most importantly, the square also contained the temple for the python vodun Dangbe, the signature symbol of Huedan and Haitian religions, a topic explored below.[7]

THE CONQUEST OF HUEDA AND
THE TEMPLE OF THE PYTHONS

The failure of Hueda's principal deity, Dangbe the python, to protect the town in 1727 echoes in the historical writing of the period (Snelgrave 1971). The people of Hueda relied on the python for protection, and they attributed past victories over Allada to its powers. Instead of placing a permanent guard at the natural boundary between Hueda and the Dahomians in occupied Allada, they performed sacrifices to the protector spirit. The Dahomian commanders observed the Huedans perform this ritual daily at the unguarded river and sent a few hundred soldiers to ford the river. Once news reached the town of their crossing, the Huedans fled without resistance while Dahomian soldiers killed and ate the temple's living pythons (Bay 1998, 60).

Snelgrave arrived in Hueda three weeks after the Dahomian conquest, leaving a narrative that matched the "patterns of [...] explanatory mode," which attributed strength to the national vodun protector. The capture, beheading, and consumption of Hueda's pythons presented a paradox because the Dahomians usually showed respect for conquered vodun by incorporating them into their religious system. The story highlights the place of the beliefs of soldiers in warfare, an attitudinal element that influences outcomes (Bay 1998, 61–62).

The python cult survived the conquest. Priests returned, pythons were gathered for the temple, and the community continued with some success. The python cult also reached Abomey, but it was never popular, perhaps because Dahomians doubted its protective power (Bay 1998, 62). The python vodun was a "purchased" spirit with few ancestral links around Abomey, and its inclusion had primarily a symbolic and political dimension.

The python vodun's relationship with Haitian Vodou's Danbala Wèdo and Ayida Wèdo is important in transatlantic history. Both Danbala and Ayida appear in Haitian Vodou's Rada Rite[8] (from Allada on the coast) and Danwonmen Rite[9] (from Abomey and the entire kingdom). How do the Dan spirits fit into the Danwonmen Rite? The Huedan lineage of the python cult perhaps became linked to the Abomeyan royal Vodun religion after Agaja's conquest in 1727. However, service to Hueda's python vodun was very likely present in the religion of the earliest Aja settlers like Dako (circa 1625), since his father was a resident of Allada. Given that the Agasuvi family ruled over Allada for several generations before migrating to the Abomey plateau, serpent veneration certainly traveled with them. The fact that the python service migrated from Allada to Dahomey is made evident in Haitian Vodou's Dawonmen Rite, which includes the spirit Dan Ayida Wèdo (i.e., in which "Wèdo" refers to Hueda). When slave raiding expanded, some of Danbala Wèdo's servants migrated from coastal areas into the Abomey hinterland, where they established congregations. Finally, the presence of snake spirits in both the Danwonmen and Rada Rites of Haitian Vodou points to the widespread presence of snake veneration in the Aja ethnic areas before the Europeans arrived.

After Hueda's conquest, Agaja visited the town and drank his first shot of European gin. Although apocryphal, the story highlights links between war, conquest, slavery, and the trade in hard liquor.

THE POLITICS OF RELIGIOUS INSTITUTIONS IN HUEDA

Jean Barbot in 1680 observed that "idols" and "fetishes" crafted of clay and wood and resembling "puppets" were displayed along the roads (Law 2004, 88). The clay figures were Legba mounds and statues near residences and the entrances of towns. The wooden statues were *bocyo*, figures that protected against negative magic (Law 2004, 88–89). In addition to Legba, Huedan spirits found in Haitian Vodou include Aizan (Ayizan in Haiti), protector of the Zobé market in Hueda and the family of Dangbe python spirits (Law 2004, 88). The king of Hueda was the head of a kin group that revered Dangbe as a *tohwiyo* (totem) of the ruling family (Argyle 1966, 16). Dangbe is still served as totem of Hueda today (Lando 2016, 102).

The people of Hueda buried the deceased within their homes (Law 2004, 88). Those tombs received annual commemorations with the sacrifice of sheep, goats, or fowl, and the consumption of the meat. Ancestral ceremonies were called *huetanu* (year-head-thing) and took place in December and January, also an important time for ceremonies of family and community renewal in Haitian Vodou.[10]

Hueda's Vodun congregations transcended familial lineage affiliation, since membership was public and not exclusive to the priest's family. The congregations of Hueda operated like churches, and there were dozens of "public fetish temples." In 1937, more than one hundred temples were counted (Law 2004, 89). The neighborhoods of Tové, Ahouandjigo, Sogbadji, Docomè, and Fonsaramè had seventy-nine temples. Although each one was dedicated to a single spirit, numerous spirits were worshiped within each congregation under the patron spirit.

The pre-Dahomian religious groups include those for Hu (also written Hou), the vodun of the sea; Dangbe, the python; Hwesi, the spirit of smallpox; and Zo, the vodun of fire. A python named Ahwanba represented Dangbe and was displayed in annual parades (Law 2004, 92). The highest-ranking Dangbe had more than one thousand initiates in 1860, in contrast to the five hundred initiated servants of Hu (Burton 1893, 139, 141). Additional public parades for Dangbe included the collection of springwater in *gozin* jars to serve as holy libation water at the shrines (Law 2004, 94). South of Hueda, water is still collected from sacred ponds for ceremonies dedicated to vodun (Lando 2016, 92).

The English slave traders built their fort near Hueda at the place where religious ceremonies for the spirit Nabbakou took place. The English had to maintain a house within the fort dedicated to the vodun. While the king of Hueda sheltered there during the Dahomian invasion, the fort was left unmolested, unlike the sacked French and Portuguese ones (Norris 1968, 42). Nabbakou protected the Huedan king in the English fort.

Prior to the Dahomian conquest of 1727, processions for Dangbe took place in Savi to the north of Hueda (Law 2004, 94). Savi was a flourishing agricultural breadbasket, producing oranges, lemons, and pineapples. However, the Dahomians destroyed it, and it remains only as a small village today (Merlo and Vidaud 1984, 284).

The French occupiers banned a few ceremonies for Dangbe after 1894, including ceremonial punishments that involved the confinement of people who had offended the vodun inside a straw hut that was ignited. Fleeing from the hut to a sacred river, the offenders were pelted with stones. The French also banned an annual procession for Dangbe, because the vodun's servants were wont to seize animals found in the streets as noninitiates hid indoors.

Distinct Dan cults proliferated around Hueda. Unlike Dangbe, the Dan vodun spirits were not incarnated in physical snakes but were symbolized by them.[11] Dan temples are situated in Hueda's Dahomian neighborhoods of Fonsaramè and Boyasaramè, providing some reason to think that the Dahomian priests of Dan arrived after Agaja's conquest and set up temples near Dangbe's temple.

The sea vodun Hu is the head of an "ocean trinity" that includes Agbe and Avlékété (Lando 2016, 45–46, 102). The name "Agbe" transferred to Haitian Vodou as "Agwe" (Brand 2000b, 46). Hu and the Hula people originate to the west of Hueda in Grand-Popo (Law 2004, 90). Agoué is a town near Grand-Popo, similar again in pronunciation to the Haitian spirit Agwe. Hu and the crocodile vodun, Tokpodun, are the lords of lagoons. Hu was the Hula people's national spirit, and Hu's priest, the Hounon, had a temple in Hueda's Sogbadji neighborhood. Kpase, the founding hero of the Hula, established Hu's shrine (Law 2004, 23).

Europeans in the 1690s noted that Hu's congregation held services with offerings by the ocean to ask for calm seas, reminiscent of those for Agwe in Haiti (Law 2004, 23). The water-drawing ceremonies for Hu required collecting both fresh and salt water. Some bottles were destined for King Ghezo's (1818–1858) ritual use in Abomey, illustrating Hueda's link to central power. An eighteenth-century source claims that two human sacrifices were thrown into the ocean for Hu, whereas nineteenth-century sources mention offerings of food, cloth, and cowries, but not humans, reflecting a shift away from ritual murder (Law 2004, 95).

Hueda's Hula residents considered themselves to be the original inhabitants, arguing that Savi was the first ethnic Hueda settlement (Law 2004, 23). Such claims are part of identity arguments set against the background of the ranking of the town's vodun spirits. Ethnic Huedans claimed that the founding hero, Kpase, established a service to Dangbe, their main spirit, prior to the Hula settlement. For the Huedans, the vodun Hu is the "younger brother" of Dangbe.

Contemporary Hueda reflects the imposed Dahomian hierarchy, with Hu ranked first over Dangbe, sapping the latter of its preeminence.

Traces of the vodun Hwesi and Zo are found in Haitian Vodou. Hwesi, the vodun of smallpox, is the Huedan manifestation of Sakpata, originating in Dassa, north of the kingdom of Dahomey.[12] Service to Hwesi was established in Hueda at the time of the Dahomian conquest in the 1720s (Law 2004, 90). It is striking that the word "Zo," Hueda's fire spirit, emerges in Haitian Vodou in the term *kanzo* (initiation by fire), a key ritual of the Sèvis Ginen initiation. The word *kã* in Fon means to "dig" or "consult," as in *kã Fa* (to consult the vodun Fa). Thus *kanzo* means "to consult Zo, the spirit of fire," illustrating continuity between Hueda and Haiti (Brand 2000b, 55).

Another important pre-Dahomian congregation was dedicated to Loko, a healing spirit residing in the tallest of the African teak trees and congener of the Haitian Loko (Law 2004, 89). Also, the spirit of thunder, So, for whom the Huedan neighborhood Sogbadji is named, appears in Haiti as Sobo, also connected to thunder.[13]

The town of Hueda had religious traditions dedicated to past kings. The town's founder, Kpase, and the king who began trade with Europeans, Kpate, in addition to the kings Agbangla, Ayohuan, and Houffon, received services. Hueda's religious quilt included congregations of Dahomian origin. A temple for the royal Dahomian dynasty is located in the Fonsaramè neighborhood (Law 2004, 90). The Dahomian spirits Mawu-Lisa have a temple in the Sogbadji neighborhood. Dahomian families from the town of Oueme who settled in Hueda brought the service of Mase, the spirit of the Oueme River.

Enslaved people retained for local labor introduced religious traditions into Hueda (Law 2004, 90). An enslaved woman from Agonli-Houegbo, east of Abomey, established a shrine for the spirit Azili in the Tové neighborhood. Azili is the namesake of Haiti's Èzili spirit family. The Dahomian army sold the woman in Hueda during the reign of Agaja, where she ended up remaining. There is a stream bearing the name Danto (as in Èzili Dantò in Haiti) to the east of Savalou, a town one hundred kilometers to the north of Abomey.[14] Given Èzili's importance in Haiti's Rada and Petwo Rites, the narrative of the spirit's origin in Dahomey and implantation in Hueda after 1720 suggests that the Èzili spirits have a Dahomian or Mahi origin.

The Yoruba spirit Shango is served in Hueda (Law 2004, 91). Like Chango in Haiti, he is a thunder spirit. Shango's establishment in Hueda is related to long-standing Yoruba trade and settlement. So's function as thunder spirit overlaps with Shango's in Hueda, just as Sobo's thunder attribute overlaps with Ogou Chango in Haitian Vodou. These religious systems are at ease with overlapping dimensions of symbolism, as there are also features that differentiate So from Shango in Dahomey or Sobo from Ogou Chango in Haiti.

Finally, free immigrants from places like the Gold Coast established vodun temples in Hueda for spirits like Adjigo (Law 2004, 91).

In addition to expensive initiations, there were numerous economic dimensions associated with Vodun in Hueda. Merchants offered donations at shrines near the royal customs counter. Members of congregations ritually begged for cowries in exchange for blessings. Ritual mendicancy generated revenue for the priests, as they expected commensurate compensation for the strenuous labor of mediating the world of people and vodun; hence the proverb, "The poor are not initiated" (Law 2004, 96–97).

Hueda stands as an ethnically diverse town whose residents embrace their multicultural origins (Lando 2016, 104). In 2003, for example, the town was 69 percent Fon, 16.5 percent Aja, 9 percent Yoruba, 0.5 percent Bariba, and 0.5 percent Dendi (Lando 2016, 104). The large number of ethnic Fon in Hueda reflects the politics of Fon settlement in regions conquered by the Fon-speaking kingdom of Dahomey. As Fon rule first took root in 1727, many people shifted linguistically to Fon dominance while maintaining other languages.

In Hueda, various ethnolinguistic groups could establish their own shrines. A priest welcomed his or her extended family and the public for major ceremonies. Each temple was organized around a central spirit or ancestor, in addition to affiliated spirits. The pattern of "composite cults" that include numerous spirits is common in Haiti and Brazil, but there are important blueprints in Hueda and elsewhere. The pattern of spirit integration is likely African, given how Huedan compounds like the one dedicated to Hevioso in the Sogbadji neighborhood included a shrine for Hu, the sea vodun (Law 2004, 92). Plus, given that stories about spirits overlap and intertwine, it is normal for them to consort together.

In both Hueda and Saint-Domingue, the slave trade produced demographic diversity, bringing people from different ethnicities and religious traditions into contact. Hueda's vodun Hu reflected the importance of fisheries and seafaring, while Dangbe reflected the accumulation of mercantile wealth (Law 2004, 92, 96). One sustaining feature of the syncretic religious culture of Hueda under Dahomian rule came from the Dahomian state. Dahomian kings acquired local religious traditions, such as the one for Dangbe that King Agaja "purchased" after his conquest. Agaja's successor, Tegbesu, "purchased" the vodun Hu. These measures secured the support of the voduns' influential initiates. In the 1770s, Europeans attributed the success of the Dahomian monarchs in subduing Hueda to their tolerance of Hueda's leading Vodun congregations, observations that point to the politics of religious syncretism (Law 2004, 96–97).

The Dahomian authorities recognized the seniority of Hu's congregation in Hueda, ranking the congregations of Dangbe, Hwesi, and Zo under it. Religious rules, like those for Mawu or Mase, were administered from Abomey.

Authorities in Abomey supervised all religious activities, accommodating conquered congregations and maintaining law and order among Vodun specialists. The Dahomian state did not tolerate rogue specialists who robbed and harmed vulnerable believers. The "Ajaho" was the administrator in Abomey charged with overseeing religions, traveling to Hueda in order to "superintend" ceremonies (Law 2004, 97).

In Saint-Domingue, the Sèvis Ginen priests drew together a multiplicity of complimentary traditions, modeling their behavior on patterns found in African kingdoms. The centrifugal coalescence of diverse elements of complimentary religious systems, as we find in the "21 Nations of Ginen" model of Sèvis Ginen, was an important political and religious pattern in Hueda, Allada, Abomey, and elsewhere.

VODUN PRIESTS WHO BENEFITED FROM DAHOMEY'S SLAVE TRADE

The royal family in Abomey's patronage of religious centers of Hueda is reflected in the clothing offered to the priests of Dangbe and Hu and the 32,000 cowries (80 *livres*, or 80 pounds) paid for each European ship that traded with the town (Law 2004, 98). This suggests that the priests of Hu and Dangbe directly received revenue from the slave trade, an arrangement between religious and political leaders. The king also supplied a bull and other animals for annual sacrifices and ceremonial feasts for Hu and Hwesi, and the Dahomian administrator attended the annual ceremony for Dangbe in Hueda after the Annual Customs in Abomey (Law 2004, 98).

KING AGAJA'S REIGN AND LEGACY

After Agaja's conquest of Allada in 1724, the Yoruba kingdom of Oyo sent diplomats to arrange for tributes, but the negotiations went badly and in 1726 the Oyo army killed and enslaved a large number of Dahomian soldiers and razed Abomey. Agaja survived in his forest hiding place (Akinjogbin 1967, 82). The Oyo army's capture and enslavement of Dahomians in Abomey is important, since they were presumably sold into the transatlantic slave market and many would have ended up in Saint-Domingue. This particular flow of enslaved Dahomians in 1726 may have contributed to the emergence of the Dahomian Rite in Saint-Domingue, one still maintained at Lakou Souvenance near Gonaïves.

Agaja's conquest of Hueda in 1727 was bold. However, the Oyo army returned to fight in 1728. Encouraged by Agaja's distraction with fighting the Oyo army, the Europeans on the coast encouraged the former slave traders of Hueda to return, leading to another assault from Agaja's Dahomian troops and the destruction of Hueda's fort on May 1, 1728. One thousand people were torn apart when the ammunition magazine exploded, a horrific casualty rate that indicates the massive stockpile of gunpowder (Law 2004, 54). This gunpowder fueled the perpetual war that the Europeans encouraged through their trading of weaponry for enslaved people (Akinjogbin 1967, 84). The Dahomian army enslaved many survivors.

At the time, Oyo slave raiders sold Dahomian captives in Badagry, while Dahomians sold Aja captives from Hueda and Allada into slavery in Hueda. The Aja, the Gedevi, and the Nago were being systematically removed from Africa. Oyo invaded Dahomey again in 1729 and 1730. By the 1730 invasion, Dahomey had lost control of Abomey, leaving Agaja with Hueda and parts of Allada. After the Oyo army withdrew, Agaja began rebuilding Abomey. The ousted Huedans and their new allies, the Popoes from Grand-Popo, planned on retaking Hueda. King Agaja defeated them by arming the rear with enlisted women (Snelgrave 1971, 126).

The kingdom of Oyo regarded the region ruled by Agaja as a tributary, much as they viewed Badagry, Oueme, and Ajase Ipo (Akinjogbin 1967, 92). After the Oyo army dealt him several defeats, Agaja abandoned his plans to limit the slave trade. The Oyo kingdom may have pressured Agaja on behalf of the slave-trading faction. Another reason may have been to purchase European firearms while raising money to pay Oyo's tribute. Agaja restricted the importation to a single port and required that he receive arms directly.

Agaja's Yovogan administrators took control of the reauthorized slave trade in 1730. Once inside Dahomey, Europeans could not depart without his permission, and he stationed his troops on the beaches to manage all activities. The slave trade, like the weapons trade, became a part of the royal monopoly. Agaja's strict controls increased the price of enslaved people, while he demanded specific items from Europeans. In 1733, in exchange for three or four thousand enslaved people, Agaja demanded 3,030 guns of various types, 10,000 pounds of gunpowder, 6 cases of musical organs, 12 or 14 melody books, and 150 pounds of large corals (Akinjogbin 1967, 104).

Agaja violated the terms of his agreement with the Oyo kingdom by attacking Badagry in 1737. In 1739, the Oyo army again razed Abomey, sending Agaja into his forest hideout. Shortly after leaving the forest in May 1740, Agaja died. Although Oyo had punished him several times, Agaja's expansion into Allada and Hueda and his control of new territory ensured Dahomey's survival until 1894. His monopoly over the slave and arms trade anchored centuries of slave trading by the royal family. The consolidation of his control over the slave trade in the 1720s was directly connected to the acquisition of the weapons required to keep

European and African threats in check. European slave traders had locked him and other African kings into a vicious cycle of dependency and eventual death.

Akinjogbin calls Agaja "one of the great military leaders" and "builders of history" (1967, 107), praise that is difficult to square given his engagement in the slave trade and his frequent humiliations at the hands of the Oyo army. Agaja put into motion generations of inhumane slave trading. The kingdom fell to the French in 1894, reflecting this long drainage of human talent and defenses from the region. The slave trade damaged Africa demographically from an early period and produced colonial capitulation in the long term (Thornton 1998, 72).

Agaja left bitter legacies of military expansionism and slave trading, emphases that shaped the careers of kings in ensuing decades. Agaja's army primed the slave trade by invading, capturing, and selling the ethnic groups that became the bedrock of Saint-Domingue; thus, he deserves to be a central figure in Haitian studies.

KING AGAJA'S SUCCESSOR, KING TEGBESU

Kings were connected to material and spiritual powers in Dahomey. Legends about Agaja's son, Tegbesu, reveal aspects of royal mythology. One story describes the flight of Tegbesu and his brothers ahead of the Oyo cavalry. Rather than accept his brother's suicidal suggestion to ignite their gunpowder to kill their adversaries, Tegbesu convinced them to wade chest-deep upstream in order to hide in a grove, ultimately saving them (Bay 1998, 81–82).

Another story relates how King Agaja sent Tegbesu as part of a tribute to the king of Oyo, in addition to enslaved people, weapons, gunpowder, bales of cloth, baskets of coral, and domestic animals. A son was demanded as a symbol of submission. Queen Hwanjile gave her son a red cloth and a protective charm. He lived, worked, and remained healthy, but he never ate food while in captivity in Oyo. When the king of Oyo heard of the lad's thriving but ascetic life, he sent him back to his mother and father. The boy brought back new products from Oyo like umbrellas, in addition to spirits like Hevioso and Sakpata (Bay 1998, 82, 111).[15]

These stories underscored Tegbesu's supernatural power and leadership abilities. His boyhood experience in Oyo explains why the king of Oyo preferred his enstoolment in 1740 over other candidates. In the early days of Tegbesu's rule, he captured and drowned his brother Zingah for plotting against him. Tegbesu ordered the execution of every man and child with the name "Bosu,"[16] since a divine sovereign sharing his name with a mortal was intolerable (Norris 1968, 5, 7).

At the time that Tegbesu was enstooled in 1740, Dahomey was embroiled in conflict with the Oyo kingdom. The Yoruba Oyo neighbors continued their harassment into Tegbesu's reign, attacking in 1742 and 1743 and threatening attack in 1748 until Tegbesu submitted and paid a tribute (Akinjogbin 1967, 111). Tegbesu continued slave trading, but his ability to gather wealth was limited since the Portuguese traders refused to pay for enslaved people in gold (Akinjogbin 1967, 115). The sale of firearms to the king's neighbors increased during Tegbesu's reign, augmenting Dahomey's insecurity. Tegbesu sold into slavery "many Dahomian princes who might have contested the throne from his own descendants," including his son Kpengla's playmate Jeromino, also called "Fruku" (Akinjogbin 1967, 116). Slave trader Robert Norris wrote that guiltless residents of entire villages "were sold for slaves, to raise supplies for his extravagance" (1968, 49). A few decades after Fruku's deportation to Brazil, the newly enthroned King Kpengla brought his childhood friend back to Dahomey.

Tegbesu executed Dahomians who were "too rich," in addition to popular citizens who threatened his ego. He executed army officers if they lost a war, a punishment also meted out in Oyo (Akinjogbin 1967, 116). Because of his despotism, Tegbesu, like Agaja before him, was faced with desertions by individuals and entire military units (Norris 1968, 50). Tegbesu was fierce and dangerous, energy that projects into the Bosou spirits in Haitian Vodou.

ROYAL VODUN AND POWER IN DAHOMEY

Vodun religion was of great importance to the Dahomian royal dynasty. Agaja's wife, Hwanjile, was a dedicated adept. She was from Aja country to the west of Abomey. Mother of two when her talents and beauty were recognized, she was brought to live in the palace of Abomey. After King Agaja's death, she became the *kpojito* (mother of the leopard), meaning the mother of King Tegbesu. The *kpojito* was a powerful administrative position in the palace that included making decisions with the king. In Dahomian society, and within Vodun, talented women enjoyed "extraordinary opportunities" (Bay 1998, 16). She possessed insights in psychology and administered religion in the kingdom. Tegbesu was her protégé to the extent that she stabilized the interregnum period that transitioned from Agaja's to Tegbesu's rule (Bay 1998, 90).

Agaja, Hwanjile, Tegbesu, and other Agasuvi vested with power used Vodun to solidify their grasp on governance, just as others used religion to compete with their governance. Religious institutions were an important source of unrest between Agaja's death and Tegbesu's enstoolment. Dahomian Vodun followers belonged to local congregations led by a male or female priest called a vodunon (vodun guardian). Congregations were linked together, and as extrafamilial social groups, they provided opportunities for different people to meet, network, share news, and promote political alternatives (Bay 1998, 92).

Tegbesu perceived religious communities as a threat. The followers of Sakpata and those who followed the "gods of the rivers and the silk-cotton trees" opposed Tegbesu and were sold into slavery, suggesting that Tegbesu did not introduce the Sakpata cult, as discussed above (Bay 1998, 92). The priesthood of the indigenous spirits of the Gedevi opposed Tegbesu (Bay 1998, 92). In selling members of congregations that opposed him, Tegbesu wiped political threats off the continent.

In the course of the battles fought between the Dahomian occupiers and the Huedan refugees and their Popo allies, Norris notes that Tegbesu's "oracles had forbidden them from attacking the enemy on the *Beach*, but had ordered that they should wait in readiness, between Griwhee and the river" (1968, 54). The term "oracle" implies that a Vodun priest who worked with the king provided military advice. Tegbesu used slavery to carry out ideological cleansing, ridding Dahomey of politically resistant forms of Vodun while enriching himself. Many of those groups found themselves in Saint-Domingue, where they overturned French colonialism in 1804. The Dahomian elite supported the slave trade because it benefited them financially and rid them of threatening competitors.

MEASURES TAKEN BY TEGBESU'S MOTHER, HWANJILE

Queen Hwanjile reordered the hierarchy of vodun spirits so that they would better reflect the dynasty's allegiances. Vodun congregations that demonstrated loyalty to the monarchy were rewarded, while congregations that were disloyal were killed or sold into slavery. Hwanjile's reordering involved an underlying political calculation. She brought some Aja spirits into the kingdom of Dahomey, most notably the creator spirits, female Mawu and male Lisa, which she established over the other Fon spirits (Bay 1998, 92). Mawu and Lisa represented the "ideological vision of power relationships at the center of the state of Dahomey" in the sense that power derived from the male king and the king's mother, the *kpojito* (mother of the leopard), each asserting influence in complementary domains (Bay 1998, 95). Today, the spirits Mawou and Lisa are served in Haitian Vodou's Danwonmen Rite, but they do not have the regal ranking they had in Hwanjile's system (Beauvoir 2008a, 187).

Hwanjile became the supreme leader of religious life in Dahomey (Bay 1998, 93). She confirmed new priests, settled political differences, authorized days for ceremonies and festivals, and ensured that congregations were financially dependent on the monarchy. The royals patronized local ceremonies and granted land to congregations. By the time of Tegbesu's death in 1774, the monarchy was in a position to influence Vodun congregations through strict regulation and financial controls (Bay 1998, 93).

THE RISE OF DIVINATION

A second development under Tegbesu and Hwanjile was the expansion of divination. This aspect of the Aja and Yoruba cultures is preserved in Haitian Vodou. The Yoruba Fa tradition of divination that originated in Ife arrived in Dahomey during Agaja's reign. Unlike the ceremonies of priest-led congregations, the Yoruba system was personal, private, and client based. Although the Fa system was foreign, Dahomey had local bokanto (diviners) (Bay 1998, 94). In Fon, *bokan-* refers to "amulets" and *-to* refers to "father"; thus, *bokanto* means "father of amulets."

The expansion of the Yoruba Fa system under Kings Agaja and Tegbesu may reflect efforts to weaken the power of the congregations and the indigenous bokanto (Bay 1998, 95). For the kings of Dahomey, the advantage of private divination was its ability to limit public prophetic interventions inside of temples during which charismatic people became possessed and made threatening political prophesies in the name of a vodun.

In Haitian Vodou, the priestly religion led by the *oungan* and *manbo* also coexists with the divination practices of the *bòkò*. The influence of Yoruba Fa divination culture is limited in Haiti, whereas the ubiquity of *bòkò* diviners suggests that the leaders of congregational Vodun as well as diviners were deported en masse from Dahomey. Religious activists and extremists were perceived as political risks for the kings.

In 1748, Tegbesu reached a peace agreement with the Oyo kingdom, allowing him to keep his army and to engage in slave raiding in areas north and west of Abomey, territories not under Oyo control. Preserving slave trading was one of Tegbesu's priorities. Once he concluded the settlement with Oyo, he focused on exporting enslaved people (Akinjogbin 1967, 125, 127). Like his father, Tegbesu strove to monopolize and expand the slave trade, concentrating it at Igelefe Fort in Hueda. This site of slave embarkation is memorialized today in the Haitian Creole expression *depi tan Jelefre* (for as long as I can remember).

SLAVE TRADING UNDER KING TEGBESU

Tegbesu centralized the slave trade at Igelefe Fort in 1744. The fact that Jelefre resonates in Haitian Creole history is evidence of his funneling of the slave trade through the fort. Tegbesu killed incompliant slave traders and consolidated his grip on the trade. He appointed his own officers to control it within the fort, and he banned Europeans from trading elsewhere in his kingdom. In 1746, 1747, and 1748, he proclaimed that anyone could travel from Epe, Oueme, and Ajara to Igelefe with enslaved people for export. Tegbesu endeavored to ensure the prosperity of his slave trading (Akinjogbin 1967, 127–28). He also colonized three areas of Hueda with Dahomians from the Abomey plateau, profoundly influencing the town's demographics (Bay 1998, 107).

Commerce in Dahomey rebounded, and by the 1750s, Hueda's trade was greater than that of the Yoruba coastal towns of Badagry and Epe (Akinjogbin 1967, 134). French, Portuguese, and English ships took approximately nine thousand enslaved people yearly. Between 1740 and 1797, a period of time that includes the reigns of Tegbesu, Kpengla, and Agonglo, the Portuguese purchased 56 percent of the enslaved people, the French 22.3 percent, and the English 21.7 percent (Peukert 1978, 105). Aja and Yoruba were captured in this period.

Since a slave was sold for a price that ranged between 24 and 32 British pounds,[17] King Tegbesu earned between 216,000 and 288,000 pounds annually, not counting his customs duties. A significant part of his revenue collection derived from exporting enslaved people (Akinjogbin 1967, 134). The condemnation of chiefs and administrators included the confiscation of their estate and the enslavement of their family and entourage (Bay 1998, 108).

For Dahomians not threatened by slave raiding, the system provided opportunities for employment. Various services were established on the beaches to facilitate the process of purchasing enslaved people. Tents served as waiting stations while enslaved people were loaded onto ships. Enslaved people were placed in stockades in forts like Igelefe as their sellers waited for the ships. The captains of the slave ships hired porters, canoe men, messengers, storekeepers, laborers, washerwomen, water carriers, rollers of barrels, slave wardens, and night watchmen. Soldiers were also stationed on the beaches (Akinjogbin 1967, 135). The Dahomian slave trade was an enormous operation that required the efforts of a significant part of the population.

THE WAR AND VIOLENCE OF SLAVE RAIDING

The narratives that come down from Tegbesu's reign are full of violence. When the residents of Jakin failed to pay a tribute in 1761, Tegbesu sent troops to kill the town's entire population. Kpengla, Tegbesu's successor, only resettled it in 1777 (Argyle 1966, 22). For the most part, however, Tegbesu's violence was motivated by the material gain from the slave trade.

Tegbesu viewed the Mahi region in the north as ideal for slave raiding. One of his favorite wives was a Mahi woman who wished for her brother to control Mahi lands, which were organized in a confederation of small states. Tegbesu claimed that Dahomian traders were penalized in Mahi country, since they were taxed arbitrarily by several chiefs rather than by a single king who could negotiate treaties (Norris 1968, 17, 19). Tegbesu wanted to select the Mahi king to ensure that he would receive a steady flow of untaxed enslaved people and goods for his trade in Hueda, and his Mahi wife's brother would perfectly serve that purpose (Argyle 1966, 24).

The Mahi hoped to live in peace next to Dahomey but declared war after Tegbesu kept meddling in their affairs. Conflict with the Mahi began in 1737, and slaughter ensued. Mahi "prisoners of distinction" were executed and the captives sold as enslaved people (Norris 1968, 20). Years later, in 1752, the twelve-month siege of Boagry resulted in a Mahi retreat and many victims. Numerous chiefs were killed and the survivors sold as enslaved people (Norris 1968, 22). A few years later, the Mahi invaded Dahomey, but they were unable to do much harm.

In 1764, Tegbesu again sent troops with his favorite son, Jupera, who perished on the trip home after an unsuccessful campaign. Tegbesu's brother-in-law never became king, and a peace accord was concluded in 1772. Although Tegbesu was unsuccessful in imposing his will on the Mahi, the campaigns enslaved people over several decades, impacting Saint-Domingue, where traces of Mahi culture are evident in cultural practices like the *mahi* drum rhythm and the Mahi Rite, which includes the spirit Loko Mahi Fado (Beauvoir 2008a, 190). Tegbesu's use of lethal violence to assert his sovereignty reflected a form of "necropolitics" connected to dehumanizing, selling, and killing people in the accumulation of power (Mbembe 2017, 163).

POWER DYNAMICS BETWEEN VODUN PRIESTS AND KING TEGBESU

The power dynamics between the monarchy and religious leaders was often rubbed raw. The high priest of Cana claimed to be the interpreter of the vodun, believing that he deserved the same honors as the king. The priest's vodun dwelled in one of the tallest trees. By his reasoning, he stood taller than other men. Tegbesu was displeased with him and knew that his popularity posed risks. Tegbesu pressured him to drop his claims and finally executed him in public with his own hands, illustrating the fate of Vodun leaders who challenged the king's power (Argyle 1966, 30).

HAVES AND HAVE-NOTS IN A SLAVE-TRADING KINGDOM

The Dahomian laborers hired by European traders were paid in cowries and brandy. The work of most occupations was compensated in this way, although sometimes cloth was offered to women instead of alcohol. Since eating well cost between 3 and 5 cowries per day, a porter who made 120 cowries in exchange for carrying one load from the beach to the fort was able to live comfortably compared to his neighbors (Akinjogbin 1967). Tegbesu and the elite lived in affluence according to the slave trader Robert Norris, who visited the kingdom in 1772. The slave trade and market economies of Hueda highlighted differences in wealth, since the elite indulged in meats like chicken, fowl, or goat whereas the poor rarely had meat at all. Prostitution was common in Hueda for European and African johns. More than 333 "girls" worked in one bordello operated by the Avloko family (Law 2004, 86).

While the slave trade depleted the population of the Bight of Benin, it generated wealth for the organizers. The wealth accumulated by the king and his generals was reflected in their impressive palaces. A small army of wives, the fiercest of whom were recruited into the Dahomian king's exclusively female palace guard, dwelled in them. The king's absolutism was evidenced in sumptuary laws that allowed the monarch alone to wear sandals and required all others to walk barefoot. However, Tegbesu's wealth was waning, illustrated by the smaller number of enslaved people (five thousand) shipped from Hueda in the year 1765, which was about half the annual number during the 1750s (Akinjogbin 1967, 139). The English abandoned Hueda in 1764 (Akinjogbin 1967, 150). The slave traders under Tegbesu had depended on traders from the Oyo kingdom, who began to divert their trade to Porto-Novo, which exported 1,500 enslaved people in 1765. Tegbesu enriched himself and his allies, but at the expense of the local and regional populations. During Tegbesu's reign (1740–1774), the massive transfer of Dahomian and neighboring populations filled French and other colonies and depleted his defenses and human resources.

THE *TOHOSU* AND *BOSU* TRADITIONS

The cult of the *tohosu*, also called *bosu* in Dahomey, involved the veneration of deceased royal children who had been born with abnormalities (Métraux 1972, 31). The *tohosu* were returned to the waters from which they came by drowning. Through their deaths, they became figments of myths extolled by the royal family and those with access to royal influence (Bay 1998, 93).

The traditions of Agaja and Tegbesu and the Dahomian dynasty seem connected to Haitian Vodou via the Bosou spirit family. It would be remarkable if ruthless slave traders like Agaja and Tegbesu could have any tradition memorialized in Haitian Vodou. Their transatlantic survival points to their political, religious, and economic power as the kings of Dahomey. Another possibility is that members of the Dahomian royal family were reduced to slavery and themselves planted the Bosou traditions in Haiti (Métraux 1972, 31). The Bosou are a powerful family of spirits resembling Dahomian kings in their ferocity.

The Bosou spirits are spread over the Bosou and Rada Rites (Beauvoir 2008b). It is striking that they do not occur in the Danwonmen Rite, however, since the Dahomian kings promoted their traditions. The presence of the Bosou spirits in the coastal Rada Rite and the Bosou Rite, however, suggests other possibilities. The Bosou traditions may have originated in the coastal region and subsequently migrated with the Alladahonu to Abomey around 1620. Another possibility is that the Dahomians created the separate Bosou Rite for this unique class of spirits.

The Bosou spirit family in Haiti includes Kadya Bosou (Bosou Rite), Bosou Dhlo (Rada Rite), Bosou Kelendjo (Rada Rite), Djobolo Bosou (Rada Rite), Bosou Achade, and Bosou Twa Kòn, among others (Beauvoir 2008b). These powerful protectors are the only ones that can work with all other spirits (Welele Doubout, personal correspondence, 2018; Jil and Jil 2009, 105). A bull's head is the animal offering made for Bosou and the symbol of his *vèvè* diagrams.

In addition to receiving *nyí* (birth names), Dahomian kings took *nyí siyensiyen* (strong names), which commemorated an exploit, an event, or a stunning act (Burton 1893, 265–66). King Dako's (1625–1650) strong names were, "As he is king, he will lay low all who do not bow to his scepter" and "A fetish charm that nothing can harm," among others. The likening of King Dako's strong name to a vodun spirit (fetish) illustrates how the Dahomian kings employed mystification to enhance their power (Burton 1893, 266).

In the case of Kadya Bosou (Agaja) and Bosou Achade (Tegbesu), the connection to the Dahomian dynasty is convincing. Kadya seems straightforwardly derived from the name (A)kadya (Agaja). King Agaja's strong name was, "Dosu asks to see, and then takes by force from the owner," a nod to his usurpations (Burton 1893, 273). One of his symbols was a European caravel boat, an image he embraced after seizing the coastal slave-trading ports.

Bosou Achade was King Tegbesu's strong name, appearing also as an important Bosou spirit name in Haitian Vodou. Even the slave trader Norris (1968) refers to Tegbesu as "Bossa Ahádee." The king's birth name, Tegbwesun, means, "Which belongs to the mysteries of the Bo-Fetish" (Burton 1893, 273). The Fon language includes numerous religious terms with the prefix *bo-*; for example, *bò*, *bōkà*, and *bōmāsi* refer to types of "amulets"; *bōgbè* and *bòlú* are "incantations"; and a *bojétó* is a "magician" (Brand 2000b, 22–24). *Bòsú* refers to a child who presents at birth with the umbilical cord around her or his neck. *Bosou* is also "leopard's blood," a title of respect used among the descendants of Agasu (Segurola and Rassinoux 2000; Jil and Jil 2009, 105). In Dahomian culture, the prefix *bo-* reflects magical properties and life force. The royal strong names Kadya Bosou and Bosou Achade project the spiritual power of *bo*. Tegbesu's other strong names include "He is like the hoe handle, he will break the legs of all nations," "The truth of another man's wife is not doubted," and "A thing in his hand shall never be taken by another person," reflecting the violence for which he was famous (Burton 1893, 275).

Bosou in Haiti is portrayed on flags and *vèvè* as a bull with three horns. In the Dahomian symbolic context, horns represent power.[18] The image of the bull used to represent Bosou may descend from the stories of Tegbesu's coronation in 1740. At that event, after wearing a tunic sown with thorns that were tipped in stinging potion, the king uttered his strong name: "The buffalo who is dressed is impossible to undress" (Bay 1998, 83). The bull imagery of the Haitian Vodou spirit Bosou seems to stem from King Tegbesu's buffalo totem.

Haitian Vodou ceremonies witnessed in July 1934 were directed at placating Bosou and other spirits (Herskovits 1937, 159–61). A service was held in the hills around Mirebalais to prevent further deaths and illnesses from tormenting a family. A table with offerings for Bosou was set up, and a *boukan* (bonfire) for Legba was built. Men who "had strong Bosu gods" took to their knees in front of the spirit's table, and the priest used fowl to touch and bless them (Herskovits 1937, 163).

After a period of possessions that took place in the drenching rain and mud, the priest calmed down the possessed worshippers and carried out the sacrifices, which were immediately prepared for feasting. Once cooked, there was a final *ranvwaye* (sending away) of the spirits that had been harassing the family. Èzili Je Wouj, Bosou Twa Kòn, Ti Kita Demanbre, and Ti Jan Pye Sèch were sent away, whereas the spirits Lemba and Simbi Djo (Dlo) were restrained. Finally, parts of the sacrificed animals were buried in receptacles, and the harassing spirits were put to rest for seven to seventeen years.

The Bosou spirit's reputation for danger is captured in the description of another ceremony that Melville Herskovits (1937, 197) attended. The possession of Bosu Trois Cornes (Bosou Twa Kòn) was so intense in the body of a young girl that several men had to hold her while various *oungan* "worked over her." One of the *oungan* shouted at Bosou, "Be off! You are not wanted here!" When Bosou left the girl, she completed a libation in front of the drums while holding a candle and was quickly sent home with assistance (Herskovits 1937, 197).

It is surprising that these monarchs profited from slave trading while transmitting venerated and feared spirits to slave colonies they helped populate. Haitian people remember the Dahomian kings better than other royalty (Jil and Jil 2009, 102). How did those slave-trading kings manage to preserve their legacies in Haiti? The question is at first confounding, given Vodouists' opposition to slavery, but as the angry and unstable dimensions of the Bosou emerge, they look more like codified forms of historical trauma.

AMALGAMATION AND SYMBOLISM IN THE ROYAL RELIGION OF DAHOMEY

In Dahomey, separate groups maintained distinct congregations, but the kings introduced a layer of political unity within the religious societies as they "amalgamated the particular cults of these groups" (Argyle 1966, 109). The monarchy was able to influence the installment of leadership in family lineages by creating the office of the *dokpwegan*. This official oversaw funerals and gave permission to new lineage heads to commence their leadership once animals for sacrifice to the ancestors had been submitted (Argyle 1966, 109).

The second part of the installment ceremony required a vodunon priest who had received training in the common ritual for Dahomey's ancestors from a house of worship that the king patronized (Argyle 1966, 109). The kings accommodated the heterogeneous spiritual lineages of the Aja people under the common banner of the Dahomian administration. The cooperation between Vodun priests and kings and the role of royal families in authorizing and patronizing rituals illustrate some of the ways Vodun was imbricated with politics and identity in Dahomey, Hueda, and Allada. State-regulated "cohesion with groomed heterogeneity" was a feature of Dahomian culture that seems detectable in the emergence of Sèvis Ginen's synthesis of Saint-Domingue's intense African diversity.

Tegbesu asserted that the spirit Agasu selected him as king, enhancing his power through spiritual alignment. He paid officers of the state to propagate the myth that Agasu protected his dynasty (Jil and Jil 2009, 104). Building temples to honor Agasu, Tegbesu rewarded the priests who promoted the royal myth. The effort of Dahomian kings like Tegbesu to connect political power with religious symbols reflected notions of order and power among the Aja.

THE END OF TEGBESU'S RULE AND HIS SUCCESSOR, KPENGLA

The Dahomian slave trade declined between 1767 and 1789, causing an economic drop. After Tegbesu's death in 1774, his son Kpengla became king. In spite of their own thievery, Europeans avoided the port of Hueda in the late 1760s and 1770s due to Dahomian treachery. Tegbesu's policy of a smooth slave trade relied on Oyo's supply of captives. The decision of Oyo traders to favor Porto-Novo, Ekpè, and Badagry to the east helped the Oyo traders, since enslaved people could be sold for larger amounts of money while avoiding the Dahomian king (Akinjogbin 1967, 144–46). Dahomey attacked Porto-Novo in 1763, 1787, 1791, and 1804, Ekpè in 1747 and 1782, and Badagry 1783 in attempts to hinder their slave trade (Law 2004, 126).

As supplies of enslaved people declined, so too did the quality of the firearms used for trading. The faulty weapons of the 1760s hurt Tegbesu's men, and French traders never rectified the problem. To remedy the decline in slave exports, Tegbesu and Kpengla desperately organized raiding expeditions in 1767, 1770, 1772, 1775, 1776, 1777, 1780, and 1781, most of which were unsuccessful (Akinjogbin 1967, 149).

By the 1760s, Tegbesu had decided that the "peaceful slave trade" was unsatisfactory, demanding wars to replenish the stocks of enslaved people and his coffers. Kpengla promised in a 1775 coronation speech to focus Dahomey's energy on the slave trade and independence from Oyo (Akinjogbin 1967, 154). Slave traders were shown "a great number of the prisoners, who had surrendered on the late occasion," a reference to captives Kpengla had made of the former Huedans, who had continued their harassment (Norris 1968, 135). Norris did not purchase the enslaved people "as they were emaciated, and appeared to be sickly." Kpengla resolved to put them to death if not purchased, since "these strangers might prejudice his people against it [his government], and infect them with sentiments incompatible with it" (Norris 1968, 135). Norris shrugged off King Kpengla's threat, writing, "[I] doubt not some of them were purchased afterwards (when their health and strength were recruited), for slaves for the *West Indies*" (135).

Several of Kpengla's attempted slave raids failed, including the loss of eight hundred Dahomian soldiers in a 1776 defeat. Raids on Mahi territory to the northwest of Abomey resulted in few captives (Akinjogbin 1967, 155). The failures of Tegbesu and Kpengla created an economic depression that stretched from 1767 to 1782 (Akinjogbin 1967, 160). In 1778, Kpengla's army captured several hundred people in the town of Appee (Argyle 1966, 22). Adding to the difficulties of life in this period, there was a famine in 1780, while Oyo demanded larger tributes.

As the conflict between Britain and the independent United States receded in 1783, the circulation of boats on the Atlantic increased. In that year, Kpengla sent his troops to march on Badagry but was repelled. They returned the next year with mercenaries and cut off six thousand heads. In 1786, Kpengla attacked Oueme, killing and capturing many people (Argyle 1966, 22).

War broke out between Oyo, its Aja allies, and the kingdom of Lagos. In 1788, the navy of Lagos, composed of forty thousand men, destroyed Badagry and captured many of its citizens, who were sold as enslaved people (Akinjogbin 1967, 167). Badagry is recalled throughout Haiti in the name of the powerful Yoruba spirit, Ogou Badagri.

In 1788, Kpengla organized slave raids, arming his men with weapons and gunpowder that he purchased on credit from the European forts. His army raided the Yoruba town of Crootoohoontoo in the Ketu kingdom. Although he was successful at first, on the march back home the Dahomians were intercepted by Ketu's army, which killed and captured many troops (Akinjogbin 1967, 172). In a raid on the Ketu kingdom in 1789, Kpengla took two thousand prisoners, of whom two hundred were sold and rest executed at the Annual Customs (Argyle 1966, 24; Dalzel 1967, 202).

Kpengla died of smallpox in 1789 at a moment when French slave-trading ambitions had somewhat waned in the Bight of Benin. Nevertheless, eleven French boats were anchored at Porto-Novo in 1786 (Dalzel 1967, 194). Although there were negotiations with Kpengla to build French forts near Epe, Cotonou, and Porto-Novo in 1786, by the time the French Revolution broke out in 1789, and the Haitian Revolution in 1791, slave trading with the French had collapsed.

THE END OF SLAVERY IN SAINT-DOMINGUE

The French colonial government of Saint-Domingue abolished slavery in 1793, whereas the metropolitan French government in Paris took measures to reinstate it in 1802. Napoleon Bonaparte sent General Charles Leclerc, his brother-in-law, to Saint-Domingue with an armada and an army of 31,131 troops on a mission to end "general liberty" (Métral and Louverture 1985). The French troops began arriving in 1802, and a total of 80,000 reinforcements arrived over a one-year period (Ramsey 2011, 50). Using a ruse, the French troops arrested and deported the popular Black governor, Toussaint Louverture, shortly after Leclerc's arrival.

The Haitian *armée indigène* (indigenous army) fought several major battles with the French army and administration of Saint-Domingue. The Haitian army, led by General Jean-Jacques Dessalines, fought the final battle of the war on November 18, 1803, at Vertières, definitively defeating the French troops and winning Haitian independence. Dessalines declared independence in Gonaïves on January 1, 1804.

CONCLUSION

The capture, sale, and deportation of people in exchange for imported goods formed the lifeblood of the triangular transatlantic trade on the West African coast. From the sailors, soldiers, and traders who plied the seaways to the investors who controlled the system remotely in Europe; from the slave-raiding Dahomian kings to the elite Black and white traders on the coast, a community arose that was single-mindedly focused on capturing and selling the weak and vulnerable, the strong and dangerous, and the criminal and indebted. The armies of kingdoms stormed into communities of innocent people living on the margins or in foreign states and took them away in coffles. Every neighbor of Dahomey, all politically resistant groups, and every delinquent inside the kingdom became a target of predation. Politically resistant Vodun groups that were deported reconstituted their quest for freedom in Saint-Domingue, achieving independence within generations.

This chapter has shown how the trade that prevailed in the transatlantic period was centered on the sale and deportation of African children, women, and men, ultimately the architects of Haitian Vodou. In addition, palm oil, cloth from Oyo, beef, ivory, and dried food were also exported. African people and things were traded for firearms and gunpowder, gold, cowries and coral, alcohol, tobacco, consumer goods, cotton and linen fabrics, iron, and luxury items (Peukert 1978, 106, 141). While snatching up goods, the elite got rid of innocent, powerless, undesirable, irresponsible, dangerous, and threatening people in society.

Every pretext was used to wage war in order to capture people, cruelties that spawned cycles of internecine violence. Gaining wealth was the goal of all the groups involved in the slave trade. The European traders and sailors and the African traders and raiders worked to secure profit and satisfy the quotas of their taskmasters, advancing up the ladders of their own careers in the process. Across the Atlantic, drugs like alcohol and tobacco were currencies in the culture of slavery. One of the extreme depressant effects of alcohol is its numbing of pain, trapping enslavers in its addictive stupor and deadening them to the inhumanity of their actions. A quarter of French cargos were loaded with alcoholic spirits, illustrating its role in fueling the French-Dahomian slave trade (Peukert 1978, 145).

Reconstructing the situation in Aja, Gedevi, and Fon communities in the slave-trading historical period contextualizes how Vodun was transformed into Vodou in Saint-Domingue and independent Haiti. The study of the African history behind the Rada and Gede cultures reveals a part of the world that Haitian Vodouists were violently torn from. The enslaver orientation of royal Dahomian Vodun and the liberator orientation of Saint-Dominguan Vodou reflected differing stances on power. Deported by Dahomian kings as political threats, many Caribbean Vodou groups had taken the path of resistance even before arriving in the French colony.

The available resources on Aja, Fon, and Gedevi history, religions, languages, and cultures are significant and merit thorough study from a Haitian point of view. The histories, societies, and cultures of the Bight of Benin deserve more attention in Haitian studies given their colossal contributions to the formation of Haiti's culture. Work in African studies represents a key frontier for Haitian and Vodou studies.

In the next chapter, religious cultures from the Bight of Benin are examined in order to lay a foundation for the reading of Haitian sacred songs. My emphasis on the kingdoms of Hueda, Allada, and Dahomey reflects their centrality in explaining Haitian Vodou's genesis. Chapter 2's focus on religion in the Bight of Benin continues the dialectical reading of Haitian Vodou's African sources in preparation for the shift in focus to Haiti that follows in chapters 3 and 4.

Chapter 2

THE AFRICAN SPIRITUAL ROOTS OF HAITIAN VODOU

The Religious Cultures of the Aja-Fon and Gedevi-Yoruba

INTRODUCTION

The political and military history of African kingdoms in the Aja-Fon and Gedevi-Yoruba region addressed in chapter 1 ventured into religious matters, since Vodun was imbricated with political power in Aja-Fon and Gedevi-Yoruba cultures. Still mindful of political matters, this chapter's focus shifts to the religious practices, theology, and structure of Vodun. The religious traditions of the Aja-Fon are relatively well known, offering insights into the societies that form the bedrock of Haitian life and culture. Since the earliest accounts, the Vodun culture of the region has fascinated observers, who have left studies providing incredible opportunities for transatlantic research.

A study of Aja-Fon and Gedevi-Yoruba religious communities offers a starting point for research on Haitian Vodou. Work on diverse African traditions is needed to gain insight into the continent-wide influences that shaped Haitian traditions. The Vodou hermeneutics proposed here uses comparative, linguistic, and historical methodologies to study the Aja-Fon and Gedevi-Yoruba religious traditions from the point of view of Haitian studies. My examination of Vodun seeks a foothold in the source societies in order to understand the religion's transmission to the recipient society of Saint-Domingue and Haiti.

FUNDAMENTALS OF DAHOMIAN THEOLOGY: SACRED BEINGS, SACRED NATURE

The Dahomians believed in a creator supreme being denoted in terms like Mawu (God) and Sê (principle, intelligence) (Le Hérissé 1910, 96). One of the deity's names is Mawu-Homêfato (God imbued with mercy) (Quénum 1999, 67).

Due to Mawu's distance from human concerns, the supreme being is not worshiped in temples, has no statues or monuments, and is only referred to in a few expressions.

Mawu created the universe and the vodun spirits that are guides to human destiny. Mawu is tied to the vodun Lisa, forming together the union of earth and sky, east and west, the upper and the lower (Brand 2000b, 62, 67). Mawu and Lisa can switch gender in the Aja-Fon cultural space, but they remain the "creator couple." In another version of the myth, Mawu created Sogbo and Sakpata as a single deity (Ifie and Adelugbo 1998, 141). Service to Lisa persists at Lakou Souvenance in Haiti, where an ancient tree serves as the spirit's residence.

The notion of the archetypical couple is common in Haitian Vodou mythology, for instance in spirit couples like the priest Loko and priestess Ayizan or the serpents Danbala and Ayida. Agaja's wife, Queen Hwanjile (circa 1704–1748), added Mawu and Lisa to Dahomey's religious system, instituting a gender-balanced "supreme couple" that reflected women's power in the kingdom. Queen Hwanjile administered religion during Agaja's reign, in addition to during the reign of their son, King Tegbesu.

The spirit Mawu is a queen served by her spirit ministers, who are "satellites" forming a "brilliant court" around her (Quénum 1999, 67). This image resembles Haitian Vodou's notion of the spirits forming facets on Bondye's (God's) diamond (Beauvoir 2008b).

The supreme being created the spirits, humankind, plants, animals, and rivers. God creates life in Vodun, whereas the vodun spirits protect and take life. Hebyoso takes life by means of lightning bolts, Sakpata by means of smallpox, or Ogun by means of war (Quénum 1999, 68). Although they are capable of killing the disobedient, spirits primarily heal the sick or provide protection.

Spirits are associated with the aspects of life over which humans have limited control. Religious inspiration sprang from veneration, love, and terror of nature (Quénum 1999, 65). Spirits link to phenomena that transcend the imagination and express a concentration of power. Thunder and lightning, smallpox, rivers, fisheries, springs, trees, serpents, or the seas call the vodun to mind. The spirits are compressed expressions of anger, impatience, jealousy, hunger, thirst, and sexual appetite (Quénum 1999, 67). Service to the Vodun is anthropocentric in that life events reflect rewards or punishments for loyalty or disloyalty (Le Hérissé 1911, 97). The vodun spirits have a double nature that is both human and supernatural. They express desire but also archetypical mythological structures that are beyond the ordinary.

Many Vodun and Vodou spirits originate in exemplary human lives, like Legba or Ogou. The greatest attributes of the exemplary human are coupled with the spirit being and promoted posthumously. Legba's wisdom and mediation are praised, while Ogou's bravery, militancy, and power are venerated.

One Dahomian creation myth describes the origins of life as a lightning bolt that left a gaping hole in one side of a gigantic *roko* (loko) tree. From that gap, the first man and woman emerged, creating the first family. The supreme being is absent from this narrative; instead, domains governed by the spirits, like lightning and trees, set the stage for the emergence of humankind.

FUNDAMENTAL TRAITS OF VODUN RELIGION AND CULTURE

In Vodun, immaterial powers emanate from nature or deified ancestors (Rouget 2001, v). The vodun spirits are ancestors recognized by the nation as royals, and they are the filaments of life and fecundity. Vodun is not "animist" because not every natural phenomenon or thing is imbued with a vodun spirit. Vodun spirits can rest in natural places, but they are not stuck there. The powerful signs of nature, including humans, are "the manifestation of a superior power" (Savary 1975, 47). Vodunists connect with the sacred through constructed or found altars where communication between the living and the immaterial powers is heightened (Rouget 2001, v). The vodun is a spirit or a "deity" of a familial, communal, national, or supranational space (Rouget 2001, v).

A category of spirit found in Vodun (but not Vodou) is the *tohosu*. "Tohosu" means "King of the Waters" (Verger 1957, 552). These were people born with abnormalities who were promptly drowned and worshiped as divinities (Verger 1957, 552; Bay 1998, 93–95). The *tohosu* were "returned home" via this infant-drowning variety of euthanasia. Offerings and sacrifices in the waters where their spirits dwelled calmed their frustrations. The rivulets around Abomey, including Agbado, Azili,[1] and Gudu, were known for their *tohosu*.

Each type of spirit has a function. The *tohosu* spirits are asked to help ensure a healthy pregnancy. Farmers call the earth vodun Sakpata to assist in harvesting. Mechanics, blacksmiths, soldiers, and politicians seek Ogou. Leaf healers and woodworking artisans beseech Loko for protection. The ancestors and vodun are invoked to correct unbalanced familial and social relationships. Vodun religion identifies and classifies the forces in the universe in order to determine which ones will work most efficaciously for the well-being of humankind (Savary 1975, 47).

The interdependence of Vodunists and the vodun spirits is understood as help requested by the venerator and the force acquired by the vodun. The blood of animal sacrifice reanimates the vital force of the vodun, allowing them to feed and reciprocate requests. The animal's blood is the agent of "life and thought," establishing the relation between the living and the ancestors. It is dripped on the altar and the ground for the spirit to feed upon (Savary 1975, 47–48).

The "pact of blood" illustrates the sacredness of blood in Vodun society. It links the partakers of a spiritual or biological family or also of a political persuasion in an unbreakable bond (Savary 1975, 48). The pact of blood that is taken with a vodun spirit creates a new line of spiritual parentage that only death can undo (Savary 1975, 48). The vodun spirit becomes the spiritual mother or father of the blood imbiber.

These ritual uses of animal blood extend seamlessly into Haitian Vodou, from animal sacrifice, to dabbing clothing and skin with blood, to consuming symbolic portions of animal blood, to the loyalty pact of blood. A pact of blood sealed the bond of the fighters led by Boukman Dutty at the Bwa Kayiman ceremony of August 14, 1791, igniting thirteen years of war against the French enslavers and leading to the foundation of Haiti in 1804.

The division of spirits between emanations of nature and humanity is found in West African and Haitian spirit systems. The sanctification of nature has a primordial place in Vodun, pointing to its place among nature religions. However, not all of nature is sanctified. A tree does not become a venerated dwelling for Loko unless the spirit Fa has determined it to be so (Quénum 1999, 89). Not every tree is sacred; instead, impressive and revealed exemplars are. Not every river, stream, waterfall, or spring has the same religious meaning as the special sites of Aja-Fon society. An impressive and ecologically important natural place has spiritual meaning because it protects the community (Lando 2016).

Protections include prohibitions on cutting trees in sacred forests, bans on fishing in consecrated waters during breeding, and the banishment of domestic animals and their fecal waste near springs used for drinking water. Legends are a tactic to protect natural resources (Lando 2016). On waterways like the L'Ahouangan and Linhouin, making noise, coughing, spitting, or hand washing are prohibited because of the dangerous water spirits that utter terrifying words from the deep. Stories circulate about boaters and canoe men whose vessels capsized or who lost things in the water (Quénum 1999, 89).[2]

Many of the vodun spirits are matched with animal totems. The python symbolizes Dangbe. The small Ziô monkey stands for the Hoho spirit of twins. The antelope represents Sakpata, and the panther is the symbol of Agasu, the Dahomian royal family's totem (Quénum 1999, 88). The dog is connected to Legba, a notable association, since Legba is matched with Saint Lazarus in Haitian Vodou, pictured in chromolithographs standing with the help of a crutch beside a dog that licks his wounds. The chameleon symbolizes Lisa, a vodun spirit who couples with Mawu, the supreme spirit who is symbolized by the moon. The tortoise is associated with troublemaking Bo spirits that are linked to hot magic and disease (Quénum 1999, 88). Sellers in Aja-Fon areas offer parts of these animals for religious uses. One of Vodun's self-preserving structural attributes is its organization, examined next.

ORGANIZATION, HIERARCHY, AND AUTHORITY IN VODUN SOCIETY

Vodun has firm structure, hierarchy, and principles. The pageantry of Aja-Fon religion reflects the people's taste for impressive external signs of faith and well-being. The temple of a vodun spirit displays hierarchy. Each titled rank receives different access to the space and roles in ceremonies (Quénum 1999, 92).

The "basic" Vodunists (*fétichistes*) are called *ahe* (*ahé* or *ahè*). They are permitted into the vestibule of the temple, making acclamations and singing sacred songs (Quénum 1999, 92). The *ahe* cannot participate in the secret traditions of a vodun (Segurola and Rassinoux 2000, 31).

In contrast, the *hunsi* are Vodunists who have undergone the lengthy formal initiation and share knowledge of the secrets of Vodun initiation. They are responsible for codifying ritual and discourse (Savary 1975, 48). The spirit possesses them during the annual celebration organized in the spirit's honor. During the five to eight days of those ceremonies, the *hunsi* no longer recognize friends and family and only speak the initiatory language connected with the spirit's ethnic origins (Quénum 1999, 92). Preparations for ceremonies are opportunities for families to make material contributions, including money, alcoholic beverages, kola nuts, sacrificial animals, and foodstuffs. The redistribution of those items among initiates reflects the ancient custom in Abomey of sharing out goods before the Annual Customs and the culture of patronage in Aja-Fon society (Savary 1975, 46).

Hunsi are male or female and are recruited among the *ahe*. After consultation with the family, the priest makes plans to take the candidate into the convent by means of a ritual "kidnapping." At the time of Maximilien Quénum's publication in 1936, initiation lasted between two and five years. Under the strict tutelage of the main initiator priest, the candidates learned the spirit's language, rite, dances, songs, and traditions (1999, 92). Novices wove sleeping mats and basketry, providing revenue to fund the expensive and lengthy initiations. The convent system produced income for the priests, since the girls provided labor on the convent's compound (Law 2004, 94).

Sickness can indicate a spirit-sent punishment on a person who has been "reserved" for initiation, but who delayed its completion (Quénum 1999, 92). In Aja-Fon Vodun, it is the younger and the unmarried who initiate, although a married person may be called. Given the long period of seclusion, husbands have been known to oppose the "kidnapping" of their spouse, fending off the Vodun priests with clubs and knives (Quénum 1999, 92).

If the "kidnapping" succeeds, the Vodun priest spreads the word that the candidate has been taken into the convent by the vodun spirit. The novice's family or spouse will begin saving money for the fastidious ceremonies that accompany her or his completion of initiation (Quénum 1999, 93). After the resurrection ritual of the initiation, the novices participate in the *ahouan-oulissi* (war captives) ritual, in which they are torn away from the bliss of communion with the vodun and break the huts for Legba while striking noninitiates in the roads (Segurola and Rassinoux 2000, 34).

The two categories of priest include the vodunon or *houmbônon* (high priest) and the *houndéva* (acolytes) who have permission to enter the *hùnkpáme* (convent) (Quénum 1999, 94; Segurola and Rassinoux 2000, 242). The priest shares a special relationship with the vodun spirit, directing the power that issues from it and ensuring that it is not damaged by misuse. Each vodun spirit has an autonomous set of "clergy" that maintains the traditions (Quénum 1999, 94). The *houmbônon* receives the respect of initiates, who only address him on their knees. His signs include a white cap, a white gown, and a sculpted scepter to hold. The main spirit he serves possesses the *houmbônon* during the annual ceremony.

Men and women serve as priests. Some vodun spirits prefer female priests, others male, others select indifferently. Priestesses often lived free from marital vows. Male priests were often the head of a family (Quénum 1999, 94). Elder priests presided over the investiture of the *houmbônon*. Clerks served under each priest in functions held for annual ceremonies. They helped organize celebrations, provided consultations, and assisted priests in discharging ritual duties. Among the clerks were the *sin-houto*, who each morning sang praises to the vodun within the temple compound, keeping time with a bell (Quénum 1999, 95). There was no prohibited place in the temple for the clerks, since they were initiated.[3]

The Vodun priesthood's power was related to the relationships priests cultivated with royalty and politicians (Savary 1975, 48). Some Vodun priests had political and economic relationships with monarchs and merchants during the transatlantic slave-trading period. Vodun priests had exceptional privileges and could influence the king (Quénum 1999, 95). The priest of Dangbe in Hueda received a share of the profits made from the sale of slaves. Vodun priests working with the royal family in Abomey were involved in the ritual murder of hundreds and even thousands of captives in the Annual Customs. Vodun communities that criticized royal Vodun could be captured and sold if too threatening, thus effacing the kingdom of dissidents.

Beside public priests, Aja-Fon religion includes private and familial traditions. The *flamine* (family priest) has special attire, a scepter, and clerks drawn from the family. The oldest male serves as domestic priest, called the *henugan* (chief of the family). He occupies the center of the family's religious culture, serving as the guardian of the ancestral temple (the *jehò*) and the rooms with ancestral altars (*asensa* or *asen*) (Quénum 1999, 95). The *henugan* sits on a throne when he receives his nomination, reflecting the ubiquity of royal notions in domestic and public religion (Savary 1975, 37).

In both rural and urban Aja-Fon polygamy, a husband and his wives share space on the plot but dwell in separate rooms or houses. Goats and fowl around the house constitute a reserve for sacrifices and feasts. The altars of the family and extended family include ones dedicated to the twins, the Abiku (spirits that kill children under twelve), the drowned *tohosu*, and the divinities that protect the dwelling and the family, including Legba, Dan, Sakpata, and Hebyoso. Domestic temples are placed on the inside and outside of houses, usually near shady groves suitable for socializing (Savary 1975, 37–38).

The term for the ancestral temple, the *jɛxɔ́* (*jehò*), also refers to the "pearl house" in the Abomey palace, serving as the temple for the ancestors of the kings. The earthen walls of the *jɛxɔ́* were molded over time from palm oil and human blood. Pearls and gold were laid into the wall, giving the place its name (Segurola and Rassinoux 2000, 260).[4] Within these structures, a variety of practices create a rich tapestry of culture.

FUNDAMENTAL PRACTICES IN VODUN

Three important components of Vodun include (1) initiations, (2) possession trance, and (3) blood sacrifice (Rouget 2001, v). Initiation takes months or years, and initiates are sworn to secrecy about it. The initiate possesses specialized secret knowledge for which he or she is admired. Possession trance connects the adept to her or his personal spirit through its brief incarnations by the spirit. The ritual involves identifying the self with the spirit. The blood sacrifice infuses the adept and the vodun with vigor. The blood sacrifice empowers the person or people for whom it is carried out, and it fortifies the vodun spirit who receives the blood. The more initiates pour blood on the altar of the vodun, the greater the spirit's power. If neglected, it exacts revenge (Rouget 2001, v).

The important root word *houn* cements basic concepts in Vodun: it is the unseen "blood" that circulates in our veins, it is the "secret," and it is the "vodun spirit" (Rouget 2001, v). *Hŭn* is the "heart" and a "drum"; *hùn* is "blood," a "Vodun divinity," and the "region Abomey," and when used as a verb it also means "to open" (Segurola and Rassinoux 2000, 239). A poetic sense of *hun* or *houn* is "opening the heart to the spirit." In Vodun (and Vodou), the adept is the *hunsi* (spouse of the spirit), the priest is the *hungán* (chief of the spirit), while the lead drummer is the *hùngán* (Brand 2000b, 46).[5]

The pouring of libations and the giving of food offerings are fundamental practices in Vodun and Vodou. Public and familial spirits are the recipients of the ritual. Pouring out water, coffee, or alcohol reflects "canonical" ritual in Vodun and Vodou ceremonies, and it is a daily gesture of veneration. In traditional Aja-Fon culture, placing the first bite of food or a few drops of a beverage on the ground for the spirits evokes a "faithful memory, a considerable and pious respect" (Quénum 1999, 90).

The art of ritual is the most important method of venerating the spirits, and it requires elaborate ceremonies. There are ceremonies to mark the phases of initiation. Congregations organize annual gatherings. A feast celebrates the new harvest of yams, corn, and millet. Prior to selling at the market, first fruits are offered to the spirits in a harvest ceremony (Quénum 1999, 86). The enthronement of a priest or king is accompanied by religious ceremonies. Most of these ceremonial functions also survive in Haitian Vodou, although the rapport with the state is less pronounced in Haiti. Of all the rituals that unite Atlantic traditions, initiation, ceremonies, and feasts are most important.

THE MAJOR RITUALS IN AJA-FON VODUN: INITIATION AND THE ANNUAL FEAST OF THE VODUN

Ritual is the art of controlling time and space by means of sounds and gestures, involving the saturation of worship with symbolic meanings. All of Aja-Fon "ritual vodun" is "massively musical." Ritual vodun spirits are served in ceremonies with a combination of the sound of songs and instruments, the gesture of dance, and the articulated language of words. In Vodun, *doing music* is an activity that "sculpts a new person" (Rouget 2001, vi). The ritual of initiation transforms the old person into a new one who bears the spiritual and physical mark of the vodun. The death is symbolic as the initiates undergo an alteration in perception as a result of a prolonged diet and "drugs" that give the ritual the appearance of death (Savary 1975, 48). From a social point of view, initiation represents the development of cooperative or solidarity social relationships (Mosala 1989, 77).

In Vodun and Vodou, the spirit decides to possess, protect, bless, or harass a person. Taking the attitude of selecting the vodun spirit is a headstrong sacrilege. An adept does not desire to join a Vodun community; rather, a vodun spirit strongly desires the person in the community. In addition to being a personal vocation, possession can be inherited. In Aja-Fon society, the decision falls back on the family. The candidate for initiation, who is usually a young girl, is not typically consulted (Rouget 1990, 92, 94).

In Aja-Fon religion, since spirits call people to initiation and service, they have power. Within that logic, none of the vodun spirits are strong enough to call the even more powerful Dahomian kings to service and submission. Instead, the pantheon of royal ancestral spirits is fully adequate. Even during the early twentieth century, the royal family strongly objected to a princess's initiation into the community of the vodun Sakpata. Although the princess had been claimed by the spirit and initiated, the royals were prepared to punish those involved.

In order to select the vodunsi and make preparations for the next year-group, the parents consult Fa several months prior to the entrance into the Vodun convent in order to learn about the suitability of the child as spouse of a vodun spirit (Rouget 1990, 95). This is a preparatory divination ritual. In some cases, initiation is undertaken in response to an accident, an illness, or a blessing. Dahomians described the spirit's calling as a "harassment" that initiation remedies (Le Hérissé 1911, 134). Adherence to Vodun is often viewed in the optic of adversity, whether collective in an environmental crisis or personal in a health crisis (Rouget 1990, 95). The enthusiasm and demand for initiation varies depending on socioeconomic conditions due to time and expense involved. Pressures from the advocates of foreign traditions like Christianity and Islam chip away at Vodun's base.

An important feature of Vodun religious communities is the "monotheistic" focus they maintain on a single spirit. Novices are initiated in convents specialized in services to a single spirit like Dangbe, Hou, or Gun—but never all three, even if they may have mythological relationships that overlap (Rouget 1990, 97). The Aja-Fon Vodunist remains in a singular relationship with one spirit and its community, even if he or she may attend the ceremonies of other spirits as a guest. In other ways, a plethora of spirits in the form of shrines for other vodun is acknowledged within temple compounds.

The novices in Aja-Vodun are called *hunyò* (vodun cadaver) or *yɔ́yɔ́* (newbies) (Rouget 2001, vi). According to some sources, the *hunyò* is someone initiated to the panther vodun Agasu (Segurola and Rassinoux 2000, 243). The "art of the Vodun initiatory rituals" is to create new people out of the *yɔ́yɔ́* by cultivating a particular representation of the world in their minds and integrating them into society through a formal affiliation with the temple (Rouget 2001, vi). Once the vodun resurrects the *hunyò*, she becomes the *hunsi* (spouse of the spirit).

Initiations in Aja-Fon communities of the late twentieth century were composed of connected rituals. A ritual marks the dramatic symbolic death of the individual as she *enters* the Vodun convent followed by a new birth a few days later (Rouget 2001, vi). On the day of resurrection (*hunfufon*), the initiate is wrapped in a burial shroud and carried in a processional outside the convent. Water is sprinkled on the initiate, and oil is massaged into the reviving body (Savary 1975, 48). The parents of a novice appear before the Vodun priest to thank him or her for "giving life to their children" (Rouget 1990, 103). Except for initiates of the vodun Sakpata, who "die" and "resurrect" in public, the resurrection rituals of other spirits occur privately in the convent (Rouget 1990, 103).

In Aja-Fon traditions, the novices begin a period of "reclusion" that lasts from months to years (Rouget 2001, vi). In the 1960s and 1970s, most initiations lasted between six months and two years. In 1978, priests in Benin signed an accord with the Marxist military government to limit initiations to three months (Rouget 1990, 120).[6]

At the time of seclusion in the convent, the parents walk the novice to the priest's property (Le Hérissé 1911, 134). The novice is introduced and the calling is examined, the goal being to ascertain readiness. The candidates for initiation stay near the priest's residence in ordinary huts. After they are trained, the priest scars them with the sign of the spirit in a private ceremony. Animal sacrifices accompany celebrations that greet the graduates.

During the first period of the reclusion, which lasts weeks or months depending on the convent, the novices are immersed in a codified ritual state described as "bewilderment" (*hébétude*) during which they carry out minor tasks (Rouget 2001, vi). Only the priests and priestesses see them. They are clad in raphia straw wrap skirts that remain unwashed, and their heads are shaved. The novices hold their heads down, assume an "ungraspable" look, and maintain "absolute docility" with their docents. As the initiation advances, "bewilderment" shifts to lucidity. As noted, in the mid-1960s novices were kept busy weaving elaborate basketwork to support the priest (Rouget 1990, 124).

In contrast to this state of bewilderment, the novices learn a secret language. Initiates of Sakpata learn Yoruba, initiates of Mawu-Lisa learn Ayizo, while initiates of Hebyoso learn the Hueda language. Previous initiates provide instruction with the priest. The *hunyò* novices learn about the different vodun, their organization in families or colleges, the use of plants, and the foods and objects that symbolize them. Novices learn about taboos and forbidden foods and practices. Initiates memorize the attitude and particularities of the vodun (Savary 1975, 53). They sing a long incantation dedicated to the spirit in the mornings and evenings. Other incantations are made facing the ground—novices kneel in a fetal position with their eyes staring at the earth as they pray for a propitious resurrection (Rouget 2001, viii). The novices take an oath to never share what they learn with the uninitiated or face the vodun's vengeance (Savary 1975, 53).

As the end of reclusion approaches, novices receive obligatory scarifications. Each congregation shares identical scarification patterns. The application of the scarifications is a painful ordeal that etches onto the skin the novice's affiliation (Rouget 2001, vi). Scarification spreads over shoulders, necks, and torsos, representing a "remodeling" of the body. This transformation turns the skin into "a sculptural matter." The scars function like beautification and public witness of devotion. Scarifications and tattoos are applied to represent a vodun spirit or lineage. In other parts of Africa, scars and tattoos may have an ethnic or familial signification and no link to possession. Scarification is a dangerous and private operation in the convent. The novices are "drugged" to endure the pain of the operation, which takes place in a setting of "effervescence, maintained by the thunder of drums" (Rouget 2001, 125–26).

One important part of Vodun initiation and possession is the "formal amnesia" that accompanies them. During reclusion in the cloister, the initiates remember nothing of family and friends. Their bewildered trance state reflects communion with the community's spirit. In a similar manner, the one possessed cannot recall what happened during possession.

Finally, several months after the resurrection ritual, the rituals for leaving the convent are held. The *sudide* rituals stretch over several weeks and include a descent into the backwaters, a ritual bath, a return to the village, the proclamation of a new name, animal sacrifice, and danced ceremonies such as trance possession for different spirits (Rouget 2001, vii). The initiate will never again be called by her former name (Rouget 1990, 131). After the *sudide*, a period of adjustment returns the initiate to normal life. Although still living at the convent, she has greater access to family and friends (Savary 1975, 53). The leaving ritual includes sumptuous feasts that have as their goal to "triumphantly display the vitality of the group" and celebrate initiation as a "victory" (Rouget 1990, 126–27).

The completion of initiation is a serious matter. The initiate's emergence from seclusion represents the appearance of a new person returning from the spirit's world. The spirit has left a permanent mark on the servant. Imbibing sacred beverages is a part of these rituals. Dawn gunfire marks the end of the initiation—it is the signal that new vodunsi await with their cry of "Here is war!" (Le Hérissé 1911, 135–36). They chase villagers like conquerors ransacking an enemy, while the priest struggles to gather them up.

The next morning, the new initiates assemble in front of the priest's home, where they undergo trials. These include being exposed to a white worm, plunging their hand into a pot of boiling porridge, and handling a hot coal or iron rod, all signs of the spirit's protective relationship with the initiate.[7] Vapors that catch flame over the boiling palm oil are signs of the spirit (Rouget 2001, 129). Once ceremonies have ended, the initiates are returned to their families, who give the priest money for the labor of initiation.

The graduates show their respect to the king and walk to the local marketplaces, stopping on the way to greet their families. Novices visit the vodun spirits they are connected to within the sanctuaries that serve them. Novices perform songs and dances associated with the spirit to collect small donations for the temple (Rouget 2001, vii). The repertoire of dances performed by the initiates during the convent's leaving ceremony is reprised at the annual celebration. The novices readjust to ordinary life, a process capped with a ritual that lifts all the prohibitions of the formerly cloistered novices. The only obligation the initiates now have is their participation in the annual celebration organized by the vodunon priest (Rouget 2001, vii, 129).

Once the initiate is back home, there are additional transitional activities like speaking the spirit's ritual language exclusively for three months as the new initiate slowly returns to Fon, Aja, or another familial language. The sacred language is used again on each occasion that the spirit returns to the head of the initiate during the sacred annual rites (Le Hérissé 1911, 137).

The annual Houéta-nou feast occurs during the rainy season from the middle of May until the end of June. During the feast, initiates dress in color-coordinated clothing and speak the spirit's language. In the mornings, the *ahouansi* beg in the marketplace to support their convent, and in the afternoons they dance in public places. Enthusiastic crowds delight in the dancing vodunsi, who demonstrate their spiritual strength through sustained dance. The return to everyday life is like the return from a long journey (Quénum 1999, 94–95).

Every aspect of initiation in Aja-Fon communities depends on the vodun of initiation. Each convent has its own traditions, lineage, politics, time frame, rituals, and culture. In addition to the ceremonies for initiation and the annual feast, a voluntary ritual for the vodun can be completed once every five days. Daily rituals like pouring out water and palm oil and offering corn are required of people initiated under Fa, the vodun of divination (Quénum 1999, 95). Next, consideration of the features of Vodun initiatory rituals provides a foundation for elaborating a "Vodou hermeneutics."

FEATURES OF VODUN INITIATORY MUSIC

In the entry, reclusion, and leaving rituals that take place in Aja-Fon Vodun, the novices sing a type of *musica reservata* (private music). They perform this vocal tradition with dances exclusively during their initiatory reclusion. Although Gilbert Rouget (2001, vii) was able to record the music, the priests did not allow him to distribute it. Nevertheless, the author comments that the music is "responsorial," or call-and-response, meaning that the parts sung by a lead singer receive a choral response. The music is monophonic in that it is sung chorally in unison. Recited in the morning and in the evening, the music is characterized by "incantation" and "longitude." The longest piece, for example, was timed at seventeen minutes (Rouget 2001, vii, 100).

This music is characterized by long melodic phrases, slow tempo, complex structure, and the employment of "chromaticism," which is a compositional technique for alternating the primary diatonic pitches and chords with others on the chromatic scale (Brown 1986, 1). The shorter "alms songs" are also responsorial and employ a chromaticism that tends toward "modulation" (Rouget 2001, vii). The novices sing the initiatory vocal music in impeccable unison, a performance that points to intense daily practice over long periods. Eyes cast down, they deliver the song in a way that exudes a sense of distance and disorientation while expressing perfection in skillful execution (Rouget 2001, 135).

INITIATION AS A MARKER OF AGE, MATURATION, AND POLITICAL ORDER IN AJA-FON REGIONS

The Aja-Fon people do not practice infant circumcision (Quénum 1999, 86). The practice is instead associated with the initiatory traditions of Gou. The vodun Gou (or Ogou) is the spirit of metallurgy and blades, childbirth, and the cutting of the umbilical cord, plus warfare and male circumcision (Brand 2000b, 42). During the Vodunist's convalescence, those circumcised under Gou may bludgeon any person's fowl without consequence. Those initiated to Gou shave their heads and carry monetary offerings for the vodun Aizan, who presides over the marketplace, illustrating the imbrication of the spirits (Quénum 1999, 86).

Vodun experts' "exceptionally dramatic" employment of the "art of ritual" in song, music, oral literature, dance, and decorative dress are important methods for recruiting novices into initiation (Rouget 2001). The initiations photographed and described by Rouget reflect the tradition's links to age and gender. The one hundred initiates photographed at Tori-Agonsa and Gôhô are mostly females under the age of twenty (Rouget 2001, 57–66). The other initiations and rituals pictured in his volume mostly involve women.

The typical number of novices undergoing Vodun initiations is between one and twelve, only occasionally surpassing that number (Rouget 1990, 120). As political and social persecution increases, however, the size of year-groups can change drastically. The fact that initiates spend a long period in "a cultural center" means that the experience is primarily offered to girls and women. Rural men are more likely than urban men to initiate. The rarity of urban candidates may reflect the corrosive effects of French influence in urban communities that were more connected to colonial culture, education, and Catholicism after the independence of Benin (Savary 1975, 53).

The motivations for initiating are complex. Initiation is pursued to fulfill a request made by a dying family member or to make good on a promise for becoming pregnant. The experience confers a higher social status on the initiate, so afterward she plays a bigger role in the family (Savary 1975, 53).

Initiation in a Vodun convent is connected to the traditional political system. Gilbert Rouget witnessed one of the first rituals undertaken by one particular year-group of initiates who attended a ceremony at the local king's residence in the nearest town. Heads freshly shaved, wearing their finest attire (a lengthy white skirt tied at the waist), shoulders oiled and newly empowered with scarifications, torsos crossed with two large sashes woven with seashells, and arms adorned with bangles, the initiates looked impeccable. They prostrated in front of the king on his couch, their seashells evoking the Atlantic Ocean as they recited in unison the lengthy, sacred song-prayers that they had memorized during their reclusion. After they completed their prostration, the king congratulated them and retired to his apartment. They would be unlikely to encounter a king again for the remainder of their lives, a fact that underscores the uniqueness of their day (Rouget 1990, 121). The new initiates displayed respect to the conventional political order.

POSSESSION TRANCE IN VODUN AND VODOU

Spirit-based religions have different methods for encountering spirits. In shamanic traditions, the specialist travels to the spirits. In Vodou and Vodun, the spirit travels to the specialist. The shaman masters the spirit, whereas the spirit of Vodun (and Vodou) masters the specialist. Shamanism is built on voluntary trance, whereas Vodun and Vodou are built on involuntary trance. The two approaches to spirits are not mutually exclusive, since the specialist of Vodun will also "travel" to the underworld to retrieve a soul in rituals that involve channeling the dead (Rouget 1990, 73–75).

Spirit possession is an ecstatic behavior. Terms like "crisis" refer to the onset of possession and its trembling and shaking, whereas "trance" refers to the durable state of possession once the spirit has settled into place (Rouget 1990, 108). Trance and possession reflect a "depersonalization" as the foreign spirit substitutes for the personal self. The substitution involves the symbolic processes of physical shaking, convulsing, and agitations, either spectacular or subtle (Rouget 1990, 46).

Ecstatic experience reflects social isolation, whereas trance possession reflects social integration. People who have ecstatic experiences, such as the Christian mystic Teresa of Ávila, write of their experiences, whereas people in trance possession are subject to complete amnesia (Rouget 1990, 49).

Trance is a transitory state of consciousness approached by trading habitual states for trance states. After a variable period of time, the one in trance returns to the original state. The visible features of trance are diverse: trembling, shivers, goose pimples, fainting, falling, a gaping mouth, lethargy, convulsions, salivation, bulging eyes, protrusion of the tongue, paralysis, thermic discrepancies like cold hands in the heat or hot hands in the cold, insensitivity to pain, the manifestation of tics, loud shouting, a fixed gaze, the cutting of the skin with blades, the grinding of glass with the teeth, somersaults, springing in the air, walking on hot coals or glass shards, bending metal, handling venomous snakes, healing illnesses, seeing into the future, speaking new, unlearned languages, entering into contact with the dead, emitting inhuman shrieks, dancing although disabled, being insensitive to flames or hot peppers, climbing trees, demonstrating a state of consciousness marked by total engagement in the trance with no attention to observers, and amnesia afterward (Rouget 1990, 56–57; Matsushita 1997). Trance involves the "intensification of an ability" and a sequence of actions that cover "something extraordinary" (Rouget 1990, 57). Trance is a transcending of the ego accompanied by the intensification of a nonpersonal disposition that takes the form of the exaltation of a great self (Rouget 1990, 57).

Trance possession in Aja-Fon communities reflects two different classes of spirits. On the one hand, among the "linage" spirits, it is barely perceptible. The possession is so "interiorized" that the unknowing observer would overlook it (Rouget 1990, 108). In the case of "national" spirits, possession is noticeable, but it does not obtain the intensity observed in Haitian Vodou (Rouget 2001, viii). Toshi Matsushita's documentary *Voodoo Kingdom* (1997) shows, however, that spectacular intensity, for example self-cutting with blades, is a feature of possession trance in Aja-Fon communities.

"Wild possession" involves possession trance prior to socialization within the initiatory community (Rouget 1990, 107). In Brazilian Condomblé, this type of possession is called *santo bruto*, whereas in Haitian Vodou it is called a *lwa bosal* (untamed spirit), in contrast to the *lwa batize* (baptized spirit). In Haitian Vodou ceremonies, "wild possessions" are not uncommon. In general, audience members may fall into various types of trance that lead them to dance and succumb to the spirit temporarily, either in their seats or on the temple's dance floor.

"Bewilderment" possession trance in Vodun, mentioned above, is linked to initiation. The novices' "bewilderment" is an "initiatory trance." The novices behave like automatons, they look "elsewhere," they cease to understand conventional language, and they sing unusual, monotonic songs (Rouget 1990, 122). During the months of initiation, the bewilderment is profound, since the novice dwells in the convent cut off from the outside world. The intensity of that "bewilderment" diminishes over the course of the initiation. The novices stay in this state of "drowsy rapture" and "reserved, timid, and interiorized trance," so different from the climactic and brief possessions of ceremonies (Rouget 1990, 128).

The "manifested trances" occur during the vodun spirit's annual celebration, and not during initiation (Rouget 2001, viii). The "manifested trances" are extroverted, intense, sometimes violent, and involve the extraordinary. One of the key requirements of participation in these trances in Aja-Fon Vodun is adulthood (Rouget 1990, 129). Whereas many young, especially female initiates are acquainted with the "bewildered" type of subdued possession that is characteristic of initiation, it is only once these girls and boys have become women and men that the spirits will use them for intense forms of possession (Rouget 1990, 129). Possession is formalized by temporal constraints, examined below.

TEMPORAL STRUCTURE, MUSIC, AND TRANCE

Possession trance in Vodun and Vodou is often, but not always, connected to ritual music and temporal structure. Musical instruments, especially percussive, are used to modify the adepts' state of consciousness. Trance possession takes place in the context of a ritual temporal structure that reflects a sequence of phases in time, including preparation, trigger, fullness, and resolution (Rouget 1990, 88).

Possession also occurs within a temporal structure with phases marked by musical structure. In Haitian Vodou ceremonies, for example, possession is prepared by singing songs for the *lwa*, engaging in formal cycles of salutation, intensifying volume and tempo, undertaking *foula* rituals of rum vaporization, and other methods. Possession's occurrence in ritual time follows signs of intensification in worship. Drums are agents of this summoning of collective energy. The *ounsi* and the spirits love the pulsations of drumming and dancing, both using the occasion to blend together. Drummers build the collective energy required for spirit possession (Wilcken and Augustin 1992, 48).

The conduct of possession depends on the initiate's level of experience. A novice, a new initiate, an experienced initiate, and an officiator have each a distinct relationship to possession, one that evolves relative to her or his role in the community (Rouget 1990, 89).

METHODS, GOALS, AND FUNCTIONS OF INITIATION

Initiation is a long process aiming to transform the structure of the individual so that she or he becomes attuned to serve as a receptacle to the spirit (Rouget 1990, 104). Vodun and Vodou specialists do not accept the initiate as they are but require that they be methodically transformed into a spirit-centered being. The initiation produces an important maturation that restructures consciousness and character. The novices emanate a calm power that distinguishes them from others (Rouget 1990, 126).

Vodun transforms individuals through a long and dramatic initiatory experience. Weeks of subdued "bewilderment," the study of a new language, intense memorization and the recitation of songs and prayers, fasting, absorbing teachings, laborious tasks like basket weaving, isolation from the wider community, intense spiritual and social bonding with the novices and leaders of the convent community, a special diet, unique clothes, the imposition of taboos and restrictions—all shake the foundations of a person's being. Rigorous spiritual and practical requirements bend individuals to transformation and in-group socialization. The public display of respect to local political leaders and devotional begging in marketplaces expose the novice to power and impoverishment, instilling lessons about having and not having.

Scarification is a major aspect of Vodun initiation, since the novice is at last physically and spiritually complete, the Vodun affiliation etched into the skin by the scarring knife or tattoo needle. This ritual marks the initiate for life, demonstrating the experience and pedigree the transformed individual has earned through a long ordeal. The scarifications show the public the person's spiritual degree while displaying the convent's traditions to outsiders who might seek initiation or services.

Initiation molds the individual, instilling a traditional education and preparing her or his coming of age in society. Initiation transforms the internal world by providing knowledge and power, and it transforms social structure by linking to a spiritual community bound by intimate secrets. Adornments, jewels, and fine clothes are offered for public admiration. Parents swell with pride witnessing the beauty, youth, and abilities in song, dance, and traditional knowledge displayed by their initiated children (Rouget 2001, 126, 127, 131).

The religious function of initiation is to prepare the novice to serve as a receptacle for the spirit. The function of the "bewilderment" is to affirm their invulnerability and indifference to the exterior world, signaling their fearless immersion in spirit. The initiation operates at once as a religious culture, a social unit, and a traditional school that prepares young people for adulthood oriented to the traditions of their ancestors (Rouget 1990, 127, 138). The next section examines the functions of naturalizing the spirits of a conquered people.

THE NATURALIZATION OF FOREIGN VODUN IN AJA-FON ROYAL RELIGION

The tendency in Aja-Fon culture to naturalize the vodun of foreign cultures is important in the formation of Haitian Vodou. The creators of Haitian Vodou absorbed diverse African spirit systems and created coherent Haitian religious systems. The Sèvis Ginen system combines African traditions like Rada, Nago, Gede, Kongo, Ibo, and Petwo into a religious system with diverse national roots. The seamless incorporation of the spirit-based traditions of other nations reflects a xenophilic orientation in Aja-Fon culture. It also reflects a form of governance and social control.

The majority of the Dahomian vodun spirits were not originally from Dahomey (Savary 1975, 54). The Aja founders of Dahomey were from Tado and Allada and brought most of the vodun with them from the outside when they conquered and settled the Abomey plateau. Nago-Yoruba and Mahi spirits to the north and Hueda and Ayizo spirits to the south were integrated into the traditions of the capital of Abomey. The royal family was the protector and administrator of the imported vodun (Savary 1975, 54). The communities of distinct foreign vodun were not permitted to fuse into new configurations, as was the case in the African syncretisms that emerged in Brazil and Haiti. The inclusion of foreign vodun was controlled so that the imported traditions could not supplant the royal religion (Savary 1975, 54). The royal family, both ancestors and the living king, were spiritual beings at the core of Dahomey's royal religious system. The royal religious culture was centered on the adoration of Agasu and his line of royal descendants. All Dahomians of note attended the Annual Customs and witnessed the ritual human murders in honor of Agasu and the deceased Dahomian kings.

Honoring regional spirits was a central feature of political and cultural cohesion in Aja-Fon and Dahomian state construction. The "public divinities" and the religious communities that functioned as their guardians were strongly venerated in the communities where they originated, but they also received homage from the rest of the country (Quénum 1999, 69). "Regional" spirits represent territories that the Dahomians conquered by military force. Recall that at its inception in 1620, the kingdom of Dahomey was no bigger than the town of Abomey. The kingdom gradually grew as the Dahomian army took territory, sold off conquered peoples, repopulated areas, and subdued survivors by integrating key features of the regional religion into the royal one.

The Dahomian kings introduced foreign spirits to their subjects. They resettled priests from conquered regions in Abomey and celebrated the new vodun in public ceremonies. Some of the resettled priests sought to entrench the prestige of their traditions on a national level. Hueda's prestigious python spirit, Dangbe, was incorporated into the pantheon of spirits venerated in the kingdom of Dahomey. The priest, his family, and his entourage were forcibly moved to Abomey.[8] Over time, the once-foreign traditions grew local roots by attracting and training a community of initiates. The naturalization of foreign spirits was valued in Aja-Fon culture, and this attitude was critical in the formation of Haitian Vodou.

Institutional religion was composed of congregational houses, and the sprawling royal family scrupulously managed congregational temples and their priests, so they were never fully independent.

SPIRITUAL CATEGORIES IN VODUN

The broadest spiritual category, the Akovodun, represents ancestors of the nation. The Tovodun are the spirits of the countryside that connect to people and places. The Hennou-vodun are spirits served as founders of a family (Quénum 1999, 69). The Akovodun were connected to the state, whereas the Hennou-vodun were domestic. Veneration of the Hennou-vodun was more widespread than service to the Akovodun (Le Hérissé 1911, 100).

Each extended family had its own Hennou-vodun. Family members knew by heart the associated mythology. The biographies of the family heroes were embroidered with rich legends of their great virtues. The expression of ancestral veneration was encoded among newborns, who received "protector names" connected to the family's Hennou-vodun. The human offspring recalled the Hennou-vodun during annual familial ceremonies (Quénum 1999, 69–70).

Even in the Dahomian capital of Abomey, the Hennou-vodun were worshiped above all other vodun. Periods of bad luck caused members of the Aja ruling classes to abandon the service of the Akovodun in favor of service to the Hennou-vodun. Of course, the royal family's Hennou-vodun was Agasu, the panther-human spirit (Le Hérissé 1911, 101).

The kings and chiefs of Dahomey established an official scheme of categorization that divided the vodun spirits into complementary groups. Each of the groups (*aouan*) had its own *hungán* congregational leader (Le Hérissé 1911, 100–12). The leadership of congregations reflected a hierarchical system of ranking and privileges, explored below.

INSTITUTIONAL LEADERSHIP

Four types of priests led the system of worship dedicated to the national vodun in the early part of the twentieth century, namely the vodunon, the hounso, the vodunsi, and the vodun-legbanon (Le Hérissé 1911, 127). The vodunon (priest) owns the spirit, the hounso carries the spirit, the vodunsi are dedicated to serving the spirit, and the vodun-legbanon incarnate the vodun Legba.

The term "vodun + non" means "spirit + possessor," or owner, and this priest lives near the place of the spirit. This residence is where the convent is situated. As the possessor of exclusive specialized knowledge about the spirit, such as its symbolic leaves, the high priest has unique insights. On the days that sacrifices were conducted for the spirit, only the vodunon priest would enter the altar room. The high priest wore a simple, white head tie, while other priests wore cowry necklaces, bracelets, and multicolored tutus, prostrating themselves by the temple's entrance (Le Hérissé 1911, 130).

Only one vodunon in Dahomey served as the priest for a vodun that was introduced by the royal family. The kings selected the official vodunon who ministered at the palace (Le Hérissé 1911, 130). The priest was chosen from among the descendants of the original priest, with preference to the firstborn. This was even the case if the person was an infant, in which case tutors oversaw the future priest's training.

The vodunon took part in neither dances nor processions, activities of the hounso. The hounso assisted the vodunon. The hounso's role was to dance while holding the sacrificial animal on his shoulders. As the hounso danced, the vodun possessed him, hence the name *houn* (spirit) + *so* (carry), or "carrier of the spirit." The vodunsi were the "spouses" or "followers" of a specific vodun spirit, participating as dancers and singers in worship, ceremonies, and processions.

Outside of their sacred functions, priests were like other citizens. They derived prestige from their priestly functions, but they engaged in the same labor as others. They were subject to the same laws as the general population. They assumed a sacred role officiating for religious events when the vodun was placed "on their head" through possession (Le Hérissé 1911, 133). The kings of Dahomey understood that specialists of Vodun could abuse the gullible, so they controlled the investiture of high priests. The king's guards exerted the monarch's prerogatives in the kingdom's temples and carried out the dismissal of displeasing priests. The most important vodun are examined in the next sections, as they are the focal points of the religion.

PERSONAL VODUN: LEGBA AND FA

The vodun spirits Legba and Fa fit within the category of "personal vodun" (Le Hérissé 1911, 137). The spirits receive service in homes and in temples led by priests, either domestic or public. Legba and Fa are "personal vodun," since each person has her or his relationship with the spirit. In the Dahomian and Haitian contexts, Legba is of equal importance. Fa is known in Haiti, but is less prominent than Legba.

In Dahomey, Legba and Fa are born and die with a person. The services to Legba and Fa do not require priestly rites due to their personal nature. Legba is capable of mischief and cruelty, but he can be assuaged with prayers and sacrifices. Legba dwells in a person's navel, which in Dahomey is considered to be the seat of emotion, whether happiness, pain, or pity (Le Hérissé 1911, 138).

Servants of the vodun display symbols of Legba near the entrances of their homes, including earthenware cups for women and children and a phallic mound of earth one foot in height and covered with a leafy shelter for the fathers of families. Some men instead display a statue of Legba seated with his hands on his knees, his penis protruding between his legs.

Legba's phallus is related to the spirit's influence in granting or refusing pregnancy (Le Hérissé 1911, 138). Besides his role in giving children, the spirit has a rather complex identity. Legba causes fortune and misfortune, including illnesses and accidents. Legba instigates a range of occurrences—the breaking of a clay jar or the disagreements of co-wives, for example, are attributed to the meddling of the husband's Legba. Legba demands service and reminds people of his importance in the form of mild or severe punishment.

Dahomians in the early twentieth century served Legba on a daily basis by addressing him in words at his symbols as they left home in the morning. Every few days, the head of the household offered him a little flour, water, and oil. If away from home for a period of time, the husband also arranged for offerings to be made to Legba by one of his wives. Symbols of "Legba crowned king" were placed at the entries of villages, where he received services once a year (Le Hérissé 1911, 139). Legba was also a king in the historical sense, ruling from his palace (Verger 1957).

PERSONAL VODUN: FA AND DIVINATION

Fa or Ifa is a second personal spirit that Vodunists revere and call upon for guidance. So central is Fa to regional culture that contemporary Muslims and Christians are known to consult the spirit's mediums (Palau Martí 1993, 233). Unlike Legba, however, only men consult with Fa and keep his symbol (Le Hérissé 1911, 139). Mawu's (God's) messenger, Fa knows and anticipates (Lando 2016, 46). Spirit of divination and fortune-telling, Fa offers guidance. Invoking Fa and learning from him requires the geomancy of reading signs from tossed palm nuts.

Ifa has an initiated community where his mythology circulates. One myth of Ifa recounts his remarkable birth. While her husband was away, one wife went to a co-wife who was menstruating and proposed a sexual liaison. The two co-wives made love on a garbage pile. After the husband returned, he noticed her pregnant belly. The child was named Ifa, and he lacked a skeleton and sat permanently in a chair. The mysterious baby spoke, bewildering everyone with his wisdom and predictions. People traveled to ask questions of Ifa and hear his responses. The indifference to taboos on female homosexuality and sex during menstruation, and on a garbage heap, reflects Ifa's extraordinary birth narrative and also hints at Haiti's norm-shattering Gede culture (Palau Martí 1993, 230).

Prior to undertaking a serious matter, a bokonon (diviner consulted for fortune-telling) calls upon Fa to give advice to his client. Matters brought before Fa include establishing the date for a journey, a marriage, or a funeral service; naming a newborn; prescribing a remedy; and offering sacrifices to send corrective energy (Le Hérissé 1911, 140). The oracles of Fa became a tool with which the king could govern.

Fa came to the Dahomians from the Yoruba town of Ife during the reign of Agaja (1708–1740). The system of divination is in the hands of the *babaláwo* priest and does not include possession. The priest initiates people into the Ifa religious community and provides divination services for clients. Learning the techniques of divination takes years of training, as does initiation into the community. Initiations lead to different degrees, each requiring sacrifices and offerings (Palau Martí 1993, 230–31).

The *babaláwo* priest greets Ifa before leaving his room in the morning. On his knees, he invokes the spirit by touching his cheeks to the ground several times. During his consultations, the priest places the divination board opposite the rising sun. Palm nuts and a cup that holds them, the board, and a powder that is spread over the board to mark the falling palm nuts, constitute the spiritual instruments. In addition, the priest uses a bell to strike the board as he calls on Ifa.[9] Ifa's offerings include red cooking oil (*huile rouge*), kola nuts, and sacrificed roosters. The offerings are placed on the palm nuts held in Ifa's cup (Palau Martí 1993, 231, 234).

The names of signs in the Dahomian context are discernably Yoruba. Prior to the introduction of Fa fortune-telling, Dahomians relied on a council of elders for divination. The Dahomians then received good advice from a Fa priest, Amonkobi, about a battle planned against the Nago, so they sent delegations to study the Fa traditions. The delegations established two traditions, Djisa and Gongon, each having a different number of signs (Le Hérissé 1911, 147).

An initiated head of the household establishes a separate room for his Fa spirit, if he can afford it. The Fa symbol is placed inside of a calabash bowl on top of an earthenware jar in a common room. In the course of a journey, a man totes along his Fa symbol, attached around his waist. Important people place the symbol on a necklace worn by a child or first wife.

Fa's symbol has to be known by the requestor in order for the spirit to communicate God's messages. Males can seek the symbol from adolescence, following their inclinations or the advice of a family Fa. The revelation of the Fa symbols occurs during ceremonies in which the bokonon hereditary diviner assists the requestor (Lando 2016, 62). The bokonon's role is to encourage the spirit to select from among symbols that appear out of the combination of signs (Le Hérissé 1911, 141). The requestor meets with the bokonon at night in a remote place when the smoky lamp of the seer creates a flickering light suitable for divination. The bokonon uses eighteen nuts that are handed to the requestor, who passes them from hand to hand and tosses them to the ground to see what symbols emerge. The lines formed by the tossed nuts resemble the form of the facial tattoos that signal spiritual affiliation. The dust that the nuts stir up when they fall represents the "personal character of the symbol" (Le Hérissé 1911, 142). In contemporary Benin, the bokonon interpreter of Fa uses a type of "rosary" that is balanced and thrown on the ground. After the toss, the traces made on the ground are interpreted (Lando 2016, 46).

The *afagbadji* (room of oracles) within the home of the bokonon is where the consultant meets his clients. The *afagbadji* or *sogbadji* is a sacred room with an altar. The client's Fa symbol presides over the consultation, and the bokonon's interpretation of Fa's signs reflects the client's relationship with the spirit. Interrogating Fa is called *kan Fa* (to consult or share Fa) (Le Hérissé 1911, 144). After death, the Fa symbol of the deceased is thrown into a crossroads close to the burial site. The vodun are evoked at the crossroads during funerals, suggesting the role that they have in conveying the spirit of the deceased safely into the afterlife (Le Hérissé 1911, 142).

Several types of bokonon are found in Dahomey and its offspring, Benin. By and large they function as "village seers" who live as farmers and earn small sums of money for consultations (Le Hérissé 1911, 145). They are responsible for the animal sacrifices required by Fa. The bokonon receives a sum for providing the animal. Some bokonon enjoy a good reputation, whereas others are reputed for dishonesty. Examined next are amulets that form a part of the bokonon's kit of magical tools.

AMULETS

Dahomian magical practices include amulets called *bo*. Although nonspecialists create amulets, the experts are the bokonon. Amulets induce or hinder events in the world. Many objects serve as magical amulets that counteract curses, attract wealth, deprive others, encourage pregnancy, prevent illness, dissuade theft, and guard against murder. A successful amulet maker attracts clients who pay in money, cloth, alcohol, or poultry. The fabrication of an amulet may require a deposit and time, depending on the ingredients required. After the craftsman completes the amulet, a brief ceremony is held to pay for it and to render it efficacious through the bokonon's uttering of an empowerment (Le Hérissé 1911, 148–49).

Amulets can be worn around the neck, biceps, forearm, waist, and ankle. Their usefulness extends only to the person wearing it or for whom it is intended. Another class of talismans is placed in front of the home, on paths, and in public places to protect against evildoers or sickness, or to send bad luck to enemies (Le Hérissé 1911, 150, 154). A *bo* amulet that caused death was once not unheard of in Dahomey. The corpse was typically found with the talisman placed nearby. A "murderous weapon that lunges in the shadows" would accompany this kind of magic. Poison was a topic of intrigue in Dahomey, but there is little direct evidence of such practices. Dahomian kings understood the risks of leaving the bokonon and the vodunon unfettered. Their agents oversaw priests and set up tribunals to handle criminal cases. Murderous amulets therefore were not common, since penalties were severe (Le Hérissé 1911, 155–56). The next sections put the service to Dangbe under a microscope, a worthy objective, given how this spirit profoundly links West Africa and the Caribbean.

THE PYTHON VODUN

The vodun spirits associated with the python are the most iconic of spirits venerated in West Africa. The python vodun is best known among the region's spirits due to observations that European visitors left in travel diaries over the course of three centuries. *Dan* means "serpent" and *-gbe* means "good," so Dangbe is the "good serpent" (Merlo 1940, 9).

Communities hosting python temples grappled with invading armies and dealt with the transition from Huedan to Dahomian rule after Agaja's conquest in 1727. The totemic python's introduction into the religious life of Dahomey only occurred after King Agaja's conquest of the coast. After the Huedan monarch Houffon was defeated, King Agaja included service to Dangbe in Abomey.

During the early twentieth century, the actual, harmless pythons representing Dangbe were seen frequently. Temple pythons could enter domiciles or courtyards and were left unharmed. A consecrated priest came to move the python to the wild or back to the temple. Temples for Dangbe were scattered throughout the kingdom of Dahomey. The most important one was in Hueda, where it still stands today with a priest, pythons, and a community of initiates.

In the Vodun communities of the Ouemenou Valley that Roger Brand (2000a, 2000b) examined, Dan and Dangbe have complementary roles in mythology and theology. Dan or "Dan ayida wedo" is a distant, abstract, and cosmic force that is rendered visible in a rainbow. The inhabitants of hilltop villages and people who live in homes on stilts tend to serve Dan because of their proximity to the sky.[10] The movements of the living in their material shell are expressions of Dan. The Oueme River represents Dan wending a path through Sakpata's landforms (Brand 2000b, 21). Here, Dan and Sakpata are interwoven spirits of matter and movement, while Dan ayida wedo links the earth and sky through rainbows, her symbol.

Dan accompanied the creator Mawu when she created the world. Dan is Mawu's agent, serving as guardian of life, movement, stability, and childbirth. The umbilical cord is his symbol (Brand 2000b, 22). After Gou (Ogou), the vodun of metallurgy, cuts it, the umbilical cord is buried under Dan's sign. Some see Dan as the "vital force" (*ace*) that extends from the creator couple, Mawu and Lisa (Brand 2000b, 21).

Dangbe is the manifest image of Dan, taking the form of actual pythons. Whereas Dan is distant and possibly dangerous, Dangbe is close and gentle (Brand 2000b, 22). The color white is associated with Dan and Dangbe, just as it is with Danbala Wèdo in Haitian communities. Among the Ouemenou Fon people, each family has its own Dangbe with an extra name reflecting things he provides, like rain and fertility.

Snake excrement is used in amulets and talismans to procure wealth (Le Hérissé 1911, 118). Some merchants carry on a trade in "the excrement of the rainbow," here a reference to Dan ayida wedo. The snake excrement is used to create "popo" charms, which help the owner acquire wealth (Law 2004, 96). The serpent spirit is sometimes represented in a circle with its mouth swallowing its tail (Le Hérissé 1911, 119). This ancient symbol, called the *uroboros*, was first attested in Egypt more than three millennia ago and is taken to represent the cyclical dimensions of the seasons and life (Hornung 1999, 77–78).

DANGBE'S AND DAN'S RELATIONSHIP TO AJA, HUEDAN, AND FON HISTORY

The historical relationship of the Aja and Huedan settlements to the serpent vodun Dangbe reflects the earliest memories of a community rooted in fishing among the lagoons and deltas that feed freshwater into the Atlantic. The veneration of python spirits is widespread across multiple ethnic groups in the Aja and Huedan regions. Huedan migrations to Aja centers like Tado, and Aja migrations from Tado and Allada to Huedan centers like Hueda, have complicated the task of identifying the origins of traditions. Oral and historical records go back about five hundred years, but the tradition is far older (Merlo and Vidaud 1984, 269).

The Houla near Badagry in present-day Nigeria venerate as their *tohwiyo* (totem) the man-eating boa constrictor (Merlo and Vidaud 1984, 270). The Aja and Huedans, however, venerate the harmless python. Dangbe is the Hennou-vodun of the Huedan royal family and its descendants while also serving as the Akovodun (vodun of the nation) for the Huedan people (Merlo 1940, 9).

As national vodun, Dangbe is "superimposed" over the Hennou-vodun of the Huedan people. "Dangbe" is generic, like Hebyoso, Sakpata, or Dan, and is specified with a second term linked to size, birth, locality, quality, and so on. The Dangbe spirits allude with their second names to animal and human features of the tradition. As for Dan, beyond the zoological meanings, theories circulate about the spirit's origins, including one wherein Dan reflects the tradition of the people and Dangbe the tradition of the elite. Dan is "plebian" whereas Dangbe is "patrician"; the former widely domesticated, the latter venerated as the Hennou-vodun in the royal family of Hueda (Merlo 1940, 12). Dangbe's community enjoyed prestige from its association with the monarchy.

The Dan spirits are numerous because of their familial links. The prominence of Danbala Wèdo and Ayida Wèdo in Haitian Vodou's Rada Rite points to their salience among captives taken to Saint-Domingue. Other Dan spirits include Dan Adjovi, Dan Sossou, and Dan Tokpon, to name but a few. Each neighborhood in the town of Hueda, including Brésil, Bova, Ahouandjigo, Fonsaramè, Tové, and Sogbadji, includes unique traditions of Dan veneration (Merlo 1940, 12–15).

In one origin myth, the priestess Ave brought a small python from Tado to the Houla people, claiming that the snake around her neck was the "benefactor of humanity." A temple and convent were established in the vodun's honor. The vodun was named Ave-Dan, which means "the serpent of Ave." The story shows the role a migrant woman had in spreading the traditions of the serpent vodun. It also shows how priests and priestesses fuse with a spirit. In another story, Ave interacts with King Agbe. Hearing of regional threats, Agbe consulted with Ave about magical means to secure victory over the threatening people of Agomé-Séva. She told him to "take the serpent in his hands" in order to avoid all harm. After he did so, his enemies took flight, relieving the Houla people. King Agbe married the powerful Ave-Dan to consolidate his power. From that time on, the Agbodjèvi descendants venerated the snake (Merlo and Vidaud 1984, 270).

Another fratricidal war broke out. This time, King Agbe was defeated and went away to "drown" with Ave, becoming "the god of the sea" in the process. The legend of Agbe's connection to Dangbe is shown in the Houla expression: "The sea belongs to Dangbe." During the fighting, Ave-Dan left Dangbe in his temple, and the survivors continued serpent veneration even after the defeat. Ongoing wars and their refugees spread the Agbodjèvi and their serpent veneration to Tori, Allada, and Porto-Novo (Merlo and Vidaud 1984, 270–71).

The Agbodjèvi were the first family to introduce prayer into Dangbe's tradition; hence they are called the *dè-non* (the ones who pray). Other families "venerate" rather than "worship" Dangbe. The Agbodjèvi associated Agbe with Dangbe because the "[s]ea did not have a consecrated animal" (Merlo and Vidaud 1984, 271). Agbe survives as Agwe Tawoyo, the foremost spirit of the sea in Haitian Vodou and classified among the spirits of the Rada Rite. The Houla stories about Ave-Dan, Dangbe, and King Agbe point to the deep African layers beneath Haitian mythology.

The Huedan priest of Dangbe at the village of Akpè claimed that the service to the python came from Hindji, which had been a village near Ségbourè on the banks of Lake Ahémé, to the west of Allada. The people of Allada agreed that Dangbe was served at Hindji. Some Alladan sources said that Dangbe Ahouanda (Ave-Dan of the Houla mentioned above) comes from Kpétou. Others speak of the town Cana, where a convent for Dangbe has stood for more than five hundred years. Those responsible for the temples of Houédacomé, Aimlonfidé, and Anigbézoun in the city of Porto-Novo also speak of Hindji. Given the destruction of Hueda by the Dahomian invaders of 1727, Hindji was likely destroyed in the wake of those wars, with the name still remembered as a source of the traditions by contemporary priests (Merlo and Vidaud 1984, 276).

The Agasuvi princes Dogbagri and Te-Agbalin, exiled from Allada after the death of King Adjahouto, were adherents of Dangbe. Although the migrants were Aja, the Huedans who were allied with the brothers also fled Tado (Merlo and Vidaud 1984, 281). Believing that Dangbe and Dossouloko had protected him from the dangers that threatened his migration, Te-Agbalin established the service to Dangbe in his new capital, Hogbonou. A narrative from the temple of Houédacomé in Porto-Novo holds that the Huedans Haholo and his son Gbého, natives of Hindji, introduced the service to Dangbe after they successfully escorted Prince Te-Agbalin to safety (Merlo and Vidaud 1984, 280).

William Bosman observed from his 1692 notes (published in 1705) that a temple for Dangbe stood in the town of Savi, located a few kilometers north of Hueda (cited in Merlo and Vidaud 1984, 284). He describes the temple as situated within an impressive woodlot "two leagues" from the king's domicile. The house of the vodun was under a beautiful tree where an old python lived. There is some doubt about whether Bosman mistakenly recalled Hueda for Savi, given the similarity of his descriptions with the still-standing temple for Dangbe in Hueda. The Dahomians, however, may have destroyed the temple in Savi, since the once large town is but a shadow of itself today. Writing in 1728, the Catholic priest Jean-Baptiste Labat[11] provided interesting details about the temple:

> [A] very spacious [house] was erected for him [Dangbe] with several courtyards and large, well-maintained lodgings. Those of the king would lack coverings and upkeep to the extent of the serpent's lodgings.

Impressive pieces of furniture were placed there, a great priest, and an entire order of initiates to serve him; even more was done: we believe it was necessary that women were dedicated to him and, in effect, the most beautiful girls were chosen to be consecrated to him, and ones were chosen each year, so that he would not lack servants. (Merlo and Vidaud 1984, 285; my translation)

Here, Labat describes features of Dangbe's traditions that are still reflected in contemporary descriptions from Rouget (2001). The annual recruitment of young girls for initiation at Dangbe's temple reflects contemporary descriptions, their youthfulness an indication of initiation as a rite of maturation.

To the north of Dahomey, the Mahi chiefdoms also served Dangbe to the extent that some scholars even suggest that the spirit originated among the Mahi people (see Law 2004, 91). However, a Hueda settlement in Mahi territory like Savalou is more likely the source of Dangbe's service in that region (Merlo and Vidaud 1984, 290). This song for Dangbe suggests that the direction of migration and cultural transfer was from the Hueda to the Mahi people:

> A Hueda engendered me [Dangbe,] then hunted me;
> A Mahi took me, then carried me away. (Merlo and Vidaud 1984, 290)

After the Dahomian kingdom was established and its armies invaded the towns of Allada in 1724 and Hueda in 1727, the vodun Dangbe took on a greater symbolic role amid brewing tensions.

The Dahomian king Agaja captured the main Vodun priests and sent them back to Abomey to establish their coastal traditions in the hinterland capital. An important reshuffling of rankings took place after Agaja's conquests: the Dangbenon was until then the supreme priest among Huedan priests but fell to second rank, replaced by the Hounon of the sea vodun. Agaja took Dangbe Drè back to Dahomey. The python refused to go further than Cana on Dahomian soil, and it was there that the spirit's temple was constructed (Merlo and Vidaud 1984, 292). While Agaja "purchased" Dangbe Drè, Huedan war refugees carried their Dangbe vodun into exile, whereas others remained at the temples in Allada and Hueda. The actions of the conqueror spread the Dangbe traditions to new places in the region but also to Saint-Domingue through the captives sold after the fighting.

In Dahomian political theology, the situation was different. As descendants of the Tadonou, the Dahomians had long served Dan, the local variant of the python spirit. They took their victory over Allada in 1724 and Hueda in 1727 as Dan's gift to the Aja-Fon people to control the coast and conduct their commerce there. Agaja built a temple in honor of the victorious Dahomian Dan in the conquered town of Hueda, the symbols of the rainbow and the snake swallowing its tail emblazoned on its walls (Merlo and Vidaud 1984, 292).

The Huedan refugees settled around Lake Ahémé to the west of Hueda and Allada, establishing temples for Dangbe. Observers in the twentieth century have struggled to distinguish among (1) traditions practiced in those temples that reflect the original Hueda settlements around Lake Ahémé prior to their displacement by the Ayizo and Aja ethnic groups, and (2) the traditions brought to the region by the refugees of Dahomian aggression (Merlo and Vidaud 1984, 292). Migration to and from various settlements helped to gradually cross-fertilize traditions over time.

The collections of the *asen* (a metal object serving as an altar for an ancestor) that represent the lineage of ancestor priests in the temple for Dangbe-To-non in the town of Kpétou reveal the many successors who have maintained the tradition. A two-hundred-year-old temple dedicated to Dangbe-Tona-houè at Guzin had sixteen priestly successors, going back to members of the entourage of exiled King Houffon (Merlo and Vidaud 1984, 292).

THE DIFFUSE TRADITIONS OF DANGBE

The traditions of Dangbe suggest a profusion of sources, including kings, priests, and common people who followed the trail of refugees or migrants. Waves of refugees infused temples at different times (Merlo and Vidaud 1984, 295). This created layers of complex historical memories maintained by different local factions. Because of the intricate history of migration that shapes the collective history of a temple, the Dangbe traditions of the Huedans and Aja are interrelated.

Informants in the early 1960s insisted that Dangbe reflects a regional heritage, not one derived from a single place (Merlo and Vidaud 1984, 296). This view seems accurate, given evidence of the veneration of the "guiding spirit" snake in the Malinke community of Kouroussa, as described in Camara Laye's anthropological novel, *The Dark Child* (1954, 16). Kouroussa is 1,800 kilometers from the Huedan coast, a distance that suggests the scale of the snake's popularity as a totemic figure.

Contemporary initiates in Porto-Novo are divided into the "Houéda-ho-mé-nou" of Huedan descent and the "Dangbe-klounon-toyi," who are the "initiates of Dangbe who are accepted by the nation"; in other words, people who are not of Huedan ethnicity but who have "converted" to the spiritual community. Only the Houéda-ho-mé-nou have the five scarifications, an ethnic and religious symbol that grants them access to ceremonies for Dangbe in Hueda. The house (*goho*) of the python takes the circular form of the most ancient models, and the prior assistant descends from a line of migrants from Tado (Merlo and Vidaud 1984, 295). The "Ligan" Dangbe priest in Porto-Novo illustrates the special status of the priesthood of Dangbe in the political order, since he was allowed the distinction of only bowing to Dangbe and not the human king. He could not, however, lay eyes on the king.

The initiates of the temple of Houédakomé call the vodun they serve Dangbe Zongbo, meaning "Dangbe-the-source." The priest at the temple of Houédakomé in Porto-Novo conserves a story about Dangbe's origins in the sacred town of Ile Ife in Yoruba country, where the python is named Mana-Mana (Merlo and Vidaud 1984, 301). The following migratory itinerary for the Dangbe traditions is theorized: Ile Ife → Mekkaw → Ketu → Adja-Tado → Allada → Cana → Porto-Novo → Badagry, and so on (Merlo and Vidaud 1984, 301). The itinerary is perhaps accurate for the Aja communities but is too narrow given evidence of snake veneration in Guinea and elsewhere. Rather, the tradition reflects an ancient feature of pan-Bantu culture.

The Adjarra Huedans also settled a few kilometers from Porto-Novo at the same time that Te-Agbalin arrived. These initiates have five facial scarifications representing the five marks on the head of the python. The priest asks Dangbe each morning to preserve the health of the Huedans. Initiates visit the temple in the Houla neighborhood of Cotonou every five days on market days. The priest sacrifices an animal when a Huedan dies among the Adjarra (Merlo and Vidaud 1984, 298). Thus war and refugee movements, in addition to migratory trends, spread service to Dangbe inside West Africa and worldwide.

The village Adjohon has a small temple dedicated to Dangbe Hwesi. Although the temple does not have a permanent python, one is presented at the large annual celebration for the vodun. The people of Adjohon conserve the historical memory of the Dahomian army's "general extermination of the first inhabitants," which forced them to reestablish traditions for Dangbe during Te-Agbalin's period of settlement (Merlo and Vidaud 1984, 298–99).

The town of Sakété has two temples dedicated to Dangbe spirits. Two pythons are served, including the short Dangbe Danguédé and the long one, Dangbe Oko, associated with farming. Both names suggest a Yoruba-Aja syncretism with the words "Oko" and "-guédé" linked to Yoruba communities (Merlo and Vidaud 1984, 301). Dangbe is also served in the village of Iguédé, a place-name that points to Yoruba settlement in the area.

In the town of Pobé, people hold that the Yoruba Mana-Mana shares the same source as the python of Hueda, originating again in Ile Ife (Merlo and Vidaud 1984, 302). While service to "Dan" is absent in the village, a service for Ol'oufa, "the rainbow," symbolized by a living snake, is present (Merlo and Vidaud 1984, 302).

Some temples are built for Dangbe as a result of a revelation. A python took refuge with a neighborhood chief, Kèkè Adjihon, who built a private temple in the vodun's honor. Among the diverse Dangbe temples, there are common and diverging aspects of the prayers, songs, and initiatory traditions (Merlo and Vidaud 1984, 299). Although sharing underpinnings, Dangbe temples develop distinct traits over centuries.

Waves of refugees leaving Tado and Allada settled along the coast in major towns like Porto-Novo, Cotonou, and Badagry, and on the edges of lakes like Ahémé and Nokoué. Some of their descendants also became refugees as a result of Dahomian aggression. These groups included closely knit ethnic groups like the Huedans, Sètoès, Toris, Azohouès, Ajas, and other victims of war. Most of the refugees shared the veneration of Dangbe, pointing to the diffuse status of the spirit's traditions.

The worship of the serpent vodun stemmed from Yoruba traditions in Ile Ife, flowed south to Tado, and spread throughout the region as war flared and refugees took to the roads. Ultimately, captives who were caught up in the slave trade in the kingdoms of Allada, Hueda, Dahomey, and Oyo spread the service of the serpent spirits to many regions in the Americas.

THE PRIEST OF DANGBE AND HIS RESPONSIBILITIES IN HUEDA

The Dangbe-Kpohounon (priest of Dangbe) has various responsibilities in the town of Hueda, where there are numerous Vodun priests (Merlo 1940, 9–18). The priest of Dangbe is in charge of services for (1) Dangbe (discussed above), (2) Aladahouin, (3) Dan (discussed above), (4) Kpase,[12] (5) Ayohuan, (6) Agbangla,[13] (7) Kinsou, (8) Gbedji, and (9) Gléhoué (Merlo 1940, 10). These generic vodun labels contain too many features to exhaustively explore here; however, there are some crucial aspects to consider. The Dangbe had three temples in Hueda for Dangbe Kpohoun (male), Dangbe Drè (female), and Dangbe Kinsou-Kinsi (twins), a trinity noteworthy for the balanced gender representation and the inclusion of twins (Merlo 1940, 10).

In the region of Porto-Novo, the arrival of displaced groups and their religious traditions also had the effect of displacing the power and prominence of existing religious groups; hence the plaintive song still sung in twentieth-century Porto-Novo: "The Serpent of the Hueda, they say, / carries the mark of the Python; / Me, I believe the contrary; / they are the marks of the viper" (Merlo and Vidaud 1984, 300). The song may point to residual bitterness about the Dahomian conquest led by Te-Agbalin, the pressures imposed by Dangbe-worshipping refugees who came during Agaja's reign, and a loss of autonomy. It suggests that the Huedan tradition embodied a degree of "viper-like" power. The confrontational style of the song also appears in the Haitian *chante pwen* examined in chapters 3 and 4. The next section examines the hierarchy and traditions of Huedan spirits.

THE HIERARCHY AND CULTURE OF VODUN IN HUEDA

Examining political and religious allegiances in Hueda helps reconstruct the religious, cultural, and political situation at the time that residents of Allada (1724) and Hueda (1727) were cast into the Atlantic slave trade by the Dahomian invaders. The political hierarchy of the Vodun temples in Hueda reflects the order imposed by the Dahomians after their conquest in 1727. The priest and temple for (1) Hou, spirit of the sea, was ranked first. The priest and temple for (2) Dangbe only became second-ranked after the Dahomian invasion of 1727. The priest and temple for (3) Hwesi, the spirit of smallpox, is third-ranked, while the "master of the flame," (4) Zo, is ranked fourth.

These temples and their priests have "jurisdiction" over the other spirits, rituals, and temples within the same neighborhood. Hou's priest and temple functions as the highest-ranked ritual authority in the Sogbadji neighborhood of southeastern Hueda, where dozens of temples are situated (Merlo 1940, 85). Each neighborhood has several vodun spirits that were ranked under the head vodun of the neighborhood.

The priest of Hou, the Hounon, also known as Dagbo (grandpa), shared responsibility with the Nagbo (grandma), a word referring to an elderly priestess (Merlo 1940, 5). The Hounon was established thanks to an ethnic Déoué family that made a living as boatmen who provided transportation between ships anchored off the Huedan coast and the beach. Seeing that there was no suitable harbor and that the sea was often choppy and dangerous, the boatmen provided irreplaceable transportation that required protection from a sea divinity.

The temples under the Hounon were situated in the neighborhood where he lived. He thus exerted local control on behalf of the administration in Abomey. The priests, initiates, and families that maintained and patronized the temples all lived in the neighborhood, forming an intimate social fabric.

The third-ranked priest in Hueda was the Hwesinon, who served the Hueda spirit Hwesi (Merlo 1940, 19). Various kings honored Hwesi. After the Dahomian invasion in 1727, King Agaja brought Hwesi and the Hwesinon back to the capital of Abomey. When he arrived in Cana, a town on the way to Abomey, Hwesi created so much tumult that King Agaja had to admit that the spirit was too strong for him. He then dispatched it back to Huedan country (Merlo 1940, 19). The kings of Abomey authorized the annual sacrifice of a bull for Hwesi.

The Zonon was the fourth-ranked priest of Vodun in Hueda, responsible for services to Zo. As the ethnic Houla monarch Kpate served Zo, this responsibility had serious political ramifications. Zo is related to Hebyoso, the lightning divinity. Before the Dahomian conquest, the Zonon and the Hounon Dagbo were considered equals, but Zo became his "vassal" in the Dahomian hierarchy. Although there is no Haitian Vodou spirit named "Zo" in Max Beauvoir's inventory (2008a), there are important traces of the spirit in Haiti. The name of Vodou's initiation is the *kanzo*, a compound word from, *kan* + *zo* (consultation of the fire spirit) (Merlo 1940, 23; Brand 2000b, 55).

THE *TOVODUN*

The *tovodun* are "public vodun" that are shared by a large population, in contrast to the royal and noble vodun, or the familial ancestors of domestic traditions, served by smaller groups (Savary 1975, 54). The *tovodun* comprise three major "colleges" (*collèges*): Mawu-Lisa, Hebyoso, and Sakpata. Each village and important place has its own protector vodun, often reposing in trees. The natural altars for these types of spirits are nestled in forests but caringly cleaned and maintained, marked by a small altar of earth and covered with a modest roof of woven mats or palm leaves. Pottery, bones, and the remains of sacrificed animals are elements of the service to the spirit and mark the holiness of the space (Le Hérissé 1911, 104–5).

HISTORICAL AND MYTHOLOGICAL DIMENSIONS OF THE MAJOR VODUN: AGASU AND ADJAHOUTO

Agasu is the "panther" totem ancestor vodun of the ruling Aja family from Tado that migrated and came to dominate Allada, Abomey, and Porto-Novo (Brand 2000b, 1). Myths of the divine panther are diffused widely in the region, since the "totem god" of the "tiger [*sic*]," called Agu, is also found in Bayelsa State of Nigeria (Ifie and Adelugbo 1998, 155). Among the Aja Agasuvi, only the king was marked with five scars on his forehead to represent his connection to the panther's claws (Le Hérissé 1911, 107).

Further details from the legend of Agasu deserve focus. As noted above, a princess from Tado named Aligbonon was in love with a panther named Agasu. One day she went to the rock of Kpovè in order to gather some rough leaves so that she could wash her calabash bowl. There she met her panther lover, and they became one flesh (Le Hérissé 1911, 106). The creature born of their union was also named Agasu, half-human, half-panther. Representations of Agasu portray the vodun with a female upper body, representing Aligbonon, and a panther's lower body, representing Agasu.

Aligbonon's children venerated Agasu and fought to elevate the prince as king and leader of the Aja people in Tado (Le Hérissé 1911, 106). The effort failed due to a formal ban on a matrilineal royal line among the Aja of Tado. Aligbonon's grandchildren renewed the struggle and attempted to install their father, Adjahouto, by force. After a violent struggle, they had to flee, taking refuge in the forest of Aida, later called the forest of Allada (Le Hérissé 1911, 106). The bellicose Agasuvi family exerted their dominance over local families and established the Agasu cult among the people they conquered. Adjahouto was revered as the founder of the Agasuvi royal lineage of Allada. The founders of the kingdom of Dahomey left Allada to seek their fortunes in Abomey. King Tegbesu, a descendent of those Aja pioneers, was eager to reestablish Agasuvi worship in Allada after the Dahomian conquest (Law 1997, 122).

King Adjahouto became a vodun spirit. Adjahouto's Agasuvi descendants projected power northward to Abomey as Europeans menaced the coast, finally establishing the kingdom of Dahomey as a means of protection, empowerment, and enrichment. Agasu remains the Hennou-vodun of the descendants of Adjahouto and the uniting ancestor of the royal family. The vodun in Agasu's entourage include king Adjahouto, Princess Aligbonon, and Wawè (Le Hérissé 1911, 107). The service to the vodun Wawè began once Aja immigrants had settled on the Abomey plateau and were able to erect a temple to Agasu. In honor of the occasion and the location, the Aja founders of Dahomey began the service to a local Gedevi vodun named Wawè. Of course, Wawè was also the name of a town near Abomey. The Haitian spirit Gede Wawè was transported to the Caribbean by Gedevi victims of the Dahomian and French slave trade, revealing layers of meaning in this word.

While Adjahouto's branch of the family left Tado for Allada in a feud, over the next centuries his descendants in Allada routinely sent offerings to placate the familial vodun in the town of Tado, the Edenic source of Agasu and the Agasuvi family (Le Hérissé 1911, 112).

HEBYOSO

Hebyoso (or Sètohoun), holding a double-headed axe, assembles the cosmic forces of rain, thunder, and lightning. His power is expressed in corrective flashes of the lightning bolt (Brand 2000b, 20). Hebyoso's powerful thunderstorms are seasonal, so the spirit's role in society recedes during dryer periods. The life-giving rain corresponds with the vodun's beneficial agency in the world (Lando 2016, 78).

The lightning vodun comes from the town of Tchango in Yoruba territory. In Haitian Vodou, one of the main lightning-related spirits is preserved in Ogou Chango. The Aja people had their own lightning-spirit served in Héviè, a place near Allada, hence the name Hebyoso (or Hevioso, or other spellings). In regions where Hebyoso was served, death by lightning was taboo and the victim was denied inhumation. Instead, the cadaver was abandoned in an isolated field to be consumed by vultures and insects (Le Hérissé 1911, 108). Such a death is punishment for dishonesty and harmfulness. The servants of Hebyoso collected the cadavers. In addition to the abandonment of the body, those killed by lightning have their skulls offered to Hebyoso (Lando 2016, 76). Hebyoso is preserved in the Dahomian Rite of Haitian Vodou with the name Kebyesou Danlè, but not in the Rada Rite, even though the spirit originates near Allada.

Hebyoso is distinct from Sakpata but shares overlapping functions in natural and agricultural domains. In the role of lightning maker and spreader of maladies, the spirits mirror one another, as Hebyoso's rainstorms feed Sakpata's plantscape. Hebyoso's clouds dripping with rain fecundate the life that grows out of Sakpata's earthen womb (Lando 2016, 78). The two vodun spirits are "brothers" whose spats lead to death and destruction for earthlings in the form of droughts, infertility, and fires (Brand 2000b, 20).

In Hebyoso's entourage is the sea spirit Hou, also called Agbe or Houalahoun. Tegbesu brought Hou back from Hueda to Dahomey (Le Hérissé 1911, 109). Houala is a town near Grand-Popo, an example of the sea vodun's name fixed in a coastal toponym. Hou is married to the spirit Na-ètè, and their daughter is the vodun Avlékété (Avrèkètè). The three are served together and associated with rip currents, the surf, and the beach. The death of a canoe man while crossing the rip currents was attributed to Avlékété. Such a death was taboo in Aja society, the body buried in the dunes instead of via a traditional inhumation (Le Hérissé 1911, 109).

AIZAN

The village of Avlékété is the source of the Haitian spirit Ayizan Velekete. She is a major divinity in Allada and along the Huedan coast (Segurola and Rassinoux 2000, 88). In contemporary Fon culture, an "Aizan" is a mound located in the market near a tall "Loko" tree (Savary 1975, 46). Aizan mounds are the guardians of the marketplaces. Some families have an Aizan to reprimand children. In the past, the construction of the mound required a ritual murder to consecrate the place, plus a combination of dirt and sand from various sources, leaves, oil, and talismans (Verger 1957, 551). Melville Herskovits and Frances Herskovits

(1938, 213) note that a "circlet of palm fronds" called an *azaŋ* is set around the base of the Aizan mound.

Offerings are made at the Aizan mound at important moments in social and religious life, including the consecration of *tohosu* spirits, initiations, the annual commemoration of royalty and nobility, and seasonal rites of the public vodun, among other practices (Savary 1975, 46). In Haiti, Ayizan's importance is reflected in her rank in ritual: Ountò, Legba, Marasa, Loko, and Ayizan in the Rada Rite. Just as the loko tree is connected to the Aizan mound in Aja-Fon society, so too are Loko and Ayizan married in Haiti.

LOKO

Loko or Atanloko is a vodun linked to the loko or *roco* tree (*Chlorofora excelsa*). Among the Fon people, there are sacred and ordinary trees. The baobab and the loko, among others, are sacred (Lando 2016, 56). In Benin, the loko tree cannot grow in a compound among humans. As the monarch of trees, the loko is viewed as the link between the spirits of the ground and those of the sky (Lando 2016, 56). The vodun Loko of Dahomey has many affiliated names and traditions such as Adanloko, Atanloko, Léléloko, and Lokozoun (Le Hérissé 1911, 114).

One of Adanloko's myths tells of the tree's sudden burst from the earth in Dôouè (Lé Hérissé 1911, 114). From the tree's branches, a husband and wife came slipping down. The man's name was "Adan," and he had many children. One day while hunting, he fell and was carried underneath a bank of clay. Adanloko's children refused to live near the clay bank that had taken their father, and they moved to live under the Agasuvi in Allada. When that branch of the Agasuvi broke away from Allada and departed for Abomey, the followers of Adanloko of Dôouè, the Adanlokovi, traveled with them to the north. The legend reveals that members of more than one family-based religious group were among the early Aja migrants to Abomey. Apparently several groups—not just the Alladan Agasuvi Tadonou—resolved to abandon the coastal regions, which were locked in the chaos of the European slave trade.

Another legend told by Aïnonvi Hountonou, a descendent of Adanloko, told of the way Adanloko turned himself into a tree to avert the demise of his soul. Having chosen the loko species of tree, which lives longer and grows bigger than others, he infused his soul into it. The Adanlokovi complete their sacrifices for the ancestors at the foot of the nearest loko. In the early twentieth century, the Adanlokovi held that loko trees spontaneously grew on the tombs of individuals who no longer received rituals from surviving family members (Le Hérissé 1911, 115).

The vodun spirits of the earth are included in Loko's "choir," and the service to Loko is obligatory when they are invoked (Le Hérissé 1911, 115). This indicates Loko's standing among the upper echelon of Aja-Fon spirits, and it is therefore of great significance that Loko is central in the Rada Rite.

DJISÒ AND DAN AYIDA WEDO

The spirit Djisò is connected to lightning, like Hebyoso. However, Djisò is older and served by the Djétovi, who helped build the Dahomian state. Djisò belongs to a range of spirits linked by the suffix -sô (or -so). Gbadè-sô is the father and Sogbo the mother of the Djisò spirits, both canonical in the Haitian Rada Rite, where they are known as Badè and Sobo. The spirit Gbadè-sô, like Hebyoso, manifests by striking humans with lightning (Le Hérissé 1911, 116).[14]

One myth about Djisò links the spirit to the Dahomian "Dan-aïdô-ouêdo" (Dan ayida wedo), the namesake of Haiti's Ayida Wèdo. According to a Dahomian legend, Dan ayida wedo serves Sogbo by taking the lightning from the clouds down to earth, leaving its trace in river valleys. The jagged patterns of lightning bolts represent the celestial expression of Dan ayida wedo (Le Hérissé 1911, 118). The Lënsouhouè spirits examined next are split between several categories.

LËNSOUHOUÈ

The Dahomian spirit Lënsouhouè, inherited in Haitian Vodou as Badè Lensoufwe and served within the Dahomian Rite, points to a complex network of spirits (Beauvoir 2008a, 187). Lënsouhouè combines the vodun and the human soul (the *yè*). Princes became Lënsouhouè after life, and the Lënsouhouè were split into underlying royal types: children who died during breastfeeding and other types of the deceased, including children, adults, and the elderly (Le Hérissé 1911, 120). The breastfeeding group are nicknamed "those who have not eaten salt," a reference to their lactose diets. Members of the Dahomian royal family served these spirits of the royal dead.

THE *TOHOSU*

One type of Lënsouhouè was "revealed" during the rule of Tegbesu. During the Dahomian king's reign, tiny, long-haired men harassed Dahomians because they had forgotten service to these spirits. To cope with the harassment, King

Tegbesu sent priests to the Mahi region for intervention. They brought back the cult of the *tohosu*, who are the kings of the water, infinite in number and inhabiting springs and lagoons. The Mahi priests claimed that they were the ones who had been harassing the Dahomians.

The *tohosu* were children born with "monstrous birth defects." They were returned as quickly as possible to the lagoon from whence they came by drowning (Le Hérissé 1911, 121). Deformed children had to be presented to two Migan judges, who authenticated the birth of a *tohosu* and authorized their ritual murder. After Tegbesu heard the instructions sent by the Mahi priests, he realized that one of his wives had given birth to a *tohosu*. This *tohosu* indicated to him where their memorial temple should be built. The divination spirit Fa told Tegbesu that his ancestors had engendered *tohosu* and that he should activate a cult to memorialize royal *tohosu*. That cult included a high priest and initiates, who were grafted to the royal Lënsouhouè cult as a third category of "spiritual individual" (Le Hérissé 1911, 122). The cult's main goal was to protect the king's wives from giving birth to infants with deformities by virtue of service to the deformed ancestral royals.

Each Dahomian king was linked to a protector *tohosu*. The *tohosu* Zomadonou was the protector of King Akaba and his twin sister, Ahangbe. In addition, twins were protected by the *tohosu* Bosouhon (Le Hérissé 1911, 123). The *tohosu* spirit of King Agaja was named Kpélou, King Tegbesu's was Adomoun, and King Kpengla's was Donouvo.

The *tohosu* had a temple where male and female priests served. The distinguishing feature of its priesthood was the absence of hereditary transmission. Once a year, the priests of the *tohosu* walked in a procession to the springs of Dido, where they conducted ceremonies linked to the rejuvenation of nature at the peak of the dry season (Le Hérissé 1911, 123). The *tohosu* priests wrapped palm leaves around their loins and remained chaste during the ceremonial period. Unlike the priests of the vodun, the *tohosu* priests did not distinguish themselves with tattoos but smeared their faces with a white china clay, which they called "the mud of the kingdom of the *tohosu*" (Le Hérissé 1911, 124). The white china clay echoes the white faces of the Haitian Gede spirits.

In their processions, the head priests, followed by assistant priests, attired themselves in multicolored fabrics (Le Hérissé 1911, 124–25). The followers of the *tohosu* ran up to the priests, kneeled, and kissed the ground in front of them.[15] Upon the priests' arrival at the shaded springs, ceremonial dances were performed before the sun went down, including single-file "snaking," dancing in quadrilles, and dancing that involved the movement of the shoulders, feet, and arms, coordinated skills acquired in the Vodun convents. After the dances, the servants of the vodun went to the spring to bathe and to fill earthenware jugs of water to carry back for their temple's altar.

The bath in the sacred springs and the visit to the marketplace after are ceremonies of purification that atone for mistakes and shortcomings with regard to serving the vodun spirits (Le Hérissé 1911, 125). Sins committed might include eating forbidden foods or even eating snake meat in forbidden leaves (Le Hérissé 1911, 125). The spring bath was a place of atonement and prayer, expressions of aqueous ecological spirituality also found in Haitian Vodou.[16] The section below examines Mawu and Lisa, the creator couple who generated the other vodun.

MYTHS OF MAWU AND LISA

Mawu and Lisa represent fecundity, the genesis of beings and the universe, and a conquering power (Savary 1975, 54). The word "Mawu" has emerged in contemporary Fon as the Christian term for God, including in the Fon translation of the New Testament. Mawu is cut off from her husband Lisa in her Christian moonlighting but remains integrally tied to him in the Vodun culture of the Fon language area.

In Vodun mythology, Mawu is a female vodun who inhabits space to the East. She is joined with Lisa, the chameleon, who inhabits the West. The moon represents Mawu and the sun Lisa (Savary 1975, 54). They made love, and the vodun Aghe, the earth, was born (Le Hérissé 1911, 126). Mawu and Lisa reflect similar manifestations in neighboring cultures, too. In Yoruba religion, Mawu corresponds to Oduduwa and Lisa to Oshala. The term "Lisa" may be etymologically related to the general Yoruba term for vodun spirits, "orisha," as in the sequence orisha → olisha → lisa (Savary 1975, 55).

Mawu's red wooden statue resembles the dawn, and she wears a seashell necklace between her large breasts. The cowry shells are symbols of her maternal power and her connection to wealth. She holds a crescent moon in one hand, symbolic of her connection to the cosmos (Le Hérissé 1911, 126). Other than this statue, Mawu is not usually represented in Dahomey, while her spouse, Lisa, is commonly painted in murals as a chameleon.

Mawu is a recent addition to the Dahomian pantheon. Nae Hwanjile, wife of King Agaja, brought Mawu's and Lisa's service to the Dahomian royal family from Adjahomé, twenty-seven kilometers to the west of Abomey, where she had been born at the turn of the eighteenth century. In 1975, the service to the vodun was under the authority of the "representative for the former queen Nae Hwanjile" (Savary 1975, 55). The service to Mawu and Lisa was emphasized in the royal family out of respect for Queen Hwanjile. The royal compounds also have temples dedicated to the couple, one to the East (Mawu) and the other to the West (Lisa) (Le Hérissé 1911, 127). Dahomian royal power had little influence in Saint-Domingue, so it is unsurprising that Mawu (Mawou in Haiti) and Lisa are diminished in Haitian Vodou.

The service to Mawu and Lisa may have spread into Dahomian towns before the tradition's integration into Abomeyan royal Vodun in the early 1700s. The survival of the spirits in Haiti's Dahomian Rite at Lakou Souvenance near Gonaïves suggests that the couple was widely venerated among Dahomians (Beauvoir 2008a, 187).

SAKPATA

The religious tradition of the vodun Sakpata has been in and out of fashion in Dahomey over the centuries. Stunned by smallpox's decimation of his army, King Agaja sent specialists to learn about Sakpata and to gain his protection. Sakpata originates in the Yoruba town of Dassa, north of Abomey, as confirmed by the Dassa dialect of Sakpata's ritual language (Brand 2000b, 76). Those priests brought back traditions for Sakpata that never fully took hold. The kings of Dahomey banned Sakpata's followers from using drums and forbade marriage between the Sakpatasi and royals. Sakpata's cult was even banned under the ninth and tenth kings, King Ghezo and King Glele. In the early twentieth century, there was a resurgence of the Sakpata cult, a fact that worried the chiefs, given how the vodun's priests could abuse inhabitants petrified of smallpox (Le Hérissé 1911, 128–29). In Haitian Vodou, Sakpata fits into the Danwonmen Rite, since the adoption of the spirit was Dahomian and never reached Allada and Hueda, where Hwesi filled a similar function. Twins, explored next, have magical and sacred qualities among various West African peoples and are central to the Rada Rite.

THE TWINS

The origin of the Haitian Creole word "Marasa," Vodou's sacred twins, is not readily traced in the Fon language. The term "Marasa" is putatively Kikongo from *mabassa*, meaning "those who come divided."[17] The veneration of twins is, however, an unmistakable feature of Aja-Fon culture.

The reverence for and fear of twins is writ large in West African societies. Malinke and Bamana societies in Guinea, the Temne people in Sierra Leone, the Win in Burkina Faso, the Yoruba in Nigeria, the Kapsiki in Cameroon and Nigeria, the Luba in the Democratic Republic of the Congo, and the Himba in Namibia, among countless ethnic groups, share deep reverence for twins, maintain complex cultural customs in their honor, and, in some cases, include them as symbols in religious life (Peek 2011, viii).

In the Fon and Yoruba contexts, dualities are deeply engrained throughout the societies. The two upper spirits, Mawu and Lisa, reflect a pairing at the center of Dahomian mythology. Oppositional complementarity is expressed throughout the religions of the region, where day and night, east and west, north and south, the vertical and the horizontal, hot and cool, the living and the dead, priest and priestess, and other dualities represent core forms of balanced culture (Lawal 2011, 82). Oppositional complementarity in transatlantic culture illustrates continuity and serves as an important signpost for Vodou hermeneutics.

In Aja-Fon society, twins are said to die and resuscitate at will and maintain strong relationships with the vodun. A small monkey is the patron animal of twin births. The twin does not perish but returns to the woods. A deceased twin is replaced by a wooden statuette that receives food and drink as though still among the living (Quénum 1999, 87). A photograph of a surviving twin with her deceased twin's wooden statuette can be found in Gilbert Rouget's study from the 1950s and 1960s (2001, 53), illustrating the continuation of the practice. Surviving twins also keep commemorative sculptures called *flanitokélé* for the deceased in Mali's Bamana society (Imperato and Imperato 2011, 55). As chapter 3 discusses, the twins are essential to the Rada Rite.

PROHIBITIONS IN VODUN

One of the circumscribing features of Vodun practice is prohibition. Each spirit has a number of symbols, items, and traditions that are acceptable or unacceptable. There are many items that the servants of the spirit embrace and use to represent spiritual service. However, there are things that are prohibited to those who serve the spirit. Some prohibitions are temporary for candidates of initiation, whereas others are permanent aspects of service.

The prohibitions reveal aspects of Vodun culture in addition to aspects of the kingdoms where they were practiced. Slave trader William Snelgrave noted that the initiates of the "national *Fetiche*" of the Yoruba people in the kingdom of Oyo were prohibited from seeing the ocean altogether (1971, 59). Instead, the Yoruba of Oyo greatly desired coral, paying traders large sums for it because it represented the national spirit.

Agasu was half a man and half a leopard. It was "sacrilegious" to display leopard skins in public (Dalzel 1967, 200). Several interesting facts about the role of leopard prohibitions can be gleaned from Oluale Kossola's narrative of nineteenth-century Yoruba life in the town of Takkoi near Porto-Novo (Hurston 2018, 26–27). Anyone who killed a leopard was required to present the animal to the local king. The hunter had to cover the leopard's head so that no woman could see it. The king would first take the leopard's whiskers, because they were considered poisonous. Next, the king would take the head, liver, gallbladder, and skin to be dried and prepared as medicines. Kossola added that "some tribes make fetish and eat de flesh, so dey eatee de medicine, you know" (Hurston 2018, 26–27). The leopard is a sacred animal and a political symbol. The prohibition against women viewing its head, or common people from taking its whiskers or using its body parts, reflects the royal usage of powerful natural symbols to represent their magnified social rank. Amulets designed to harm an enemy in Dahomey included leopard whiskers, monkey skulls, animal tibias, and others (Le Hérissé 1911, 155).

Some spirits prohibited their devotees from eating fowl with white feathers, others from eating fowl with black feathers (Snelgrave 1971, 59). Some spirits prohibited the consumption of mutton. Although he was dismissive in his observations, Snelgrave noted that the prohibitions were scrupulously kept.

The initiates of Dangbe could not eat the meat of rams, as could not the members of the "tribe of Hueda" (Merlo and Vidaud 1984, 274). The clan that served Dangbe Hwesi was prohibited from consuming the flesh of a hippopotamus. Groups that served the serpent spirit were prohibited from eating python meat, but those that served other spirits were not (Merlo and Vidaud 1984, 274). Food prohibitions are symbols of adherence to a Vodun initiatory group. The initiates adopt a handful of prohibitions that represent the initiatory community, but there is no need to impose on others these idiosyncratic practices that are rooted in a secret initiation.

CONCLUSION

This chapter has focused on the Aja-Fon religious and cultural heritage of Haitian Vodou. The investigation has included consideration of the primary African sources that shaped the Rada Rite and the Gede Rite. This chapter has gone deeper into the background of the Rada Rite than the Gede Rite, since the latter's sources are less well known, given that there are few records of the Dahomian conquest of their lands. Conquest, enslavement, and intermarriage changed and even erased Gedevi history. Their remoteness from the coast also prevented European travelers from visiting and writing about them. However, as this chapter has demonstrated in numerous places, traces of Gede culture are detectable in the Aja-Fon region, where Gedevi migrants and refugees settled after Agasuvi and coastal migrants seized their lands and established Dahomey.

Comparative research on African source cultures is a leading edge in Haitian Vodou studies. Signal efforts have advanced research on the Kongo connections that influenced Vodou in Saint-Domingue and Haiti. The spirit-based religious systems of the Aja-Fon and Gedevi-Yoruba people were systematic theologies kept and cherished by hierarchical organizations that transmitted specialized religious and cultural knowledge in a private and initiatory educational culture. The Vodun priesthood is centralized around a charismatic and authoritative leader, male or female, who takes charge of a vast tradition focused on one spirit. The community of each spirit is trained and initiated in a convent, while annual celebrations reunite the members. Traditions of divination, mythology, songs, dances, prayers, and spirit possession reflect cultural systems that respond to adherents' deepest search for meaning.

An intricate world of connections link Vodun and Vodou. The Aja-Fon Vodun lexicon shows innumerable affinities with the Haitian Creole Vodou one. The origins of many Haitian Vodou terms are confirmed in instances when similar phonetic and semantic traits are found in West Africa. Towns like the Dahomian capital of Abomey and coastal towns like Allada and Hueda were beacons of influence in the formation of Haitian Vodou's Rada and Gede Rites. Dahomian armies captured and sold the Gedevi founders of the Gede Rite and the Alladan and Huedan founders of the Rada Rite to French slave buyers bound for Saint-Domingue. At the same time, elements of the local populations were judicially enslaved or captured by outside raiders and sold into the slave trade bound for Saint-Domingue. The Rada Rite, the Gede Rite, the Nago Rite, the Dahomian Rite, and others that survive in Haiti today are lineages to that history.

Aja-Fon religion and culture especially flourished as a topic of research in French-language publications in the later twentieth century. Analyses of Aja-Fon religious cultures try to meet practitioners and practices on their own terms. Comparing closely related traditions serves the goal of developing interpretations that are recognizable to Vodunists and Vodouists. Vodou hermeneutics seeks to interpret sacred texts and traditions within a "family" of relevant traditions to ensure the representativeness of the reading.

The dual African and Caribbean focus of this transatlantic project extends from the ancestral, linguistic, and cultural connections that bind the Aja-Fon and Gedevi-Yoruba people with Haitians. The dialectical approach builds on a comparative method in order to underscore the connections between the traditions. The first two chapters of this book have analyzed the historical, political, economic, and religious situation in the regions of Africa where the founders of Vodou in Saint-Domingue originally became entangled as enslaved people. The next chapters explore how the traditions of the Bight of Benin took form in Haitian Vodou's Rada Rite and Gede Rite through the lens of the songs of Rasin Figuier and Rasin Bwa Kayiman.

Chapter 3

THE RADA RITE IN HAITI

Rasin Figuier's *Vodou Lakay*

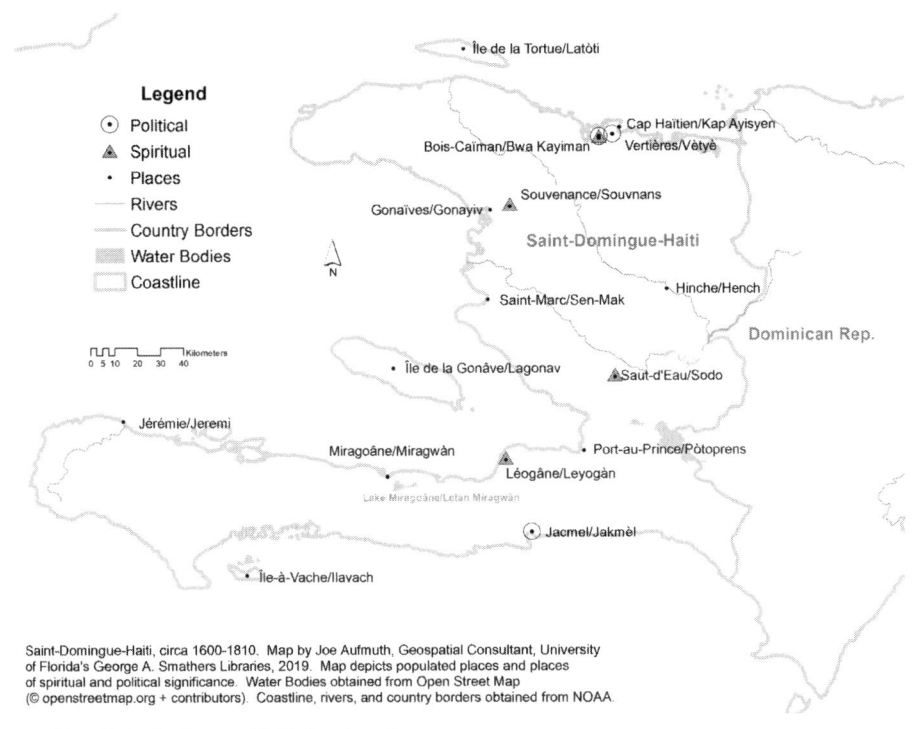

Map of Saint-Domingue and Haiti, circa 1600–1810.

INTRODUCTION

The songs of Rasin Figuier's album *Vodou Lakay* (Vodou at Home) (2004), examined in this chapter, and the songs of Rasin Bwa Kayiman's album *Guede* (2004), examined in chapter 4, belong to the immense canon of Vodou's sacred

Figure 1. Rasin Figuier's *Vodou Lakay* album cover. Photo courtesy of Amey Owen.

songs.[1] Rasin Figuier's album focuses on the Rada Rite and Rasin Bwa Kayiman's album focuses on the Gede Rite, but both cohere to the orbit of Sèvis Ginen (Ginen Service). These two albums scratch the surface of a massive tradition that is becoming better known thanks to *rasin* albums and publications like Max Beauvoir's collections of Vodou songs and liturgies (2008a, 2008b). These are ultrafine recordings by top-notch outfits.

The vast corpus of Vodou sacred literature, especially songs, reaches the Haitian public in temples, Lakou courtyards, and homes, over radio, television, and the internet. Singing or listening to *rasin* music is a part of daily life. Great *oungan* and *manbo* and their initiates are dedicated vocalists. For instance, oungan Alisma's initiates at Société Linto Roi Trois Mystères in Miami meet several times a week to practice songs and to study.

For centuries, Vodou culture was strictly an oral tradition passed down via family and community lines. Vodou songs increasingly entered the realm of print after the 1920s and the realm of sound recordings since the 1930s (Lomax et al. 2009). Publications by Milo Marcelin (1949, 1950), Michel Laguerre (1980), Max Beauvoir (2008b), and Benjamin Hebblethwaite et al. (2012) include hundreds of Haitian Creole Vodou songs, but they are still only a fraction of Vodou's total material. As impressive as these books are, the impact of *rasin* recordings via marketing in boutiques and mass distribution on radio programs, compact discs, DVDs, and digital files is likely even greater, and hence my focus on the influential *rasin* groups Rasin Figuier and Rasin Bwa Kayiman.

In the Haitian diaspora, the sale of compact discs in Haitian shops has spread the circulation of songs. Rasin Figuier's *Vodou Lakay* and Rasin Bwa Kayiman's *Guede* were both published on the bicentennial of Haitian independence in 2004 on Jean Altidor's record label, Mass Konpa, based in Miami. I first discovered these *rasin* artists and purchased their albums while visiting Haitian shops in Miami. As a Haitian music lover, I have always purchased and listened to Vodou music; these are ancient pulses that I resonate with. Recordings of sacred music like that of Rasin Figuier and Rasin Bwa Kayiman are of great importance for historians, linguists, and ethnomusicologists. As my appreciation grew, I resolved to study the songs using historical, linguistic, and critical methods and to learn about the African sources they spring from.

THE RASIN FIGUIER ALBUM THAT INSPIRED THIS CHAPTER

Rasin Figuier's album *Vodou Lakay* focuses on the spirits of the Rada Rite, in addition to a few others like the Nago Rite. Jean Altidor's Mass Konpa (sometimes spelled "Kompa") record label and film production company, which produced the album, releases entertainment and art for consumers in the Haitian diaspora and Haiti. Its music catalogue is a mix of secular and sacred music.

The group's name, Rasin Figuier (Roots of the Fig Tree), reflects the sacred status of the *pye figye* (*Ficus* spp.) in Haiti. The fig tree, like the *mapou*, is never cut. Common around cemeteries, the fig tree serves as *repozwa* for spirits like Bawon Samdi, Gran Bwa, Èzili, and Danbala (Tarter 2015, 102). The artists who perform on Rasin Figuier's album *Vodou Lakay* reflect the traditional Vodou orchestral arrangement:

(1) Lead vocalist, Fritert Pierre
(2) Second lead vocalist, Raymond Salomon
(3) Chorus members, Mariette Sylvestre, Seurette Louis, Marie Dadie Eustache, Josette Delva, Raymond Jérôme, and Michel Christophe
(4) Chorus arranger, Serge Loseille
(5) "Maestro arranger," Eldet Sérôme
(6) Second drummer, Cajuste Jean Evens
(7) Third drummer, René Alix
(8) First base drummer, Dérolus Jean Frenelt
(9) Second bass drummer, Walter Menelas
(10) Third bass drummer, Ulver Pierre

The songs of Rasin Figuier and Rasin Bwa Kayiman include several singers and percussionists, reflecting a traditional structure balanced between a rhythm section and vocals. The traditional Rada battery includes the low-pitched *manman*, the medium-pitched *segon*, and the high-pitched *boula* (Wilcken and Augustin 1992, 32). These hardwood drums have cowhide heads attached with wooden pegs. Uniting the botanical and the animal world, drums symbolically connect humans to the universe (Jean-Michel Yamba, cited in Dirksen 2019a, 55–56). As a result of foreigners extracting hardwoods, mahogany trees have disappeared, and drums are now made of wood from the fig, trumpet, and breadfruit trees (Dirksen 2019a).

The lead drummer plays the *manman* with a stick in the right hand and with the left hand free, as does the player of the *segon*. The *boula* player holds two sticks. The *boula* is the first to strike for the *oundjènkon* (lead singer), but the *manman* indicates for the ensemble to stop (Wilcken and Augustin 1992, 33). In addition, the *ogantye* (cowbell player) plays the iron *ogan* (iron cowbell) with an iron stick, providing a time line around which the drummers beat or extemporize (Wilcken and Augustin 1992, 40). The similarity of the word *ogan* to the spirit of metallurgy Ogou cannot be coincidental. The sacred *ason* (rattle), covered with a mesh of multicolored beads or snake vertebrae and with a bell tied to it, is also a part of the ensemble. An *oungan* or *manbo* holds the *ason* and bell in the right hand and uses them to lead the cycles of salutation but also to set the tempo or signal the end of playing (Wilcken and Augustin 1992, 41). An *oundjènikon* receives choral responses from the choir of *ounsi*.

The ensemble reflects Vodou's highly organized society, which focuses on steadying human contact with ancestors and nature. Since the drums are agents in human interactions with spirits, they are baptized and bowed to, touched by the *ason*, illuminated by candles, sprinkled with libations, and traced with *vèvè* at their bases (Wilcken and Augustin 1992, 48). Ountò, the drum spirit, is even greeted in some Rada ceremonies before Legba. The next section presents the history of the Rada Rite.

HISTORICAL DIMENSIONS OF RADA

The word "Rada" comes from the name of the town of Allada or Arada, as it was once known in the colony of Saint-Domingue. The Rada Rite and its spirits are among the more prominent traditions of Vodou in Haiti. However, there are twenty-one rites in Sèvis Ginen, including Rada, Petwo Fran, Gede, Nago, Kongo Fran, and others (Beauvoir 2008a). Although many scholars present Rada and Petwo as though they were dual systems that dominate Vodou, the situation tends to be multipolar in Sèvis Ginen, as several rites are observed.

Most of the rites are only undertaken after the Rada spirits have received greetings.

The term *lwa Ginen* (Ginen spirits) refers to the Rada spirits (Beauvoir 2008a, 187–96). Vodou rites are made up of strictly defined lists that group spirits together on the basis of their region of origin in Africa (Métraux 1972, 28). In addition to rites, Vodou also classifies spirits by *fanmi* (family), because some spirits have "family members" in more than one rite. For example, the Rada spirit Legba Atibon has family members within Rada like Legba Gran Chimen but also in the Petwo Fran Rite like Legba Bwa and in the Zandò Rite like Legba Zandò. Legba originated in the Bight of Benin, but his relatives emerged in western Central African rites following the pattern of spirits "migrating" from the rites of the Bight of Benin founding populations into the western Central African rites that derive from populations that arrived after them (Hebblethwaite 2015a).

At one hundred spirits, the Rada Rite has the largest cohort, serving as a "catchment" rite derived from traditions that originate over a large region (Jil and Jil 2009, 92). At the same time, the Danwonmen (Dahomian) Rite with ten spirits, the Gede Rite with thirty-seven spirits, the Ibo Rite with nine spirits, the Mahi Rite with one spirit, and the Nago Rite with forty-nine spirits collectively illustrate how several rites that originate in the Bight of Benin region are attested within Sèvis Ginen (Beauvoir 2008a, 187–96). In general, Rada reflects the traditions of Allada, Hueda, and Tado.

The founders of the Rada Rite were among the earlier enslaved people taken to Saint-Domingue (circa 1680–1730). Western Central African people arrived in the colony as captives after the 1720s. The new arrivers introduced rites and spirits that were taken up into the various preestablished "founder" rites like Rada, creating an African synthesis called Sèvis Ginen (Bellegarde-Smith 2004, 25).

STRUCTURAL FEATURES OF THE RADA RITE: REPEATED FEATURES AND ONE-OFF FEATURES

Rasin Figuier's *Vodou Lakay* reflects a Rada Rite ceremony in miniature, making it helpful to examine basic aspects of the ceremony. The Rada ceremony maintains a set of repeated patterns while gradually introducing one-off features. The repeated patterns in temples like Société Linto Roi Trois Mystères are expressed in these ways:

(1) All of the *ounsi* initiates wear white clothing from head to toe.
(2) At least one *oungan asogwe* or *manbo asogwe* is present to lead the cycle of salutation, possibly more.

(3) The *oungan* or *manbo* holds an *ason* (sacred rattle) and a bell in the right hand.
(4) In the left hand, the *oungan* or *manbo* holds a white-painted metal cup to pour water libations for the spirits at the stations.
(5) A silk scarf that matches the color of the spirit to be greeted is tied around the neck of the *oungan* or *manbo* who leads the cycle of salutation.
(6) Several initiated assistants walk behind the *oungan* or *manbo* holding candles, an animal such as a chicken destined for sacrifice, a bottle of Florida water, or a white cup of water with leaves floating in it.
(7) An assistant carries an object that represents the spirit.

The term "cycle of salutation" in (2) above is the repeated cyclical pattern in the Rada Rite. Each spirit receives at least one cycle. It is a "cycle" because the *oungan*, *manbo*, and their assistants complete it by circulating counterclockwise around the temple's *potomitan* (center post) while sequentially greeting the *stations of salutation*. Once the *ason* has been passed to the priest who will lead the cycle and the colored scarf that represents the spirit has been tied around her or his neck, the following sequence of gestures unfolds:

(1) The *oungan* or *manbo* raises the *ason* in the air to signal the start of the cycle of salutation and to indicate that the congregation must rise in respect. The drumming becomes focused.
(2) The priest circles around the *potomitan*.
(3) After completing a half circle, the priest and assistants salute the *first station*, the four cardinal points. After, they circle the *potomitan* again, stopping briefly before they stride toward the drummers.
(4) The drummers speed up the tempo to welcome the priest and entourage. The priest and entourage ritually salute Ountò, the spirit of the drums, and the *ountògi* (drummers) by the priest touching the drums, and his or her chest, with the *ason* and by the group fully prostrating before them. This is the only full prostration in a cycle of salutation, and it completes the *second station*.
(5) The priest and entourage circle the *potomitan* again, forming a circle to greet the spirits through the symbolic center post, the *third station*. The priest touches the *ason* and his or her chest while speaking deliberately to the spirits through the *potomitan*.
(6) The practitioners circle the *potomitan* again, stopping to salute the door to the *badji* (altar room) and initiation chamber for a salutation at the *fourth station*. They complete three Vodou bows there.
(7) A *fifth station* involves greeting the shrine of the specific spirit celebrated at the ceremony.

(8) Last, the priest quickly raises and lowers the *ason* to indicate the end of the cycle of salutation, while the worshippers complete a *dogwe* ritual by touching the ground with the right hand and tapping the chest twice.

(9) The cycle of salutation is complete, but typically a free-form type of worship will persist through a few additional songs. It is an auspicious time in Vodou ceremonies for a spirit to descend into a worshipper.

Wedded to the fixed features of the cycles of salutation in the Rada Rite are one-off features that are included during the appropriate cycle of salutation. The one-off features take the form of a specific ritual, or the display of specific colors, symbols, objects, songs, rhythms, or activities (like spirit possession) that match the greeted spirit. The characteristics of the spirits will be discussed below, so it suffices to illustrate a few particularities of Atibon Legba.

The one-off features of Legba's cycle of salutation include the *ounsi* who carries crutches that symbolize Legba's age, serving as supports for the possessed should he appear. If Legba arrives, the crutches are placed under a horse's armpits to hold up the spirit. Crutches in place, sweeping regal yellow and purple cloth adorn the shoulders of the spirit, and a silk scarf is tied around her or his head to indicate the spirit's installment. After the spirit has descended, Legba inspects his shrine and ritually greets the worshippers, who bow, kneel, and cross their arms to shake the great king's pinky fingers with their opposite pinkies.

RESEARCH ON THE RADA RITE

Melville Herskovits (1937, 310–13) collected three lists of the Rada and Petwo spirits from three informants near Mirebalais, and they all agree in substance. Additional spirits that single informants cited were also confirmed Rada spirits, including Grann Alouba, Siligbo (Silibo), Loko, Marasa, and Sobo. Some of Herskovits's informants mentioned the "21 classes of *loa*," a reference to the "21 Nanchon Ginen" of Sèvis Ginen, including "Rada, Petwo, Dahomey, Ginen, Kongo, Nago, Ibo, and Wangòl" (Herskovits 1937, 149). The informants' descriptions suggest that they had knowledge of Sèvis Ginen.

Milo Marcelin's volumes *Mythologie vodou (rite arada, I, II)* (1949, 1950), are important studies of the Rada Rite. His books offer hundreds of transcribed Vodou songs in Haitian Creole, complete French translations, and a critical apparatus (the songs of which were reprinted and translated in Hebblethwaite et al. 2012, 73–125). In his introduction, Félix Morisseau-Leroy describes meeting Marcelin at Vodou ceremonies, where they took delight in eating, drinking, singing, and dancing with their friends, priests, and devotees of Vodou. He enjoyed the confidence and affections of a great number of initiates (Morisseau-Leroy, cited in Marcelin 1949, 8). Marcelin frequently cites unnamed *oungan* and *manbo*; his eye for detail demonstrates keen participant observation. Although he was not a Vodou "apostle," Marcelin was a "free thinker" who "considered religiosity to be the general property of the human spirit" (Morisseau-Leroy, cited in Marcelin 1949, 8).

Marcelin (1949) may be the first author to describe the Rada Rite following the *règleman* (ordering) of the spirits. His book's order resembles a standard Rada ceremony with Atibon Legba, Ayizan Velekete, Loko Atisou, Danbala Wèdo, Ayida Wèdo, Mètrès Èzili (Lavyèj Karidad and Sent Elizabèt), Grann Èzili, Agwe Tawoyo, Mètrès Lasirèn, and Agasou Gnenen flowing naturally from one to the next.

Shortly after Marcelin's groundbreaking study, Maya Deren's *Divine Horsemen: The Living Gods of Haiti* (1953) was published. The Rada Rite represents the "basic African tradition" in Haiti, and it reflects "the emotional tone of their place of origin" (Deren 1953, 60). The kingdoms of Allada, Hueda, and Dahomey were "absolute" and "well-organized" monarchies where cooperative work groups completed agricultural work (61). The rigid hierarchical structure of those kingdoms is reflected in the inflexible structure and tone of the rite and its rituals. Deren suggests that the calm, benevolent, and disciplined system of the Rada Rite was inadequate on its own for addressing the violent culture of the colony of Saint-Domingue, a need that the Petwo Rite filled with its "hot" and "dangerous" spirits (61, 84).

The basic entrance into Vodou, the *kanzo* initiation, takes place under the sign of the Rada Rite. The Rada spirits reflect "an educational initiatory force" (Deren 1953, 85). The Rada *oungan* spirit, Papa Loko, and the *manbo* spirit, Ayizan Velekete, work with the initiator priests of the societies they protect. The initiation is described as *kouche pou Danbala* (sleeping for Danbala), occurring under the auspices of the great serpent spirit of Hueda (Richman 2005, 130). The role of the Rada spirits in the *kanzo* initiation is an important reason for the Rada Rite's centrality in Haiti.

Publishing his study shortly after Deren, Alfred Métraux examined Rada as an anthropologist. The Rada traditions held the greatest prestige during the 1950s (Métraux 1972, 86). As a result of the confidence they inspire, Rada spirits are the first greeted in a ceremony. When they are not dancing in the heads of their followers, Rada spirits rest in Ginen. Bedecked in white clothing, worshippers praise the Rada Rite spirits with shouts of *Ayibobo!* or *Abobo!* These spirits are "gentle," "benevolent," "regal," "slow," or "cool" (87). Rada spirits work slowly for their servants, whereas Petwo Fran spirits work quickly, but the latter bring greater risk. Failure to secure a request from Rada spirits may carry the requester to hotter spirits. The Rada spirits do not kill people out of malevolence but as punishment for grave wrongs. Failure to serve the *lwa* is the cause of a generally mild punishment. The Rada spirits wait patiently for their servants to fulfill their obligations and warn them in dreams or possession that a feeding ceremony should be completed (Métraux 1972, 88–89, 98).

Karen McCarthy Brown draws on her relationship with manbo Mama Lola's community. She lists six rites and advances the idea that Rada and Petwo have "come to dominate," adding that Ogou's Nago Rite may be an exception. She also suggests that in the "countryside," the presence of diverse "nations of Vodou spirits can still be found" (Brown 2001, 100). The Rada spirits are "sweet-tempered," "dependable," and imbued with "wisdom." They connect to the family as *lwa rasin* (root spirits), and several of them go by familial titles like *papa* or *manman*. The Rada spirits receive sweets (Marasa), water (Ayizan), or eggs (Danbala), basic commodities that are reflections of "coolness" (Brown 2001, 100–101).

Like the spirits themselves, the altar room for the Rada spirits is white or decorated with light colors, offering a "peaceful atmosphere in compliance with the serenity that characterizes the Rada gods" (Saint-Lot 2003, 107). Sèvis Ginen is multipolar with several dynamic rites in addition to Rada and Petwo including Gede, Makaya, Danwonmen, Kongo Fran, Kongo Savann, Nago, Zandò, and others. The next section examines the large number of spirits in the Rada Rite.

THE VAST RADA SPIRIT FAMILY

Oungan Max Beauvoir lists 102 Rada spirits, in addition to their family category (2008a, 193–96). His list of the spirits in Sèvis Ginen's twenty-one principle rites was compiled after decades of fieldwork and experience as an *oungan*, providing a one-of-a-kind resource.

Spirit name	Family name
1. Danyi	Dangbesi
2. Adjehoun	Pyè
3. Agaou Bèt Sansan (Agaou Beast without Blood)	Agaou
4. Agaou Konble (Konbe?) (Agaou Full-to-the-Top)	Agaou
5. Agaou Lèfan	Agaou
6. Agaou Misan Wèdo (Agaou Misan from Hueda)	Agaou
7. Agaou Potokoli	Agaou
8. Agaou Tonè (Agaou Thunder)	Agaou
9. Agaouwemen/Agaouyèmen (Agaou from Yèmen)	Agaou
10. Agasou Dam Selele (Agasou Lady Selele)	Agasou
11. Agasou Mawoude	Agasou
12. Agasou Wèlo	Agasou
13. Agasou Yangòdò	Agasou
14. Agasou Yèmen (Agasou from Yèmen)	Agasou

15. Agwe Mede	Agwe
16. Alazon Pyè	Pyè
17. Atakwa Mèdji	Marasa
18. Atidanyi Boloko	Dangbesi
19. Atyasou Yangòdò	Atyasou
20. Ayigba	Legba
21. Ayizan Gwèto	Ayizan
22. Ayizan Velekete	Ayizan
23. Belekou Djòdjò	—
24. Bosou Dhlo	Bosou
25. Bosou Kenendjo	Bosou
26. Danbala Pyè Wèdo	Dangbesi
27. Dan Ayida Wèdo	Dangbesi
28. Djobolo Bosou	Bosou
29. Dosou Loko	Loko
30. Èzili Dantò	Èzili
31. Èzili Pyè	Pyè
32. Faro Mèdji	Marasa
33. Filomiz Pyè	Filomiz Pyè
34. Gran Bosou Komblamen	Bosou
35. Grann Adanyi Kodan	Dangbesi
36. Grann Adanyi Wèdo	Dangbesi
37. Grann Adja	Grann Èzili
38. Grann Alouba	—
39. Grann Adjasouyangòdò	Atyasou
40. Grann Ayizan	Ayizan
41. Grann Bòsin	Dangbesi
42. Grann Silibo Vavoun	Grann Èzili
43. Grann Tèsi Freda	Grann Èzili
44. Hountò (Sacred Drum)	—
45. Jan Bazil	Jan
46. Klèmerzin Klèmey	Klèmerzin Klèmey
47. Komè Loko (Sister Loko)	—
48. Labalèn (The Whale)	Èzili
49. Labèl Venus (The Beautiful Venus)	Èzili
50. Legba Atibon	Legba
51. Legba Avadra Bowa (Legba Vagabond Cute King)	Legba
52. Legba Azouka	Legba
53. Legba Gran Chimen	(Legba of the Great Path) Legba

54. Legba Katawoulo	Legba
55. Legba Kay (House Legba)	Legba
56. Legba Kele Hounde	Legba
57. Legba Kolokoso	Legba
58. Legba Misègba	Legba
59. Legba Sanyan	Legba
60. Legba Ti Yanyan (Little Brightly Colored Legba)	Legba
61. Legba Zankliyan	Legba
62. Loko Djè	Loko
63. Manbo Anayza Pyè (Priestess Anayza Pyè)	Pyè
64. Manbo Dechouke (Priestess of Uprooting)	Grann Èzili
65. Manbo Delayi Mede (Priestess Delayi of Mede)	Èzili
66. Manbo Lasirèn (Mermaid Priestess)	Èzili
67. Manman Jimo (Mother of Twins)	Marasa
68. Manman Wou	Èzili
69. Marasa Dogwe (Patron of Consecutive Twins)	Marasa
70. Marasa Dosa (Patron of Daughter Born after Twins)	Marasa
71. Marasa Dosou (Patron of Son Born after Twins)	Marasa
72. Marasa Elou	Marasa
73. Marasa Jimo (Marasa Twins)	Marasa
74. Marasa Kay (House Marasa)	Marasa
75. Marasa Kreyòl (Creole Marasa)	Marasa
76. Marasa Zensa	Marasa
77. Marasa Zensou	Marasa
78. Mèt Agwe Taroyo	Agwe
79. Mètrès Altagras	Èzili
80. Mètrès Sèvèrin Bèl Fanm	Èzili
81. Minis O'Dan	Dangbesi
82. Naete	Èzili
83. O'Dan Misan Wèdo	Dangbesi
84. O'Dan Wèdo Dienke	Dangbesi
85. O'Dan Wèdo Yèmen	Dangbesi
86. Papa Jimo	Marasa
87. Papa So	Sobo
88. Pyè Aleman	Pyè
89. Pyè Dambara [Danbara]	Pyè
90. Pyè Fere	Pyè
91. Sesilya	—
92. Silibo Vavoun	Èzili
93. Sobo Khesou	Sobo

94. Sobo Naki	Sobo
95. Sobo Wandile	Sobo
96. Vye Legba	Legba
97. Wa Loko Alade	Loko
98. Wandile Janpyè	Pongwe
99. Agwe Taoyo [Tawoyo]	Agwe
100. Legba Choukèt	Legba
101. Madmwazèl Chalòt (Miss Chalòt)	—
102. Tenayiz (Dam) (Lady Tenayiz)	—

The 102 spirits listed for the Rada Rite fall within nineteen families. For example, the family name Dangbesi connects all of the serpent spirits. The spirits' names are often related to the family name. Dangbesi links to Danbala, Dangbe, and O'Dan. In the Fon language, *dàn* means a "serpent" and spirit represented by a piece of iron shaped like a serpent. The family name Dangbesi comes from *Dangbe + si* (Dangbe's spouse), a word still current in Fon (Segurola and Rassinoux 2000, 121).

Several spirits have names that cannot be derived from the spirit family's name: for example, Adjehoun in the Pyè family, Grann Silibo Vavoun in the Èzili family, or Faro Mèdji in the Marasa family. The spirit Adjehoun contains the ubiquitous word *houn*, meaning "drum," "blood," and "spirit" in Fon (Segurola and Rassinoux 2000, 238). The name "Silibo" stems from a Dahomian family name (Courlander 1973, 327). A handful of spirits like Sesilya, Hountò (the spirit of the drum) and Grann Alouba have no family listed in their entries. Most of the family names stand for great Vodou spirits that receive cycles of salutation in the Rada Rite. The order of the spirits and the codified ritual embedded in ceremonies are preserved by *règleman* (ritual rules). In addition to their main name, most of the Rada spirits have revealing epithets. Some of them appear to be surnames of people who served them and became iterations of these spirits: Alazon *Pyè* (Pierre); Atakwa *Mèdji* or Wandile *Janpyè* (Jean-Pierre). Other epithets reflect symbolic features of spirits; for example, the ones attached to the Marasa reflect the spirits' patronage of twins, triplets, and the children born after them (Courlander 1973, 324).

Epithets may annex Creole words that provide insight into the spirit's character; for example, Legba Kay (House Legba) reflects protections at home. Several spirits include familial, social, or political epithets like Grann Ayizan (Granny Ayizan), Papa So (Papa So), Manman Jimo (Mother of Twins), Madmwazèl Chalòt (Miss Chalòt), Mètrès Sèvèrin Bèl Fanm (Mistress Sèvèrin Beautiful Woman), and Minis O'Dan (Minister O'Dan). Legba Gran Chimen (Legba of the Great Path), like other spirits with the name "Gran Chimen," protects travelers on their journeys (Courlander 1973, 319). The spirit Agaou Tonè (Agaou Thunder) is linked to the sky and lightning.

Epithets may point to mythological figures such as Labèl Venus (the Beautiful Venus) or Manbo Lasirèn (Manbo Mermaid), or to marine animals such as Labalèn (the Whale). Evidence that the Rada Rite emanates in part from Aja culture is suggested in the spirit names that include the ethnonym; for example, Grann *Adja* and Grann *Adja*souyangòdò. Harold Courlander noted a female *lwa* named Adja whom he described as having the "arts of pharmacy" (1973, 325). The spirit Adja shows those arts to her initiates when she carries them away to the woods to reveal the secrets of roots and herbs. Adja Bosu is another Adja spirit identified as Dahomian by Courlander (1973, 325) and not included in Beauvoir's list. The village name Avlékété is added in Ayizan *Velekete*. Likewise, the surnames in Grann Adanyi *Wèdo* and Grann Tèsi *Freda* are probably derived from the town of Hueda.

Lastly, several features of the Rada Rite reflect the royal Aja and Dahomian religious cultures. The official spirit of the Agasuvi Aja royal family, Agasou (Agasu in Fon), born of Princess Aligbonon and her leopard lover, Agasu, functioned as the ancestor of leading families in Tado, Allada, Abomey, and Porto-Novo (Segurola and Rassinoux 2000, 20). The fact that Agasou appears in the Rada Rite and not in the Danwonmen Rite of Haitian Vodou suggests that the service to Agasou was incorporated into public Alladan religion, whereas in Dahomey it was exclusive to the royal family.

The Bosou spirits venerated by the kings of Dahomey also appear in Haitian Vodou's Rada Rite, except for Kadya Bosou in the Bosou Rite. In the Fon language, *Bòsú* and *Bōsi* are the male and female "spouses of the Bo." The Bo is an amulet, talisman, spell, or curse created with leaves and other admixtures (Segurola and Rassinoux 2000, 103). The Fon root word *bo* can also be found in the Haitian Creole word *bòkò* (fortune-telling priest). As with Agasou, the Bosou spirits and the *tohosu* cult reflect shared traditions of Allada and Hueda that "migrated" to Dahomey with the latter's Aja founders. These collective traditions were folded into the Rada Rite in Haiti.

There are spirit classifications in Beauvoir's list of Rada spirits that raise questions. Most practitioners consider Èzili Dantò to be a Petwo spirit and Èzili Freda to be a Rada spirit. Beauvoir, however, categorizes Èzili Dantò as a Rada spirit and Èzili Freda Danwonmen as a spirit in the Danwonmen Rite (2008a). Jistis Liben notes that Vodou does not impose a rigid structure on its adherents and that "each homestead strikes in the way it knows" (personal correspondence, 2018). For Liben, Dantò is Petwo and Freda is Rada in the tradition of his upbringing, and that is also how numerous scholars have found it (Brown 2001, 246; Saint-Lot 2003, 141; Déita 2006, 48).

As Beauvoir presents a list without explanations (2008a, 187–96), it is difficult to reconcile differences. I have witnessed several Rada Rite ceremonies in which Èzili Freda received a cycle of salutation and possessed one of her followers. At ceremonies I attended for Èzili Dantò on her feast day in mid-August, the worshippers wore white clothes and a red scarf tied around their head during the daytime. Oungan Michelet Alisma of Société Linto Roi Trois Mystères explains that although Èzili Dantò is a spirit in the Petwo Rite, saluting her in that rite requires completing the Rada Rite *first*, hence the white attire (personal correspondence, 2018). Although Dantò is a Petwo spirit, the Rada Rite ceremony canonically precedes her Petwo Rite. The canonicity of the Rada Rite in Sèvis Ginen ceremonies shows how Rada spirits like Èzili are able to migrate into the Petwo, Nago, or Kongo Rites that follow it.

MOTIVATIONS FOR WORKING WITH RASIN FIGUIER AND RASIN BWA KAYIMAN RECORDINGS

These chapters provide transcriptions, translations, and analyses of the leading Haitian Vodou studio albums published by Mass Konpa Records in Miami. Although hundreds of Vodou songs have been collected in the past century, few of the texts are linked to sound recordings like this project. Georges Vilson's *Kandelab* books, *Notated Haitian Folk and Vodou Songs* in two volumes (2013, 2015), include a set of compact discs. However, the author recorded the material without percussionists or choir; thus, it scarcely resembles the congregational setting. Vilson's books provide valuable music notation but do not interpret the songs. *Alan Lomax in Haiti* (Lomax et al. 2009), a book plus ten compact discs, contains historical material but suffers from the low-fidelity sound quality of the 1930s recordings, and its underwhelming liner notes give only partial transcriptions of the songs. Lois Wilcken's project to digitize the recordings of Frisner Augustin's ensemble, La Troupe Makandal, is a signal effort. A new release of La Troupe Makandal's album *Èzili* (first recorded in 1986) includes Wilcken's liner notes, lyrics, and translations with explanatory texts (Wilcken 2017). Expanding on her approach, I work with the high-fidelity recordings of my personal favorite *rasin* artists.

The music was recorded live in a studio in Haiti, the sound engineered so that the lyrics are audible. In my fieldwork experience, the lyrics of songs recorded in the ceremonial context with a single microphone are difficult to hear because there are many competing sounds. The drumming, clapping, conversations, ritual events, and a dispersed and ambulating circular choir make hearing lyrics a challenge. Although the albums under scrutiny here were not recorded in a worship setting, they are authentic songs performed by practitioners under the best conditions. Unlike a ceremonial context, which can stretch over several hours, the *rasin* recordings I work with provide a compressed idea of the ceremony.

RASIN FIGUIER'S *VODOU LAKAY*

Rasin Figuier's complete album is sequentially introduced in the next sections. The first five songs (1.a–1.e) reflect the content of "track 1" on the compact disc. Although the CD has six tracks, within each track, several distinct but connected songs are assembled. For example, track 1 on *Vodou Lakay* includes five songs, but the rhythm is played uninterrupted throughout the track. There is only a pause in sound between each of the six tracks. These Rada songs about life, order, and rootedness are a small part of the sacred literature in Vodou's expanding canon, but they offer a representative sample of this rite and its culture.

Priyè Ginen

1.a

Dyò ta nou de o.
Dyò ta nou de o, frè o.
Se nan Ginen ki genyen lwa e.
Dyò ta nou de o, frè o, frè o.

Se nan Ginen—ki genyen lwa e.
Dyò ta nou de o, frè o.

Ginen Prayer

1.a

Dyò ta nou de o.
Dyò ta nou de o, oh brother.
Hey, Ginen has lwa.
Dyò ta nou de o, oh brother, oh brother.
It is Ginen—that has lwa, hey.
Dyò ta nou de o, oh brother.

Rasin Figuier opens their album in a style that evokes the beginning sequence of Rada ceremonies in Sèvis Ginen temples. These sequences form lengthy chanted invocations called *priyè Ginen* (Ginen prayer), accompanied by the *ason* (rattle) but no drum pulse (Fleurant 1996, 17). Sitting in a circle or semicircle, initiates recite the prayer from memory for around forty-five minutes. They take a solemn posture fitting their concentration on the spiritual tradition. The *priyè Ginen* is a time for guests to remain respectfully silent.

On this condensed version of the prayer, the *ason* is shaken vigorously, drum rolls build anticipation, and hand clapping breaks into the recording. In the ritual context, however, the *priyè Ginen* is a rich oral document containing information about the spirits, the saints, and the priestly lineage of a given Vodou community. This area of Vodou has received little attention, with the exception of Max Beauvoir's *Lapriyè Ginen* (2008a), which provides the transcription in Haitian Creole of prayers and litanies (*litani*).

The first two lines of song 1.a illustrate a common feature of songs: strings of opaque words that Vodouists call *langaj* (Vodou ritual language), expressions understood by priests and initiates but not by ordinary speakers of Haitian

Creole. The first word of the song, *dyò* (or *djò*), refers to the breath of life that encircles the earth, forming an abode of spiritual beings (Beauvoir 2008b, 28). *Dyò* also refers to those initiated together into Vodou during the same *kanzo* initiation. The second of *Lapriyè Ginen*'s five major texts is titled *Litani Djò* (Djò litany), a document in which the formulation "Sen Djò" (Saint Djò) occurs in the second and third lines of seventy-three out of seventy-nine parts (Beauvoir 2008b, 87–116). For example, no. 66 is: "Yeah all Rada escorts. Saint Djò *do kowa gwa*. Yeah all Rada escorts, our lives are in God's hands, oh *sanyan*" (italicized words are examples of *langaj*).[2] The "Saint Djò" invocation repeats for every important category, including *Gran Pè Etènel* (Eternal Great Father) and the Catholic saints in addition to Vodou and African sources like the spirits. Sen Djò includes the initiated members of the Sèvis Ginen houses, Hounsi Bosal, Hounsi Kanzo, the *manbo* and *oungan* leadership, and the Hountògi drummers. All Vodou categories are within the Sen Djò: *the sacred breath that encircles earth*.

Line 3 affirms Africa and its spiritual dimension in the dyad *Ginen-lwa*, linking sacred history and experience with sacred ancestral geography.

1.b

Yabòdò antaye, ansi an
Ayibobo—Ayibobo, medam.

Nou pral antre nan sobagi a.
—Abobo!
Nou pral antre nan sobagi a la.
Sobagi ladogwesan Mina o.

Avan n antre, fò nou jete dlo.

Nou pral antre nan sobagi a.
—E ago e!
Nou pral antre,
ounsi kanzo ladogwesan.
—Abobo!
Nan sobagi a,
nou pral antre nan sobagi a la.

Sobagi ladogwesan Mina o.

1.b

Yabòdò antaye, ansi an
Ayibobo—Ayibobo, ladies.

We are going to enter the sanctuary.
—Abobo!
We are going to enter this sanctuary.
Oh the sanctuary of the Mina heritage.

Before we enter, we must pour out water.

We are going to enter the sanctuary.
—Hey ago hey!
We are going to enter,
ounsi kanzo of the heritage.
—Abobo!
Into the sanctuary,
we are going to enter into the sanctuary.

Oh the sanctuary of the Mina heritage.

Song 1.b opens with a call-and-response formula that is commonly heard at Vodou ceremonies: *Yabòdò antaye*, called by a *manbo*, and the choral response, *ansi an!* In other transcriptions, it appears in this as: *Djavòdò montayi*, and the response, *Wonsiyon!* (Beauvoir 2008b, 143). These expressions, unknown to most Haitian Creole speakers, have a meaning recognized in Vodou: *Do the Vodou spirits walk with you?* And the response is, *Yes, we are Vodou* (Welele Doubout, personal correspondence, 2017).

Although the words are challenging to link to the Fon language, there are some possibilities: *Yabadaóóó* is a Fon response given to the congratulatory expression *ajámácóóó* (Segurola and Rassinoux 2000, 525). The expression *ansi* or *wonsiyon* appears to be related to the standard Haitian Creole word *ounsi* and originates in the Fon word *hunsì*, "initiated spouse of the spirits." The *hunsì* (and *ounsi*) receive secret teachings and a new spiritual identity during their initiation (Segurola and Rassinoux 2000, 242). The commonly heard expression *yabòdò antaye* that opens the song functions as an organizing formula alerting worshippers about the Rada sacred activity about to commence.

The *manbo*'s formula and the synchronized chorus of several women reflect one of Vodou's key underlying patterns: a strong leader who holds a community together, either woman or man, and a tight-knit group of initiated choir members who are choreographed in their service to the spirits. Women and men sing lead parts, with women outnumbering men in the choir.

The first part of the song is about walking into the sacred space of the *sobagi*— the inner sanctuary of a temple in which the altar forms the focal point. It contains a concrete altar with objects that represent the *lwa*, initiates, and offerings. The door to the *sobagi* is one of the "stations" of the temple that is saluted during each cycle of salutation during a ceremony, and thus is a pillar of Vodou.

In contemporary Benin, the official residence of the national Vodun chief, Daagbo Hounon Houna, is called the Sogbadji. In the Fon language, the word *sɛgbeji* means "original purity" while the words *sɛ* or *so* in Fon refer to "God" (Segurola and Rassinoux 2000). Sogbadji also refers to a neighborhood and its vodun temple in the town of Hueda (Law 2004, 54). The pouring of libations at the *sobagi* is a common trope in Vodou songs, as illustrated in this line: "We're going to pour water at his Sobagi," suggesting that this song comes from the center of the tradition (Beauvoir 2008b, 123).[3]

The praise expressions *ayibobo* in line 2 and *abobo* in line 4 ("praise to the spirits") are related ritual acclamations situating worship within the Rada Rite. They are used in between songs as an expression of jubilation equivalent to "hallelujah" and are related to the Fon language's acclamation, *awòbóbó* (Fadaïro 2001).

The terms *sobagi ladogwesan* in line 6 refer to the Vodou community's (*ladogwesan*) altar room. Vodouists, like all worshippers, gather around a sacred place, the *sobagi*. *Dogwe* or *djògwe* means to be "protected" from evil like spells and *kout poud* (poisonous powder) (Beaubrun 2013, 125).[4] The *dogwe* is a ritual gesture that concludes the cycle of salutation for each spirit in which the priest points the *ason* to the ground while the audience touches the ground and double-taps the left side of their chest with the same right hand.[5]

The phrase "we must pour out water" makes reference to the obligatory libation ritual. Water is a host for the spirits. Lakes, ponds, springs, streams, rivers, and droplets are spiritual symbols. Water basins for spirits are common in temples. Priests carry vessels of water with sprigs of herbs floating on top as they perform a cycle of salutations. Water and herbs are fundamental tools for healing. Saluting the drummers and the *potomitan*, priests pour water libations and bow their heads to the ground. Water libations *feed* the *lwa* who dwell in the earth. Water symbolizes purification and agency in this rite focused on life.

The song contains expressions like *ago*, perhaps related to the Fon expression *agòo* ("attention here," "be vigilant," or "I am here") (Segurola and Rassinoux 2000, 24). *Ago* (or *ago e*) is so common in Haitian Vodou that it should be analyzed functionally as an emphatic word that requests contact with the *lwa*. *Ago* is sung with force at the end of a line to evoke sacred power, and it demarcates a transition between songs like the praise term *ayibobo*.

This song tells of the *ounsi kanzo* entering the sanctuary. They are the initiates, the core of any temple community because they completed the *kanzo* initiation. They completed the *kouche* (lying down) in the *djèvo* (initiation room) for several days, fasted, were fed by spirits (who possess the initiators), studied, sang, and practiced oral tradition and rituals. Some *kanzo* initiations, like those at Société Linto Roi in Miami, for example, require the memorization of printed sacred texts (oungan Michelet Alisma, personal correspondence, 2014). The confinement of the *kouche* is a time when the *lwa* connect to initiates and instruct them through dreams (Métraux 1972, 69).

There are several types of ranking in initiation. While many complete the *kanzo* to become *ounsi senp* (first degree) or *ounsi soupwen* (second degree), fewer become *oungan asogwe* or *manbo asogwe* (highest degree of priesthood). The *kanzo* initiation confers hierarchical titles and functions in the Sèvis Ginen system.[6]

The last line, "Sobagi ladogwesan Mina o" (Oh the sanctuary of the Mina heritage), closes with the African name Mina. The term *Anmin* from *Rit Anmin* (*Anminan*) also memorializes the ethnonym Mina in the name of a Vodou rite. Mina refers to a language, more commonly called Gen, and the people who speak it along the coastal region overlapping Benin and Togo (see also Jil and Jil 2009, 145; Kangni 1989; Hebblethwaite 2015a, 76). Words like *sobagi*, *ounsi*, *ladogwesan*, and Mina are signposts pointing to Rada's roots on the coast of the Bight of Benin.

Bonjou Papa Legba	*Hello Papa Legba*
1.c	1.c
Bonjou Papa Legba, gwo lwa mwen.	Hello Papa Legba, my great lwa.
—Abobo, wi, bonjou, m ap di Alegba.	—Abobo, yes, I'm saying, hello to Alegba.
Bonjou Papa Legba, gwo lwa mwen.	Hello Papa Legba, my great lwa.
Alegba, ban m ti moso.	Alegba, give me a little piece.
Bonjou Papa Legba, gwo lwa mwen.	Hello Papa Legba, my great lwa.
Wi, bonjou Papa Legba, gwo lwa mwen.	Yes, hello Papa Legba, my great lwa.
Alegba papa, ban m ti moso.	Alegba, Papa, give me a little piece.
Bonjou Papa Legba, gwo lwa mwen.	Hello Papa Legba, my great lwa.

Song 1.c is about Papa Legba, called Atibon Legba or Alegba, the keeper of the crossroads, the master of roads, and the guardian of entries (Marcelin 1949, 15). Legba is likened to an underlying force of nature: "Alegba you are wind, push us along, we are butterflies, we'll carry news for them" (Beauvoir 2008b, 100).[7] As gatekeeper, Legba is associated with the *potomitan* in temples, since it is a gate for spirits. Legba is the first spirit greeted in the Rada Rite, and he receives the *mayi* dance before his invocation, the *yanvalou* in his presence, and the *mayi* again before he leaves (Marcelin 1950, 24).

Legba is referred to as *gwo lwa mwen* (my great *lwa*) in the song in reference to his high status. Legba's position as first among spirits is canonical in a pan-African context. In contemporary Fon society, Legba is the spirit of order and disorder and the messenger of other deities (Fadaïro 2001, 115). In Fon religion, Legba's approval is obtained at the beginning of ceremonies with offerings of water, alcohol, and a special food made of corn flour and red cooking oil. In the Nigerian context, Legba is remembered as a king who was deified, a memory kept in Haiti (Déita 1993, 34; Verger 1957). The primacy, intercession, intimacy, and royalty of Legba are shared tropes in Aja-Yoruba and Haitian thought.

As the first spirit, Legba opens the "gates" (*baryè*) and "paths" (*chemen*) for his followers to interact with other spirits. One song makes this clear: "Open the gate Atibon (Legba), so we can pass over to the Lwa!" (Beauvoir 2008b, 243).[8] Legba is the master of the crossroads: "Legba stays in the great path in order to rule" (Beauvoir 2008b, 242).[9] Legba is called "Master of the Great Path"[10] in reference to his role as a protector of travelers and entryways (Beauvoir 2008b, 101).

Legba is an old spirit who requires assistance (Déita 1993, 34). When he possesses a priest in a ceremony, he takes the form of an elderly man who is so crippled and ancient that he cannot support his own weight. Under Legba's force, an able-bodied priest collapses to the ground to be quickly helped up by initiates, who wedge his *beki* (crutches) under his armpits as supports. During his cycle of salutation, the priest's crutches are carried for display by one of his initiated assistants.

This song demonstrates the relationships between the servants and their spirits, and it points to the legacy of migrations that spread Legba veneration in West Africa and the African diaspora. The worshippers greet the spirits with "hello," because they appear before them when they mount the priest or other initiates in ritual. When Legba appears in a Vodou ceremony, after observing Saint Lazarus's shrine, his focus is on greeting his servants. They stand in line to greet him and receive his blessings. Taking turns, each person bows and spins in a formal curtsy as they approach him. They kiss the ground before him, remain on their knees, cross their arms, and offer their pinkies. Legba himself wipes the sweat from his brow and then wipes it on theirs. His strengths are mediation, wisdom, and leadership. The *ti moso* (little piece) requested from Papa Legba suggests a portion of his protection.

Miyanvalou mwen	*My Miyanvalou*
1.d	1.d
Miyanvalou mwen, ago ago!	My Miyanvalou, ago ago!
—Abobo!	—Abobo!
Miyanvalou mwen, ago ago!	My Miyanvalou, ago ago!
Miyanvalou mwen, ago ago!	My Miyanvalou, ago ago!
Gran Chemen bare mwen.	Gran Chemen blocks me.
Miyanvalou mwen, ago ago!	My Miyanvalou, ago ago!
Ankò chemen bare nou la!	Again the path blocks us here!
Miyanvalou mwen, ago ago!	My Miyanvalou, ago ago!
Miyanvalou mwen, ago ago!	My Miyanvalou, ago ago!
Gran Chemen bare mwen.	Gran Chemen blocks me.
Miyanvalou, ounsi kanzo mwen, ladogwesan mwen!	Miyanvalou, my ounsi kanzo, my heritage!
—Abobo!	—Abobo!

Mezanmi,[11] Gran Chemen bare nou la.	Oh my friends, Great Path blocks us here.
Miyanvalou mwen, ago ago!	My Miyanvalou, ago ago!
—Gran Chemen bare mwen.	—Gran Chemen blocks me.

Song 1.d opens with the word *miyanvalou*, which is a variant of the term *yanvalou*. The *yanvalou* is the central drum rhythm and dance of the Rada Rite, delighting the spirits (Welele Doubout, personal correspondence, 2017). The *yanvalou* rhythm features a compound meter that permits both binary and ternary divisions of the beat,[12] allowing for complex drumming patterns to emerge from a "two-against-three" rhythmic structure (Chris Ballengee, personal correspondence, 2019). The tempo of the *yanvalou* is eighty slow pulses per minute with drum breaks called *kase* that are introduced on cue to capture intensification in ritual. The break contradicts or attacks the main rhythmic pattern (Wilcken and Augustin 1992, 52). The *kase* occurs canonically as the *oungan* or *manbo* salutes the stations in a ceremony, whereas it also occurs spontaneously when a drummer detects the signs of spirit possession. Although Vodou drumming is aesthetically beautiful, its main function is to bring spirits down (Wilcken and Augustin 1992, 52).

The dancer of the *yanvalou* embodies the motion of a serpent, curling the spine in an upward to downward flow while circulating the shoulders. The back is somewhat lowered and the arms are held to the hips with the elbow, bending to form a triangle. The *yanvalou* dance was used to greet royalty (Jil and Jil 2009). The Fon words *àvalú* and *j'àvalú* are employed "to pay homage to, to present one's respects to a superior or a group prior to beginning an important action" (Fadaïro 2001, 114). *Àvalú* is to pay the highest tribute: *Un j'àvalú Māwū* (I give praise to God) (Segurola and Rassinoux 2000, 72). In this song, the possessive noun phrase *miyanvalou mwen* means "the honorable tradition that is mine" (Jil and Jil 2009, 93).

"Great Path" (*Gran Chemen*) in line 5 is Atibon Legba. Although he is not explicitly mentioned in the song, "Legba Gran Chemen" is one of his manifestations in the Rada Rite (Beauvoir 2008a, 127, 194). In several Vodou texts, metaphorical aspects of the Great Path capture aspects of Legba's identity: his age, stature, and guidance for travelers. We learn that Gran Chemen has "blocked" (*bare*) the narrator. Other songs for Gran Chemen also touch on the theme: "Gran Chemen is tall, we're blocked" (Beauvoir 2008b, 201).[13] We do not know how the narrator is blocked, but in other songs about Gran Chemen, one hindrance is illness.

The song again returns to the core expressions *ounsi kanzo mwen* (my *ounsi kanzo* [initiated servant of the spirits]) and *ladogwesan mwen* (my heritage), imprinting Sèvis Ginen's initiatory terminology into the song. In a Haitian context in which diverse schools of Vodou are practiced, *kanzo* is a pedigree. One of the main currents of this song is the spirit's interference. The song is a supplication about a consternating situation, a misfortune that tests the narrator's mortal fiber and for which the spirit must lift barriers.

Ala pouvwa	*Oh What Power*
1.e	1.e
Ala pouvwa Ayisyen genyen.	Oh what power Haitians have.
—Abobo!	—Abobo!
Yo pran ason lwa m nan,	They took the ason of my lwa,
yo voye l jete.	they threw it away.
—E ago e!—E ago e!	—Hey ago hey!—Hey ago hey!
Bondye bon, Lesen bon,	God is good, the Saints are good,
Marasa bon.	the Marasa are good.
Yo pran ason lwa m nan,	They took the ason of my lwa,
yo voye l jete.	they threw it away.

This well-known song (1.e) affirms the power of Haitian culture and identity (Beauvoir 2008b, 98). However, the mood of the song is tragic in tone, since the power of some Haitians has been used to throw away Vodou's main symbol of the priesthood, the *ason* (sacred rattle). In the face of that aggression, the narrator asserts that God, the Saints, and the Marasa are good. They form a fixed sort of trinity in many songs (Marcelin 1950, 135).

The *ason* is a rattling instrument and ritual tool that the *oungan* and *manbo* use to salute, call, and send away the spirits (see fig. 2).

A single gourd forms the rattle and handle, while multicolored beads representing the spirits are strung around the exterior of its head. The *ason* is a fundamental part of Sèvis Ginen as the main tool earned in initiation and used in the priesthood. To become a priest is to *pran ason an* (take the *ason*). The sacred instrument is used in ritual, music, spirit invocation, healing, and symbolism. The priest holds it in the right hand and uses it for greetings at the stations within the cycles of salutation. A nonpriestly initiate can also have an *ason* at her or his house for personal use, but during ceremonies only *oungan* and *manbo asogwe* may use it. In the Fon language, *asogwè* or *asogò* is the term used for the *ason*, while *asogwe* refers in Haitian Creole to the one who takes the *ason* as priest (Segurola and Rassinoux 2000, 66). The taking and the throwing away of the *ason* is a grave offense, along the lines of burning a Bible.

Figure 2. An *ason* (shaker). Photo taken by Ben Hebblethwaite at the Tropenmuseum, Amsterdam, 2016.

Song 1.e evokes the goodness of God, the Saints, and the Marasa. The Creole term *Lesen* (the Saints) does not exclude Catholic saints, although it is synonymous with the word *lwa* in Haiti. Another Vodou song confirms this overlap: "Pray for the saints! Shout *abobo* for the *lwa*!" (Marcelin 1950, 135).[14] The Catholic lexical field within Vodou originates in the forced conversion of enslaved people to Christianity. The prohibition of non-Catholic, non-Christian religions resulted in the emergence of camouflaging practices.

Catholic features (like *sen* from *saint*) that were altered semantically in the colonial period presented numerous advantages. For example, knowledge about Catholic culture had appeal, as enslaved people in Saint-Domingue wished to understand French culture and its religion, one of the main projections of French power in the colony. The assimilation of Catholic saints disguised and preserved Vodou culture while subverting Catholic symbols. Vodouists have been so successful that Haitian clergy have abandoned the display of chromolithographs.

The Marasa, the third term in the trio, appear in Rasin Figuier's songs following the order of the Rada Rite, immediately after Papa Legba. Although the term "Marasa" has no match in Fon, the concept of twins, the "Hoho," is of great importance in the Vodun of Benin, especially in families with multiple childbirth. Little clay pots that are joined together honor and symbolize twins, and families with twins conduct annual ceremonies before the earthenware (Lando 2016, 47).

The Marasa are the "Divine Twins," spirits of twins, triplets, quadruplets, and so on. The Marasa spirits have numerous manifestations, like Marasa Dosou Dosa (Zensou, Zensa), Marasa Jimo, and Marasa Bwa. Service for the Marasa is strongest in families with offspring from multiple childbirth. Honorifics for children born after the Marasa include Dosou, Dosa, and Dogwe (Déita 1993, 137). In this way, Vodou provides a way for all of the children to feel special. The Marasa are associated with the family, parents, children, and the love that binds them, as illustrated in this song: "Marasa, here is the water, here is the food! Family, assist your family. Parents, assist your parents" (Beauvoir 2008b, 298).[15]

A hearty pot of *manje marasa* (twins' food) is prepared at ceremonies. Sweet potatoes, potatoes, plantains, yams, pumpkin, eggplant, squash, millet porridge, ground corn, red beans, peas and rice, and herring bouillon are combined with meat from sacrificed pigeons, chickens, turkeys, or goats (Marcelin 1950, 136).[16] The Marasa receive the cooked food in the morning, and in the afternoon children eat the lion's share left behind.

According to Vodou mythology, the Marasa suffered the pain of forcible separation from family during the slave trade, and so they now support the living who have likewise suffered separation and personal tragedy. This song illustrates their consolation: "I come from Ginen, I don't have family. Marasa is family"[17]; and "I don't have family, who is going to speak for me? Marasa is family!"[18] Another important role of the Marasa is intercession with God; for example, "Marasa spirits, beseech God on my behalf"[19]; or, "Marasa spirits, call God for me"[20] (Beauvoir 2008b, 298–99).

At ceremonies in the Rada Rite, the Marasa's cycle of salutation includes a spread of sweets, bread, and pastries on a woven rice-husking disc (*laye*). Servers offer initiates and the audience one of the treats on the *laye* at the close of the cycle of salutation, illustrating a communal feature of the ceremony.

Stories circulate about the influence that human twins exert upon families and on the revenge that they take if displeased or jealous (Déita 1993, 135). To temper their envies, families must treat them identically (Marcelin 1950, 132). If jealousies are left unchecked, a twin can hurt her or his twin or a family member. They should receive a service on Christmas, the Epiphany, and Easter Saturday

(Marcelin 1950, 137). Having an extra finger at birth is also attributed to the influence of the Marasa (oungan Michelet Alisma, personal correspondence, 2014).

This account of the *ason* that was thrown away is the central tension—the solution suggested is the steadfast affirmation of Rada's philosophy of life, order, and rootedness in God, the Saints (spirits), and the Marasa. The presence of the Marasa in this trio underscores the distinctness of this category. God is one, Marasa is two, and the Saints are many. Furthermore, a trio of concepts is a recurrent structure in Vodou songs and Haitian society: for instance, *twa wòch dife* (three fire stones [for cooking]), *twa fèy, twa pawòl* (three leaves, three words [initiatory words]), *Marasa Twa* (Marasa Three), *Twa Wa* (Three Kings), and *Latrinite* (the Trinity). God, the Marasa, and the Saints form a triple defense and a concise summary of Vodou theology.

Manyanva	*Utmost Respect*
2.a	2.a
Manyanva, manyanvalou Loko.	Respect, utmost respect to Loko.
—Abobo!—E ago e!	—Abobo!—E ago e!
—Asanble kilti sa!	—Assemble this culture!
Mayanva, nou wè!	Respect, we see!
Manyanva, manyanvalou Loko.	Respect, utmost respect to Loko.
Ki di sa a, manyanvalou e!	Who says this, respect, hey!
Manyanva ounsi kanzo Ladogwesan yo.	Respect ounsi kanzo of the Heritage.
Manyanvalou Loko.	Respect to Loko.
Lanj Gabriyèl ki di sa a—	The angel Gabriel said this—
Manyanvalou e!	hey manyanvalou!
Papa Loko ki di sa—manyanvalou e!	Papa Loko said this—hey respect!

Song 2.a is for Papa Loko (Loko Djè), the *third* spirit after Legba and the Marasa in the Rada Rite. Loko is the spirit of trees and plants. Loko is a priest who minds the *ounfò* (temple) and protects the priesthood. He confers the *ason* through initiation. The *fête de l'arbre* (celebration of the tree) takes place on the last Friday in May and is the occasion of ceremonies in which people who were healed by Loko place chipped cups or plates at the foot of his trees around Haiti. Supplicants light his candles and hang clothing worn during the period

of illness in the tree's branches as a testimony of the spirit's grace. Taking a bath in a curative spring, a sick person suspends her or his clothing from a tree so that Loko will do healing work (Marcelin 1949, 44–45). As a spirit of healing, priestly knowledge, and plant-based medicine, Loko's qualities reflect the best attributes of priests. Always loved, he is criticized in some songs for being too talkative and indiscreet (Marcelin 1949, 48).

He is honored with the *yanvalou* drum rhythm and dance, hence the expression, *miyanvalou Loko*. Loko is present in other West African rites of Sèvis Ginen like the Ibo Rite.[21] Once in Haiti, Loko also migrated into the Central African Makaya Rite.[22] Spirits from the rites of the founder ethnicities in Saint-Domingue, in particular the Aja- and Fon-speaking people, tended to migrate into the rites of the ethnic groups that appeared later in colonial history.[23]

Loko appeared in a ceremony to greet his servants with a pickaxe propped up on his shoulder at Société Linto Roi in Miami, a variant of the big stick that Milo Marcelin (1950, 41) describes him as holding. Loko loves farmers, and he is deeply attached to nature (Déita 1993, 97). He is linked to Emperor Dessalines, Haiti's first ruler (1804–1806): "Lanperè Desalin o Loko Dewaze" (Beauvoir 2008b, 255). Furthermore, there is an oral tradition that Dessalines served Loko (Marcelin 1949, 42). Loko is associated with empowering magical charms (*pwen*) in some songs: "King Loko, you already gave me the Charm" (Beauvoir 2008b, 255).[24] As the patron of sanctuaries and ceremonies, he watches over initiations.

The name Loko in Dahomey/Benin and Saint-Domingue/Haiti is linked to a majestic tree. The *iroko*, *roko*, or loko tree is among the tallest in West Africa, considered sacred alongside the baobab (Lando 2016, 56). Loko and *iroko* are Fon, Ibo, and Yoruba words for the gargantuan African teak trees (*Milicia excelsa*) (Segurola and Rassinoux 2000, 339). In Benin, people do not reside in compounds that include an *iroko* tree, since the species is an intermediary between earth and sky spirits, requiring some distance from settlements (Lando 2016, 56). Maps of Dahomey and Benin show places that have the name, including Loco-Atoui, Lokokanmé, Lokonkouané, and Lokossa.[25] Sacred trees and forests are natural ceremonial and ecological sites protected for centuries (Lando 2016, 58). In Haiti, Loko's *pye repozwa* (resting tree) is the *Jatropha curcas* (*medecinier béni*) (Marcelin 1949, 41). The tree-cutting taboos observed in Dahomey with respect to sacred trees are also widely noted in the Caribbean (Tarter 2015).

The song mentions that the angel Gabriel wills the assembly of Vodouists. "Angel" comes from the Greek word *angelos* (a translation of the Hebrew *mal'ākh*, "messenger") (Olson 1990, 29). The angel Gabriel here echoes Loko, adding gravity to the request. Biblical features point to an attitude of naturalizing foreign influences. Vodouists are aware of Gabriel's standing in Catholic and biblical tradition. His incorporation points to "cultural appropriation" and parallelism in Vodou. Gabriel complements Loko, implying that they operate on similar spiritual levels. As can be seen with Catholic chromolithographs, the long-term effect of the inclusive attitude is the gradual Vodouization of foreign features. The cultural politics of Vodouization expresses xenophilia as well as a subversion of hegemony, raising the observation that cultural appropriations may reify central control, or instead resist and disrupt it.

Va Loko

2.b

Frè Loko, Loko Vade.
Va Loko, Loko Vade.
Miyanvalou Loko, Loko Vade.
Va Loko, Loko Vade.
Miyanvalou Loko—Loko Vade.

Go Loko

2.b

Brother Loko, Loko Vade.
Va Loko, Loko Vade.
Respect Loko, Loko Vade.
Go Loko, Loko Vade.
Respect Loko—Loko Vade.

Song 2.b is a second song of praise to Loko. Loko Vade is one of the manifestations of the Loko *lwa* alongside Azagon Loko, Loko Atisou, Loko Kisigwè, and others (Hebblethwaite et al. 2012, 259). The variants "Loko Vade" and "Loko-De" appear in several songs (Marcelin 1949, 42). In addition to Papa Loko (Daddy Loko), he is called Frè Loko (Brother Loko), and is therefore a spirit who is like a beloved family member. Likewise, Bondye, Loko, the *manbo* and *oungan*, and the congregation link up in a spiritual family. In domestic, national, and royal Dahomian expressions of Vodou or Vodun, the concept of family travels on a biological and spiritual continuum.

Agaou Gwonde

2.c

Agaou gwonde o—Yabòdò!
Agaou gwonde nan peyi a.
Agaou gwonde o.
Agaou gwonde nan peyi a.
Se fò,
ou mèt mete lepyè a, e.
Agaou gwonde e nan peyi a.

Mwen di se fò

Agaou Roared

2.c

Oh Agaou roared—Yabòdò!
Agaou roared in the country.
Oh Agaou roared.
Agaou roared in the country.
It is strength,
you can put your feet back, hey.
Hey Agaou roared in the country.

I say it is strength

—ou mèt mete lepyè a.	—you can put your feet back.
Eya, Agaou gwonde nan peyi a.	Oh yeah, Agaou roared in the country.
Agaou gwonde,	Agaou roared,
ounsi kanzo Ladogwesan o!	ounsi kanzo of the Heritage!
—Abobo!—E ago e!	—Abobo!—E ago e!
Agaou gwonde—nan peyi a!	Agaou roared—in the country!

The title of song 2.c, *Agaou Gwonde* (Agaou Roared [or Rumbled]), captures the formidable character of this powerful spirit, associated with storms, lightning, and earthquakes. When Agaou possesses a person (see Beauvoir 2008b, 193), he is known for his *vole* (jumping), energy, and tree-climbing abilities (Welele Doubout, personal correspondence, 2018). The words "put your feet back" make reference to the ground in Agaou's flight. As Welele Doubout notes, "Agaou doesn't mess around," meaning that he is feared and respected.[26] Agaou punishes his horses for disloyalties such as conversion to Protestantism (Marcelin 1949, 103–4).

Songs in other collections refer to Agaou as a "handsome man," a "guy with a sickle," a "general," and a "Vodou priest" (Beauvoir 2008b, 89–90).[27] One song line, "Oh Agaou comes from Anminan,"[28] suggests that the spirit originates among the Mina people now settled in coastal Togo and southwest Benin. His epithets show that Agaou is linked to religious, masculine, natural, and beastly descriptors, reflecting totemic and perhaps military attributes. Agaou receives several ingredients in his sacred food, including millet stuffed into a mixture of sweet potatoes, yams, plantains, and crushed okra, as if each ingredient represented a dimension of his power (Marcelin 1949, 105).

Agaou's descent can be "dangerous" in the sense that the spirit's horse may engage in what appears to be dangerous behavior. At a Petwo-Kongo ceremony for Agaou at Société Linto Roi in Miami, this aspect of the spirit's character was visible. The *oungan* was dressed in multicolored attire with red strips of cloth tied around his shoulders and waist, and his head was coiffed with a bright red bandana. The spirit's horse toked on a cigar and greeted his followers. Taking a large swig of rum, he sprayed mist three times on the chest of an initiate. Puffing on the cigar, he blew smoke over his machete as a blessing before embracing his servant with a formal greeting, which entails moving his head from right to left and touching his servant's forehead with his own, in a three-part gesture. Pulling several of his followers from the audience, Agaou belted out a song about himself in his thunderous voice. With the flat part of his machete, the spirit pounded his horse's chest three times. Drawing a few worshippers near, Agaou took a moment to give his advice. Moments later, with the flat part of his machete blade, he slapped the *potomitan*.

As the possession moved to its culmination, assistants of the priest laid a small red cloth on the ground next to a small statue of the spirit's corresponding saint, Saint Michael. A pile of glass shards was spread on the red cloth, and Agaou's horse, the *oungan*, stood on top of the glass shards barefooted. As the possessed *oungan* stood on the shards unharmed, the Vodou *ounsis* circled around him, sang, and danced while holding his offerings of cake and food above their heads in a single-file processional. The spirit was there to revel in the preparations his followers had made. As this unfolded, the worshippers sang, "What magical powers Agaou possesses,"[29] a reference to the unscathed horse standing on shards of glass.

This song typifies the style of repeating a small number of the spirit's attributes. The word *gwonde* (roared) occurs more than eight times in the basic transcription, illustrating the aesthetic of conciseness and incantation. Similarly, the song praises the *ounsi kanzo*, revealing through repetition the elevation of initiation.

Ayizan Gogo	*Ayizan Gogo*
2.d	2.d
Ayizan gogo,	Ayizan gogo,
—Abobo!	—Abobo!
Ayizan golado, Ayizan gogo,	Ayizan golado, Ayizan gogo,
Ayizan golado m,	my Ayizan golado,
ala fanm a yo fre.	oh how fresh their women are.
—E ago e!	—E ago e!
Ala fanm a yo fre, ago e.	Oh how fresh their women are, ago hey.
Ago, nou la, Danbala Wèdo.	Ago, we are here, Danbala Wèdo.
Ago, nou la, Ayida Wèdo.	Ago, we are here, Ayida Wèdo.
Mare frè ki	Tie up the brother
pral kondwi m ale, ago e.	who is going to escort me away, ago e.
Ayizan gogo, Ayizan gogo,	Ayizan gogo, Ayizan gogo,
Ayizan golado!	Ayizan golado

Song 2.d calls upon the female spirit Ayizan, protector of freshwater, markets, public places, doors, and gates (Marcelin 1949, 29). Legba, Loko, and Ayizan walk together in Vodou ceremonies. An elder *manbo*, Ayizan is Loko's spouse, equaling him in every domain. Chapter 2 examined the deep transatlantic affinities reflected in Ayizan Velekete and her coastal linguistic cousin in Benin, the village of Avlékété.

Ayizan "dances in the heads" of many *manbo* priestesses (Marcelin 1949, 33). Although she is a distinct spirit in Haiti, in Dahomey/Benin the "Aizan" are erected in the center of markets to watch over businesses and expel evil spirits (Lando 2016, 47). Ayizan is the "great divinity of Allada and among the Pedah people," and the "vodun of the market in Hueda" and of the "brush" (Brand 2000b, 20). In the Rada Rite, Ayizan appears immediately after her husband, Papa Loko. Ayizan has several names, including Ayizan Gwèto (Beauvoir 2008a, 194). Gwèto (or Gwètò) is one who possesses wisdom (Beauvoir-Dominique and Dominique 2003, 90).

Welele Doubout notes that the names *Ayizan golado* and *Ayizan gogo* in lines 1 and 3 are "places" where Ayizan is served (personal correspondence, 2016), an intuition perhaps reflected in Dahomian place-names like Gololouhoué, Golo-Djigbé, Golo-Tokpa, and Gogbo (US Office of Geography 1965, 32). Cartographic analysis reveals that toponyms are common features in the naming of Vodou spirits.[30]

Ayizan is the spirit that protects temples, and, as Loko's partner and counterpart, she attends to initiation. One song declares "Ayizan is great," and another calls her "manbo Ayizan,"[31] reflecting her patronage of priestesses (Beauvoir 2008a, 121). Several songs point to a spirit linked to movement, for example "Ayizan walks,"[32] "Ayizan went strolling,"[33] and "I'm going to saddle my horse in order to do a tour of the country"[34] (Beauvoir 2008a, 121–22). Another important attribute of Ayizan is her abhorrence of alcohol, an attitude that permeates the Rada ceremony until Èzili Freda's cycle.

The *palmier royal* (*Roystonea regia* or Florida royal palm) symbolizes Ayizan, and Haiti generally. The palm tree's fronds are associated with power and freedom, appearing in the coat of arms in President Alexandre Pétion's Haitian flag. Traditionally, palm leaves covered the *peristil* (temple dance floors) in order to enshroud the worship space in Ayizan's purifying atmosphere. Sick people, pregnant women, and menstruating women cannot participate in a ceremony "if they don't have their Ayizan on them, because, being impure, they would spoil the ceremony" (Marcelin 1949, 32).

Offerings are placed on palm leaves. After Ayizan's cycle, the *ounsi* initiates braid out of palm leaves a loose palm-frond staff in her honor. They spend several minutes weaving it together while singing to the beating drums. When the woven staff—also called the *ayizan*—is completed, one initiate, usually a female, carries it wrapped in a white cloth over her shoulders with both arms slung over the ends.

The culmination of the Ayizan sequence now draws near. Guided by the shaking *ason* held by an *oungan*, the female carrier of the *ayizan* palm staff dances and greets the canonical stations in the temple. Near the end of the salutations of the stations, the drummers' tempo quickens, and the priest who guides the one carrying the *ayizan* intensifies his attitude. Eyes locked on the carrier of the *ayizan*, the priest speaks assertively, calling forth the spirit from deep within the worshipper's body. Commanding the spirit, the priest's head cocks slightly to one side as he calls on Ayizan. While making the last circumambulation around the *potomitan* with the priest, dancing and spinning with increasing force, briefly, but vigorously, the bearer of the *ayizan* transforms into Ayizan. Surrounded by priests and initiates who protect the spirit's spinning horse from harm, they swiftly guide her out of the public *peristil* dance area and into the privacy of the altar room, where the spirit departs and the person returns.

Another domestic ceremony for Ayizan recorded by Marcelin (1949, 35–36) entailed the *ounsi*'s creation of an *ayizan* from the royal palm leaf. Rather than possessing an initiate, however, the presiding *oungan* called the spirit through a *zen* (clay jar) covered in white satin and channeled Ayizan. A week or two later, the *zen* was installed with food offerings on the family altar so that Ayizan could be called upon when needed.

Song 2.d implores Danbala Wèdo and Ayida Wèdo to tie up a "brother" who threatens Ayizan, revealing the personal intervention of the spirits. The threats of the "brother" also reveal tension in the familial discourse, compared with the affectionate tone of song 2.b for Loko.

Wèdo

3.a

Djobodo antaye, ansi an, ayibobo!

Ayibobo, medam!

Wèdo, m rele Wèdo,
ki lwa sa?
Danbala Wèdo!
—Abobo!—E ago e!
M ape mande ki lwa sa,
yo di m se Wèdo.
Vini mande o ki lwa sa,
yo di m se Wèdo la,
lwa m nan!

Wèdo

3.a

Djobodo antanye, ansi an, ayibobo!

Ayibobo, ladies!

Wèdo, I call Wèdo,
Which lwa is this?
Danbala Wèdo!
—Abobo!—E ago e!
I am asking which lwa is this,
they tell me it's Wèdo.
Come ask which lwa this is,
they tell me it's Wèdo here,
my lwa!

Songs 3.a–3.c are all dedicated to Danbala Wèdo, the serpent spirit. His traditions in Haiti and those of his counterpart, Dangbe, at the Temple of the Pythons in Hueda, Benin, resonate in communities around the world (Alexander 2017).

In Haitian Vodou, Danbala Wèdo and Ayida Wèdo, husband and wife, belong to the Dangbesi family (Beauvoir 2008a, 194–96). They are associated with fecundity, force, nature, rainbows, purity, the cause of initiation, good fortune, and goodness (Marcelin 1950, 55). Danbala and Ayida are worshiped as sky spirits in Haiti and Dahomey. Physical snakes do not usually represent Danbala Wèdo in Haitian temples; instead, white eggs, flour, and an iron serpent statue on the altar are used (Marcelin 1950, 56).

In Rada Rite ceremonies, when Danbala descends upon a worshipper, he or she falls to the ground to slither and roll like a serpent. This sequence of events is only briefly visible, as the spirit's horse is quickly covered with a white sheet before edging toward the altar room. Danbala possessions may involve the dispensing of wisdom or the precipitous climbing of a tree. The spirit is eventually coaxed down, given an offering, and covered with a white sheet to send the spirit off (Marcelin 1949, 62–63).

Danbala Wèdo and Ayida Wèdo intertwine their bodies under the water to support the earth. Snakes master the elements as they climb, glide, and swim in a natural temple of water, springs, caves, roots, and trees. The snake's natural qualities of adaptability and omnipresence reflect the Rada values of nature and ecology. Danbala Wèdo and Ayida Wèdo were the first *lwa* created by God, a myth that points to the centrality of the animal world in Vodou thinking (Jil and Jil 2009, 86).

The Danbala sequence in song 3.a opens with the ritual formula "Djobodo antaye, ansi an, ayibobo" (Do the Vodou spirits walk with you?—Yes, we are Vodou!). Here, the formula demarcates the transition to the next cycle of salutation and serves as a formal boundary giving way to the three-song sequence for Danbala. This homage to Danbala Wèdo reflects a common layering of three songs during the cycle of salutation.

The terms used to refer to Danbala include "Master Danbala"[35] and the affectionate "Papa Danbala," the "the snake spirit."[36] Danbala is "sacred,"[37] and he is associated with the purity of "Guinea or ancestral Africa,"[38] as opposed to the alleged corruption[39] of "the Creoles"[40] (i.e., the culture of the Saint-Domingue colony and its sequels). He and Ayida require a "water basin"[41] where they rest (Beauvoir 2008b, 153–55; Marcelin 1949, 58).[42] Ayida Wèdo is called "Mistress Ayida"[43] or "Danbala's Mistress."[44]

In Benin, the serpent spirit Danbadahwèdó is attested in the Fon language (Segurola and Rassinoux 2000, 121). Ayidohwèdó in Benin's Vodun culture is linked to the rainbow, just as Ayida Wèdo is the rainbow spirit in Haiti. Dan in Benin is the patron of space, matter, and movement, like the water in the Oueme and Wo Rivers (Brand 2000b, 26). Ayida Wèdo is a spirit of freshwaters whose colors are blue and white (Marcelin 1949, 69).

Song 3.a is organized around a statement, a question, and an answer: the calling of Wèdo, a question about who Wèdo is, and the answer, *Danbala* Wèdo.

In line 5, the pronoun "I" clarifies who is asking, and in line 6, "they" (*yo*) provide the answer. Line 7, "Vini mande ..." (Come ask ...), invites communication with the *lwa*. The final line captures the narrator's relationship to the spirit—it is *her* spirit.

Danbala Wèdo Lasous o	*Oh Danbala Wèdo of the Springs*
3.b	3.b
Danbala Wèdo	Danbala Wèdo,
lasous o, m a prale.	oh to the springs, I am going.
M poko rive,	I had yet not arrived,
m tande teta nan dlo mande,	I heard tadpoles in the water ask,
kote y a wè mwen?	where will they see me?
M poko rive la,	I had not arrived there yet.
m tande O'Dan o do.	I heard O'Dan from behind.
M poko parèt la	I had not appeared there yet
epi m tande O'Dan.	and I heard O'Dan.
M pral salye drapo mwen	I am going to salute my flag
pou m ale ...	so I can go ...
epi wouch ...	and woosh ...
Abobo! E ago e!	Abobo! E ago e!
Danbala Wèdo,	Danbala Wèdo,
m pral salye drapo lwa m nan!	I am going to salute the flag of my lwa!
O do m ap salye drapo mwen	Upon my back, I will salute my flag
pou m ale!	so I can go!
Ayida Wèdo,	Ayida Wèdo,
m pral salye drapo lwa m nan!	I am going to salute the flag of my lwa!
O do, m ap salye drapo mwen	Upon my back, I will salute my flag
pou m ale!	so I can go!

Song 3.b immerses listeners in Danbala's natural environment, reflecting the ecological dimension of Rada. Features of the sacred natural world include the *sous* (spring), Danbala's resting place, and the talking *teta* (tadpoles) who ask about the song's narrator (Déita 2006, 14). According to Marcelin (1949, 111), the *teta nan dlo* is one of Agwe's epithets. The song suggests parallel worlds, one of living beings and the other of their spirit namesakes.

Danbala Wèdo, Simbi, and Loko are considered the "Masters of the Water,"[45] dwelling near sacred springs and protecting or punishing people through them (Marcelin 1950, 56). If two snakes live near a river where two basins have formed, the basins are dedicated to Danbala and Ayida (Marcelin 1950, 71). Before arriving at the spring, the narrator "hears" the talking tadpole and O'Dan.[46] After discovering the proximity of Danbala, the song shifts to the salutation of the ritual flags, a part of ceremonial worship in which the two sacred flags of a temple are presented publicly.

Two flags representing the founding spirits of the temple are displayed: spirits like Danbala and Èzili are commonly paired in those roles. The sequined ritual flags of Vodou display images of saints or *vèvè* (diagrams of spirits), designed from beads and sequins that are sewn onto colored cloth. In the sequence, the *laplas* (master of ceremonies) leads the *pòt drapo* (flag bearers) in a quick-paced dance around the *potomitan* while clasping a sword tied with a red scarf. The presentation of the flags takes place before the sequence dedicated to Ogou, spirit of defense and war. The red scarf tied to the sword's hilt indicates Ogou's involvement. A closing feature of the flags sequence includes the *ounsi* and members of the audience, who briefly touch the base of the flagpole. As in the Marasa cycle, a tactile ritual illustrates the participative, unifying rituals of the Rada Rite.

Nou tout blan	*We Are All in White*
3.c	3.c
Sa se Rasin Figye!	This is Rasin Figuier!
O nou tout blan e!	Oh we are all in white!
—Abobo!	—Abobo!
Danbala Wèdo, basen reken an ki tonbe nan Figye a, eya,	Danbala Wèdo, the basin of sharks who fell into the Figye, oh yeah.
O nou tout blan e!	Oh we are all in white!
—O nou tout blan, medam!	—Oh we are all in white, ladies!
Basen sa pase Danbala Wèdo.	This basin is because of Danbala Wèdo.
Basen sa pase Ayida Wèdo.	This basin is because of Ayida Wèdo.
O nou tout blan, e.	Oh we are all in white, hey.
Nout tout blan, medam.	We are all in white, ladies,
—Ayibobo!	—Ayibobo!
Ki tonbe nan figye a ?	Who fell into the fig tree?
—Eya nou tout blan e.	—Hey yeah, we are all in white.

Song 3.c's title, *Nou tout blan* (We Are All in White), refers to the color of the clothing worn by worshippers of the Rada Rite, in addition to Danbala's own color. White eggs, flour, chalk, cloth, and sheets stand for the purity of Danbala Wèdo and the Rada Rite. In addition to the reference to "white," some other songs mention "blue," which is also Danbala's color, in addition to rose (Marcelin 1949, 64). White stands for the moral strength of the ancestry.

Although Danbala's basin has positive connotations, this song refers to the threatening "basin of sharks."[47] Yvrose and Jerry Gilles (personal correspondence, 2016) suggest that song 3.c shows that the ancestral heritage provides servants of the spirits with a moral compass to navigate through the basin of sharks, which is the world of predation where greed and ferocity drive the powerful to devour the vulnerable. The shark basin is a place where small fish, like the members of Rasin Figuier, would fall prey to the sharks, were they not to embody the virtues and moral strength of Danbala and Ayida. In adherence to their path, the members of Rasin Figuier exclaim the moral and spiritual preparations needed to survive the wickedness of this world.

Èzili Freda Dawomen

3.d

Èzili Freda, o Alada Dawomen,
o kay mwen.
—Abobo!
M ape rele mètrès
ki soti anba dlo,
se fanm chans mwen.
—E ago e
—Pale, pale, pale medam, wi!
Si Zota pa ta o kay mwen.
M ape rele mètrès—manbo—
ki soti anba dlo,
se fanm chans mwen.
M ape rele mètrès
ki soti anba dlo
—se fanm chans mwen

Èzili Freda Dawomen

3.d

Ezili Freda, oh Alada Dahomey,
oh my home.
—Abobo!
I will call the mistress
who comes from under water,
she is my good luck woman.
—Hey ago hey!
—Speak, speak, speak ladies, yes!
If Zota wasn't in my house.
I will call the mistress—manbo—
who comes from under water,
she is my good luck woman.
I will call the mistress
who comes from under water—
she is my good luck woman.

In song 3.d, Èzili Freda is presented with an Alladan and a Dahomian connection, and indeed the Èzili spirits appear in both the Rada Rite and the Danwonmen Rite (Beauvoir 2008a, 187).[48] Èzili is the spirit of beauty, flirtatiousness, and unconventional love. Prostitutes, homosexuals, and virgins serve the fierce Èzili Dantò (Dayan 1995, 63; Tinsley 2018, 69). She is pictured with long, seductive hair and wearing luxurious clothing (Marcelin 1949, 77). She loves champagne, perfume, lotion, soap, toothpaste, toothbrushes, and makeup.

Èzili Freda is the sensual and lovely member of the family, hinted at in her preference for pale rose or pink (Marcelin 1949, 85). She shows the traits of the self-absorbed lover, satisfying various male *lwa* as their mistress, including Agwe Tawoyo, Danbala Wèdo, and Ogou Badagri, for whom she wears three rings (Marcelin 1949, 78). As their lover, she is also the *matlòt* (rival) of Agwe's wife, Lasirèn, and Danbala's wife, Ayida Wèdo, spirits with whom she argues in the mythology (Déita 2006, 48).

Possessing women or men in a ceremony, Èzili Freda fawns, primps, pouts, admires her reflection in mirrors, brushes her hair, washes her face, sprays Florida water perfume, and displays an air of self-centeredness. She likes to be pampered, to have her mirror handed to her, to be offered jewelry and served champagne. Èzili Freda is an alluring, light-skinned figure, while Èzili Dantò is a maternal Black figure, a mimicry of the sexualization and excess of mixed race women and the maternalization and violation of Black women in Saint-Domingue (Alexandra Cenatus, personal correspondence, 2018; Dayan 1995, 64). There are "good," "evil," "elderly," and "shriveled" manifestations of Èzili, reflecting the multiple guises of women in the colony (Dayan 1995, 56).

Some have claimed that Èzili is a Haitian spirit (Dayan 1995, 58). However, the spirit Azlì or Azili is still served today in the Fon language area of Benin. Azlì dwells in the waters of Lake Azili that surround the island of Agonvè, located on the left bank of the Oueme River (Brand 2000b, 7). In addition to their common traits, major differences include leprous male manifestations of Azlì in Fon culture (Tossounon 2012).

Line 1 focuses on Èzili Freda's origins. The insertion of the vocative voice suggests the irretrievability of these lost homes: "Oh Allada Dahomey." As is the case with many Vodou spirits, the name situates Èzili geographically in Allada. Although this song is the product of Haitian Creolization, it demonstrates the importance of African geographical encoding in Caribbean songs. It also suggests that the song comes from a period after the Dahomian conquest of the kingdom of Allada in 1724, perhaps coming from the Alladan captives sold by King Agaja after 1724.

Line 4 says that Èzili Freda is a "mistress," repeating her moniker "Mistress Èzili."[49] Èzili brings her servants good luck as revealed in the fixed expression *fanm chans* (good luck woman). Line 8 encourages female independence and agency. The mention of "Zota" in line 9 is unclear, but it may be a personal admonition. Lines 10–15 reprise lines 4–6, adding that Èzili is a *manbo* while reiterating that she is loved for the good fortune she brings about.

Dieula

3.e

Do, Ewa! Do, Ewa! Do, Ewa!

Èzili k ap dodo la.
Dodo Jozèt!
—Anhan!
Dodo Sara!
—Anhan!
Dodo Rita!
Gade, Dadi k ap dodo la.
M a di, dodo Jozèt!
—Rasin Figye k ap dodo la!

Dieula

3.e

Do, oh God! Do, oh God! Do, oh God!

Èzili is sleeping here.
Sleep, Jozèt!
—Oh yeah!
Sleep, Sara!
—Oh yeah!
Sleep, Rita!
Behold, Dadi is sleeping here.
I will say, sleep Jozèt!
—Rasin Figye is sleeping here!

In song 3.e, the Haitian Creole name Dyela means "God is here." Names prefixed with *Dye-* (Dieu), like "Dieudonné," are common, so Dyela is likely dedicated to a person. The theme of the song is *dodo* (to sleep) in its familiar form. The first line's three utterances of *do*, interrupted by the exclamation *Ewa!* (oh God!), seem to involve the truncation of *dodo* to *do-* combined with *ewa*. The term *ewa* refers to the supreme being, offering a comment on the title Dieula (God is here) (Welele Doubout, personal correspondence, 2019).

The spirit Èzèt and her followers, including Jozèt, Sara, Rita, Dadi, and the members of Rasin Figuier, are sleeping. The song may be a *chante pwen* (song of criticism) that criticizes the members of the group for their excessive resting. Even though Haitians say that spirits never sleep (*lwa pa dodo*), Èzili's sleeping in this song may represent the group's inaction in an unnamed area (Welele Doubout, personal correspondence, 2017).

Agwe, Vodou miwa

4.a

Djobodo antaye, ansi an,
Ayibobo—Ayibobo!
Ayibobo, medam—Ayibobo!
Agwe, Vodou miwa e.
Abobo, e ago e

Agwe, Vodou Mirror

4.a

Djobodo antaye, ansi an,
Ayibobo—Ayibobo!
Ayibobo, ladies—Ayibobo!
Agwe, mirror of the spirits.
Abobo, hey ago hey

Agwe Tawoyo, Vodou miwa e.	Agwe Tawoyo, mirror of the spirits.
Agwe, Vodou miwa, ase.	Agwe, mirror of the spirits, of power.
Agwe, Vodou miwa e.	Agwe, mirror of the spirits, hey.
—E Ago e!—Abobo!	—E Ago e!—Abobo!

In song 4.a, Rasin Figuier calls upon Agwe Tawoyo, the admiral, minister of the navy, and supreme master of the sea and all islands (Marcelin 1949, 103–4). One of his titles is *Mèt* (Master) Agwe Tawoyo. Waves and tides, islands, navigation, and safe harbor are the signs of this oceanic spirit (Marcelin 1949, 107). Agwe's *vèvè* displays his boat, named *Imamou*, and in ceremonies it takes the form of a wooden chair and oar. During an Agwe possession, the horse sits in his wooden chair, rows with his ritual oar, makes the mouth of a fish, and bulges his eyes.

Dahomian King Agaja's royal symbol was a boat like the one used to represent Agwe's *vèvè*. Agwe's color is light blue, although his worshippers remain clad in white for his services (Marcelin 1949, 103). There are a few other Agwe *lwa* in the Rada Rite, including Agwe Mede and Agwe Tawoyo. Master Agwe is married to Lasirèn, a mermaid *lwa*. In one song for Agwe, he is called "Dahomian Guy," suggesting that the song reflects the period after King Agaja of Dahomey took Allada in 1724, as is also seen in song 3.d for Èzili (Beauvoir 2008b, 94). A song reproduced by Max Beauvoir (2008b, 95) tellingly includes the name Allada and a reference to Dahomian King Agaja: "Agwetawoyo Kimba Alada, Kadja Dosou."[50]

Agwe's mistress, the *lwa* Èzili, also resides in the sea. Some songs chide him about his sexual proclivities: "Agwe you can't go out with two women, / You have to send one away, oh!" (Beauvoir 2008b, 93).[51]

Agwe is a judge of character, as demonstrated in this song: "Agwe Tawoyo was the one who called me, / I'm going to see what the living do to me, / Earthly sinners are not good, they are bad!" (Beauvoir 2008b, 95).[52] His interventions on the sea can be salvific. Like the other spirits of the Rada Rite, he works in tandem with God, for example: "Agwe Woyo, I'm not in a hurry! / There is nothing here besides God in the heavens" (Beauvoir 2008b, 94).[53] The *lwa* disappears into God, illustrating the notion of a spirit as a facet of God's radiance.

Agwe's service takes place on the seaside, where a wooden raft is prepared with offerings in his honor. The *bak Agwe* raft is released into the open sea to feed him (Déita 2006, 23). Landlocked communities like Lakou Souvenance honor Agwe at his tree (Saint-Lot 2003). Songs for Agwe in other collections address the spirit's connection to the *sea* and the *island* (much like song 4.b below): "Agwe Woyo, I was right there on the sea / Agwe Woyo, I was right there by the island" (Beauvoir 2008b, 94).[54] A Fon expression close to the Creole

Agwe Tawoyo is found in *agbetawoyó* (the sound of the sea), suggesting "the ocean in its immensity" (Segurola and Rassinoux 2000, 28).

Agwe is described as the "mirror of the Vodou spirits."[55] The term *miwa* includes the French sense of a reflecting "mirror," like the surface of the sea or a basin (Welele Doubout, personal correspondence, 2016). As Welele Doubout explains, *miwa* is also a reflection of the people, the ancestors, and the community that raised a person. The shimmering surface produces a mirror connecting the living with the ancestors. The spirit's symbolic link to the mystical aspect of reflections on water is confirmed in a song Beauvoir collects: "Agwe, Vodou spirit mirroring power" (2008b, 94).[56] *Ase* in line 7 is a Fon word for the essential power of being, spirit, destiny, fate, and God (Segurola and Rassinoux 2000, 404).[57]

Agwe Woyo

4.b

Agwe Woyo, Agwe Tawoyo,
move tan bare m—abobo!
—e ago e!
Sou lamè a mwen ye.
Laklas, zile a mwen ye.
Agwe Woyo, Agwe Tawoyo,
move tan bare m—e ago e!

Agwe Woyo, nèg wala zangi a.

—move tan bare m.
Agwe Woyo, nèg dlo sale a.

—move tan bare m.
Batiman Agwe Woyo debake.
—Abobo!
An anrivan m nan zile a,
m resevwa yon tan.
Batiman Agwe Woyo debake.
Kaptenn Sèvo mande: kijan n ap fè?

Koki lanmè reponn: n ap fè konsa,

se pou lavi zanfan yo.

Agwe Woyo

4.b

Agwe Woyo, Agwe Tawoyo,
Bad weather traps me—abobo!
—hey ago hey!
I am on the sea.
Class, I am on the island.
Agwe Woyo, Agwe Tawoyo,
bad weather traps me—hey ago hey!

Agwe Woyo, man of the
wala eel.
—bad weather corners me.
Agwe Woyo, man of the salt
water.
—bad weather corners me.
Agwe Woyo's boat arrived.
—Abobo!
Upon my arrival on the island,
The weather welcomed me.
Agwe Woyo's boat arrived.
Captain Sèvo asks: what will we do?
Seashell answered: we'll do like this,
it's for the lives of the children.

Batiman Agwe Woyo debake.	Agwe Woyo's boat arrived.
An arivan m nan zile a,	Upon my arrival on the island,
m resevwa yon tan.	The weather welcomed me.

Song 4.b provides key notions about Agwe's protections. On a literal level, the song describes being caught in bad weather at sea, facing the dangers of the natural force, while supplicating for Agwe's help, the dolphin-like spirit who guides lost ships (Déita 2006, 22). The song falls into the terror of a powerful storm at sea. The theme of the storm is thrice followed by the assuring promise of the *zile* (island), introducing a safe harbor in the narrative. Agwe's palace on the sea is "a reef of floating corals" called "Three Islands"[58] (Déita 2006, 22). The song relieves the sense of mortal danger by introducing Agwe's boat, usually called *Imamou* but here generically called the *batiman* (ship).

Fishermen hold annual ceremonies for Agwe to thank him and ask for protection (Marcelin 1949, 108). *Move tan* (bad weather) is a metaphor that represents the struggles faced in the course of life. Lines 6–7, 8–9, and 10–11 are a reiteration of the narrator's endangerment on the sea and a display of Agwe's diverse appellations: "Agwe Tawoyo, man of the wala eel" and "man of the salt water." With each call to the spirit, the plight of the narrator is underscored responsively: "bad weather corners me." However, the tension of the cries is soothed in line 12 with the mooring of Agwe's boat.

Abobo in line 13 suggests a break in the song. Lines 14 through 22 shift the narrative forward. The point of view is no longer distressed but bodes of a safe arrival. New figures emerge, including Kaptenn Sèvo (Captain Brain), who asks Koki (Seashell, referring to Agwe), "What are we going to do?" Seashell replies that help is coming for "the lives of the children."

The last three lines comfort us in the serenity of the safe island. Songs about deliverance from the dangers of the sea reflect the timeless experiences of fishermen and seafarers, including the traumas endured by enslaved people in the Middle Passage and by boatpeople today.

Balizay

5.a

Aoche Nago—Awo!	Aoche Nago—Awo!
Nèg Nago di kochè! Yòbòdò!	Nago men say flay! Yòbòdò!
Balizay o, m a rele Ogoun Balizay o.	Oh Balizay, oh I will call Ogoun Balizay.
M rele Ogoun Balizay o.	Oh I call Ogoun Balizay.
Chapo panama m tonbe.	My panama hat fell off.

Balizay o, eya, rele Balizay o.	Oh Balizay, yeah, oh call Balizay.
Chapo panama m tonbe.	My panama hat fell off.

Song 5.a, entitled "Balizay," is a cycle of three songs dedicated to Ogou, and consequently it points to the Nago Rite, a close relative of Rada. Although not all the spirits in the Nago Rite have the name Ogou, the majority do (Beauvoir 2008a, 191–92). Ogou belongs to a famous family of *lwa*, including national spirits like Sen-Jak Majè, the father and chief of the family, and a variety of "sons" like Ogou Badagri, Ogou Feray, and so on (Marcelin 1950, 41–78).[59] Ogou is a spirit of power, politics, war, metal, defense, and protection.

The opening acclamation *Aoche Nago* means "By the power of the Nago *lwa*." The word "Nago" refers to the traditions of Yoruba origin. There are Nago temples and altars dedicated to the Ogou *lwa* in Haiti (Marcelin 1949, 104). The Ogou spirits are also included in Rada altars (Marcelin 1950, 45). *Awo*, the response given above to *aoche Nago*, is a "collective reference for believers of the Yorùbá religion" (Fama 1996, 21). *Awo* may be related to *lawo*, a Yoruba term that appears to be a source for the word *lwa* (Jil and Jil 2009, 125). I take *Awo Achè Nago* to mean "By the grace of the Nago spirits." In the syllable *-che* in *aoche*, the palatalized Yoruba equivalent of the Fon term *acè* (or *se*, *ze*, or *aze*) and Creole *ase* appears.[60] Recall that *ache*, *acè*, and *ase* are powerful transatlantic concepts designating power, vital force, and the power of the vodun. The proximity of the Yoruba, Fon, and Creole words points to the deep commonalities among the languages and cultures of these peoples.

The second line references male Nago identity and mentions that the Ogou-lwa "flay or cut" (*kochè*) adversaries. The notion of "flaying" implicates animal sacrifice. Ogou Balizay is matched with Saint Florian (Marcelin 1950, 77). In Haitian Creole, *balizay* means "clearing a field" and "erosion," suggesting that this epithet is related to the spirit's sweeping force. Some Ogou names include epithets associated with places like Ogou Badagri, which refers to the town in coastal Nigeria. Others reference powerful historical figures like Ogou Achade, whose name points to King Tegbesu of Dahomey, who took the strong name "Achade." Powerful military leaders like Tegbesu and the Haitian emperor Dessalines were linked to the spirit Ogou, because their legacies of warfare were interpreted in a Vodou mythological context modeled on Ogou's template of the intrepid African warrior. King Tegbesu became assimilated to the concept of Ogou as the historical figure became "depersonalized" (Deren 1953, 32).

Olicha	*Olicha*
5.b	5.b
Olicha, Olicha Fawo e.	Olicha, Olicha Fawo e.

Olicha, Olicha Fawo e.	Olicha, Olicha Fawo e.
Fawo e, Fawo e!	Fawo e, Fawo e!
Fawo e, Fawo e,	Fawo e, Fawo e,
nou pral janbe pas la,	we are going to cross the pass,
Alesou Fawo Pyè.	Alesou Fawo Pyè.
Olicha, Olicha, Fawo e!	Olicha, Olicha, Fawo e!
E e, abobo! Fawo e, Fawo e!	Hey hey, abobo! Fawo e, Fawo e!
nou pral janbe pas,	We are going to cross the pass,
Alesou Fawo Pyè.	Alesou Fawo Pyè.
Olicha Nago, Olicha!	Olicha Nago, Olicha!
—Abobo!	—Abobo!

In song 5.b, "Olicha" honors "Olicha Fawo" (line 1), also known as "Alesou Fawo Pyè" (line 6). Olicha appears in songs alongside Ogou (Hebblethwaite et al. 2012, 57–58). Olicha the magician knows about healing and harmful plants, having a mixed reputation for using plants that kill and cure (Marcelin 1950, 72; Hebblethwaite et al. 2012, 274).

Students of Yoruba and Cuban religions may recognize "Olicha" in the word òrìsà (spirit). The words are likely related, since alternation in "liquids" like *r* and *l* and palatalization from *s* to *ch* (i.e., /ʃ/) are common in language contact.[61] Haiti's Olicha only refers to a particular spirit, not to the spirits in general.[62] The retention of near-synonyms like Olicha (a particular spirit) and *lwa* (spirit) from Yoruba, *vodou* (spirit) from Fon, and *lespri* (spirit) from French reflects the multilingual sources of Vodou. Vodou's Creolization demonstrates a coherent synthesis and restructuring of diverse cultural sources.[63]

Although the *lwa* Alesou Fawo Pyè does not appear among Beauvoir's list of spirits and rites (2008a, 187–96), many of the *lwa* in his list include the term *pyè* (stone, rock). Examples include Pyè Fere, Pyè Aleman, and others. How did these spirits in different rites acquire the epithet Pyè in their name, ultimately becoming a spirit family that cuts across numerous rites? Beauvoir's system of classification, which organizes spirits by the "Rite," "Name," and "Family" (2008a, 187–96), offers a starting point. The names of *lwa* that include the name Pyè are classified within the family Pyè, just as the diverse manifestations of the Ogou spirits are in the Ogou family. The term *pyè* refers to a sacred rock taken from a special place chosen by the *lwa* (Welele Doubout, personal correspondence, 2017).[64] The *lwa* in the rock delivers energy to the rock's owner. At one domestic ceremony in the hills above Léogâne, stones that held the family spirits were bathed, polished, and oiled (Courlander 1973, 44–45).[65]

Song 5.b returns to supplicate Olicha Fawo in line 4 while asserting the main tension in line 5: "we are going to cross the pass." The unspecified pass could reflect the Middle Passage or another harrowing experience. The phrase "we are going to cross the pass" reflects the concerns of all vulnerable travelers and leads to an "Olicha model" for traversing passages accompanied by ancestors like Alesou Fawo Pyè.

Ti Gason, Ti Gason	*Little Boy, Little Boy*
5.c	5.c
Ti gason, ti gason,	Little boy, little boy,
Manman w voye w chache dlo.	Your mother sent you to find water.
Li pa voye w chache bwa.	She did not send you to find wood.
Si ou tande tire, si yo ba wou,	If you hear shooting, if they give it to you,
ba yo tou.	give it to them, too.
—Ou mèt tande tire,	—You may hear shooting,
si yo ba wou,	if they give it to you,
ba yo tou.	give it to them, too.
Ti gason, ti gason,	Little boy, little boy,
manman w voye w chache dlo.	your mother sent you to find water.
Li pa voye w chache bwa.	She did not send you to find wood.
Ou mèt tande tire,	You may hear shooting,
si yo ba wou,	if they give it to you,
ba yo tou.	give it to them, too.
—E aoche!	—E aoche!

Song 5.c is a *chante pwen* that conveys a warning in an indirect, nonconfrontational style (Richman 2007, 90). The little boy is the focus, and his mother stands behind instructing him. The fact that the water and the wood alternate in lines 2 and 3 suggests that the boy has not grasped his assignment. Line 4 turns to "shooting" and retaliating (*ba yo tou*). There is a degree of nonchalance in the expression "Ou mèt tande tire" (You may hear shooting), as if the song reflects a time when shooting could occur at any moment and required a response.

Song 5.c opens with a hint of tension in the boy's failing memory but escalates with the verb *tire* (shoot). The only Vodou-specific word, *aoche*, points to Ogou's militant Nago Rite. The content of the song reflects Ogou's concern for defensive measures when facing threats.

Bonus track

6.a

O papa Desalin,
Voye on ti priz limyè pou nou,

ak yon ti kras konsyans,
pou n ka chita ansanm,
pou n sove peyi nou.
Nou pati!

Rasin Figye, bon bagay!

Alfabetizasyon se chemen je klere

pou 2004 ka vin pi bèl.

Ayiti, yo di w
pral bèl, se vre.

Alfabetizasyon, se chemen devlòpman

pou peyi nou ka vin pi bèl.

Lè tout moun fin konn li,

peyi nou va mache.
N ap fè 2004 la,
n a di viv Ayiti.
Viv Ayiti ayisyen, viv Ayiti!

—Alfa!
Ayiti pou peyi m: viv Ayiti!

—Peyi a pral bèl o,

mon Dye!
Tout moun vin konn li,

Bonus track

6.a

Oh papa Dessalines,
send a glimpse of light for us,

with a little bit of conscience.
so we can sit together,
in order to save our country.
Let's take off!

Roots of the Fig Tree, good stuff!

Literacy is the path of knowledge

so that 2004 can become more beautiful.

Haiti, they say you
are going to be beautiful, it's true.

Literacy is the path of development

so that the nation can be more beautiful.

When everybody knows how to read,

our country will function.
We will celebrate 2004,
we will say long live Haiti.
Long live Haitian Haiti, long live Haiti!

—Literacy!
Haiti is my country: long live Haiti!

—Oh the country will be beautiful,
my God!
Once everybody knows how to read,

peyi nou va mache.	our country will move forward.
—N ap fè 2004 la, n a di,	—We will celebrate 2004, we will say,
viv Ayiti!	long live Haiti!

Songs 6.a–6.d reflect the *chante pwen* genre, which focuses on social and cultural criticism. These critiques provide insight into Rasin Figuier's views on politics and contemporary events. Still rooted in a Vodou outlook, the songs focus on social criticism and alternate between encouragement and lament in their assessment of the Haitian human condition. The *chante pwen* framework is grounded in critical analysis, showing how Vodou songs are neither separate from nor inimical to critiques of power. In some respects, *chante pwen* reflect a facet of Vodou's liberation theology.

Song 6.a opens with an invocation to Jean-Jacques Dessalines (1758–1806), champion of Haitian independence. In 1791, at age thirty-three, Dessalines joined the rebels in fighting the French, helping Boukman Dutty, Jeannot Bullet, Jean-François Papillon, and Georges Biassou (Oriol 2002, 188). Named a division general by Toussaint Louverture in 1800, by 1802 he commanded the West and the South with Toussaint. He made use of scorched-earth tactics against Charles Leclerc's French pro-slavery troops.

Dessalines laid his arms down after Louverture's capture in June 1802 but returned to fight in October 1803. The soldiers of the indigenous army recognized him as the most experienced fighter, naming him commander in chief. Swiftly winning decisive battles, Dessalines declared Haitian independence in Gonaïves on January 1, 1804. In the early months of his rule, he carried out the massacre of the remaining French white people. He named himself governor general for life, then emperor, a megalomaniacal prelude to his assassination on Pont-Rouge in 1806.

According to one tradition, Dessalines covered his head in a red cloth to honor Ogou (Marcelin 1950, 33). Although some scholars suggest that he became a "god" in Vodou, it is not clear whether Dessalines is a spirit who is totally independent from Ogou or whether some Ogou possessions take on Dessalinian attributes (Dayan 1995, 17). In song 6.a, Dessalines is an inspirational figure who sends out light and knowledge, leading to dialogue that saves the country.

The invocation of Dessalines in song 6.a draws from the prestige of the national hero to add urgency to the theme of literacy. Rasin Figuier's reference to Dessalines in a song about literacy aligns the group's sympathies with the ideological tradition of Haiti's disenfranchised Black, Creole-speaking majority.

Education and literacy are essential to the Vodouist world view, contrary to the claims of Protestant and Afrophobic polemicists who falsely link Vodouists to illiteracy and worse (Hebblethwaite 2015b; Joseph 2016, 89). Racine Figuier argues that literacy is the only way to attain the "more beautiful" bicentennial of 2004. Literacy is the path of "knowledge" and "development," positions that mirror those of Creolists who urge the adoption of majority language policies in Haiti (Dejean 2006). Hopes were high in the years before a bicentennial year that was supposed to represent Haiti's achievements. Instead, the year 2004 devolved into a political struggle that culminated in the removal of President Jean-Bertrand Aristide, founder of the Fanmi Lavalas political party. He was threatened and fled, describing the event as a kidnapping. He ended up in South Africa, where he lived in exile for several years.

6.b

Moun sa yo, ki moun yo ye?

Yo bliye ki sa nou te fè pou n te ba yo pouvwa.
—Anmre, nou pa t dòmi nan nwit, se vre.
Moun sa yo, ki moun yo ye?

Yo bliye ki sa nou te fè pou n te ba yo pouvwa.
Gen nan yo

ki vle sa chanje
Gen nan yo

ki pa gen volonte.
Yo pa vle n avanse.

Mezanmi, gad sa yo fè nou!

Gad sa yo fè n, Ayisyen,

gad sa yo fè nou.
Gad sa yo fè, mezanmi,

gad sa yo fè nou.
Yo kraze peyi n, o Bondye.

6.b

These people, which people are they?

They forgot what we did to give them power.
—Help, we did not sleep at night, it's true.
These people, which people are they?

They forgot what we did to give them power.
There are those among them

who want this to change.
There are those among them

who have no will.
They don't want us to progress.

My friends, look what they did to us!

Look at what they did to us, Haitians,

look at what they did to us.
Look what they did to us, my friends,

look what they did to us.
They destroyed our country, oh God.

Mezanmi gad sa yo fè nou.	Oh heavens, look what they did to us.
—Woy, woy, woy, mezanmi, gad sa yo fè nou,	—Oh my, oh my, oh my, oh heavens, look what they did to us,
woy, woy, woy!	oh my, oh my, oh my!
Mezanmi, yo kraze peyi a,	Oh heavens, they destroyed the country,
woy, woy, woy. (bis)	oh my, oh my, oh my! (bis)
Mezanmi, moun yo divize nou.	Oh heavens, the people divided us.
—Woy, woy, woy, Mezanmi, yo divize nou.	—Oh my, oh my, oh my, Oh heavens, they divided us,
Woy, woy, woy.	oh my, oh my, oh my!

From hopeful strains in song 6.a, Rasin Figuier shifts to a pessimistic mood above. The politicians have forgotten the voters. They are in it for self-gain and not the enhancement of the community, a problem Haitians call *patripòch* (patriotic pocket). The song asserts in lines 8–9 that some of those elected want self-serving practices to cease, while others, in lines 10–11, do not want to change. Without naming them directly, this lament accuses members of the political class of harming and fracturing the Haitian people.

6.c	6.c
Twòp san koule o, nou di ase, twòp san koule nan peyi a.	Too much blood spilled, we say enough, too much blood spilled in the country.
Ayiti, twòp san koule, se vre.	Haiti, too much blood spilled, it's true.
Twòp san koule o, an verite.	Oh too much blood spilled, in truth.
Twòp san koule nan peyi a.	Too much blood spilled in the country.
Zotobre tonbe, malere mouri o!	Big shots fell, oh the poor died!
Lavalasyen tonbe. Konvèjans mouri o. Se pa fòt nou,	Lavalas supporters fell. Konvèjans supporters died. It is not our fault,

se fot zanmi ipokrit yo	it's the fault of our hypocritical friends
—ki fè sa rive la e.	—that this happened here.

Songs 6.b and 6.c resemble the plaintive psalms of Hebrew sacred literature. Five reiterations about spilled blood intone the tragic mood. The notion of "too much blood" projects an ethics derived from Vodou practice, a standard of measuring suffering and loss of life. The spilled blood extends from Dahomian ritual murder, to the Middle Passage and death-camp conditions in Saint-Domingue, to the political violence of contemporary Haiti. The song reveals how the angry rhetoric of warring political factions exacerbates the violence endured by the poor.

Song 6.c refers to political parties that vied for power after the ousting of Jean-Claude Duvalier in 1986. Founded in 1991, Fanmi Lavalas (Landslide Family) was the party of President Jean-Bertrand Aristide, while the opposition coalition, Konvèjans (Demokratik) (Democratic Convergence), was founded in 2000. Konvèjans was a coalition of parties, members of the Haitian elite, and foreign allies such as the International Republican Institute, a US-based nonprofit (Dupuy 2005).

In the song's narrative, Lavalas supporters fell and those of Konvèjans died, the messaging deftly walking between the rival political parties to focus rather on the tragic deaths of the poor trapped in the political violence.

6.d

Ayisyen, si n te gen inyon,	Haitians, if we were united,
n ta rive deja.	we would have already prospered.
Peyi mwen, o peyi mwen!	My country, oh my country!
O peyi mwen o,	Oh my country,
ou pa prale.	you aren't going anywhere.
Ale m ale, m ale, m ale,	I'm really going, I'm going, I'm going,
m ale, wi, m prale.	I'm going, yes, I'm going
Lavalasyen, si n te gen inyon,	Lavalas supporters, if we were united,
n ta rive deja.	we would already prosper.
Peyi mwen, o peyi mwen,	My country, oh my country,
o peyi mwen, o adje!	oh my country, oh grief!
Ale m ale, m ale,	I'm really going, I'm going,
m ale, wi, m prale.	I'm going, yes, I'm going.

Konvèjans, si n te gen inyon,	Convergence, if we were united,
n ta rive deja.	we would have already prospered.
Peyi mwen, o peyi mwen,	My country, oh my country,
o peyi mwen, o adye!	oh my country, oh grief!
Kote lwa yo?	Where are the lwa?
M rele lwa yo, m pa wè lwa yo.	I call the lwa, I don't see the lwa.
Anba, ye, anba, ye, anba, ye!	Under, yeah, under, yeah, under, yeah!
Ayisyen, si n te gen inyon,	Haitians, if we were united,
n ta rive deja.	we would have already prospered.
—Ale m ale, m ale, m ale,	—I'm really going, I'm going, I'm going,
wi, m prale.	yes, I'm going,
Peyi mwen, o peyi mwen,	My country, oh my country,
o peyi mwen, adye.	oh my country, oh grief.
Adye, adye, adye!	Oh grief, oh grief, oh grief!

While song 6.a includes a passing exhortation to *Dye* (God), all the other songs on the sixth track critique political violence and intimidation. While song 6.d is also political, it includes a final verse that returns to the theme of the *lwa*. The narrator's response to the disunity in the country is to "go away" with a sense of despair at the Haitians' inability to establish "union." The union envisaged is one in which cooperation and prosperity could emerge between political parties. The formula "if we were united" is repeated after "the Haitians," "Lavalas," and "Konvèjans," pointing to inclusivity and acknowledging that a better world is possible.

The second part of the song returns to the theme of the sacred: "I call the lwa, I don't see the lwa. / Under, yeah . . ." The lines close the record on an urgent note, while a strain of frustration about the slow response of the spirits is detected. Doubt is affirmed straightforwardly while the holy is "under, yeah, under," a reassurance that the spirits are just below the feet. After this brief cycle of supplication, doubt, and affirmation, the song returns to the theme of fleeting unity and an admission of exasperation in the repetition of "oh grief." These final songs assess Haiti's recent history and offer blunt criticism on the role of political divisiveness in fueling economic and social hardships.

Those negative forces are the antithesis of Rada's concern for life, order, and rootedness.

CONCLUSION

Rasin Figuier's album *Vodou Lakay* is a traditional roots Vodou recording with acoustic rhythmic instrumentation and ceremonial worship songs sung in call-and-response style by a choir and a lead singer. The quality of the studio recording makes *Vodou Lakay* an ideal introduction to Rada songs. The lyrics, arrangements, and delivery provide an illustration of the concerns of Vodou sacred music. The majority of the songs deal with the spirits of the Rada and Nago Rites, providing a corpus for the investigation of the mythology, the spirits, the historical memory, and the ideas that structure the tradition. The songs reveal Vodou's cosmology and values, in addition to shedding light on social and political concerns.

The study of the historical, political, and religious situation between approximately 1600 and 1800 in the Aja-Fon and Gedevi-Yoruba areas laid a foundation for the interpretation of Rasin Figuier's songs in this chapter. This "Vodou hermeneutics" has brought various disciplines to bear on a multifaceted phenomenon. The core methodology in these chapters is a dialectical approach that reads in both directions to recover Africa's impact on Haiti and Haiti's current significance for understanding Africa's past and present. Creole Vodou songs preserve African features from a multitude of sources, propelling this project to more engagement in African studies.

The Rada Rite philosophy emphasizes the axioms of life, order, and rootedness, whereas the Gede Rite examined in chapter 4 focuses on death, healing, and sexuality. The final *chante pwen* above focusing on the political morass in Haiti represent a point of contact between the Rada and Gede Rites, as they express extreme pessimism toward politics as well as frustration about access to the *lwa*. There are times when Rada Rite worship is not sufficient to mediate the disruptions and trauma of daily life. On those occasions, it is appropriate to seek other ritual paths within Sèvis Ginen, and, among the striking choices, the Gede Rite has helped servants of the spirits articulate and grapple with the extreme forms of displacement and alienation experienced in 2004.

Chapter 4

THE GEDE RITE IN HAITI

Rasin Bwa Kayiman's *Guede*

INTRODUCTION

The Gede spirits reflect conception, birth, childhood, senescence, and death, rising from and speaking to moments of transformation (Smith 2010, 2, 159). The Gede transmute the living through healing or death (Brown 2001, 359). Ancestral spirits of a universal order, the Gede protect and heal children and transfer people into death. Gede's theological function is linked to the idea that "death is a source of power" that the living can harness through ritual (Smith 2010, 9).

The Gede spirits have historical roots in the Gedevi (Igede) people of the Aja-Yoruba region. Chapter 1 examined the collapse of the Gedevi people on the Abomey plateau as the Aja-Fon founders of Dahomey surged. However, unlike the story of the Dahomian victors, far less is known about the defeated Gedevi people. Haitian Gede songs provide an important portal for reconstructing ancient Gedevi culture.

Gede's possessions express hunger, sexuality, and humor. He eats rapidly with his hands and may throw his food. He comports himself around women with an aroused attitude. The Gede spirits are the last to be greeted in ceremonies, disruptively snubbing social conventions by comically stealing objects (Marcelin 1950, 145). His raw humor, satire, and concern with sex and death shed light on our humanity and "work alchemical changes on the mood of a Vodou family," transforming solemn ritual into laughter (Brown 2001, 361). His bawdy mockery dissolves tensions and reminds people to live authentically. The Gede spirits appear at the end of ceremonies, just as death comes at the end of life. The Gede are among the few spirits that will venture into public spaces, especially when the possessed parade in Port-au-Prince (Marcelin 1950, 146).

The Gede celebrations in Haiti begin on All Saints' Eve (Halloween) with revelry that extends past midnight. On the All Saints' Days of November 1 and 2,

Vodouists visit cemeteries to remember the dead and take part in personal and public rituals among the graves. The cemetery is a place for memorializing the dead, petitioning the ancestors, offering food, flowers, and libations, conducting healing rituals and possession performances, and taunting with an obscene humor called *betiz* (Smith 2010, 117). Although ritual activity is concentrated in the first week of November, it is common for temples to schedule their main ceremony on one of the weekends of the month.

There are ceremonies of the utmost seriousness in which the pelvic spirit appears. At the temple of the priest Grandizè Nèg Lafrik Ginen (sèvitè Bonapat) in Gonaïves, I attended a ceremony in early November 2014 during which Gede's pelvic grinding manifested in a woman who rubbed the *potomitan*. There were twenty women dressed in black and purple, all initiated under sèvitè Bonapat. At one point, he, too, became possessed and rubbed the flames from the candles he held all over his head, hands, and chest. The community set out a sumptuous table with cake, food, and drinks for the ancestors, offering small sums of money there. In addition to the ceremony's traditional drumming, singing about the *lwa*, dancing, and possession events, there were times of solemn prayer. Heads bowed, the initiates gathered around a food-laden altar to share French and Creole prayers, some Catholic, others Vodouist.

In November, there are parties and nightclub events with Gede themes. At one event that I attended in Gonaïves on the eve of November 1, performers presented Vodou dance and music in the "folkloric" style. Absent was priestly ritualizing with the *ason*. However, after midnight dozens of people in the audience around the stage succumbed to the Gede and found themselves indecorously pseudo-humping the floor as well as each other, cavorting theatrically in Gede's playful mockery of sex under the pounding drums. The unfolding scene of several Gedes on the loose was rambunctious fun, provoking hilarity in the audience.

In this chapter, I examine the identities of the Gede spirits, the structure of the Gede Rite, and aspects of service to the Gede spirits in order to explicate Rasin Bwa Kayiman's songs. The Gede traditions are analyzed via an extensive corpus of songs, especially those compiled by Milo Marcelin (1950) and Max Beauvoir (2008b), in addition to personal and scholarly sources. The Gede reflect the abject in that their experience reflects the worst of the Dahomian conquest, capture, and sale; the Middle Passage; and the stigma and torture of Saint-Domingue. The Gede Rite is suited to the traumas of economic globalization, including the plight of boat people and disposable migrants, separation from family in diasporas, and the ordeals of sex work in the sexual economy. Studying the Gede Rite is an encounter with spiritual traditions that engage with the agony and ecstasy of sex, birth, and death.

HISTORICAL DIMENSIONS OF GEDE

Chapter 1 examined the history of the Aja-Fon and Gedevi-Yoruba regions, including the rise of Dako and his allies around the Abomey plateau in the 1620s. Dako and the Dahomians killed off the leaders of the local Gedevi-Yoruba people and took political and military control of the region. The Dahomians sold the Gedevi off to the European slave traders, and they gradually intermarried with survivors.

The Gedevi-Yoruba maintained their services to their divinized ancestor, who was materialized in a rock (*bétyle*) that originated in Ile Ife, the spiritual center of the Yoruba world. The rock helped the Gedevi destroy their enemies. The neighboring Dovi and Mitogbodji communities also held services for a great stone that leaned up against a baobab tree. Spirits dwell within stones, and they empower the owner (Merlo and Vidaud 1984, 272).

The Gedevi people included skilled magicians, morticians, and gravediggers before the Dahomian period (Bastide 1967, 146). After the Dahomian conquest, they were obliged to provide burial services, placing them at the bottom of Dahomian society (LaMenfo 2011, 204). The Gedevi religion was focused on the Gede spirits, the ancestors of the Gedevi nation. It is not known how closely the ancient Gedevi religion resembled Haiti's Gede Rite, but children, healing, death, and the cemetery seem to be original emphases. As was the practice among the conquering Aja people, they incorporated aspects of the Gedevi mythology into their culture. The Gedevi people became the "lords of the earth" to the Aja conquerors (LaMenfo 2011, 204).

Just as the Dahomians fused elements of the Gedevi-Yoruba traditions into their religion, so, too, in Haiti are the Gedevi traditions a part of Sèvis Ginen, in which the Aja Rada Rite enjoys prominence. Scholars include under the banner of Sèvis Ginen the following rites: Rada, Gede, Ibo, Nago, Zandò, Bizango, Anmin, Bosou, Boumba Mazwa, Danwonmen, Gede Petwo, Kaplaou Ganga, Kita, Kongo Fran, Mahi, Makaya, Matinik-Djouba, Petwo Fran, Seneka, and Wangòl (Beauvoir 2008a, 187–96). On the ground, however, priests of Sèvis Ginen work with a subset of inherited rites, not all of them.

In Dahomey, the state's "buying" of the traditions of conquered people hastened social integration. One account of the fate of the Gedevi people claims that the Aja conquerors sold them into slavery to escape from their "spells" (Bastide 1967, 146). This claim points to the Dahomian use of mystification to attack the Gedevi, and it suggests their resistance.

Although servants of the *lwa* in the Sèvis Ginen tradition embrace the Gede Rite, the *Vodou lakou* (compound Vodou) traditions practiced in the Gonaïves region stick to single rites. According to sèvitè Bien-Aimé of Lakou Souvenance, his community strictly serves the "*lwa* Ginen" that are the "*lwa* Dawonmen."

Member of the *rasin* band Boukman Eksperyans and lifetime student of Vodou Mimerose Beaubrun describes her spiritual journey into Haiti's spirit-based traditions (2013). She asked sèvitè Bien-Aimé questions that persist in Haiti about the Dahomians:

> "In that case, is the character of the lakou Fon or Gede?" I [Beaubrun] included the Gedes because the Dahomey site belonged to them before the Fons. According to my reasoning, I told myself that the Gedes took their natural place in Rada rituals and in all the lakou of a Dahomey character. I situated the Gedes in the same pantheon.
>
> "I [Bien-Aimé] don't know what you [Beaubrun] are talking about when you refer to 'Fon.' But as far as the Gede is concerned, this lakou does not have this character. Our lwa are instead '*dawonmen*' *fran-Ginen* (they originated in a 'pure' vodou rite from Dahomey)." (Beaubrun 2013, 173)

The narrator pressed sèvitè Bien-Aimé for an explanation and was told that although the Gede are respected, they are not welcome to dance freely in Lakou Souvenance because they are "not Ginen" (Beaubrun 2013, 174). Mimerose Beaubrun knows that the Gedevi people were the original inhabitants of the Abomey plateau and that the rise of the Aja-Fon kingdom of Dahomey resulted in their subjugation and enslavement. If Dahomey is "Ginen," how could the religion of the Gedevi people, who predate the conquering Dahomians, *not* be "Ginen"? Isn't Gede the ultimate "Ginen"? While Lakou Souvenance exclusively practices the Danwonmen Rite, Beaubrun's historical question about the Gedevi who were sold into slavery by Dahomian enslavers sheds light on the reconciling power of Sèvis Ginen. Unlike the Lakou traditions around Gonaïves, the Sèvis Ginen system reflected in Beauvoir (2008a, 2008b) and centered in Léogâne and Port-au-Prince seamlessly integrates Gede and other rites.

Some *oungan* and *manbo* draw a distinction between practices that are Ginen and those that are not. They claim that some spirits are "Ginen" and others are not. Manbo man Choune, for example, claimed that Ginen *lwa* do not make the same demands as Kongo, Rada, or Petwo *lwa* (Beaubrun 2013, 185). The non-Ginen *lwa* ask for the sacrifice of a chicken but take instead the life of the supplicant's child, she claimed (Beaubrun 2013, 186). Throughout Beaubrun's travels to Vodou Lakou and temples, she encountered assertions about what is acceptable Ginen and what is not. In a rural domestic setting, I have noted that some *oungan* use the term "Ginen" to refer to inherited ancestral spirits in distinction from those from public temple-based traditions in which spirits may be *achte* (purchased) via initiation or other rituals. Used in a given temple, Lakou, or family, the word "Ginen" essentially means "authentic" and "genuine," in determining acceptable practices. Although a few people argue about the place of the Gede Rite in Vodou, its formal inclusion in Sèvis Ginen places it at the center of my concerns.

RESEARCH ON THE GEDE RITE

An early reference to Gede is Antoine Innocent's 1906 novel *Mimola, ou L'histoire d'une cassette* (*Mimola, or the Story of a Casket*), which offers scenes from a *boule zen* ceremony, including detailed ethnographic descriptions of the worshippers (Innocent and Laval 1935, 141–52). The *oungan* invoked the name of God, the Virgin Mary, and various spirits, including "Legba avadra atibon," "Loco atissou azamblo gidi," "Ogou badagri," and "Guédé hounssou." The mention of Gede in this list is important, since it shows how the spirit is listed alongside Rada and Nago spirits in this early twentieth-century manifestation of Sèvis Ginen.

The French travel writer Eugène Aubin's book *En Haïti* (1910) reports on experiences with Haitians who classify Gede within a "Ginen" system that includes spirits like Legba, Loko, Danbala, and Agwe (99). Aubin offers a description of his visit to manbo Téla's annual "celebration of the house" in mid-August at the Bellot family farm in the hills overlooking the Cul-de-Sac plain. The main *ounfò* was dedicated to Danbala, and a second one was split between the Kongo and Nago Rites. The trees on the property were dedicated to various spirits, including a *cirouéllier* (*monben*) tree decorated for "Guede Baron Samedi" with a black cloth, bones, and skulls (Andrew Tarter, personal correspondence, 2019; Aubin 1910, 99). Aubin's book also includes a photograph of oungan Plaisimond's *ounfò* near Mariani, with its large cross for Bawon Samdi outside the temple (206).

Elsie Clews Parsons notices that Port-au-Prince is a stronghold for Gede culture (1928, 158). The son of an *oungan* brought Gede's *banda* dance from Port-au-Prince back to Léogâne after studying in the capital. The *banda*'s movement of the hips and buttocks imitate "the act of fecundation" (Marcelin 1950, 145). Gede Nibo speaks with a nasal tone and eats "casaba," peppers, and herring. His jaws are tied with white cloth and his nostrils are stuffed with cotton wool, reflecting how the dead are dressed at burials (Parsons 1928, 158). One song illustrates Gede Nibo's love for children: "I am going to give you money / to take care of the children" (Parsons 1928, 158). Bawon Samdi of the Gede Rite is noted as a fearsome "grande diable" on a scale that eclipses Ogou. Bawon tries to make people laugh and attempts to stop them if they do (Parsons 1928, 162).

Zora Neale Hurston, in her 1938 ethnographic study *Tell My Horse*, also shows how the Gede spirits are fully integrated into Sèvis Ginen (1990, 164). In her chapter on the Secte Rouge secret society, she notes that followers of Gede attacked the former for encroaching on a bridge they deemed sacred, suggesting some fighting between different Vodou groups (215). Haiti's Black working classes serve the Gede, the burlesque possessions offering up a form of social class criticism. They are "the deification of the common people of Haiti," since they say what the peasant wants to say (Hurston 1990, 219). The proverb "Gede pa dra" (Gede isn't a sheet) means that the spirit's function is not to conceal people's fears.

Hurston errs in suggesting that Gede is neither European nor African, as it plainly comes from the Gedevi people. While the Gede have no temple, they do have a niche on every *oungan*'s property, usually in the form of a cross or tomb (Hurston 1990, 219). She describes the apparel, foods, and drinks the spirit prefers but again errs in suggesting that there is no service or ritual for Gede. In November, many Vodou communities organize services and rituals for Gede. Gede's unflinching drinking and washing of his face with hot-pepper-infused rum is a sign of his possession at those ceremonies. Hurston describes several Gede possessions, including one in which a lesbian possessed by Gede committed suicide, hinting at the traumas homosexual Haitians endure (1990, 222).

The African-born (*bosal*) enslaved people who served Gede were ousted from the docks of Port-au-Prince because they inspired fear (Hurston 1990, 222–23). The Gede community moved to Miragoâne, a town situated 102 kilometers to the west of the capital, and there the community prospered. Mentioned earlier, the bridge crossing Lake Miragoâne was their meeting place. In the 1930s, the Gede service had spread in the West and South but was not yet known in L'Artibonite or the North (Hurston 1990, 223). Today, service to Gede is active in cities like Gonaïves. In the North, a system involving the Pyè spirits fills a similar function. Hurston suggests that the variety of epithets exemplified in "Baron Cimeterre," "Baron Samedi," and "Baron Croix" reflect a single underlying type: the Lord of the Dead (1990, 223). She importantly emphasizes that Baron and Gede reflect features of a common Gede culture.

Milo Marcelin's *Mythologie vodou* volumes (1949, 1950) are landmarks in the hermeneutics of Vodou songs. He was in the first generation to compile and publish a selection of songs, making his work an important source. Of the 262 songs he compiled, 43 at the end of his collection are for Gede, reflecting the *règleman* (liturgy) of a Vodou ceremony. Gede is "handsome" and dressed in "white," "black," and "yellow," appearing like a president, deputy, or senator (Hebblethwaite et al. 2012, 177, songs 219, 250). A song for Bawon suggests his recalcitrant character: "Bawon of the Cross, / who says he is stronger than God" (Marcelin 1950, 147). Bawon spirits are "pretentious," taking themselves to be superior to the other spirits and even to "the Christian God" (Marcelin 1950, 147).[1]

The *vèvè* for the Bawon spirits are composed of cornmeal or ashes (Marcelin 1950, 146). Public cemeteries and domestic grave sites are marked with Bawon's cross, where offerings are placed on his feast days (Marcelin 1950, 147). A black rooster is sacrificed for Bawon on the Day of the Dead in early November, and the tombs in Haiti's countryside are decorated with skulls, bones, and black cloth (Marcelin 1949, 144). One informant rejected the idea that Bawon Samdi was a "bad *lwa*," reasoning that "if he is paid to do bad things, he'll do it—it is his trade. But if you are a good *child*, and you serve him well, and he is happy with you, he'll do anything for you" (Marcelin 1950, 168).

Bawon Samdi's protective interventions for his servants are the reason people serve him (Marcelin 1950, 170). In one narrative, the wife of a sergeant in the Garde d'Haïti and her two children were being escorted by an officer on a voyage late in the evening. As they passed a cemetery in a forest, men singing to the rhythm of clanging iron approached. Several held candles, leaving the woman, her children, and the officer panic stricken. Acting quickly, she led them into the cemetery, where they lay down in front of the Kwa Bawon, a large cross that represents Bawon Samdi in Haitian cemeteries, and pulled a blanket over them. The men circled the cemetery three times while singing and then walked away, allowing the travelers to continue their journey. Asked how she got her idea, she explained, "Bawon himself sent it. I am his *child* and I risked great danger. He took me under his protection" (Marcelin 1950, 171).

Aspects of Haitian rural culture are revealed in Gede spirits like Bawon (Marcelin 1950, 170–71). An avid cockfighter explained that his cowardly fighting cock took flight at the sight of a hen. To remedy the situation, he took it on a Monday before the Kwa Bawon, where he lit a black candle, poured out some white rum libations, cut the rooster's crest off, and buried it. On Sunday, he took the rooster to a cockfight and put him in a duel with the meanest rooster in the venue, owned by a sergeant in the Garde d'Haïti who was protected by the *lwa* Osanj.[2] The man took out his black *mouchwa* (scarf) and reminded Bawon of his request in the cemetery. In the arena, his rooster "raised his head to the sky, lowered his head to the ground, turned left and right, and attacked his adversary." Flipping in the air, his rooster buried his spur in the heart of the opposing cock, killing it instantly. No offer, including a cow and a goat, would convince him to part with the Bawon-empowered rooster. He left with his pockets full of money for the next few Sundays.

Shortly afterward, the man fell ill and spent a month in the hospital. After his discharge, he discovered that a neighbor had purchased his moneymaking rooster from his mother by means of a ruse. He went to the neighbor and threw his money at him but failed to secure the rooster. He discovered that the deceptive neighbor had entered the bird in a fight in Haiti's biggest *gagè*, the Grand-Orient, and placed a 1,000-gourde bet on him. The original owner returned to the cemetery and turned the earth where he had buried the rooster's crest, reminding Bawon that the rooster had been stolen from him and that it was high time to "break the engagement" (Marcelin 1950, 170–71). Bets were

20 to 5 in favor of his former rooster. Knowing of his advantage, he placed all his money on the opposing rooster and again walked away with a large sum of money after his former rooster fled the fight.

Maya Deren dedicates a lengthy passage of her book *Divine Horsemen* (1953) to Gede in a section titled "Ghede: Corpse and Phallus; King and Clown." Gede is the "phallic deity," the "Lord of Resurrection," the "lord of that eroticism that [...] is beyond good and evil," who taunts hypocrites and the holier-than-thou with his pelvic thrusts (102). Gede, like Legba, must be notified about marriages, births, disputes, and problems. His sexual humor, mimicry, and mockery provide temporary reprieve from his role in producing sickness, healing, dying, and death, but his jokes never completely release people from their mortal fear (Deren 1953, 112).

Gede is "insensate" to the "fiery liquid" sprayed in his eyes and to the rum infused with hot peppers with which he rubs himself (Deren 1953, 105). Gede is a wandering and starved beggar who gobbles down ritual food. His appearance at inappropriate times in the ritual order reveals his trickster character. A parade of Gedes in the 1920s walked past the sentries of the National Palace to demand money from President Louis Borno, who indeed paid them, attesting to his public dimension (Deren 1953, 107). A glimpse of this incident is reflected in this song: "Gede Nibo is a handsome fellow! / He dresses himself all in white / to go to the (presidential) Palace" (Hebblethwaite et al. 2012, 117).

The Bawon spirits are called upon for magical purposes, such as digging up zombies in the graveyard for use as slave labor or for empowerment. *Bòkò* ask Bawon to turn victims into animals or to inflict *baka* (spirit wounds) (Deren 1953, 113). More importantly, Bawon and Gede guard and heal children. On one occasion, as a last resort for a dying child, a ceremony was organized to call Gede for help (Deren 1953, 114). Black chickens and a large black goat were sacrificed, and Gede agreed to help. He anointed the child on his altar with blood from the sacrificed goat and, reaching between his legs, brought up a seminal emission with which he rubbed and healed the child. Gede had possessed a female *manbo*, and there was no way to account for the fluid (Deren 1953, 114). The next section focuses on theological aspects of the Gede spirits.

THEOLOGICAL CHARACTERISTICS OF THE GEDE SPIRITS

Mambo LaMenfo (2011, 197) classifies Vodou spirits as (1) the "lwa" or "elevated spirits" like Legba, the Marasa, and Danbala, representing universal features of experience; (2) the "mistè" (mysteries) or "mò" (the dead) who were at one time living humans and were subsequently promoted as spirits; and (3) the "zansèt yo" (ancestors) who work for family members as "personal mistè" as the "elevated dead."

In this system, the Gede fit into category (2): they are the unknown, unnamed, and unconsecrated dead that spring from humankind and reflect universal aspects of existence and nonexistence. In one of Vodou's creation myths, the decent of the Rada spirits across the earth's waters caused many deaths, producing the Gede. The Gede spirits are kept separately from the spirits of other rites because they are not linked to specific people and are not "elevated" (LaMenfo 2011, 202). Like people who die abandoned, perishing with no burial, who were murdered or succumbed to a mass tragedy, the Gede never received the "cleansing rites" for the dead and thus must be handled with special techniques. Since the Gede are unclaimed and unconsecrated dead (category 2), they are never incorporated into the altars of the *lwa* (category 1) or the ancestral dead (category 3) (LaMenfo 2011, 203). The Gede's attachment to death necessitates a separate altar or niche in their honor.

REPRESENTING THE GEDE SPIRITS

The Gede spirits wear purple and black, and the servants of the spirits clad themselves in the colors at ceremonies in November. The Gede spirits are characterized by genital symbolism and engage in theatrical pelvic thrusting with other Gede while receiving phallic objects from assistants, using them to mimic sexual penetration (Hurbon 1993, 95). Females possessed by Gede may wash their vaginas with hot pepper–infused rum (Smith 2010, 9).

The Gede spirits deride death, jesting with mortality in order to process its impact (Hurbon 1993, 95). In their popularity, they are joyously received in ceremonies. They speak with a disconcerting nasal tone, used in Haitian cinematic representations like Arnold Antonin's *Les amours d'un zombie* (2010) as well as in Frankétienne's novel *Dézafi* (1975).

Gede interrupts gender roles by making women dress as men and men dress as women (Hurston 1990, 224). In 2007, Katherine Smith observed an ambulating parade of Gede spirits dressed in drag. They danced clasping bones like phalluses while the crowd yelled "Gede Masisi!" (Gay Gede!) (Smith 2010, 117). Cross-dressing is also a part of *bann rara* (*rara* band) parades, as I witnessed in Gonaïves around Easter in 2014.

Like all of Sèvis Ginen's rites, the spirits in the Gede Rite are organized in a hierarchy and in family relationships. The Gede Rite includes dynamic spirits that express a wide range of spiritual, philosophical, and social functions, the main features of which are examined next. Bawon Samdi is the father of all of the Gede spirits; he is depicted as a tall and thin Black gentleman with a long beard (Marcelin 1950, 153). Bawon Samdi is the "leader of the Gede and [...] the escort of the dead" (Hurbon 1993, 95). The term "escort" refers to spirits that form a group around a major spirit like Bawon Samdi. Bawon Samdi is called the Mèt Simityè (Master of the Cemetery), the chief of the sojourn of the dead (Déita 2006, 68).

Bawon Samdi is the "brother" of Bawon Lakwa and Bawon Simityè. Bawon Lakwa is also called Azagon Lakwa (Great Cross) (Marcelin 1950, 172).[3] Bawon Lakwa fetches the dead from mortuary parlors and accompanies them to the cemetery, as one of his songs explains: "Bawon Lakwa [...] carries him away! / Carries him away to the cemetery" (Marcelin 1950, 172).[4]

When a person is possessed by Bawon Samdi, he or she falls to the ground and lies stiffly like a corpse (Brown 2001, 360). His jaw is wrapped in white cloth, his nostrils and ears are stuffed with cotton, and he is powdered like a cadaver (Brown 2001, 360). The servants of the spirits mournfully gather around the corpse. In one of manbo Mama Lola's ceremonies, the mournful seriousness was only disrupted when the Gede spirit Ti Malis displaced the horse's Bawon Samdi, changing solemnity into celebration (Brown 2001, 361).

At the request of a family, Bawon Samdi judges whether a death was natural or unnatural (Smith 2010, 117). As Bawon Samdi is a spirit that authorizes sorcery in matters that relate to death, magicians call upon him. He decides which of the buried dead may or may not be used for magic (Smith 2010, 118). Grann Brijit is Bawon Samdi's wife and the mother of the Gede spirits. She is said to be a Black woman and is called *grann* (granny) (Marcelin 1950, 177). Her *repozwa* (resting trees) are the purple mombin (*Spondias purpurea*) and the banyan fig (*Ficus benghalensis*) (Marcelin 1950, 177). On the rare occasions on which she possesses a servant, Grann Brijit takes the gait of a cadaver and the demeanor of mourning, as reflected in this song: "You say Mother Brijit is lying down, / she is sleeping! / When she wakes, every last initiate will bow!" (Hebblethwaite et al. 2012, 120, song 234).

Grann Brijit is the daughter of Ounsa Wangòl and the sister of Gede Nibo. Her sacrificial animal is a black hen. Like her husband, macerated *clairin* (white rum) is her preferred drink. Her symbol is a pile of stones laid near Bawon Samdi's cross (Déita 2006, 70). Ounsa Wangòl impregnated Grann Brijit, and she gave birth to the "evil and cannibalistic spirits of the Petwo Rite," suggesting that the Gede Rite influenced elements of the Petwo Rite. Every cemetery in Haiti has its Bawon and Brijit. If the first person buried was a male, then Bawon Samdi rules over the cemetery; if the first person buried was a female, then Brijit takes charge (Déita 2006, 68).

The trademark symbols of the Gede spirits—the top hat, black and purple clothing, a cane, dark glasses with a missing lens, a cigar, and white rum—bring to mind the image of a magician who partakes in vices (Hurbon 1993, 95). The single-lensed glasses symbolically express Gede's connection to the dead and the living (Smith 2010, 3). Plus, like a penis, his glasses have only one eye (Brown 2001, 362).

Figure 3. Rasin Bwa Kayiman's *Guede* album cover. Photo courtesy of Amey Owen.

Protector of children, Gede accessorizes pacifiers and baby rattles (Brown 2001, 362). His traditions include mock funerals with coffins that pallbearers lift in the air as they march through the center of town (Brown 2001, 362). Gede Brav is Bawon Samdi and Grann Brijit's greedy, argumentative, and wayward son. Their other son, Jan Simon Britis (Jean Simon Brutus), however, is intellectual, prophetic, and pure (Déita 2006, 78, 80). Jan Simon Britis is Gede Nibo's chief assistant, presiding over tribunals as a severe judge (Marcelin 1950, 194).

In a myth that depicts sexual violence, the female Gede Loray (Gede of the Storms) was born after Agawou Tonnè raped Wanman Wèdo. Agawou Tonnè had chained her up under the sea. Like Gede Loray's conception in rape, her birth occurred during a storm, making the spirit afraid of water. Her possessed horse throws a fit if she encounters water. Grann Brijit adopted Gede Loray and convinced Bawon Samdi that she was their daughter (Déita 2006, 80).

Roman Catholic saints also represent the Gede spirits. Bawon Samdi is identified with Saint-Expédit, cross in hand and casket at foot, and Saint-Radegonde, who founded Sainte-Croix Monastery (Marcelin 1949, 154). Grann Brijit is identified with Sainte-Brigitte, patroness of Ireland (Marcelin 1949, 177). Some identify Gede Nibo as Saint-Louis de Gonzague, others as Saint-Gérard de Majella, since he holds a crucifix and has a skull on his bed stand (Marcelin 1950, 181). Rasin Bwa Kayiman's album cover features the image shown in figure 3. The spirits are put to work by *oungan* and *manbo* by displaying the image of the saint or sometimes turning it upside down.

RITUALS AND SERVICES OF THE GEDE FAMILY OF SPIRITS

Bawon Samdi and Grann Brijit are called in the ritual for the dead referred to as the *desounen*, involving the placation and separation of the *lwa mèt tèt* (main spirit served by the deceased) and the *gwo bonnanj* (the part of the deceased that returns to God) from the body of the deceased (Deren 1953, 44). The *mèt tèt* spirit is quickest to help but also the most exacting; thus, securing its release satisfies all spiritual obligations. The *desounen* is the "remission of the divine heritage" whose purpose is to ensure that the corpse rests in peace without the turmoil of attached spirits (Deren 1953, 45). The *gwo bonnanj* descends into the watery abyss for one year and a day, whereas the *lwa mèt tèt* freely seeks a new host.

The *desounen* ritual reflects Vodou's handling of death and grieving, providing a therapeutic ritual over this final rite of passage. Bawon Samdi and Grann Brijit receive *vèvè* and animal sacrifices, while the officiating *oungan* becomes possessed by the dead's spirit and advises the deceased person's living family (Charlier and Gray 2017, 22).

One year and one day after a death, a ritual called *retire anba dlo* (reclamation from the waters) is organized. A ceremony led by a priest and assistants calls the soul of the deceased to communicate with the living via a *govi* (clay pot). The prayers of the *oungan* are directed to Legba, Bawon Samdi, and Gede. The priest channels the voice of the deceased, who enquires about the welfare of the living family members and complains about their neglect of the dead (Deren 1953, 50). "Speaking to the dead" is a part of Vodou's outlook on the afterlife, offering a method for transforming grief into veneration.

The *desounen* and *retire anba dlo* ceremonies reflect familial and domestic traditions. Public Vodou societies also organize a vigil and Novena after a member dies (Métraux 1972, 263; cited in Smith 2010, 51). The community calls forth the soul of the dead from the watery abyss to dwell permanently in a *govi* in the altar room, where it is treated like a minor spirit. Atop the altar, the dead respond to the petitions and prayers of living family members and friends.

In the diasporic context, Vodou communities are also deeply involved in funerals. Société Linto Roi Trois Mystères includes funeral services for initiates. Members of the society work together to mark with dignity the passing of one of their own, including wearing coordinated attire and sashes emblazoned with the society's name while maintaining a formal demeanor only interrupted by bereaved weeping.

THE GEDE SPIRIT FAMILY

The following list of the spirits in the Gede Rite (from Beauvoir 2008a, 187–88) provides insight into historical and linguistic aspects of the Gede tradition:

Spirit name	Family name
1. Bawon Gran Bwa	Bawon
2. Bawon Kafou	Bawon
3. Bawon Kara	Bawon
4. Bawon Kriminèl ("Criminal")	Bawon
5. Bawon Lakwa	Bawon
6. Bawon Lento	Bawon
7. Bawon Loran	Bawon
8. Bawon Samdi	Bawon
9. Bawon Simityè	Bawon
10. Bawonlin Lakwa	Bawon
11. Brav Gede Nibo	Gede Nibo
12. Bwa Landeng Lakwa (Dick in the Cross's Ass)	Gede Nibo
13. Gede Drivayè (Waifing Gede)	Gede Nibo
14. Gede Fatra (Trash Gede)	Gede Nibo
15. Gede Kriyòl (Creole Gede)	Gede Nibo
16. Gede Lensou	Gede Nibo
17. Gede Loray (Gede of the Storms)	Gede Nibo
18. Gede Nouvavou	Gede Nibo
19. Gede Pikan (Gede of Thorns or Spicey Gede)	Gede Nibo
20. Gede Ramase (Pick Up Gede)	Gede Nibo
21. Gederounsou Mazaka [Gede Ousou]	Gede Nibo
22. Gede Wawe [Wawè] (Gede of Wawe)	Gede Nibo
23. Grann Brijit (Granny Bridgit)	Bawon
24. Grann Pele (Granny Pele)	Bawon
25. Jan Giyon	Jan
26. Jan Krab (Crab Jean)	Jan
27. Jan Loran	Jan
28. Jan N'Zinga	Jan
29. Jan Zonbi (Zombie Jean)	Jan
30. Lènto Fè (Iron Lènto)	M'Poungwe

31. Senfò Yewe	—
32. Ti Chal Lakwa (Little Charles of the Cross)	Gede Nibo
33. Trase Fouye Lakwa (Trace Dig the Cross)	Gede Nibo
34. Vye Bawon (Old Bawon)	Bawon
35. Manman Travo (Mother of Works)	—

In addition, Beauvoir (2008a, 188) adds the following four spirits for the Gede-Petwo Rite:

1. Gede Zarenyen	Gede Nibo
2. Gedevi Welo	—
3. Jan Simon Britis	Gede Nibo
4. Kaptèn Zonbi	—

There are a few Gede Rite spirits that do not make Beauvoir's list (see also Métraux 1972, 9; Courlander 1973, 322–23). For example, Gede Vi is important. The name Gede Vi points to the ethnonym *Gedevi* ("children of Gede"), a reference to the ethnic group itself. Gede Vi is a healing *lwa* like Gede Nibo (Marcelin 1950, 193). Some informants viewed Gede Vi as the "son of Gede Nibo" or "Gede Nibo's wife" (Courlander 1973, 323).

Among the spirits on Beauvoir's list, Gede Loray and Gede Zeklè reflect lightning and storms. Like Sobo, Ogou Chango, or Kebyesou, they use bolts of lightning to slay people. Gede Loray is an "evildoing" female *lwa* of storms and "violent death." She possesses her servants during storms (Marcelin 1950, 196). The name Balewouze (Sweep and Sprinkle) alludes to the ritual of purifying sacred space. Jensiman Britis is a graveyard assistant for Gede Nibo. Bawon Pikan is a gravedigger. Azagon Lakwa (Great Cross) plants crosses over newly dug graves. The epithets of these spirits point to death, the world of the cemetery, burial, decay, insects, and transformation into dust (Courlander 1973).

A few spirits have permuted names, like Gede Nibo Mazaka compared with Gederounsou Mazaka (Beauvoir 2008b, 187; Courlander 1973, 323). The multiplicity of spirits and human families that serve them, in addition to the admixtures that naturally occur over time as family ancestors are fused with spirits and as families incorporate new members through unions, contribute to the rich accretions of names. They reflect important traces of historical memory attached to the deepest realm of identity and culture, representing a significant area of interest for comparative linguistics and historical studies.

Max Beauvoir's (2008b) and Harold Courlander's (1973) inventories of the Gede Rite present research opportunities. Little is known about these striking spirit names and their epithets. Why, for example, are there several Bawon and Gede spirits, and how did they all come to be? How does one deal with the profusion of names in terms of the historical context? Do Gede and Bawon myths express monogenetic, polygenetic, or diffusionary traits? The enslaved Gedevi founders of the Gede Rite were dispatched to the four corners of Saint-Domingue, and over time they diffused their Gedevi families' traditions into the colony. Forces of synthesis like Sèvis Ginen brought the disparate rites from around the colony under a single umbrella that diffused the tradition with each newly initiated priest.

Many of the Bawon and Gede epithets are transparent Haitian Creole terms that reveal an aspect of the spirit's attributes, for instance Gede *Drivayè* (Waifing) and Gede *Fatra* (Trash); or that reflect a feature of Gede's irreverence, for example *Bwa Landeng Lakwa* (Dick in the Cross's Ass). The name "Gede Zarenyen" (Gede the Spider) reflects the spider-like gesticulation of the person possessed by this Anansi-esque spirit (Métraux 1972, 91). As is often the case, the second part of the spirit's name can be an African place-name. For example, Gede *Wawe* (Wawè) includes the toponym Wawè, a Gedevi town near Abomey that was conquered by the Dahomians (Glélé 1974, 102). Gede Wawe (Gede Tiwawè or Gede Tiwawè Panchè) sows mischief in his appearances (Courlander 1973, 323).

As for Gederounsou Mazaka or Gede Ousou (Gede Youaredrunk), this "evildoer" is known for swilling copious drafts of alcohol while remaining sober (Marcelin 1950, 196). His courtship with his wealthy sister, Gede Loray, is not something the judge Jan Simon Britis accepts (Marcelin 1950, 196). The Gede name Jan N'Zinga is common in Angola. Gede Kriyòl, in contrast, is bluntly colonial. There is also the spirit Jan Zonbi (Zombie Jean), a name that points to the place that zombies occupy in the Gede Rite.

Jan Zonbi is at home in the Gede Rite, since the zombie in Haitian Creole folklore is a person who has been poisoned and has seemingly died, been buried, and raised from the dead by the poisoner magician. In the folklore, the zombie is an automaton who works as a slave for a master unless she or he tastes salt, in which case becoming a threat to the victimizer. Courlander (1973, image 30) photographs two men who are "probably" possessed by Jan Zonbi. Jaws bound with gauze and nostrils stuffed with cotton, they roll in a large bonfire. Through this cast of spirits, the Gede Rite animates the cemetery, populating the landscape with mythology that explicates death.

GEDE, BAWON, BRIJIT, AND THE CEMETERY

The cemetery is a public religious site where servants of the spirits meet (Smith 2010, 86). Port-au-Prince's main cemetery is treated like a large outdoor *ounfò* in which designated places (*repozwa*) represent important spirits from various rites, including a tomb for Danbala Wèdo, an oak tree (*bwadchenn*) for Gran

Bwa, an open recess for Èzili Dantò, a tree for Èzili Mapyang, a small grave for Gede Ti Pis Lakwa, and a big cross called Kwa Bawon for Bawon Samdi, the ritual focus of the cemetery (Smith 2010, 86). The sacred *mapou* tree (*Ceiba pentanahan*) planted beside the cemetery serves as a *repozwa* for Gede spirits (Tarter 2015, 101).

According to Karen McCarthy Brown (2001, 380), there is predatory sexual behavior among the Gede, and the lack of female Gede spirits indicates male domineering in Haitian society. However, there are some female Gede of importance. Grann Brijit, addressed in detail below, appears as an elderly, frigid spirit. Another female Gede spirit is Gedelia, who possessed manbo Mama Lola. Karen McCarthy Brown spotted Gedelia iconography on a tap-tap bus in Haiti, but little is known about her. In song 1.a below, the Gede named Sizann Lakwa (Susanne of the Cross) appears. Mentioned above is also the frightening Gede Loray. Although female representations of Gede spirits may be fewer than male ones, the songs of Rasin Bwa Kayiman examined later in this chapter place women's sexual and social concerns in sharp focus. Gede culture is an arena in which gender politics emerges as a central issue.

The Kwa Bawon is a concrete cross that serves as the spiritual crossroads of the cemetery, a place where resolution is sought in matters of life and death (Smith 2010, 86). On days designated for spirits, their servants leave candles and offerings at the spirit's *repozwa* in the cemetery. The Kwa Bawon is a focal point where servants of the spirits gather to call on Gede's assistance and communicate with "ancestors who lie buried in a great anonymous heap of bones," referring to the charnel house where skeletons are tossed once rent for a temporary tomb is no longer paid (Brown 2001, 369–71).

THE DEAD, MAGIC, AND MORALITY

The practice of magic involves the bending of reality for personal benefit. Since the Gede spirits drag people into or pull them back from death, they are called upon to facilitate the most serious forms of magic, whether socially constructive or destructive. The known dead and the Gede are called on to quicken justice, healing, fortune, and equilibrium in social relations. When other avenues of social promotion and remediation are limited, contacting the dead or the Gede presents an opportunity (Smith 2010, 122). The "occult economy" reflects a desire for survival as much as consumption in a setting where these are limited (Smith 2010, 153). Gede invites a critique of capitalism and the commodification of human life, encompassing a range of normative and nonnormative practices. The following accounts hint at these concerns.

The healer and magician Antz, who works inside of a tomb in Port-au-Prince's main cemetery, illustrates the complex and contradictory magical services associated with the Gede spirits (Smith 2010, 105). Antz called upon *djab* (antisocial spirits) and *mò* (dead souls) for his clients, and was a malefactor (*malfèktè*) because he cast spells and sent spirits that other *oungan* or *manbo* would not work with (Smith 2010, 93). Such magicians serve desperate clients who need quick interventions.

Calling on the powers of a purchased spirit like Djab Andèy (Spirit in Mourning), Antz received fast financial gains, but it would kill him and his child within seventeen years of his first taking up such work (Smith 2010, 93). A client served by Djab Andèy could expect financial windfalls, but the client would have to pay a significant sum for the assistance. Djab Andèy is a "predatory capitalist" type of spirit in that he seeks quick gratification, regardless of the damage it causes in the world. However, there are also cases of Antz using Djab Andèy's power to attain virtuous ends, such as causing impotence in a delinquent father until he paid child support (Smith 2010, 121).

In calling on the powers of an inherited spirit like Gede Avadra (Vagabond Gede), Antz's working conditions were stark. During a mental health crisis, Gede Avadra had led Antz to live in the cemetery. Mounted by Gede Avadra in front of Bawon's Cross, Antz healed a child who had suffered under a deadly spell (Smith 2010, 98). Gede Avadra's mother and father, Grann Brijit and Legba, had abandoned Gede Avadra at the cemetery gates, reflecting the plight of parentless children and the tragedy of *restavèk* (child domestic workers) (Smith 2010, 102). Since Gede Avadra is a homeless orphan, the healer-magician Antz had to sleep for four days outside of the cemetery prior to beginning the treatment of the child (Smith 2010, 101). After using Gede Avadra's services, Antz could not accept money for the work. As "the voice of the dispossessed," Gede Avadra functions as the "moral foil" to Djab Andèy's predation, the spirits functioning as "inversions of each other" (Smith 1010, 120).

In a different narrative, three Dominican prostitutes purchased a *zonbi astral* from oungan Ti Benn in order to improve their powers of sexual attraction and increase their earnings from sex work (Smith 2010, 128). The *zonbi astral* was "invaginated" in a "transubstantiation" ritual in which the power of the dead was transferred to the genitals of the prostitutes. The bodiless zombie was called to work for the clients, but it had to be fed ritually to remain active (Smith 2010, 147). The ritual took place in Titanyen (Lil' nothing), a town located eighteen kilometers north of Port-au-Prince where victims of crime or state violence are infamously dumped (Smith 2010, 129). The surplus of the unnatural dead makes it a site charged with magical potential. Ti Benn told the prostitutes that the zombie would bring them wealth but would likely limit the length of their lives to five years (Smith 2010, 146).

The fee for the magic was approximately the equivalent of US$130 per month, money that would be kept in a hole near Gede's cross (Smith 2010, 148). The magical operation involved the crushing of a human skull into a fine powder with a mortar and pestle. Since the skull was from someone who had died an unnatural death, their soul lingered with their body and could be captured as a bodiless astral zombie capable of bewitching the clients of the prostitutes. The powdery essence from the skull was mixed with perfume, plant material, and other ingredients and then set on fire inside of a basin (Smith 2010, 149). The *oungan* then instructed the women to thoroughly wash their vaginas in the extinguished magical liquid, including rubbing it into their crotches. The *oungan* explained that the procedure combined the "white magic" of making the women more attractive with the "black magic" of making men pay more readily (Smith 2010, 149). Making use of a recently departed's soul in the form of a zombie is morally ambiguous, because the magic can be utilized for healing, profiting, or harming (Smith 2010, 154). Katherine Smith argues that zombies that heal or protect reflect "normative Vodou," whereas zombies coerced for harm reflect nonnormative expressions of sorcery and magic (2010, 154). The importance of ceremonies in honor of Gede increased over the twentieth century in Haiti, a matter examined next.

THE GEDE RITE, FAMILY ANCESTORS, AND MIGRATION

How did displacement from rural to urban areas change ritual practices? The construction of domestic tombs for ancestors became increasingly limited, and burials were concentrated in cemeteries. Worship and ritual started to shift from private domestic space to public communal space. Gede began to function like a surrogate for the ancestral dead (Smith 2010, xi–xii).

In rural areas, services for the dead are domestic and linked to family Lakou, which is property associated with multigenerational settlement. The Lakou and the large tombs that Haitian families erect for their dead are the sites of these rituals. Haitian rural residents have abandoned traditional land to reside in cities, where electricity, running water, education, employment, services, and passages to foreign opportunities are more available.

In rural ancestral veneration, the spirits of deceased family members possess their living children. Philo, the mother of manbo Mama Lola, became possessed by her mother's spirit and, more rarely, her father's (Brown 2001, 364). Mama Lola received her mother's spirit in dreams and through petitions in the cemetery. In some cases, an ancestor spirit can become the *lwa mèt tèt*. In other cases, the arrival of a great universal spirit is treated like the appearance of a familial ancestor if that ancestor actively served the spirit during his or her lifetime. The arrival of Agwe was taken as the appearance of Mama Lola's mother, since the spirit of the sea was her *mèt tèt* (Brown 2001, 368).

As Haitians have become a migratory people uprooted from their homeland and familial burial sites, practices that honor the personal ancestral dead at domestic burial sites have shifted to practices that honor the universal ancestral dead, the Gede. Direct contact with the ancestors in Lakou via tombs has shifted to the urban and diasporic Gede Rite of Sèvis Ginen.

Gede spirits straddle multiple ancestral layers. In the absence of domestic entombment, they represent missing family members, in addition to the "collective dead," the "national dead," and the "spirit of the people" (Smith 2010, xii). Gede has become "a generalized spirit of all the dead," substituting for the ancestors (Brown 2001, 368). The increased importance of the carnivalesque public Gede celebrations of November 1–2 is rooted in the rural exodus that shifted commemorations of the dead from private to public spaces (Smith 2010, 86). The next section turns to an examination of Rasin Bwa Kayiman's record *Guede* (2004), an album that offers direct access to the living Gede tradition.

RASIN BWA KAYIMAN'S ALBUM *GUEDE* (GEDE SPIRITS)

Rasin Bwa Kayiman's album *Guede*, released by Jean M. Altidor's Mass Konpa Records in 2004, focuses on the spirits of this important rite. Altidor's record label, which is based in Miami, releases dozens of albums and films annually, constituting a significant catalogue of Haitian entertainment.

The music of Rasin Bwa Kayiman's *Guede* illustrates the sacred music of the Gede Rite. The album is arranged in a traditional Vodou orchestral formation, just as Racine Figuier is:

(1) Lead vocalist, Sergo Pierre (founding maestro of Rasin Bwa Kayiman)
(2) Chorus members, Marie Maude Joseph, Nounoune Jacker, Solmene Deliane, Ysmarie Valles, and Kelita Jean Louis
(3) First drummer, Edy Chery
(4) Second drummer, Louicito Aldor
(5) Third drummer, Archelus Julien
(6) First bass drum, Davir Desir
(7) Second bass drum, Ronald Mathieu
(8) Third bass drum, Saget Arius
(9) *Fer* (iron) or *ogan* (iron cowbell), Francklin Pierre
(10) Secretary, Julien Archelus
(11) Founding member, Sergo Pierre

(12) Invited artists, Pierre Woodly, Pierre Fritzbert, Silvina Regatte, Marie Matte, and Mamoune

Both albums in this book are constructed in similar ways: a charismatic lead vocalist who sings and calls to a chorus that sings and responds, several drummers, and a cowbell player form the Vodou orchestra. As was the case in chapter 3, the entire *Guede* album's seven tracks are transcribed and translated below in sequential order. Once again, within each track, several songs flow from the one into the other.

Yo, n ap rele yo — *Them, We Are Calling Them*

1.a

Yo, m ap rele yo.	Them, I am calling them.
Gede Nouvavou, m ap rele yo.	Gede Nouvavou, I am calling them.
Kwa Lakwa, m ap rele yo.	Cross of the Cross, I am calling them.
Trase fouye lakwa, m ap rele yo.	Trace and dig the cross, I am calling them.
Jan Simon Britis Lakwa, m ap rele yo.	Jan Simon Britis the Cross, I am calling them.
Adja, nou rive.	Adja, we have arrived.
Yo, n ap rele yo.	Them, we are calling them.
Gede Nouvavou, n ap rele yo.	Gede Nouvavou, we are calling them.
—Kwa Senbo!	—Senbo's cross!
Yo, n ap rele yo.	Them, we are calling them.
Gede Nouvavou, n ap rele yo.	Gede Nouvavou, we are calling them.
Gede Nouvavou, n ap rele yo.	Gede Nouvavou, we are calling them.
Adja, nou rive.	Adja, we have arrived.
Dje, mwen di kwa Senbo, n ap rele yo. Ti Marasa Lakwa, n ap rele yo.	God, I say Senbo's Cross, we are calling them. Little Marasa of the Cross, we are calling them.

Kwa Lakwa, n ap rele yo.	Cross of the Cross, we are calling them.
Mòpyon Lakwa, n ap rele yo.	Crabs of the Cross, we are calling them.
Sizann Lakwa, n ap rele yo.	Sizann of the Cross, we are calling them.
Adja, nou rive.	Adja, we have arrived.

Song 1.a is an opening salvo that cuts to the marrow of the relationship between the Vodouists and the spirits: it is one of *calling* spirits in song, drum, and dance, but also oration and writing. The first line of the song calls on a plurality of spirits but also emphasizes the spirit Gede Nouvavou. The expression "Cross of Crosses" in line 3 is one of the many monikers for the Gede spirits. People bear crosses in life, but the cross of crosses is death itself. In line 5, the Gede spirit Jan Simon Britis also makes an appearance.

Gede Nouvavou is an *oungan-lwa* and a beggar who spreads rumors. He is the brother of Gede Ti Ware and Gede Ousou, the last children of Bawon Samdi and Grann Brijit (Marcelin 1950, 198). A two-line song for Gede Nouvavou reveals that he rests in a mango tree: "Gede Nouvavou has a mango tree! It is a spirit's resting tree."[5]

The Cross of Crosses, mentioned in line 3, is the intersection of life and death. The center of the cross is where Bawon, Brijit, and the Gede take charge of the passage from life to death. The "Cross" is a crossroads (*kafou*) linking the living with the ancestors under the water. In line 4, the images of *trase* (to trace) and *fouye* (to dig) point to the seeking of Vodou spirits. *Trase* calls to mind the tracing of *vèvè* cosmograms by priests. *Fouye* is a common verb in songs and folklore, such as "Chache fouye, w ap jwenn" (Dig and you will find), a proverb I saw painted on a wall in a Léogâne compound. The lyric "trace and dig the cross" calls for an engagement with the Gede and the good and bad they bring: life, its sexual euphorias, and death (Jil and Jil 2009, 220).

Line 5 calls out to Jan Simon Britis. This powerful and brainy judge is the son of Bawon Samdi and Grann Brijit, and, as Gede Nibo's chief assistant, he wears distinguished attire, including tucking a white jasmine flower in a buttonhole in his jacket (Marcelin 1950, 194). His servants place a white jasmine flower in a glass of water on his reception table (Déita 2006, 80).

The line "Aja, we have arrived" symbolically calls out to the Aja people after an arrival in the Caribbean. The song seems to express solidarity with the Aja people, who, like the Gedevi, were sold by powerful African governments and traders to European enslavers. "Aja, we have arrived" is a message of survival.[6] In addition to the coastal ethnic group and its language, the word "Aja" also refers to the elderly female *lwa* who instructs her initiates about roots and herbs. She may also compel them to eat glass (Courlander 1973, 325). Glass-eating spirits still appear in ceremonies, as I witnessed at Société Makaya in Miami. Although the spirit was allowed to manifest for a few minutes, the community expelled it as the possession performance became more dangerous. Glass-crunching spirits that use their teeth to break bottle shards demonstrate the spirit's power of protection over the servant.[7] Complex words like "Aja" reveal a palimpsest woven from layers of meaning, each one visible in traces.

The expression "Kwa Senbo" (Senbo's Cross) in line 9 is another important linguistic clue to approaching the song. The word *senbo* is related to the Fon word *sègbó*, meaning "Great Spirit" or "God." Lines 15 through 18 give a series of fascinating appellations. Ti Marasa Lakwa (Little Marasa of the Cross) is noteworthy, since the Marasa or "Twin" spirits of the Rada Rite, examined in Chapter 3, pop up in a Gede name. The expression "Kwa Lakwa" (Cross of the Cross) mockingly epitomizes the cross as if death could be outdone by more death. Likewise, Mòpyon Lakwa (Crabs of the Cross) playfully scorns death while embodying it, too, in the form of a horrible pubic pest. In a similar vein, among the Gede there is Ti Pis Lakwa (Little Flea of the Cross). These names deride the Gede and death itself. Finally, Sizann Lakwa (Susanne of the Cross) presents a female Gede figure.

The song is about God, Gede Nouvavou, and other Gede spirits. As the last line suggests, the message is also one of departure, the Middle Passage, and arrival in the colony, preserving a fragment of that harrowing journey and revealing Gede as a spirit that handles exile, displacements, and migrations.

1.b

Di chè mesye, manman mwen nan won,

l ape danse.
Chè mesye, manman mwen nan won,

l ape danse.
Si w renmen fanm sila, fò w renmen l,

Simityè Lakwa e.
Lakwa devan, simityè dèyè.

Dye lakwa devan,
simityè dèyè.
Si w renmen fanm sila, fò w renmen l,

1.b

Say dear men, my mother is in the circle,

she is dancing!
Dear men, my mother is in the circle,

she is dancing!
If you love this woman, you have to love her,

Cemetery of the Cross.
The cross is in front, the cemetery is behind!

God of the cross is in front, the cemetery is behind.
If you love this woman, you have to love her,

Simityè Lakwa e.	Cemetery of the Cross.
Di chè mesye, lakwa yo nan won,	Say dear men, the crosses are in a circle,
y ape danse.	they are dancing.
—Dye o kwa Senbo!	—God oh Senbo's cross!
Chè mesye, lakwa yo nan won,	Dear men, the crosses are in the circle,
y ape danse.	they are dancing.
Si w renmen fanm sila, fò w renmen	If you love this woman, hey you have to love
Simityè Lakwa e.	the Cemetery of the Cross.
Lakwa devan—simityè dèyè!	The cross is in front—the cemetery is behind!
Dye lakwa devan	God of the cross is in front
—simityè dèyè!	—the cemetery is behind!
Si w renmen fanm sila, fò w renmen	If you love this woman, hey you have to love
Simityè Lakwa e.	the Cemetery of the Cross.
Di chè mesye papa mwen avè mwen,	Say dear men, my father is with me,
l ape danse.	he is dancing.
—mmm!	—mmm!
Chè mesye, manman mwen avè mwen,	Dear men, my mother is with me,
l ape danse.	she is dancing.
Jan m te renmen papa m pou l al nan	Hey, I loved my father too much for him to go to
Simityè Lakwa e.	the Cemetery of the Cross.
Jan m te renmen manman m tout al nan	Hey, I loved my mother too much for her to go to
Simityè Lakwa e.	the Cemetery of the Cross.
Lakwa devan—simityè dèyè.	The cross is in front—the cemetery is behind.
Kou pa manman devan,	My mother's turn is in front,
gade kou pa m dèyè la	look my turn is behind there.
Jan m te renmen fanmi m	Man, I loved my family too much for
tout al nan Simityè Lakwa, mesye.	all of them to go to the Cemetery of the Cross.

Si n renmen fanm sila—fò n renmen	If you love this woman—you have to love
Simityè Lakwa e.	Cemetery of the Cross.

Song 1.b opens with a beautiful line that captures the perspective of a son and a daughter gazing at the splendor of their mother, who dances in a circular pattern across the dance floor of a Vodou ceremony. She is "in the round," twirling on an earthen surface. Line 5 returns to the theme of love: "you" have to love the mother as does the Gede Rite protector, Simityè Lakwa. The Gede spirits are called on to love and defend the living while stalling death. Line 7 takes up a Vodou spatial metaphor with the two adverbs "in front" and "behind." A frequent formulation, "God in front, the spirits behind," sparingly encapsulates Vodou theology.[8] However, in this case, "the Cross" is in front and "the Cemetery" is behind, suggesting that "the Cross" is the passage into "the Cemetery."

Line 8, "God of the cross is in front," provides further confirmation of the modeling of this lyric on the common expression, "God is in front, the spirits are behind." Lines 9 through 11 return to the narrator's perspective on his mother dancing in the ceremony, poignant nostalgia that points to the tradition's multigenerational, familial foundations.

The first through third verses have similar themes, but each adds important details. In verse 2, the topic is "the crosses" rather than "mother," representing the Gede spirits that are dancing. Verse 3 adds the "father" and the "family," creating a complete image of the household.

Line 24 points to the tension of family, friends, and ourselves passing by way of the cross and cemetery to join the ancestors. Lines 29 through 32 contemplate the loss of parents and the loss of self to the living. Those who dance with us today, die in front of us tomorrow, advancing our turn in mortality. Line 33 insists on the theme in reprising the saying, "The cross is in front—the cemetery is behind!" The expression is rephrased to include the death of the narrator's mother and the narrator: "My mother's turn *is in front*, look my turn is right behind." The song shifts perspective to the period after the death of the narrator's family, illustrating that loving other human beings necessitates a mortal tension. This song points to intergenerational communion and engagement with the Gede Rite to resolve those pains.

1.c	1c.
Bawon, men timoun yo.	Bawon, here are the children.
Bawon Lakwa, men timoun yo.	Bawon of the Cross, here are the children.
Bawon Samdi,	Bawon Samdi,

men timoun yo nan simityè.	the children are in the cemetery.
Vle pa vle, fò lavi n chanje	No matter what, our lives must change
—nan lakou lakay.	—in the yard back home.

Bawon Samdi, Bawon Lakwa, and Bawon Simityè form a triad of diverse attributes (Marcelin 1950, 146). For example, Bawon Simityè takes care of the cemetery, while Bawon Lakwa supplies the dead (Marcelin 1950, 173). Bawon hears about people's deepest frustrations, threats of exile, and requests for strength (Beauvoir 2008b, 132).

Priests have developed a ritual system for appeasing, memorializing, and communicating with the dead. Bawon mediates that communication: "Bawon of the Cross, show me the three words of the prayer, / So that I can speak with the dead."[9] Children are threatened with Bawon's wrath for their effronteries: "Bawon, oh Bawon, Bawon, oh Bawon, here are naughty children cursing at the adults, take them away to the cemetery."[10] One song is clear about what domain Bawon controls: "Oh Bawon, it is you who leads the seven dead to the cemetery."[11] The song suggests that Bawon is God's assistant in matters of death. In this way, it illustrates how the *lwa* make known the attributes of God.

Song 1.c shows Bawon Samdi's love for children. He and the Gede must heal and protect children, especially sick ones. The presence of the names Bawon Lakwa and Bawon Samdi illustrates how members of a spirit family occur together in songs. After three cries to Bawon, the third line calls out to the children in the cemetery who pay him their respects. They arrived there on November 2 in order to visit and clean the graves of their deceased family. The final lines are a cry to Bawon for social change, an expression of social consciousness that will become more pointed.

1.d	1.d
Bawon o, m a rele Bawon o!	Oh Bawon, oh I will call Bawon!
Bawon o, m a rele Bawon o!	Oh Bawon, oh I will call Bawon!
Bawon Lakwa moutre m twa mo priyè a anvan m ale	Bawon of the Cross show me the three words of prayer before I leave
pou m ka pase avè mò yo.	so I can pass through to the dead.
Bawon Bitasyon	Bawon of the Farm
(Bawon Samdi, Bawon Kriminèl)	(Bawon Samdi, Bawon Kriminèl)
moutre m twa mo priyè a	show me the three words of prayer
—pou m ka pase avèk mò yo!	—so I can pass through to the dead!

Song 1.d opens with supplications to Bawon. In lines 3–4, we learn that the narrator seeks knowledge of "three words of the prayer," a lyric for Bawon Samdi examined above about contact with the ancestors. Here, the formulaic, "three words of prayer," is the step taken to "pass through to the dead," to receive news from the dead.

In line 6, the epithet "Bawon of the Farm" connects the spirit to cultivation. Bawon Kriminèl (Criminal Bawon) is also mentioned, providing an allusion to a bloodthirsty life-taker. Bawon Kriminèl is sometimes known for antisocial magic involving murder and zombification (Smith 2010, 86). His *repozwa* (resting place) in the cemetery of Port-au-Prince is near the tomb of the abusive dictator François Duvalier, in ruins since revolters smashed it on February 7, 1986. Some people, like the artist Pierrot Barra, view Bawon Kriminèl as a source of justice (Smith 2010, 110).

1.e

Bawon o, Bawon Lakwa o,

m prale.
—Kwa!
—Dye, Bawon, ale, mesye, Lakwa!

Bawon o, Bawon Lakwa o,

m prale.
Bawon o, m prale.
Bawon o, m prale.
M a kite peyi a, m ale.
Bawon Loran, m prale
—m pral kite peyi a ba yo!

Bawon Bitasyon, m prale!
—m pral kite peyi a ba yo!

Bawon Kriminèl, m prale
—m pral kite peyi a ba yo!

1.e

Oh Bawon, oh Bawon of the Cross,
I am leaving.
—Cross!
—God, Bawon, go, man, the Cross!

Oh Bawon, oh Bawon of the Cross,
I am leaving.
Oh Bawon, I am leaving.
Oh Bawon, I am leaving.
I'll leave the country, I'm off!
Bawon of Loran, I am going
—I will leave the country for them!

Bawon of Farms, I am going!
—I will leave the country for them!

Criminal Bawon, I am leaving
—I will leave the country for them!

Song 1.e has a call-and-response structure with the *manbo* singing the first two lines and the chorus responding with "Kwa!" (Cross!). Line 4 seems odd grammatically, but it is reasonable to interpret it as an expression of frustration directed at Bawon, God (Dye), and the passage into death, "the Cross."

The notion of "leaving" Haiti is common in Haitian songs, reflecting the memorialization of migration in songs (Richman 2005). Song 1.e does not explain the narrator's motives, but the attitude is one of frustration and abandonment. The sour mood is especially expressed in the response given in line 11: "—I will leave the country for them!"—in which the country is turned over to antagonists who remain behind.

The name Bawon Loran is probably linked to a place or a family name. Beauvoir's list of spirits in the Gede Rite (2008a, 187–88) includes Bawon Loran and Jan Loran, suggesting wide recognition. The names Bawon Bitasyon and Bawon Kriminèl reappear with the narrator's assurance that the country will be abandoned on account of *them*, unnamed members of society who threaten the narrator's well-being. The name Bawon Bitasyon (Bawon of Farms) illustrates the encoding of rural and Lakou culture in songs. The theme of the singled-out servant of the spirits contending against a band of antagonists is common, reflecting the endless siege that vulnerable Vodouists have endured in the Caribbean. The repetition of names suggests that the singer blames Bawon for a part of the woes experienced.

1.f	1.f
Pran o wi wa—kondwi m ale!	Take me oh wee wah—drive me away!
Pran o wi wa—mennen m ale!	Take me oh wee wah—lead me away!
Pran zonbi o wi wa—kondwi m ale!	Oh take zombie wee wah—lead me away!
Nèg Leren, ou bwè tafya w ap vin fè tenten w anba toujou—kondwi m ale kay zonbi o wi wa ki mennen m ale.	Man of Leren, you drink liquor, you'll still come do your fooling underhandedly—lead me away oh to the zombie's house wee wah who took me away.

Song 1.f seamlessly appends to song 1.e but shifts in substance away from the *lwa*. In lines 1 and 2, the song's narrator seems to be captured and reduced to a zombie state. The words "zombie" and "me" that appear in line 3 should be one and the same individual. The expression *wee wah* is zombie onomatopoeia that imitates their squeals. The song makes a subtle appeal to children with this playful expression.

The themes are serious, however, since an evil magician typically captures and "zombifies" his victims with a toxic powder. A few hours after being buried alive by means of the powdered anesthetic, the magician and his helpers gather at the grave. Uttering incantations and cracking his whip, they unbury "the dead" and revive the zombie, who slowly emerges from the anesthesia. The zombie has suffered brain damage in the casket caused by oxygen deprivation. Zombified, next to her or his casket, cognitively and emotionally devastated, the victim can be "driven away" ("kondwi m ale") or "led away" ("mennen m ale") at the end of a whip and enslaved.

A sociological explanation for zombification can be found in the history and culture of Haiti's Vodou secret societies (Beauvoir-Dominique and Dominique 2003, 139–72). Secret societies like the Chanpwèl, Bizango, Makanda, Zobòp, Vlengbedeng, and others are rumored to practice shape-shifting magic and cannibalism, their members reportedly having the ability to fly. In addition to a magical function, secret societies provide protection and judicial services for their community. Grouping together the most dangerous spirits reflects the seriousness of their proceedings.

Secret societies took root in the most remote regions of Haiti, where access to the courts and police were absent. In the event of land disputes, crimes of murder or adultery, acts of selfishness, insults, theft, slander, or lack of respect or harm rendered to a society member, the offending individual was denounced (*vann*) to the members of the secret society. Accuser and accused were brought before the members of the society, and an "emperor" (*anperè*) read the judgment of the General Staff Group (Gwoup Deta Majò). If one of its members asked for clemency on behalf of the accused, the unanimous judgment of the General Staff Group was broken, and the accused was acquitted. On the other hand, if unanimity was upheld, the sanction could range from a fine to zombification (Beauvoir-Dominique and Dominique 2003, 139–72).

The source of trouble in the song appears to be the "man of Leren" and his heavy drinking, which led him to publicly harass the song's narrator. The narrator finds him or herself at the zombie's house—having been taken away. The call of the narrator to be driven away is difficult to interpret, but it certainly reflects victimization. There is tension at this song's core, but here there is no resolution, only enslavement.

P ap plase ankò	*Won't Be a Common-Law Wife Again*
2.a	2.a
Kwa Senbo—kwa!	Senbo's cross—cross!
Kwa Lakwa—kwa!	Cross of the Cross—cross!
Kwa dèyè kwa—kwa!	Cross behind crosses—cross!

M p ap plase ankò, anye!	I won't be a common-law wife again, oh my!
Kote Marimod ki te plase o?	Oh where is Mary-Maude who took a common-law partner?
—Se vre!	—It's true!
—Mezanmi, pawòl la ap pale, vin tande!	—Oh man, the truth is being spoken, come listen!
—Rele machann kilòt, soutyen, slip, deyodoran [...]	—Call the panty merchant, bras, underpants, deodorant
Kòman mezanmi, nou pa bezwen m la?	Wow, my goodness, you don't need me here?
M p ap plase ankò, mesye.	I won't be a common-law wife again, guys

Kote Marimod ki te plase o?	Oh where is Mary-Maude who was a common-law wife?
Mezanmi, vin wè Marimod k ap tiye mòpyon, anhan	Oh my, come see Mary-Maude who is killing crabs, oh yeah!
Mezanmi, vin wè Marimod k ap tiye mòpyon, anhan!	Oh my, come see Mary-Maude who is killing crabs, oh yeah!
Nan bounda Julyè se pèt-pèt.	Up Juliette's butthole are lots of farts.

The three-line ritual formula for invoking the Gede Rite opens song 2.a, indicating the canonical feature of the formula. Within it, eight occurrences of the word *kwa* (cross) propound the core theme of death. The designations *Kwa Senbo* (Senbo's [God's] Cross), *Kwa Lakwa* (Cross of the Cross), and *Kwa dèyè kwa* (Crosses behind crosses) all express a note of extremity and point to the presence of the supreme being at the very head of the rite.

Songs 2.a and 2.b offer glimpses of Gede's characteristic *betiz* (vulgarity). The main theme of a woman's abandonment of *plasaj* (common-law partnerships) offers a poignant critique of this Haitian institution. A *plasaj* relationship between a man and a woman describes "the extramarital unions of respectable people" (Leyburn 1998, 187). In the traditional Haitian custom, the man is expected to remain faithful to his *plase*, whether one or several. A woman will only agree to enter a *plasaj* union if the man has prepared a modest furnished house on land that they and their children can farm. Generations of Haitian peasants have opted for *plasaj* relationships.

The first three lines of the song signal the Gede tradition with the calls of *Kwa Senbo, Kwa Lakwa,* and *Kwa dèyè kwa*. Thereafter, however, the song focuses on the practical issue of the singer's refusal to enter into another common-law partnership. In line 4, that resolve is affirmed. The song's narrator asks what happened to Mary-Maude, who also entered such a union. Something scandalous occurred, and the neighbors are summoned to learn of it. The line "Wow, my goodness, you don't need me here?" suggests that Mary-Maude got thrown out of her partnership when the commitment of her partner waned. The song's narrator has suffered misfortune similar to Mary-Maude's and wants nothing to do with *plasaj*, calling for the market sellers to gather near to hear her complaints.

The third part of the song, beginning with line 14, is an oblique comment on the condition of Mary-Maude, who now figures in a comic burst centered on the killing of genital crabs, perhaps a reference to the condition that her husband left her with and, at the same time, a nod to the mischievous Gede spirits who revel in jokes about pubic pests. Finally, the song ends on a note of *betiz* regarding Julyè's flatulence. The style and language is base and childish, and smacks of Gede's slapstick humor while delivering a frontal critique on the prevailing sexual political culture.

2.b

Ti Nènè, ou di w anvi raze mwen.

Si w ap raze mwen,
atansyon tèt nan langèt mwen

—He-hey!
—E sa se pa anyen, sa se plim pan!

Ti Nènè, ou di w anvi raze mwen.

Si w ap raze m, atansyon

nen [tèt] langèt mwen.
Gade chita ti Nènè k ap fè resò

douk sou douk anba langèt solid o.
Zo e zozo e!

2.b

Little Nènè, you said you want to shave me.

If you are going to shave me,
watch out for the head of my clitoris

Oh my!
—Hey, this isn't nothing, it's a peacock feather!

Little Nènè, you said you want to shave me.

If you are going to shave me, watch out

for the head of my clitoris.
Look at sitting Nènè who is spring-loaded

fucking under a serious clitoris.
Hey bone, hey cock!

Song 2.b takes up several curious sexual or semisexual themes. Ti Nènè, in lines 1–3, is welcome to shave off the narrator's pubic hair provided she takes care not to cut her clitoris. The choir replies with the characteristic expression of surprise, *He-hey!* Line 5 is a humorous response suggesting that Ti Nènè does not wield a razor but a peacock feather, itself an implement for inducing sexual ecstasy in some bedrooms.

The reference to the shaving of pubic hair is repeated, building tension, since a razor in the proximity of a clitoris produces discomfort. The idea is arresting but dissipates into laughter. In lines 9–10, the narrator describes Nènè bouncing like a wound-up spring on her lover's penis. Alternately, the song is about sex between women, and the *zozo* is their dildo. Nènè has a "serious clitoris" because she knows how to satisfy her sexual desires, revealing the ways Haitian songs demonstrate awareness of the central role of the clitoris in female sexuality (McAlister 2002, 74). Of course, orgasm as a "little death" returns full circle to Gede's death motif.

The song closes on a phallic note: the phrase *zo e zozo e* derives from *zo* (bone) and *zozo*, meaning "bone-bone," the Creole word for "cock." Overall, the song reveals Gede's sexually affirming aspect while still inflecting danger into the mood. This danger, the threat of genital mutilation, evokes the intolerable death of erotic pleasure.

3.a	3.a
Kwa Senbo—kwa!	Senbo's Cross—cross!
Kwa Lakwa—kwa!	Cross of the Cross—cross!
Kwa dèyè kwa—kwa!	Cross behind crosses—cross!
Gede nan mòn.	Gede in the mountains.
Ala on move Gede, Gede nan mòn.	What a mean Gede is Gede in the mountains.
—Kwa!	—Cross!
—Dye o, kwa Senbo!	—Oh God, Senbo's cross!
Gede nan mòn.	Gede in the mountains.
Ala on move Gede, Gede nan mòn.	What a mean Gede is Gede in the mountains.
Lavi miyò, miyò pase byen!	Life is better, better than wealth!
Gede nan mòn trase fouye lakwa,	Gede in the mountains trace and dig the cross,
Jan Simon Britis Lakwa!	Jan Simon Britis of the Cross,
M ap rele Mòpyon Lakwa!	I am calling Crabs of the Cross!
Ala on move Gede, Gede nan mòn!	What a mean Gede is Gede in the mountains!
—Kwa!	—Cross!
Gede nan mòn,	Gede in the mountains,
Ti Marasa Lakwa,	Little Marasa of the Cross

M rele Ti Bèbèt Lakwa.	I am calling Little Bèbèt of the Cross
M rele Sèt Tèt Lakwa.	I am calling Seven-Headed Cross,
Ala on move Gede, Gede nan mòn.	what a mean Gede is Gede in the mountains.

After opening with Gede's ritual formula, song 3.a complains of the anger of "Gede in the mountains." Line 10 is a wise saying about life's supremacy over wealth. The song urges a retreat to the countryside as a way of delinking from the oppressive neocolonial gridlock of cities. In line 11, Gede in the mountains is connected to core ritual and conceptual terms with "the cross" as the direct object of the serial verb: "trase fouye lakwa" (trace [and] dig the cross), suggesting that the Bawon and Gede spirits should be consulted about our mortality.

There is tension around the idea that Gede in the mountain is "mean." However, line 11 asserts the important point that Gede has a place at the center of objectives: *trase fouye* is an injunction to seek truth. *Trase fouye* also brings to mind the proverb of warning, "If you keep digging, you'll find your granny's bones" (Patrick Bellegarde-Smith, personal correspondence, 2018).[12] *Trase fouye* is a call to the source even as Haitian people are faced with the threats of displacement, dehumanization, and famine-inducing economic policy.

Lines 12–13 list Gede spirit names, which accumulate until the close of the song. Jan Simon Britis of the Cross, the judge who appeared in song 1.a, and Crabs of the Cross, which appeared in songs 1.a and 2.a, are supporting Gede spirits that add an incantatory litany to the song. The list springs into a complex throng of Gede spirits, including Little Marasa of the Cross, Little Bèbèt of the Cross, and the Seven-Headed Cross, a playful but horrific grouping of spirits that flash the face of death—a seven-headed cross—across our minds. Although the song's focus is on Gede in the mountains, he is surrounded by a hydra of spirits that uncover haunting aspects of Gede symbolism.

3.b   3.b

M anba Gwo Wòch o!	Oh I'm underneath Big Rock!
—Kwa!	—Cross!
E mwen trase fouye a,	Hey, I traced and dug,
m anba Gwo Wòch o,	Oh I am underneath Big Rock,
ou pa wè m ap navige?	don't you see that I am navigating?
—Dye o Kwa Senbo!	—Oh God, Senbo's cross!
Anba Gwo wòch o!	Oh underneath Big Rock!
E mwen, m Mazaka Lakwa	Hey, it's me, I am Mazaka of the Cross

m anba Gwo Wòch o,	I am underneath Big Rock,
ou pa wè m ap navige?	don't you see I am navigating?
Sa ki mande pou mwen,	Those who ask for me,
m anba Gwo Wòch o.	oh I am underneath Big Rock.
Sa k mande pou lakwa yo,	Those who ask for the crosses,
m anba Gwo Wòch o.	oh I am underneath Big Rock.
Se mwen Gede Nibo,	Oh it is me Gede Nibo,
m anba Gwo Wòch o,	I am underneath Big Rock,
ou pa wè m ap navige?	don't you see that I am navigating?

Song 3.b is the first to reference Gwo Wòch, meaning literally "Big Rock." The spirit's name calls to mind the practice of associating spirits with impressive rocks where they commonly rest, just as they did in Dahomian and Gedevi societies (Le Hérissé 1911, 194). On both sides of the Atlantic, rocks are sold to clients for the powerful spirits that reside in them.

The song's narrator is *underneath* the spirit, suggesting its profound influence, one reinforced by the choral response of *Kwa!* (Cross) in line 2, which indicates the Gede Rite. In line 3, the "trace and dig" motif returns. However, this time the result of the ritual activity is positioned under Gwo Wòch's influence. Line 5 clarifies the song's tension in a question about navigation. The term *navige* (to navigate) is common in songs for Agwe and Èzili, denoting guidance on the sea and in the storms of life. After this revelation, the chorus responds with a formula that expresses ultimacy: "Dye o, Kwa Senbo" (Oh God, Senbo's cross!).

Line 11 inquires rhetorically about those who ask about Gede, only to be told that he and the rest of "the crosses" are underneath Gwo Wòch. The spirit name Gede Nibo is added as if synonymous with Gede Mazaka Lakwa. This elliptical song addresses a quest (*navige*) so broad that all listeners belong to it. Defying straightforward interpretations, it stays focused on God and the spirits, and it suggests that the concern can be dealt with by retreating under the "Great Rock."

3.c

Kwa Marasa anye, o sizo,	Marasa Cross oh yeah, scissors
M pa Marasa ankò,	I am no longer Marasa,
mwen pran verite langèt li	I heard the truth about her clitoris
Manman pran verite koko li …	Mother heard the truth of her pussy …
Manman pran verite pèpèt li …	Mother heard the truth of her spring-box …

Song 3.c explores the sexual theme elliptically. Kwa Marasa, presumably twin Gede spirits, are highlighted with *betiz* that explores a sexual encounter between two lesbian lovers (like in song 2.b). The term *sizo* (scissors) refers to two female lovers who spread their legs wide apart facing each other in order to grind their vaginas together to-and-fro, drawing out each other's sexual euphoria. But the satisfaction sought in the scissoring leads to tension and renunciation in line 2.

The truth has been discovered about the lover's clitoris, vagina, and *pèpèt* (popper), which we render as "spring-box" to capture Gede's uncouthness. The last three lines point to the playful and explicit side of Gede songs. Gede culture revels in expressions of symbolic sexuality, including homosexuality. In a Gede possession trance, I have seen how two men, two women, or a man and a woman can mimic sexual acts together. The words *langèt* (clitoris) and *koko* (pussy) in lines 3–4 embed the song in a raw sexual world in which "mother" is learning of her offspring's sexual activity.

Song 3.c addresses the spirit Kwa Marasa. Although other collections do not include songs for this spirit, there are other spirits with "Kwa" inserted in the initial position to form compound names such as Kwa Asingbo and Kwa Lento (Beauvoir 2008b, 232–33). The prefix "Kwa" assists in the incorporation of a given spirit into the Gede Rite. The name "Kwa Marasa" incorporates "Marasa," which originates in the Rada Rite. Both the Gede Rite and the Rada Rite emanate from the cultural space of the Yoruba and Aja regions, and hence the concept of the Sacred Twins probably existed among the Gedevi prior to the Atlantic slave trade. However, it is also possible that the Marasa part of Kwa Marasa "migrated" into the Gede Rite during the colonial or neocolonial periods. This song points listeners to the sexually expressive Gede culture while opening avenues for theoretical questions in Vodou hermeneutics and transatlantic history.

4.a

Kwa Senbo—kwa!
Kwa Lakwa—kwa!
Kwa dèyè kwa—kwa!

Ala chay o, ala chay o!

Ala chay o, ala chay o!

—he hey!

4.a

Senbo's Cross—cross!
Cross of the Cross—cross!
Cross behind crosses—cross!

Oh what a burden, oh what a burden!

Oh what a burden, oh what a burden!

—hey hey!

—Dye, ala chay pou manbo a	—God, what a burden for the manbo
(oungan an) pote—fyawfyaw!	(the oungan) to carry—fyawfyaw!
Levanjil yo di tout oungan	The evangelicals say that all oungan
se malfektè.	are evildoers.
Nou pral nan tribinal la,	We are going to the courthouse,
nou pral jije avè yo, ala chay o.	we are going to judge them, oh what a burden.
Ala chay o, ala chay o!	Oh what a burden, oh what a burden!
Ala chay o, ala chay o!	Oh what a burden, oh what a burden!
Levanjil yo di tout manbo	The evangelicals say that all oungan
se lougawou.	are blood-suckers.
Nou pral nan tribinal la,	We are going to the courthouse,
nou pral jije avè yo, ala chay o.	we are going to judge them, oh what a burden.

Song 4.a introduces the theme of interreligious strife. Although it opens with the formula of the Gede Rite, the song primarily aims criticism at lying Christians, illustrating the critical concerns of the *chante pwen* genre. As a commentary on relations between servants of the spirits and evangelical Christians, the song reflects the asymmetrical rivalries between Vodou and Protestantism that have accelerated since the US occupation of Haiti (1915–1934).

The mood of the song is frustration, as the victims of the false accusations are seeking justice by means of the courts. The song describes how evangelicals have wrongly accused *manbo* and *oungan* of evildoing. To set matters right, the *oungan* and *manbo* take their complaint to a secular judge. The evangelicals slanderously claim that the *manbo* and *oungan* are criminals (*malfektè*) and werewolf-like bloodsuckers (*lougawou*), casting the stones of prejudicial terms that are commonly employed from pulpits across Haiti and throughout the world where Christians organize to curse and destroy other religions, particularly African traditional religions. Evangelicals have attempted to rewrite Haitian history by demonizing the blood pact that the combatants took part in at the Bwa Kayiman ceremony in August 1791 (McAlister 2012). Although blood pacts are rituals that herald initiation and enjoin secrecy and loyalty in the African and African Atlantic world, evangelicals in Haiti and the United States prefer an eisegetical interpretation of history in which they are a "pact with Satan" (Hebblethwaite 2015b; Rouget 2001, 20–21).

The anti-Vodou rhetoric and violence of extremist Catholics and Protestants have snuffed out hopes for rational interfaith dialogue in Haiti. Decades of toxic propaganda from North American and Haitian pastors and missionaries continue to fuel the loathing and persecution of African spirituality emanating from noxious churches. The song is about the religious strife that riddles Atlantic history and the present. The response to the irrationality is not violence and stupidity of an equal order, but instead a determined legal riposte that confronts the enemy using the rational channels of the courts. Even if the judicial system is the best place to resolve these problems, the final words of the song imply that a satisfactory court case will involve much hardship. Death in this song is the variety that Christians produce in their colonization and missionization.

4.b

Souvan m gen lanbisyon.
—Se vre!
—Sa se pa anyen, sa se plim pan!

M pral konyen pou degouden o!

Souvan m gen lanbisyon.
M pral plimen pou degouden o.

Souvan m gen lanbisyon.
Si w pa vòlè,
kanmenm, w ap pran sida o,
nan tou langèt ou!

4.b

I often have ambitions.
—It's true!
—That isn't nothing, that's the peacock's feather!

Oh I'm going to fuck for two bucks!

I often have ambitions.
Oh I'm going to suck for two bucks!

I often have ambitions.
Even if you don't steal,
oh you'll still catch AIDS all over your clitoris.

Song 4.b again deviates from the mythological domain of the spirits to explore social dimensions of life in Haiti in the *chante pwen* genre. The female-voiced song is the first of several that deals with a strong-willed prostitute turning tricks for tiny sums of money. The notion of "ambitions" in line 1 is a reference to lust for money. The method for obtaining the money is to "fuck" for "two bucks," the song employing the vulgar term *konyen* (to fuck) with its rhyming monetary counterpart, *degouden* (bucks). The same idea is expressed in lines 5–7, now *konyen* replaced with the synonym *plimen* (to screw). Anxiety erupts through the lyrics in the final lines. The first seven lines build sexual tension around the image of a prostitute's rapid-fire fucking for fistfuls of bucks. Lines

8 and 9 arrest the vision of money and fucking with two bombshell revelations. Thievery and sexually transmitted diseases may hasten the sex worker's passage to death.

Song 4.b fits the pattern of judgment, derision, and correction typical of the *chante pwen* genre. The cause and effect in the song's narrative delivers the final, fatal judgment: the quest for money in sex work is dangerous. The description of the clitoris infected with AIDS adds a viral crassness to the closing judgment, once again anchoring the song in Gede's extreme style. The song sarcastically notes that even though the prostitute does not steal, she will end up with AIDS nonetheless. This Gede *chante pwen* warns that sex work will kill her long before other occupations.

4.c

Si m ap taye, kite m taye!

—Nan devan m, mesye!
Si m ap konyen, kite m konyen [taye],
depi m piti, m ap konyen [taye].

M gwo, koko nan bounda.

Vakabon pa veye m—kite
m plimen [taye].
Si m ap plimen, kite m plimen.

4.c

If I'm screwing, let me screw!

—In front of me, guys!
If I'm fucking, let me fuck,
I have been fucking since I was small.

I'm grown up, pussy on my ass.

Don't watch me vagrants—let me shag.
If I am shagging, let me shag.

Song 4.c asserts the sexual independence of a female-voiced narrator who wants uninterrupted sexual satisfaction. The vulgar terms for sexual intercourse in the song range among *taye*, *konyen*, and *plimen*, all variants of "fuck," adding irreverence and urgency to the song. The pressure is on to release sexual frustrations in a private place, beyond the prying eyes of voyeurs.

The assertion in line 4 that the narrator has engaged in sexual activity from a young age introduces a taboo sexual theme into the song. The basis for the narrator's sexual behavior is a history of sexual activity beginning in youth. Sexual encounters in that context usually include predation; thus, the song may suggest a hidden tragic narrative of rape or incest. This may form the backdrop to the story of prostitution taken up in song 4.b. A second tension expressed in the song is the absence of privacy and the voyeurism of *vakabon*, "vagrants" peeping at the sexual scene. Privacy is a luxury that many working-class people in Haiti lack, a situation reflected in the demand that the voyeurs avert their eyes.

One of the more striking assertions of adulthood and sexual independence is reflected in line 5's quip about having "pussy on my ass." This points to the idea that sexual independence is literally built into her body. Her sexual organs were designed for use. This short song's five vulgarities—*taye, konyen, plimen, koko,* and *bounda*—maximize Gede's vulgar flair. The song ends with the cycle of sex, pleasure, birth, and death condensed in grinding loins.

4.d

4.d	
Ti tou, ti tou, ti tou	Little hole, little hole, little hole
—kalanbè fin manje langèt ou!	—smegma has eaten your clitoris!
Ti tou, ti tou, ti tou	Little hole, little hole, little hole
—gade jan l fin manje koko w!	—look how it has eaten your pussy!
Ti tou, ti tou, ti tou	Little hole, little hole, little hole
—men mòpyon fin manje langèt ou!	—crabs have eaten your clitoris!
Ay andan kay la mesye— gen kalanbè!	Hey inside the house—there is smegma!
Nan kwen kay la, mesye —gen [chaje] kalanbè!	Man, in the corners of the house —there is smegma!
Lè w gad nan mitan kay la, mesye,	When you look in the middle of the house, man,
—gen kalanbè!	—there is smegma!
Lè w gade sou kabann nan, mesye	Man, when you look on the bed
—gen kalanbè!	—there is smegma!
Tout se kalanbè!	It's all smegma!

In the vein of songs 4.b–4.c, this one offers images of oral sex and genital secretions. Lines 1, 3, and 5 repeat the expression "little hole" three times like an incantation about sexual orifices. Smegma, which is composed of shed skin, moisture, and skin oils, is produced around male and female genitalia. The narrator's clitoris and vagina have been "eaten" by smegma, an observation about unkempt, oversexed genitals. The verb *manje* used outside the context of eating food can mean "to imprison," "to kill," "to poison," and so on. The smegma-stricken clitoris and vagina form a prelude to the crabs of line 6, painting a bleak portrait of the subject's genital health.

The previous two songs examine an unrepentant nickel-and-dime form of prostitution. Song 4.d expands on the unpleasant and possibly fatal dangers facing sex workers. Lines 7–15 elaborate on the smegmatic problems in the "corners of the house," in the "middle of the house," and "on the bed." The closing expression, "It's all smegma," concisely summarizes the writhing and agonized sexual world ushered in by this trio of songs. Beyond the sexual words like "clitoris," "pussy," and "crabs" that point to the Gede Rite, the expression "little hole" connects us to our own ultimate burial in a hole.

5.a

Kwa Senbo—kwa!
Kwa Lakwa—kwa!
Kwa dèyè kwa—kwa!

Konminezon mare, sou do m yo ye.

Konminezon mare!
—Men asosi grenadya zo

devan bwa kochon, al konyen!

—Sa se pa anyen, sa se plim pan!

Yon bouzen ki di konsa: vòlè ki vòlè

jwenn viza pou l vwayaje,
alevwa pou bouzen—pa gen danje, way!

5.a

Senbo's Cross—cross!
Cross of the Cross—cross!
Cross behind crosses—cross!

They are plotting, they are behind my back.

They are plotting.
—Here is balsam apple-grenadine boner

in front of pig dicks, go fuck!

—This isn't nothing, this is a peacock feather!

A whore who said: even thieves

get visas to travel,
why not a whore—there is no danger, oh my!

Song 5.a opens with the ritual formula of the Gede Rite, but it is a *chante pwen* about betrayal and unfairness. The female-voiced song again takes up the theme of the prostitute's tragic station in society. Lines 3–4 express the fear that enemies are plotting the downfall of the narrator, who is presumably also the prostitute.

The theme of plotting is common in Vodou songs, and the terms *konplo* and *konminezon* are used to convey a sense of peril and vulnerability. Here we encounter the "death" of rational peace of mind and its replacement with fear and paranoia. Line 6 is absurdist, yet the message remains vulgar with the mention of pig dicks. The "peacock feather" for sexual tickling is also found in songs 2.b and 4.b with identical phrasing, showing that it is a fixed formula.

In lines 9–11, the prostitute voices her frustration at witnessing the issuance of a travel visa to a thief while she, a sex worker who has committed no serious crime, is denied the privilege. Thieves have money and influence, while the harmless *bouzen* (prostitutes) pose no threat but face incalculable odds in life. This series of songs take the point of view of prostitutes, illustrating Gede's role as the patron *lwa* of sex workers. The laments of prostitutes are directed toward the Gede spirit family, one that is comfortable with all the guises of human sexuality.

5.b	5.b
Arete bouzen yo, pinga n bat yo.	Arrest the whores, don't you all beat them.
Arete bouzen yo, pinga w bat yo.	Arrest the whores, don't you beat them.
Arete bouzen yo, pinga w bat yo.	Arrest the whores, don't you beat them.
Se degouden y ap chèche.	They are just looking for fifty cents.

Song 5.b is a short *chante pwen* that criticizes the mistreatment of prostitutes by the police, charting the theme of "death" as the abject condition of sex workers who are victims of poverty and police violence. While noting the prostitutes' arrest, the song warns (*pinga*) officers not to beat them for eking out a precarious living in the sex trade. The images reflect an attitude of compassion and defense for the rights of prostitutes, condemning their harsh treatment.

5.c	5.c
Yon sèl somèy, yon sèl somèy,	One of a kind rest, one of a kind rest,
yon sèl somèy,	one of a kind rest,
n ap reveye l anba zozo.	we are waking her up with cock.
Yon sèl somèy, yon sèl somèy,	One of a kind rest, one of a kind rest,
yon sèl somèy,	one of a kind rest,
reveye l anba zozo.	wake her up with cock.
Kalanbè w pa gen de somèy.	Your smegma doesn't get rest.
—se reveye l anba zozo!	—wake her up with cock!

Song 5.c offers a message about interrupting a resting woman with sexual demands. Here, the erect penis does the intrusive waking. Repeated in triplicate, the theme of the woman's rest is central as the invasive member prods her, the antithesis of her repose. Line 7's quip that there is no rest for smegma underscores the urgency of the male sexual demands. Here, Gede's phallic domain reflects ways in which the penis impinges on women, such as through sex work or nonconsensual interruptions of sleeping.

5.d	5.d
M te pale machann marinad la!	I told the marinade seller!
M te pale machann marinad la!	I told the marinade seller!
M te pale machann marinad la	I told the marinade seller
pou l pa mouye farin a dlo sa.	not to saturate the flour with this water.
Marinad la gen gou koko medanm yo.	The marinade tastes like the women's pussies.
—Move gou en!	—Bad taste huh!

Song 5.d indulges in Gede's vulgarity. Thrice the song's narrator exclaims that she has spoken to the marinade seller to not mix flour with a marinade that tastes like "women's pussies." The response that the marinade has a "bad taste" punctuates the distasteful imagery. The term *koko* (pussy) occurs in four songs in this short collection, showing Gede's concern with vaginas and penises. The vagina's smell, its secretions, its sexual function, its role in giving women pleasure through oral sex or coitus, and the difficult conditions of sex workers are illustrated in several songs. Here, *madan sara* (market sellers) are in the scope of the Gede Rite.

6.a	6.a
Gede Nibo dèyè lakwa a,	Gede Nibo is behind the cross,
san m ap koule,	my blood is flowing,
san m ap koule vre.	my blood is really flowing.
Gede Nibo dèyè lakwa a,	Gede Nibo is behind the cross,
san m ap koule.	my blood is flowing.
Gede Nibo dèyè lakwa a, ago e!	Gede Nibo is behind the cross, hey ago!
Papa Gede Ti Pis Lakwa,	Papa Gede Lil' Louse of the Cross,
ago ago e!	hey ago ago!
San m ap koule vre.	My blood is really flowing.

—Anba san Lakwa,	—Under the blood of the Cross,
Jeneral Lakwa, ago ago e!	General of the Cross, hey ago ago!
—Sèt Tèt Lakwa,	—Seven Heads of the Cross,
Mòpyon Lakwa, ago ago e!	Crabs of the Cross, hey ago ago!
—Simityè Lakwa,	—Cemetery of the Cross,
Sizann Lakwa, ago ago e!	Suzanne of the Cross, hey ago ago!

Song 6.a is the second of three that include Gede Nibo. Gede Nibo, also known as Brav Gede, is sexually promiscuous (Courlander 1973, 322). Brav Gede is greedy and daring (Marcelin 1950, 193). Gede Nibo represents a "family" of *lwa* that includes Gede Drivayè, Gede Fatra, Gede Kriyòl, and Gede Lensou, among others (Beauvoir 2008a, 188). Donning a black jacket, pants, and top hat, cigarette tucked between his lips, cane in hand, Gede Nibo interrupts ceremonies, begs for money, and rubs hot peppers onto the tongue and eyes of his horse (Courlander 1973, 323).

In one myth, the spirit Ogou Badagri found Gede Nibo as a stone on the banks of Lake Miragoâne. Ogou Badagri took the Gede stone home, and Loko baptized it. Gede Nibo's ritual beverage is white rum macerated with twenty-one types of hot peppers, creating a drink called *pise tig* (tiger piss). In line 1, Gede Nibo is behind the cross, nestled behind the spot where life and death meet. In lines 2, 3, 5, and 9, the same utterance is repeated, "My blood is really flowing," referencing menstrual bleeding. The song alternates between calls to Gede Nibo and Lil' Louse of the Cross and the cry "my blood is flowing." The flowing blood and the ghastly "seven-headed" manifestation of Gede produce a macabre mood.

A new name, General of the Cross, appears, illustrating a martial title for a Gede spirit that is reminiscent of General Ogou Badagri. The martial expression hints at an army of Gede swarming the cross, afflicting and alleviating people with the many paths to and from death, including bleeding and clotting.

6.b

Gede Nibo ki kote w prale?	Gede Nibo where are you going?
Mazaka Lakwa ki kote w ap rive?	Mazaka Cross where will you arrive?
—Kwa!	—Cross!

Gede Nibo ki kote w prale?	Gede Nibo where are you going?
Jipitè Lakwa, ki kote w ap rive?	Jupiter of the Cross, where will you arrive?
Premye novanm nan ki rive,	The first of November that has arrived,
m pral danse on Gede.	I am going to dance a Gede.
Se de novanm nan ki rive,	The second of November that has arrived,
m pral danse on Gede.	I am going to dance a Gede.
M pral lakay Fifi,	I am going to visit Fifi,
m pral danse on Gede.	I am going to dance a Gede.
Gede Nibo ki kote w prale?	Gede Nibo where are you going?
Mazaka Lakwa ki kote w pral danse?	Mazaka cross where are you going to dance?
—Kwa!	—Cross!
Gede Nibo ki kote w prale?	Gede Nibo where are you going?
Jan Simon Lakwa,	John Simon of the Cross,
ki kote w ap danse?	where are you going to dance?
Premye novanm nan ki rive,	The first of November that has arrived,
m pral danse on Gede.	I am going to dance a Gede.
Se de novanm nan ki rive,	The second of November that has arrived,
m pral nan tout Gede.	I am going to dance a Gede.
M pral lakay Mago,	I am going to visit Margo,
m pral danse on bon Gede.	I am going to dance a good Gede.
M pral lakay Fabyen.	I'm going to Fabien's house.
M pral lakay Kleyan,	I'm going to Cléant's house,
kay Manbo Mago.	to Manbo Mago's house.

Song 6.b tells the story of going to ceremonies on the first and second of November, the first days of the Fèt Gede (Gede Feast) national holiday. The song's message is a joyous announcement about the arrival of Gede's

month. In its allusions to various ceremonies, it hints at a widespread Gede culture.

The song's narrator calls out to Gede Nibo, Mazaka Lakwa, and Jipitè Lakwa to find out their plans, adding a litany of accumulating power to the text. Gede Nibo is a hermaphrodite spirit (Marcelin 1950, 181). The lemon tree is his *pye repozwa*, and he receives a black rooster and a black goat for his sacrifices. Residents of Miragoâne claim that he was born under the bridge that provides access to the town. In one variant of Gede Nibo's origin myth, Loko found him in a rock by Lake Miragoâne. Back home, Gede Nibo transformed into a child. Not wanting a child, Loko was happy when General Ogou Badagri adopted the young Nibo. Gede Nibo works as Bawon Samdi's "Minister of the Interior" (Marcelin 1950, 183). Vodouists represent Gede Nibo with a small tomb placed in front of the Kwa Bawon. A black candle is lit in the spirit's honor alongside macerated white rum. Gede Nibo is called upon to put a person in contact with family members who live far away or have recently died (Marcelin 1950, 186).

Jipitè Lakwa stands out for including a reference to "Jupiter," which is possibly a patronym, the planet, or the Roman deity Jupiter. The song asks about the arrival of the Gede spirits in the opening lines of the first and second verses (1–5 and 12–17). The narrator is traveling to a Gede celebration in order to dance and find out. Beyond the good news that Gede will be feted in a fitting manner, the final part of the song gives information about the calendar: celebrations will be held at various homes in the month of November. Reciprocal visits to cooperating communities are reflected in the references to several hosts: manbo Mago, Fabyen, and Kleyan. Avoiding the conflict of earlier songs, song 6.c expresses a celebratory tone.

6.c	6.c
Kwa Senbo, kwa lakwa!	Senbo's cross, cross of the cross!
Kwa sou kwa, kwa dè kwa	Cross on cross, cross behind cross
Bawon nan mitan	Bawon is in the middle
—se li k papa tout kwa yo.	—he is the father of all the crosses.

In song 6.c, Kwa Senbo, the "Cross of the Supreme Spirit," is called upon in line 1. The Gede "kwa" formulas appear in lines 1–2 in order to show that in the multiplicity of Gede spirits, one towers the highest: Bawon, the father of the Gede "crosses." As father of the crosses, Bawon's God-like status comes into focus. There is a reassertion of phallocratic order after a series of blistering critiques via sex workers, *plasaj*, and woman-to-woman sex songs. The ideology of the father is a return to a patriarchal impulse.

6.d	6.d
Anmwe o vin wè yo, tande on pawòl o!	Oh help, come see, oh listen to this!
—He hey!	—Hey hey!
Anmwe o vin wè yo, tande yon koze o!	Oh help come see them, listen to this talk!
Tifi a al lopital, l al fè dilatasyon,	The girl went to the hospital to get a dilation,
doktè leve l mete l sou tab operasyon,	the doctor lifted her and put her on the operating table,
[men] bistouri a chape,	the scalpel slipped,
li chire langèt li.	it slit her clitoris.

Song 6.d begins with an invitation to hear gossip that has a frightening twist. This cautionary song about the threat of genital mutilation and the death of erotic pleasure takes the form of a *chante pwen*. The song criticizes modern health care, which allows accidents that can cause permanent wounds or death. A pregnant woman has gone to the hospital to receive what appears to be a cervical dilation prior to childbirth. Instead, the doctor mishandles his scalpel and accidentally cuts her clitoris. Assuming the song's narrative to be based on an actual event, it may have been sung originally in public in order to direct criticism at the hospital where the procedure went awry. Whether the clitoris is being harmed such as in this song or pleasured such as in song 7.b, this sensitive sexual organ belongs to Gede.

7.a.	7.a
Ane sila a	This year
lajan trase p ap nouriti w ankò.	traced money will no longer nourish you.
—Dye balanse, pa gouye la!	—God shakes, don't grind here!
Ane sila a	This year
lajan pikan p ap nouriti w ankò.	thorny money will no longer nourish you.
Nou p ap travay ankò,	We will no longer work,

nou pa nan konkirans—	we are not in competition—
premye janvye a, n a wè sa o!	the first of January, oh we will see this!

Song 7.a is an elliptical *chante pwen* about a change in conditions involving a shift away from ill-gained "thorny money" with strings attached, to a space of liberation and unity. The response, "God shakes, don't grind here," suggests that God's *balanse* (shaking, etc.) rules supreme—no amount of writhing leaves any impression.

Abandoning the ambition that spawned the thorny money is difficult, but "God shakes." In line 8, the narrator announces that the truth will be revealed on January 1. This is both New Year's Day and Independence Day in Haiti, followed on January 6 by the Lèwa (Epiphany), an auspicious time of the year for Vodou celebrations. Nourishing pumpkin soups are served to commemorate the day. At this distinct time, the problems of "thorny money" and competition will be reconciled.

7.b

7.b	7.b
Men ki kote ou kòmanse swe?	Well where did you start sweating?
—anba langèt mwen kòmanse swe.	—I start sweating below my clitoris.
Men ki kote ou kòmanse swente?	But where do you start to ooze?
—anba langèt mwen kòmanse swente.	—I start to ooze below my clitoris.
Anba langèt mwen [ou]	Below my [your] clitoris
—m kòmanse swente!	—I start to ooze!

Song 7.b is a *chante pwen* that explores a sexual theme focused on bodily fluids and the question of *where* the addressee begins to sweat. The sweat flows from under the clitoris, oozing from Gede's own secreting glands. The body's fluids engage in the course of conception that Gede ushers in, during his grinding.

This song stands out next to several others for its unbridled embrace of sexuality. Other songs in this collection mention the risks that a clitoris encounters, while this one embraces it as a source of pleasure and satisfaction. Gede is concerned with the totality of genital experiences, both those that affirm and those that threaten genital health. An illustration is the way Gede rubs hot peppers on the horse's genitals in an effort to warm himself up among the living. The hot peppers on the crotch reflect the genitals as a vector for sweating, oozing, excitement, pain, and life's spasmodic intimacies.

7.c

Pa manyen m, pa manyen m—mòpyan!	Don't touch me, don't touch me—crabs!
Pa mòde m, pa pike m—mòpyan!	Don't bite me, don't sting me—crabs!
Si ou pèsekite m—mòpyan!	If you persecute me—crabs!
M ap tiye w si lè dezan—mòpyan!	I'll kill you within two years—crabs!
Pa mòde m, pa grate m—mòpyan!	Don't bite me, don't scratch me—crabs!
Pa pike m, pa nève m—mòpyan!	Don't sting me, don't irritate me—crabs!
Si ou enève m—mòpyan!	If you irritate me—crabs!
M ap tiye w [si lè …] dezan—mòpyan!	I'll kill you within two years—crabs!

The last song on the album offers defensive imperatives. Vodouists have been persecuted throughout the Americas to the extent that African traditions have been driven into extinction in most places, surviving fragmentarily under the cloak of Christianity is some cases. The persecution of Vodouists continues to this day by the same antagonists: local and foreign Christians of the Catholic and Protestant cults and their allies in the state.

Here, the message is clear: if the persecution continues, the narrator will kill the enemy within a period of two years. This song advocates for defensive violence under specific conditions. The strike is neither preemptive nor driven by avarice. Rather, the narrator has been touched, bitten, stung, scratched, irritated, and persecuted. The decision to kill is in self-defense, the consequence of sustained threats and aggression. At the end of each line, a single response (*mòpyan*) beats a steady rhythm anchoring the song, one last time, to Gede and his sphere. Here, *mòpyan* (crabs) is an intensifier that adds emphasis to the singer's rage. The repetition of *mòpyan* adds an incantatory bite to the song. Those who persecute Vodou can be killed under Gede's sign.

CONCLUSION

Rasin Bwa Kayiman's album *Guede* provides an intense point of access into the Gede Rite, one of Sèvis Ginen's canonical traditions, which enjoys particular prominence in Haiti in November. The parties and ceremonies for Gede in public and private cemeteries are important ways to remember the dead. Gede culture is celebrated in temples, public squares, community centers, nightclubs, private residences, and graveyards. From formal religious ceremonies, to Gede-inspired folkloric galas, to roving bands of people possessed by the Gede, the month of November is a time in Haitian communities when Vodou's culture spills into public spaces.

The album *Guede* illustrates spheres of influence that include sexuality, genitalia, diseases, and death. Songs deal with the threat of evangelicals and warn persecutors of death. The songs provide a glimpse of social conditions, such as prostitution and voyeurism. Like the *rara* songs of Haiti's roving springtime street bands, those for Gede display irreverence to the dominant culture's moral posture (McAlister 2002, 73). The vulgar language and outrageous propositions of Gede songs unmask power and disrupt the habitual. The songs demonstrate the multifarious functions of spirits like Bawon Samdi, Gwo Wòch, and Gede Nibo that help their servants grapple with the ecstasies, agonies, and absurdities of our sexual culture and our unstoppable march toward death.

Chapter 3's study of Rada songs and chapter 4's examination of Gede songs illustrate the compartmentalization of themes in Haitian Vodou. The emphases on life, order, and rootedness exuded by the ensemble of Rada spirits is kept distinct from the themes of sexuality, healing, and death expressed by the Gede spirits. While kept discretely within their own rites, both orbit naturally within Sèvis Ginen, which organizes the twenty-one rites into ethnic groupings with distinct thematic and emotive emphases. These ancient rites memorialize the history, culture, and people caught up in the displacement and alienation of the transatlantic period. In the face of that hell, Vodou is a religious system designed for transcendence and empowerment.

Chapter 5

CHAINS AND RAINBOWS OVER THE ATLANTIC

European and African religions and the Atlantic slave trade were bound together as invisible interlocking chains. Powerful royalist Christians and their royalist Vodunist counterparts led enslaver classes. The political systems, belief systems, and daily operations in those European and African kingdoms were finely tuned to maximize the extraction of African enslaved people and the collection of financial windfalls. While these crimes against humanity generated ill-gotten gains over a period of centuries, the divided and racist aftermath of the contemporary world demonstrates the enduring radioactivity of the slave trade's hatred, violence, divisiveness, and dehumanization.

In some ways, the enslaved people served spirits and held religious practices that were typologically comparable to the ones served by the royal families of the kingdoms of Dahomey, Allada, and Hueda. In other ways, the violence and grandiosity of royal politics and religion were diametrically opposed to the local traditions of the people the royals preyed upon. In some cases, victims resisted enslaver kingdoms and were captured as punishment. In other cases, people were randomly swept up in the wide net of slave raids. Other people were accused of crimes, failed to pay debts, or committed adultery and were adjudicated to the slave trade. Raiding and trading of enslaved people by the kings, armies, mercenaries, and traders of Dahomey, Allada, and Hueda was a core feature of the region's economic system.

Sold to French slave traders, the founders of the Rada and Gede Rites carried their traditions through the Middle Passage, inscribing traces of trauma and salvation in the songs. As long as enslaved people breathed, the chains of bondage would never overcome Ayida Wèdo's Rainbow (*O Vodou lakansyèl* Oh Spirit of the rainbow) (Marcelin 1949, 70). Enslaved people resisted the French government in Saint-Domingue, toppling it in late 1803, only 106 years after the colony was founded. In *Stirring the Pot of Haitian History*, Michel-Rolph Trouillot looks to the values of the native-born culture—land, Vodou, and the Haitian Creole language—to explain the cohesion of the Haitian freedom fighters during the Haitian Revolution and War of Independence (1791–1803). Those values also offer contemporary Haitians with paths to land reform, interfaith dialogue and respectfulness, and Haitian Creole majority rule (Trouillot, Past, and Hebblethwaite 2021, 53). Land, Vodou, and Haitian Creole are the foundations of the "Vodou Temple of Freedom" (Trouillot, Past, and Hebblethwaite 2021, 60).

Scholars of Haitian and Vodou history have not yet deeply examined the participation of the kingdoms of Dahomey, Allada, and Hueda in the French Atlantic slave trade. Haitianist authors have not thoroughly explored the history and mechanisms of enslavement in African kingdoms. The violence of royal power and the epistemic violence of religious power in the context of slave raiding and selling should receive more examination. The ritual murders at Dahomey's Annual Customs were a royal Vodun practice that necessitated the capture and execution of people on religious and political grounds. Hearing of the demands of European abolitionists, Dahomian kings and anti-abolitionists argued that selling captured people was moral because the number of victims killed in Dahomey's Annual Customs decreased, perpetuating revenues from the slave trade into the 1870s (Claffey 2007; Law 2002, 258). The insularity and absolutism of the royal family's religion projected an attitude of exclusive religious supremacy and divinely appointed power, traits that thinly masked the crimes of mass enslavement. The Vodunists enslaved by the royal families of the region practiced thoroughly different types of Vodun, mostly familial or communal in nature.

I undertook this analysis of the history, politics, and religion of the Bight of Benin because it informs the interpretation of the cultures that constructed the Alladan ("Rada") and Gedevi-Yoruba ("Gede") aspects of Haitian Vodou. Enslaved people transmitted those cultural systems in a colonial plantation society that was scarred with agricultural death camps for Africans and Creoles. The powerful Rada and Gede legacies are expressed in the albums of the important contemporary *rasin* artists highlighted in earlier chapters, providing a testament to the survival and universality of Haitian Vodou. I have endeavored to develop a theory and practice of "Vodou hermeneutics" that engages with the tools of multiple disciplines in the task of interpreting the songs of Rasin Figuier and Rasin Bwa Kayiman. As an academic researcher, my goal has been to build consensus among scholars and practitioners about the meanings of Vodou songs and culture. While, as a noninitiate, my knowledge has been constrained, academic libraries have afforded me panoramic information.

I interpret the *rasin* songs in the context of fieldwork in Vodou communities. My work relies heavily on Haitian and African studies, linguistics, language documentation practices, literary criticism, historiography, comparative studies, sociology, religious studies, and ethnomusicology. A multidisciplinary approach was essential, since my goal was to interpret contemporary songs that have ancient roots in transatlantic history. My focus on the Bight of Benin and Saint-Domingue/Haiti only examines a subset of the sources of Haitian Vodou, leaving unexamined the equally important Nago and Kongo Rites, among others.

As a beginner Haitian Creole language student in the 1990s, I purchased the music of Boukman Eksperyans at Von's Record Store in West Lafayette, Indiana, to learn about Haitian culture. I quickly understood that *rasin* music provided firsthand access to Vodou religion and culture, and I was smitten by the sound and message. The superiority and mysticism of the music and lyrics encouraged me to learn more. I knew that if I could become fluent in Haitian Creole language and culture, then I would greatly deepen my personal culture. Of course, that is the case with all the languages and cultures that we study. In the course of learning about *rasin* music, I was lucky to befriend J. L., who traded me his Creole for my English in meetings at a coffee shop. Recently transplanted to Indiana, he spoke to me of his mother's mighty Vodou culture, her songs, mythologies, and beliefs. Having limited notions about a country I had never visited and a language I barely knew, my friendship with J. L. in West Lafayette and my encounter with Haitian Vodou music profoundly influenced my academic interests, ultimately taking me on a path to complete a PhD at Indiana University focused on the Creole spoken by the Haitian community in Miami.

After starting to work at the University of Florida in 2003, I got to know more about Vodou and *rasin* music recordings. I still peruse the shelves at Haitian boutiques in Miami for *rasin*, *konpa*, *wege*, *twoubadou*, and even *levanjil* albums. Traveling there over the years, I had the privilege of meeting music producer Jean Altidor, the owner of the record label that released some of Rasin Figuier's and Rasin Bwa Kayiman's albums. He operates a variety shop in North Miami called Mass Konpa, where he sells the movies and albums he produces.

In 2015, I showed Jean the Haitian Creole transcriptions and English translations I had done from various albums that belonged to his music catalogue. I explained to him that I hoped to publish a book focused on the interpretation of the Rasin Figuier and Rasin Bwa Kayiman recordings in a transatlantic historical context. Jean immediately expressed his support, and he has remained steadfast in his encouragement.

In 2016, work began on the interpretation of the albums. As skeletal drafts that examined the songs emerged, I sketched out the chapters focused on Aja-Fon and Gedevi-Yoruba history, politics, and religion. As the work progressed, I could see the importance of simultaneously analyzing Africa and the Caribbean as distinct worlds in a dialectical historical relationship. This approach seeks to recover Africa's impact on Haiti and Haiti's significance for understanding Africa's past and present. While the African sources are treated independently from Haitian ones, the dialectical reading uncovers points of contact and separation.

The introduction to this book provides an account of the history of Saint-Domingue in order to present the reader with an idea of the built world and social structures that enslaved people encountered in the colony. A sketch of the core features of Haitian Vodou, the tradition's theological underpinnings, and its philosophies and practices offers an overview of the Haitian context that I seek to explicate through the lens of the Bight of Benin.

At the outset of this project, I was less aware than I should have been about the African kings who sent armies, raiders, and traders to capture, divide, and sell neighboring peoples to the European slave traders waiting on the coast. The coastal kings of Hueda and Allada gave licenses for slave traders to construct warehouses and forts. American students in my classes assume that European slave raiders rounded people up in a manner resembling what is described in Alex Haley's 1974 novel *Roots*. The study of the kingdoms of Dahomey, Allada, and Hueda in chapters 1 and 2, however, forced me to look at the real inner workings of a slave trade that was the main source of revenue for regional African economies. These kingdoms and their laws, armies, and patterns of slave raiding, as well as their royal and public Vodun religious cultures, reflect intersecting parts of transatlantic historical memory, each profoundly and subtly informing the emergence of Haitian Vodou.

I have attempted to break with the stubborn persistence of accounts of Haitian history that exclusively reflect "postdisembarkation" orientations to analysis. Many books focused on the history of Haiti and Vodou are hermetically separated from the histories and cultures of African people, as if to suggest that the long conversations inherited from Africa ceased to resonate in the Caribbean. Kings like Dako, Wegbadja, Houffon, Agaja, and Tegbesu deeply impacted the Caribbean. After Dahomey was established around 1625, Dahomian kings ordered the enslavement and sale of vast numbers of Gedevi-Yoruba people. King Agaja's order for the Dahomian army to invade Allada in 1724 resulted in the enslavement and sale of eight thousand residents, while their invasion of Hueda in 1727 resulted in the enslavement and sale of eleven thousand residents, illustrating events from African history that receive little mention in Haitian studies even though captives from those towns significantly impacted the colony.

The focus on Vodun religious traditions, practitioners, festivals, and politics in chapters 1 and 2 reveals a religious establishment that accommodated the slave trade of the Aja (Allada and Hueda) and Aja-Fon (Dahomey) kings. The kings and royal families in those towns administered and patronized influential

Vodun priests and bokonon diviners who received a cut of the profits from the slave trade. At the behest of the kings, royal Vodun priests presided over the mass ritual murder of war captives in Abomey at the Annual Customs, the victims' blood an essential food for the dead kings and a portentous sign of the worthlessness of common human life. Royal Vodun was an intimate part of Dahomey's political ideology and state apparatus. Kings and their priests used ritual murder and the slave trade to neutralize enemies. If they became too ambitious or powerful, influential priests and their congregations were captured, murdered ritually, or sold. The political and military ascendancy of Vodouists in Saint-Domingue and Haiti is a clear sign that royal families in the Bight of Benin used the slave trade to eliminate politically astute religious communities.

Royal Dahomian Vodun and European royal Catholicism mirrored each other asymmetrically. Royal Catholics and royal Vodunists supported and financially benefited from the slave trade. The enslaved people in the colony had fleetingly fallen victim to the royal slave trade, a system controlled by governmental, military, trading, and religious powers that were diametrically opposed to them. But despite the complicity of African royal families and Vodun priests, their victims in the colonies did not become disillusioned with service to the spirits.

Exposed mostly to the brutal side of Christians, enslaved people in Saint-Domingue naturally kept their ancestral religions while adopting Christian symbols compatible with Vodou. Over time, *oungan* and *manbo* fused national African traditions into Sèvis Ginen, which reflects an impressive array of African rites. For the most part, the victims of the slave trade would only acquire a limited idea of the royal Dahomian religion, and never would they see it as a shared tradition. As many enslaved people were deported for practicing a militant variety of Vodun, the religion could emerge as a source of resistance and power in the colony.

Chapter 2 examines the Vodun traditions that emanated from the temples and convents of the Bight of Benin, including the organization, leaders, and culture of the religion. Strong leaders transmitted tradition by recruiting candidates for initiation. They expressed a form of absolute authority that reflected the power of kings and queens. These keepers of culture maintained temple compounds and held court over vast oral and musical traditions. They labored to transform and mature the personalities of initiates while preparing them for a life of spirit service. Powerful priests swayed politicians, but most were simple agriculturalists who were deeply respected for their spiritual works. Most of these traditions persist into the present.

The sections on Vodun focus on the basics of a shared heritage including possession trance, musical traditions, leadership, and forms of learning in initiation. The politics of incorporating foreign spirits into the Dahomian state after conquests models the integrative centrifugal force of Haitian Vodou. The telescopic analysis of Vodun spirits like Dangbe, Agbe, and Loko anchors the interpretation of related Haitian *lwa* like Danbala, Agwe, and Loko in their origins, demonstrating dialectically the profound historical relationships that connect and distinguish Africa and the Caribbean. The study of Vodun in Dahomey, Allada, and Hueda provides a corpus needed to advance the comparative and empirical goals of Vodou hermeneutics in chapters 3 and 4.

The linguistic documentation of the songs of Rasin Figuier in chapter 3 and Rasin Bwa Kayiman in chapter 4 required several months of work, as numerous Haitian Creole specialists listened to the recordings on compact disc, analyzed the transcriptions, and checked the translations. A "Vodou hermeneutical" methodology emerged in a gradual process involving thinking about the texts in light of our fieldwork, comparing them with other Vodou texts, situating them in a transatlantic lens, conversing and corresponding about their meanings with experts and initiates, and finally connecting dots and synthesizing through book learning and writing.

In approaching the Haitian Creole Vodou songs, I consulted historical works about the Aja, Fon, and Yoruba peoples to get a picture of the world from which enslaved people were taken. Linguistic analyses of Vodou and Vodun religious vocabularies helped to pinpoint a vast array of transatlantic connections. Cartographical and historical research helped me identify place-names in the Bight of Benin and Haiti, and Joe Aufmuth's maps in this volume offer invaluable assistance in identifying the geography of the events examined. I delved into poetics and literary criticism in the explication of the songs' genres, symbols, themes, structures, literary devices, rhetorical traits, and ideologies. Haitian, Vodou, and Vodun studies were the cornerstones of my discussions throughout.

My close readings and interpretations of Vodou songs in chapters 3 and 4 reveal the ancient and recent memories they contain. Vodou songs are portals into the mythology, history, and culture of the servants of the spirits. Rasin Figuier and Rasin Bwa Kayiman's lyrical, melodic, and rhythmic statements illustrate some of the deepest concerns of Haitian Vodouists in the intimate form of spiritual music. These Haitian Creole songs echo Aja-Fon and Gedevi-Yoruba cultures and identities, demonstrating powerful and persistent transatlantic relationships.

The colonization of Saint-Domingue by the French—and the Americas by Europeans more generally—ignited vast upheavals of war and slave raiding between African communities, fueled the ruthless system of selling and shipping people, and imposed apocalyptic conditions on millions of people caught up in it. In spite of the independence that was won in 1804, Haiti's ruling elite remained entrenched in the use of the French language in the new republic, reflected today in a neocolonial order in which only 5–10 percent of the population, the ruling class, are bilingual in French and Creole, while 90 percent of the population is monolingual in Haitian Creole. The exclusion of Haitian Creole speakers from the francophone Haitian state, schools, and businesses is one of Haiti's most pernicious impediments to development (Dejean 2006; Hebblethwaite 2012). In the face of that societal disaster, one of the efforts toward decolonization reflected in this book is the prioritization of Haitian Creole language and culture in order to mirror Haiti's national identity. Creole is the only means to social and economic development in Haiti, deserving prominence throughout Haitian studies.

I often think that I need to decolonize my own headspace before attempting as much in Haitian studies. How could I, the son of English and Afrikaans colonial families from Rhodesia, Lesotho, and South Africa, privileged with long exposures to Belgium, France, the Netherlands, Quebec, the Czech Republic, Germany, the United States, and Haiti, imagine it possible to decolonize research on Saint-Domingue and Haiti, Allada, and the Abomey plateau? And how could I insist on promoting Haitian Creole over French when I have spent my life benefiting from English global dominance?

If I had allowed the racial essentialism that permeates the cultures of South Africa and the United States to take control of me, I could have undertaken work in linguistics insulated from the historical problems of slavery, racism, and religious prejudice. Turning aside the criticism of the "disciplinarian" Haitianists, I felt it was more important to explore a multidisciplinary methodology of Vodou hermeneutics. I got entangled in this research topic, since it served as a wide window into a lacuna in Haitian studies but also into the slave societies that so thoroughly haunt the contemporary world. Given all the attachments of my birth, I have tried to honestly interrogate the ideas and attitudes I inherited from the colonial and neocolonial worlds I live in, but surely I fail in places.

The emphasis on the point of view of Vodunists and Vodouists contributes to decolonizing research, because the knowledge transmitted comes in large part from people and communities that inherited and devotedly practice the traditions. At the same time, staunchly colonial works by slave owners like Robert Norris ([1789] 1968) and Moreau de Saint-Méry (1797) are unavoidable but can be read critically. Printed and recorded Vodou songs, the words of Vodouists and Vodunists, and the words of those who have lived in the communities have been my primary sources. As an academic, my partnership with Jean Altidor's Mass Konpa record label and their interstellar artists Rasin Figuier and Rasin Bwa Kayiman reflects constructive linkages between Vodou communities and academic researchers. The presentation of their songs in

Haitian Creole and English and my engagement with Fon and Yoruba sources offer access to Haiti's transatlantic identity and shatter notions of Vodou's isolation.

As I publish on Haitian Creole (Hebblethwaite et al. 2012), Jamaican Creole (Hebblethwaite 2019b), and Arabic influences in German (Hebblethwaite 2016) and French (Hebblethwaite 2019a) within the field of "song studies," my analyses and interpretations focus on the peoples, languages, cultures, and histories that form the sources of the songs. Those publications provide language documents from the artists and develop interpretative studies drawing from scholars who work within the communities. The focus on Creole in this book is a mental and practical reorientation distanced from metropolitan priorities, a disposition that embraces Haitian Creole's role in the completion of decolonization (Meehan 2009, 30). Research on Haitian Vodou must prioritize the religion's first language, Haitian Creole, a reality illustrated since Jacques Roumain's (1943) and Milo Marcelin's (1949, 1950) pioneering collections of Vodou songs and prayers. Far more work is needed to collect and interpret Haitian Vodou songs and sacred texts. The next generation of transatlantic scholarship on Haitian Vodou should draw from deeper mastery of the Fon, Yoruba, and Kikongo languages. I offer a preliminary research methodology to explore transatlantic connections, but it only scratches the surface of potential discoveries.

Vodou hermeneutical work on the preservation, translation, and interpretation of Haitian Vodou texts draws from both sides of the Atlantic. It is hoped that the approaches to interpretation undertaken in this project will inspire further work on the diverse rites of Sèvis Ginen, including the Nago Rite, the Petwo Rite, and the Kongo Rite. Exploring Haitian Vodou's roots in African history reveals a religious culture inextricable from political, economic, and social structures. Haitian Vodou songs are the crystallization of centuries, allowing listeners to experience the vividness of the present while immersing in a historical "spring" with no bottom. I cherish these ancient and contemporary songs because they pulsate and chant with a soaring power that gives the world new meaning.

NOTES

INTRODUCTION

1. The term "priest" refers to a male or female Vodou priest.
2. The ideologues included authors, clerks, administrators, scholars, priests and pastors, and the like.
3. Between 1760 and 1792, the enslaved sugar plantation workforce was composed of 42 percent men, 36 percent women, and 22 percent children and rose to 33 percent men, 40 percent women, and 22 percent children in the years 1796–1797 (Geggus 1993, 79).
4. The western Central African ethnic groups purchased by coffee planters included the Bantu Kongo and Mondongue, and the Bight of Biafra groups included the Ibo, Bibi, and Moco ethnic groups (Geggus 1993, 81).
5. Compare this to the Lakou communities around Gonaïves that serve single rites.
6. Although there are historians who write about this part of Haiti's history, Marie Vieux-Chauvet's novel *Love, Anger, Madness*, first published in French in 1968, is a striking rendering.
7. Although the majority of coffee plantations had fewer than 99 enslaved people, twelve large estates (having between 100 and 399 enslaved people) held 37 percent of all enslaved people in the coffee industry (Geggus 1993, 77).
8. The cultivation of indigo required planting, harvesting, carrying mature plants, scraping its paste into a bucket, and drying the plant product in boxes and barrels. On those plantations, African enslaved people had to place the product in stone vats where salts dissolved the paste, dyestuff coagulated, and starchy materials floated to the surface (de Cauna 2009, 24).
9. The word *nāgbō* refers to a "great woman," a "vodunsi who resuscitates the candidate of initiation from spiritual death to rebirth in Vodun" (Segurola and Rassinoux 2000, 240, 362).
10. Another definition of Ginen is a "person who thinks according to the teachings embedded in the immaterial ancestral inheritance" (Beauvoir 2008a, 12).
11. At the height of his career as *oungan*, Max Beauvoir was named Ati (from *atín* in Fon, meaning "tree"), the highest title of respect for a senior specialist of Haitian Vodou. (For the Fon word, see Segurola and Rassinoux 2000, 69.)

12. The term *makanda* is defined by Karl Laman (1964, 479) as "paw print of a dog or cat"; absent is any reference to "charms" or poison.

13. *Magnétisme* or "mesmerism" refers to possession performance in colonial writing, the analogy taken from an ecstatic European movement that colonial administrators looked down upon.

14. The term *fonda* is unattested in Laman (1964). *Bila* means to "praise" (Laman 1964, 37). Laman glosses the term *mayòmbe* as "magistrate, superior chief, prince, governor and honorific title," and Mayòmbe is a heavily wooded region north of Boma in the Democratic Republic of the Congo (514).

15. This is Moreau de Saint-Méry's list: Sénégalais, Yoloffes, Poules/Poulards, Bambaras, Quiambas, Mandingues, Bissagos, Sosos, Aradas, Caplaous, Mines, Agouas, Socos, Fantins, Cotocolis, Popos, Fons, Fidas/Foëdas, Mais, Aoussas, Ibos, Nagos, Dahomets, Ibos, Mokos, Congos, Mayombés, Mousombés, Mondongues, Malimbes, Mozambiques, and Quilois (1797, 25–39).

16. See Elizabeth McAlister (2002, 29) on the function of *rara* kings and queens to perform short dance routines in honor of a person who is saluted in exchange for a small amount of money.

17. Moreau de Saint-Méry's comment about "secrecy" (1797, 46–47) may also reflect the fact that initiates are sworn to secrecy regarding the *kanzo* initiation ritual. Of course, safety and security in the oppressive colonial context were certainly the main reasons to maintain secrecy about Vodou practices.

18. In Fon, *vèvè* means to "supplicate," so the Haitian *vèvè* is a diagrammatic supplication to the spirits (Segurola and Rassinoux 2000, 462).

19. Today at Société Linto Roi Trois Mystères, several dozen *pakèt inisyasyon* are displayed in *oungan* Alisma's altar room.

20. Petwo was also the surname of a line of Kongo kings, including Don Petwo IV and Jan Petwo. Don Petwo opposed slavery and converted to Christianity (Jil and Jil 2009, 200–10; Hebblethwaite et al. 2012, 279).

21. There are also several place-names called "Petro-Congo" in the present-day Democratic Republic of the Congo (according to Google Maps), and one of them lies on the Congo River, which was a route taken by African slave traders.

22. See chapter 3 for a discussion of the word *dyò* (sacred breath) in Vodou.

23. These included "the ceremonies, rites, dances, and meetings in the course of which are practiced, in offering to so-called divinities, sacrifices of cattle or fowl" (Ramsey 2011, 184).

24. Major novels by Jacques Roumain (1947), Jacques Stephen Alexis (1957), Marie Vieux-Chauvet (2009), and Frankétienne (1975) demonstrate long-standing crises around the environment, migration, exploitation, and authoritarianism.

25. Karen Richman (2005) builds on Gerald Murray (1977, 1980) and Serge Larose (1975).

26. See also Maya Deren's descriptions of mortuary rites (1953).

27. The original Creole is: "[L]wa yo toujou pale. Lwa yo kontan anpil pou pale ak sèvitè yo. Anyen pa chanje nan fòs lwa yo genyen nan dimansyon mistik yo, men yo adapte yo chak segond" (Welele Doubout, personal correspondence, March 10, 2018).

NOTES

CHAPTER 1

1. The salutation of princes in Porto-Novo, Benin, is "O kú Tadonù, o kú Ajánù" (Greetings, man of Tado; greetings, man of Aja) (Glélé 1974, 39).

2. Palm tree fronds are the main feature of the cycles of salutation for Ayizan Velekete in the Rada Rite.

3. Norris advocated for the slave trade, so he is attempting to demonstrate Dahomey's disposition to continue supplying enslaved people.

4. The Treaty of Rijswijk was signed in 1697 between France and the Grand Alliance of England, Spain, the Holy Roman Empire, and the United Provinces of the Netherlands.

5. These details about treatment are according to reports from the 1780s.

6. Robin Law (2004, 67) calls this narrative a "traditional stereotype."

7. The Dan serpent-spirits manifest through Danbala Wèdo, Ayida Wèdo, O'Dan, and others in Haitian Vodou.

8. In Rada, they appear as Ayida Wèdo, Danbala Wèdo, Danwezo, Minis Odan, O'Dan Misan Wèdo, O'Dan Wèdo Dienke, and O'Dan Wèdo Yemen (Beauvoir 2008a, 187–96).

9. In the Danwonmen Rite, they appear as Danyi, Danbala Pyè Wèdo, and Dan Ayida Wèdo (Beauvoir 2008a, 187–96).

10. See Carrié Paultre and Bryant C. Freeman (2001) for an example in Haitian literature.

11. According to one narrative, Dan originated in the Mahi region north of Dahomey and was introduced after the Dahomian conquest (Law 2004, 91). However, a Huedan community settled in the Mahi town of Savalou in the mid-sixteenth century. Servants of the Vodun Dangbe around Savalou wear the same scarifications as the servants of Dangbe in Hueda (Merlo and Vidaud 1984, 289).

12. Sakpata is preserved in the Danwonmen Rite.

13. The term "So" appears in the name Hevioso (Hebyoso), which means "So of Héviè," a village twenty kilometers north of Hueda (Law 2004, 90). The Ayizo people brought So to Hueda from Héviè.

14. See *Carte de l'Afrique de l'ouest au 1/50,000e (Type Outre-Mer); République du Dahomey* at the University of Florida's George A. Smathers Libraries' Map and Imagery Library (Institut Géographique National, 1951–1968).

15. Another tradition suggests that Agaja introduced the Vodun Sakpata into Dahomian religion, perhaps after Tegbesu returned from Oyo (Segurola and Rassinoux 2000, 403). A third tradition claims that Adjahouto, the seventeenth-century Aja king, introduced Sakpata (Brand 2000b, 76).

16. Written "Bossa" in Norris 1968.

17. In 1967 prices.

18. The number three in spirit names like Bosou Twa Kòn and Marasa Twa refers to the grouping of spirits into three domains: the sky, the land, and under the water.

CHAPTER 2

1. The name of the rivulet Azili is striking for its resemblance to the name of the major Rada Rite spirit of Haitian Vodou, Èzili (Verger 1957, 552).

2. This legend resembles the Haitian legend of the spirit Djobolo Bosou, who punishes people who fail to serve him by drowning them on Lake Miragoâne. Jacques Roumain's 1944 novel *Gouverneurs de la rosée* (*Masters of the Dew*) also records the Haitian myth of a vengeful spirit who is called the "Mistress of the springs" (1947, 16).

3. Haitian Vodou temples like Société Linto Roi in Miami also have numerous assistant priests who help the highest-ranked priest, oungan Michelet Alisma.

4. The word *jehò* is possibly an antecedent of the Haitian Vodou term *djèvo*, the sacred room in which the novice stays during her or his initiation.

5. Haitian Vodou shares related vocabulary: the *oungan* is "the priest," the *ounsi* is "the initiated adept," the *Ountò/ountò* is "the spirit of the drum/the drum," and *ountògi* are "drummers." Although the word for blood (*hùn*) has been replaced in Haitian Creole with *san* (from the French *sang*), the core religious meanings of Aja-Fon *houn* remain in Haitian Vodou.

6. Haitian Vodou's *kanzo* initiation lasts about ten days; however, months or years of preparation precede it.

7. The *boule zen* ritual in Haitian Vodou's *kanzo* initiation preserves the initiatory rites.

8. Perhaps members of the public in Abomey were pressured to attend the ceremonies of foreign vodun, as Maximilien Quénum (1999, 69) suggests.

9. Likewise, a Haitian Vodou priest or priestess holds the bell and the sacred rattle.

10. Those dwelling close to the earth serve the vodun Sakpata.

11. Père Labat (1663–1738) is best known for his writings on Martinique in the Caribbean.

12. Kpase (Kpassè) was the erstwhile king of Saï, who founded the farm Gléhoué, the sixteenth-century predecessor to Hueda. Kpassè's myriad forms include a sacred forest, a silk-cotton tree called Kpase-Loko, and protector spirits called Kpase-Gou and Kpase-Dan (Merlo 1940, 15).

13. Agbangla, known as Ahoho Agbangala, was the eighth king of Saï. Buried in Dokomè in the Sogbadji neighborhood of Hueda, he became a venerated vodun after his death (Merlo 1940, 16).

14. The *-sô* family of spirits presents a case in which a popular "child-spirit" served in Dahomey fails to reemerge in Haitian Vodou, whereas the parent-spirits do survive.

15. Prostration is a sign of devotion that persists in Haitian Vodou. For example, the *laplas* (master of ceremonies) kisses the ground three times in front of the *oungan* in the Rada Rite, and the *oungan* or *manbo* kisses the ground before the drums.

16. Places like Sodo (Saut d'Eau), Basen Ble (Bassin Bleu), and Basen Zim (Bassin Zim) in Haiti are Vodou pilgrimage destinations known to the entire population.

17. Marilyn Houlberg (2011, 275) provides no source for the claim, and I have not been able to identify the specific spelling in Pierre Swartenbroeckx (1973) or Karl Laman (1964). Laman does give *mbàasa* ("division in two") (1964, 523); links to *Marasa*, however, are not obvious.

CHAPTER 3

1. The songs discussed in chapters 3 and 4 can be purchased on compact disc from the Mass Konpa Mizik Shop, 11628 NE 2nd Avenue, Miami, FL 33161, (786) 486-5893. The CDs are also for sale at www.discogs.com.

2. "(1) Eya tout eskòt Rada yo. (2) Sen Djò e. [...] (3) Eya tout eskòt Rada yo. Sen Djò do kowa gwe. (4) Eya tout eskòt Rada yo, lavi n nan men Bondje o sanyan."

3. The Creole original is: "Nou pral jete dlo devan Sogbagi li."

4. Additionally, the term *dogwe* also appears in connection to the *lwa* Marasa. The Fon term *dógbè* means "to make a team" or "form an association," notions reflected in Haitian Vodou's collaborative culture (Fadaïro 2001, 100; Höftmann 2003, 149).

5. The gesture is still observed in Fon culture: the term *akɔ́n* refers to the gesture of touching the ground and the chest with the hand as a sign of confidence in the word of the vodun spirit (Segurola and Rassinoux 2000, 41).

6. For example, *sèvitè Ginen* (servants of Ginen), *oungan* (male Vodou priest), *manbo* (female Vodou priest), *hounsi yehwe* (initiate), *hounsi desouni* (initiate), *hounsi bosal* (initiate), *hounsi kanzo* (initiate), *hountògi* (drummer), *boulatye* (drummer of the *boula*), *katalye* (drummer of the *kata*), *laplas Ginen* (master of ceremonies), *pòt drapo* (flag bearers), and *konfyans kay* (confidents of the house) (Beauvoir 2008a, 96–97). The term *oungenikon* (choir leader) should be added to this list.

7. "Alegba ou se van, pouse n ale, nou se papiyon, n a pote nouvèl ba yo!"

8. "Ouvè baryè Atibon (Legba), pou nou pase a Lwa yo!"

9. "Legba rete nan gran chemen an pou l kòmande."

10. "Mèt Gran Chemen."

11. *Mezanmi* is not "my friends," like the French *mes amis* from which the Creole interjection is derived. It expresses exasperation and surprise more than solidarity.

12. The meter of the *yanvalou* generally corresponds to 12/8 time.

13. "Gran Chemen an wo, nou bare!"

14. "Lapriyè pou sen yo! Kriye abobo pou lwa yo!"

15. "Marasa men dlo, men manje! / Fanmi ranmase fanmi o. Paran ranmase paran."

16. A common feature of food served to the spirits is the variety of ingredients. In a service from the 1940s, worshippers sang *Marasa men dounou* (Marasa, here is our food) while serving the ritual food (Marcelin 1950, 135). The Creole song preserves the Fon expression *dù vodún nū* (eat food offered to a spirit), providing independent evidence that the Marasa are from the Aja-Fon linguistic area (Segurola and Rassinoux 2000, 154, 470).

17. "M sòti nan Ginen, / M pa genyen fanmi, / Marasa eyo."

18. "M pa genyen fanmi, / sa k va pale pou mwen? / Marasa eyo!" (Hebblethwaite et al. 2012, 71).

19. "Marasa yo, priye Bondje pou mwen."

20. "Marasa yo, rele Bondje pou mwen."

21. For example, Loko Davi and Lokosi Dayòk Freda (Beauvoir 2008a, 187–96).

22. For example, Loko Azanblo Gidi (Beauvoir 2008a, 187–96).

23. See Hebblethwaite 2015a for a study of "spirit migration."

24. "Wa Loko, ou menm ki ban mwen Pwen an deja."

25. Other place-names with the root word Loko- include Locowoui, Locokohoué, Lokoli, Lokodana, Lokokoukoumé, and Lokopa (Institut Géographique National 1968; US Office of Geography 1965).

26. "Agaou pa jwe."

27. The original Creole terms are *bèl gason*, *nèg sèpèt*, *Jeneral*, and *Hougan*.

28. "Agaou o ki sòti Anminan."

29. "Ala yon maji Agaou genyen."

30. Another famous example is Ogou Badagri, whose name stems from the town Badagry in coastal Nigeria, a major hub for slave deportations.

31. "Ayizan gwo" and "Manbo Ayizan."

32. "Ayizan mache."

33. "Ayizan ale pwonmennen."

34. "M pral sele chwal mwen pou m al fè letou peyi a."

35. "Mèt Danbala."

36. "Lwa koulèv la."

37. "Sakre."

38. "Ginen."

39. As an anonymous reviewer noted, it is legitimate to argue that Creolization creates artifacts and practices that fall across a spectrum, some representing corruption and others, like Sèvis Ginen, a consolidation of resistance.

40. "Kriyòl yo."

41. "Basen."

42. Temples like Société Linto Roi Trois Mystères in Miami have shrines with water-filled basins for Danbala and Ayida.

43. "Mètrès Ayida."

44. "Mètrès Danbala."

45. "Mèt Dlo."

46. The python spirit called Adum or Odum is also found in Nigeria's Bayelsa State, suggesting a broad diffusion of O'Dan's mythology (Ifie and Adelugbo 1998, 155).

47. "Basen reken."

48. Èzili spirits also appear in the Kongo Savann Rite, the Makaya Rite, the Nago Rite, the Petwo Fran Rite, the Seneka Rite, the Wangòl Rite, and the Zandò Rite.

49. "Mètrès Èzili."

50. Here, the name Kadja Dosou may point to the historical figure King Agaja of Dahomey, who ordered the invasion of Allada, its occupation, and the sale of its surviving population. "Dosu" refers to the Dahomian king's "strong name," since he was born after twins (Bay 1998, 78).

51. "Agwe ou pa ka kondui de fanm, / Fò w voye youn ale o!"

52. "Agwetawoyo ki voye rele mwen, / Mwen prale wè sa pou vivan yo fè mwen, / Pechè d latè yo pa bon, yo move!"

53. "Agwe Woyo, m pa prese o! / Nanpwen anyen la pase Bondje nan syèl la."

54. "Agwe Woyo, nan lamè a m te ye la a / Agwe Woyo, bò zile a m te ye la a."

55. "Vodou miwa."

56. "Agwe, Vodou miwa ase," or "Agwe Vodou miwa aze."

57. Also written as *sè*, *se*, *ase*, and *ache*.

58. "Twa Zile."

59. Ogou Achade and Ogou Balendjo are also well known.

60. On *ase*, see Brand 2000b, 8, 26.

61. Japanese-English and Korean-English are commonly cited examples for [l] and [r] contact phenomena (Ladefoged and Maddieson 1996). Palatalization of [s] to [ch] is

common in Gallo-Romance languages, Creole languages, and standard English, for instance *undershtand* (Wartburg 1950).

62. Max Beauvoir includes Orichala in the Nago Rite and O'Lisha Oko in the Matinik-Djouba Rite (2008a, 191–92). Orisha Oko, a spirit of agricultural fecundity and wealth, is considered a major deity of the Yoruba pantheon (Adepegba 2008, 109).

63. Other examples include terms like *oungan* (priest) from the Fon word *hungán* (priest) (Rouget 2001, 97), versus *gangan* (priest) from the Kikongo word *nganga* ("prêtre idolâtre" [*sic*]; Laman 1964, 683).

64. The owner of the rock derives from it the energy to work in Vodou as a specialist (*oungan*, *manbo*, *bòkò*, etc.) (Welele Doubout, personal correspondence, 2018). The discovery of a sacred *pyè* (stone) is an important part of the narrative of the calling-to-the-Vodou-priesthood. According to Déita (2006, 84), the Pyè *lwa* replace the Gede *lwa* in the north and northwest of Haiti. In ceremonies in Saint-Marc, the Pyè *lwa* are venerated before the Gede *lwa*. Pyè Balawe, for example, is the corollary of Gede Loray. The Pyè share similar characteristics with the Gede, including corresponding Catholic saints and ritual colors of purple and black.

65. One of those spirits in the rocks was Nananbouclou, the spirit of herbs and medicines (Courlander 1973, 45, 320).

CHAPTER 4

1. Some of the themes captured in Marcelin's songs (1950) include: Bawon and Gede are served white rum (song 224), called upon for protection from enemies (songs 231–232), Gede Ousou carries a dagger (song 239), Gede Nibo lives behind the cross (song 240), Gede Nibo receives food and money to protect children (song 242), is wearing a coat and top hat (song 245), a black scarf (song 246), has a "cinnamon butthole" (song 248), grinds when dancing (song 250), and asks for a feather, his tool for erotic tickling (song 253). Gede Nibo heals the sick (song 254). He receives rum, chicken, plantain, and sweet potatoes, and he saves the children (song 255). Gede is both a king (song 256) and a flying beetle (259). Gede Nouvavon reposes in a mango tree (song 262). Gede is called a "hypocrite" for letting slanderers talk (song 260). In one song, Gede Nibo complains that he only gets respect when he is needed for healing, but is accused of being a "demon" after the patient is well again (song 244) (see Hebblethwaite et al. 2012, 117–25).

2. Osanj is one of the Ogou spirits (Hebblethwaite et al. 2012, 274).

3. The Fon word *azangùn* (great) is also used in the Fon expression *loko azangùn* (the great *roko* tree [and spirit]) (Segurola and Rassinoux 2000, 89).

4. "Bawon Lakwa [...] kondi l ale! / Kondi l ale nan simityè."

5. "Gede Nouvavon gen yon pye mango! Se yon pye repozwa" (Hebblethwaite et al. 2012, 124; see also Tarter 2015).

6. In present-day Benin and Togo, there are dozens of towns that attest to the Aja presence, such as Adjaha, Adja-Ouèrè, Adjaka, Adjara, Adjara Dévoukamé, Adjamé, Adjara Voko, Adjago, and Adjakpéhokon (Institut Géographique National 1951).

7. Recall that the word "Aja" also refers to a person who is spiritually mature (Beaubrun 2013).

8. "Bondye devan, lwa yo dèyè."

9. "Bawon Lakwa, montre m twa mo priyè a, / Pou m sa pale avèk mò yo" (Beauvoir 2008b, 132).

10. "Bawon, Bawon o, Bawon, Bawon o, Men timoun radi k ap joure granmoun o, / Kondui y ale nan simityè" (Beauvoir 2008b, 132).

11. "Bawon o, se ou menm ki kondui sèt mò nan simityè" (Beauvoir 2008b, 132).

12. "Chache fouye w ap jwenn ak zo grann ou."

DISCOGRAPHY AND BIBLIOGRAPHY

SELECTED DISCOGRAPHY

Boukan Ginen. 1995. *Jou a rive*. Danbury, CT: Xenophile.
Boukman Eksperyans. 1991. *Vodou Adjae*. New York: Mango.
Chandèl. 2003. *Mea Culpa*. Brooklyn: Geronimo Records.
Kanpèch. *Ogou*. 2001. Brooklyn: Geronimo Records.
King Kessy. n.d. *Voudou Djam* [*Vodou djanm*]. King Kessy.
Koudjay. 1999. *N ap tan-n yo*. Brooklyn: Chancy Records.
Mambo Diela. *Guédé sans limite*. Brooklyn: Geronimo Records, 1996.
Racine Barak. 2003. *Nèg pa Bondye*. North Miami: Mass Konpa Records.
Racine Mapou de Azor. 1999. *Samba Mové, Pot-pourri*, vol. 2. Brooklyn: Geronimo Records.
Racine Mapou de Azor. 2002. *Live Samba Mové #4*. Brooklyn: Geronimo Records.
Racine Figuier [Rasin Figuier]. 1999. *Dantò*. Brooklyn: Geronimo Records.
Racine Figuier [Rasin Figuier]. 2000. *Men chay la*. Opa-Locka, FL: Mass Konpa Records.
Racine Figuier [Rasin Figuier]. 2002. *Se don nou*. Opa-Locka, FL: Mass Konpa Records.
Racine Figuier [Rasin Figuier]. 2004. *Vodou Lakay*. North Miami: Mass Konpa Records.
RAM. 1997. *Puritan Vodou*. New York: Island Records.
Rasin Bwa Kayiman. 2003a. *Pap fè ti nèg konfyans*. North Miami: Mass Konpa Records.
Rasin Bwa Kayiman. 2003b. *Sa m fè moun yo*. North Miami: Mass Konpa Records.
Rasin Bwa Kayiman. 2004. *Guede*. North Miami: Mass Konpa Records.
Rasin Okan. 1999. *Sakrifis la di*. Brooklyn: Hip Muzik.
Tokay. 2003. *Bandonen yo*. Brooklyn: Geronimo Records.
Various artists. 1997a. *Angels in the Mirror: Vodou Music of Haiti*. Compiled by Elizabeth McAlister. Roslyn, NY: Ellipsis Arts.
Various artists. 1997b. *Musiques paysannes d'Haïti / Peasant Music from Haiti*. Paris: Buda Musique.

BIBLIOGRAPHY

Adepegba, Cornelius O. 2008. "Associated Place-Names and Sacred Icons of Seven Yoruba Deities." In *Orisa Devotion as World Religion: The Globalization of Yoruba Religious

Culture, edited by Jacob K. Olupona and Terry Rey, 106–27. Madison: University of Wisconsin Press.

Akinjogbin, I. A. 1967. *Dahomey and Its Neighbours, 1708–1818*. Cambridge: Cambridge University Press.

Alexander, Kevin. 2017. "In Benin, Up Close with a Serpent Deity, a Temple of Pythons and Vodun Priests." *Washington Post*, January 26.

Alexis, Jacques Stephen. 1957. *Les arbres musiciens*. Paris: Éditions Gallimard.

Antonin, Arnold, dir. 2010. *Les amours d'un zombi*. Centre Pétion-Bolivar, Port-au-Prince.

Argyle, William J. 1966. *The Fon of Dahomey: A History and Ethnography of the Old Kingdom*. Oxford: Oxford University Press.

Aubin, Eugène. 1910. *En Haïti: Planteurs d'autrefois, nègres d'aujour-d'hui; 32 phototypies et 2 cartes en couleur hors texte*. Paris: Armand Colin.

Averill, Gage. 1997. *A Day for the Hunter, a Day for the Prey: Popular Music and Power in Haiti*. Chicago: University of Chicago Press.

Bastide, Roger. 1967. *Les Amériques noires: Les civilisations africaines dans le Nouveau Monde*. Paris: Payot.

Bastide, Roger. (1935) 2003. *Social Origins of Religion*. Translated by Mary Baker. Minneapolis: University of Minnesota Press.

Bay, Edna G. 1998. *Wives of the Leopard: Gender, Politics, and Culture in the Kingdom of Dahomey*. Charlottesville: University of Virginia Press.

Beaubrun, Mimerose P. 2013. *Nan Dòmi: An Initiate's Journey into Haitian Vodou*. San Francisco: City Lights.

Beauvoir, Max. 2008a. *Lapriyè Ginen*. Port-au-Prince: Edisyon Près Nasyonal d'Ayiti.

Beauvoir, Max. 2008b. *Le grand recueil sacré, ou, Répertoire des chansons du vodou haïtien*. Port-au-Prince: Edisyon Près Nasyonal d'Ayiti.

Beauvoir-Dominique, Rachel. 2019. *Investigations autour du site historique du Bois Caïman*. Montreal: Éditions du Centre International de Documentation et d'Information Haïtienne, Caribéenne et Afro-Canadienne.

Beauvoir-Dominique, Rachel, and Didier Dominique. 2003. *Savalou E*. Montreal: Éditions du Centre International de Documentation et d'Information Haïtienne, Caribéenne, et Afro-Canadienne.

Bellegarde-Smith, Patrick. 2004. *Haiti: The Breached Citadel*. Toronto: Canadian Scholars' Press.

Bellegarde-Smith, Patrick. 2006. "Resisting Freedom: Cultural Factors in Democracy; The Case for Haiti." In *Vodou in Haitian Life and Culture: Invisible Powers*, edited by Claudine Michel and Patrick Bellegarde-Smith, 101–15. New York: Palgrave Macmillan.

Bellegarde-Smith, Patrick, and Claudine Michel, eds. 2006. *Haitian Vodou: Spirit, Myth, and Reality*. Bloomington: Indiana University Press.

Bosman, William. 1705. *A New and Accurate Description of the Coast of Guinea, Divided into the Gold, the Slave, and the Ivory Coast*. London: Rose and Crown.

Brand, Roger. 1975. "République du Dahomey en bref." In *Dahomey: Traditions du peuple fon*, edited by Roger Brand and Claude Savary, 1–30. Geneva: Musée d'Ethnographie.

Brand, Roger. 2000a. *Cultes vodoun et textes oraux des Wéménou du sud Bénin*. Munich: Lincom Europa.

Brand, Roger. 2000b. *Ethnographie et vocabulaire religieux des cultes Vodoun*. Munich: Lincom Europa.

Brown, Karen McCarthy. (1991) 2001. *Mama Lola: A Vodou Priestess in Brooklyn*. Berkeley: University of California Press.
Brown, Matthew. 1986. "The Diatonic and the Chromatic in Schenker's 'Theory of Harmonic Relations.'" *Journal of Music Theory* 30, no. 1 (Spring): 1–33.
Burton, Sir Richard Francis. 1893. *A Mission to Gelele, King of Dahome: With Notices of the So Called "Amazons," the Grand Customs, the Yearly Customs, the Human Sacrifices, the Present State of the Slave Trade, and the Negro's Place in Nature*. London: Tylston and Edwards.
Campbell, Joseph. 1959. *The Masks of God: Primitive Mythology*. New York: Viking Press.
Casimir, Jean. 2009. "From Saint-Domingue to Haiti: To Live Again or to Live at Last!" In *The World of the Haitian Revolution*, edited by David Patrick Geggus and Norman Fiering, xi–xviii. Bloomington: Indiana University Press.
Casimir, Jean, Walter D. Mignolo, and Michel Hector. 2018. *Une lecture décoloniale de l'histoire des Haïtiens: Du Traité de Ryswick à l'occupation américaine (1697–1915)*. Port-au-Prince: Jean Casimir.
Charlier, Philippe, and Richard Gray. 2017. *Zombies: An Anthropological Investigation of the Living Dead*. Gainesville: University Press of Florida.
Chisholm, Hugh. 1911. "Treaty of Ryswick." *Encyclopaedia Britannica*. 11th ed. Cambridge: Cambridge University Press.
Claffey, Patrick. 2007. *Christian Churches in Dahomey-Benin: A Study of Their Socio-Political Role*. Leiden: Brill.
Courlander, Harold. (1960) 1973. *The Drum and the Hoe: Life and Lore of the Haitian People*. Berkeley: University of California Press.
Daly, Mary. 1974. *Beyond God the Father: Toward a Philosophy of Women's Liberation*. Boston: Beacon Press.
Dalzel, Archibald. (1793) 1967. *The History of Dahomy: An Inland Kingdom of Africa, Compiled from Authentic Memoirs by Archibald Dalzel*. London: Frank Cass.
Dauphin, Claude. 2014. *Histoire du style musical d'Haïti*. Montreal: Mémoire d'Encrier.
David, Philippe. 1998. *Le Bénin*. Paris: Éditions Karthala.
Dayan, Joan. 1995. *Haiti, History, and the Gods*. Berkeley: University of California Press.
De Cauna, Jacques. 2009. "Vestiges of the Built Landscape of Pre-Revolutionary Saint-Domingue." In *The World of the Haitian Revolution*, edited by David Patrick Geggus and Norman Fiering, 21–48. Bloomington: Indiana University Press.
Déita [Mercedes Foucard Guignard]. 1993. *La légende des Loa du vodou haïtien*. Saint-Marc, Haiti: Déita.
Déita [Mercedes Foucard Guignard]. 2006. *Répertoire pratique des loa du vodou haïtien / Practical Directory of the Loa of Haitian Vodou*. Saint-Marc, Haiti: Reme Art Publishing.
Dejean, Yves. 2006. *Yon lekòl tèt anba nan yon peyi tèt anba*. Port-au Prince: Fondasyon Konesans ak Libète.
Deren, Maya. 1953. *Divine Horsemen: The Living Gods of Haiti*. New York: Book Collectors Society.
Desmangles, Leslie Gerald. 2006. "African Interpretations of the Christian Cross in Vodou." In *Vodou in Haitian Life and Culture: Invisible Powers*, edited by Claudine Michel and Patrick Bellegarde-Smith, 39–50. New York: Palgrave Macmillan.
DeWalt, Kathleen Musante, and Billie R. DeWalt. 2011. *Participant Observation: A Guide for Fieldworkers*. Lanham, MD: Rowman and Littlefield.

Dirksen, Rebecca. 2019a. "Haiti's Drums and Trees: Facing Loss of the Sacred." *Ethnomusicology* 63, no. 1 (Winter): 43–77.

Dirksen, Rebecca. 2019b. "Meditations on the Usefulness of Museums: Putting *Sacred Drums, Sacred Trees: Haiti's Changing Climate* to Work." Paper presented at the Haitian Studies Association annual conference, Gainesville, Florida, October 19.

Dorange, Norluck, dir. 2009. *The Oblivion Tree*. Oblivion Tree Project, Orlando.

Dorsainvil, Justin. (1931) 1975. *Vodou et névrose*. Port-au-Prince: Éditions Fardin.

Dubois, Laurent. 2013. *Haiti: The Aftershocks of History*. New York: Picador.

Dubois, Laurent, and John D. Garrigus. 2006. *Slave Revolution in the Caribbean, 1789–1804: A Brief History with Documents*. Boston: Bedford/St. Martin's.

Dupuy, Alex. 2005. "From Jean-Bertrand Aristide to Gerard Latortue: The Unending Crisis of Democratization in Haiti." *Journal of Latin American Anthropology* 10, no. 1 (April): 186–205.

Eagleton, Terry. 1978. *Criticism and Ideology: A Study in Marxist Literary Theory*. London: Verso.

Ernst, Carl W. 2011. *How to Read the Qur'an: A New Guide, with Select Translations*. Chapel Hill: University of North Carolina Press.

Fadaïro, Dominique. 2001. *Parlons fon: Langue et culture du Bénin*. Paris: L'Harmattan.

Fama, Aina Adewale-Somadhi. 1996. *Fama's Èdè Awo: Òrìṣà Yorùbá Dictionary*. San Bernardino, CA: Ilé Ọ̀rúnmìlà Communications.

Firmin, Joseph-Anténor. (1885) 2004. *De l'égalité des races humaines*. Port-au-Prince: Ateliers Fardin.

Fleurant, Gerdès. 1996. *Dancing Spirits: Rhythms and Rituals of Haitian Vodun, the Rada Rite*. Westport, CT: Greenwood Press.

Foà, Edouard. 1895. *Le Dahomey: Histoire, géographie, mœurs, coutumes, commerce, industrie, expeditions françaises (1891–1894)*. Paris: A. Hennuyer.

Forbes, Frederick E. (1851) 1966. *Dahomey and the Dahomans: Being the Journals of Two Missions to the King of Dahomey and Residence at His Capital in the Years 1849 and 1850*. London: Frank Cass.

Frankétienne. 1975. *Dézafi*. Port-au-Prince: Ateliers Fardin.

Galerie Degbomey. n.d. "Cyprien Tokoudagba, 1939–2012, Benin." Available at http://www.galeriedegbomey.com/cyprien-tokoudagba.html.

Geggus, David. 1991. "Haitian Voodoo in the Eighteenth Century: Language, Culture, Resistance." *Jahrbuch für Geschichte von Staat, Wirtschaft und Gesellschaft Lateinamerikas* 28, no. 1: 21–49.

Geggus, David. 1993. "Sugar and Coffee Cultivation in Saint Domingue and the Shaping of the Slave Labor Force." In *Cultivation and Culture: Labor and the Shaping of Slave Life in the Americas*, edited by Ira Berlin and Philip D. Morgan, 73–100. Charlottesville: University Press of Virginia.

Geggus, David. 1996. "Sex Ratio, Age and Ethnicity in the Atlantic Slave Trade: Data from French Shipping and Plantation Records." In *Slave Trades, 1500–1800: Globalization of Forced Labour*, edited by Patrick Manning, 257–78. Brookfield, VT: Variorum.

Geggus, David. 2001. "The French Slave Trade: An Overview." *William and Mary Quarterly* 58, no. 1 (January): 119–38.

Geggus, David. 2009. "Saint-Domingue on the Eve of the Haitian Revolution." In *The World of the Haitian Revolution*, edited by David Patrick Geggus and Norman Fiering, 3–20. Bloomington: Indiana University Press.

Geggus, David, ed. 2014. *The Haitian Revolution: A Documentary History*. Indianapolis: Hackett.
Ghilardi, Adrian, Andrew Tarter, and Robert Bailis. 2018. "Potential Environmental Benefits from Wood Fuel Transitions in Haiti: Geospatial Scenarios to 2027." *Environmental Research Letters* 13, no. 3: 1–11.
Gilles, Jerry M., and Yvrose S. Gilles [Jil, Dyeri, and Ivwoz S. Jil]. 2009. *Remembrance: Roots, Rituals, and Reverence in Vodou*. Davie, FL: Bookmanlit.
Glélé, Maurice Ahanhanzo. 1974. *Le Danxomę: Du pouvoir Aja à la nation Fon*. Paris: Nubia.
Haley, Alex. (1974) 2014. *Roots: The Saga of an American Family*. Boston: Da Capo Press.
Hall, Robert A. 1953. *Haitian Creole: Grammar, Texts, Vocabulary*. Menasha, WI: American Anthropological Association.
Hebblethwaite, Benjamin. 2012. "French and Underdevelopment, Haitian Creole and Development: Educational Language Policy Problems and Solutions in Haiti." *Journal of Pidgin and Creole Languages* 27, no. 2: 255–302.
Hebblethwaite, Benjamin. 2015a. "Historical Linguistic Approaches to Haitian Creole: Vodou Rites, Spirit Names and Songs; The Founders' Contributions to Asogwe Vodou." In *La Española: Isla de Encuentros / Hispaniola: Island of Encounters*, edited by Jessica Stefanie Barzen, Hanna Lene Geiger, and Silke Jansen, 65–86. Tübingen, Germany: Narr Francke Attempto Verlag.
Hebblethwaite, Benjamin. 2015b. "The Scapegoating of Haitian Vodou Religion: David Brooks's (2010) Claim That 'Voodoo' Is a 'Progress-Resistant' Cultural Influence." *Journal of Black Studies* 46, no. 1 (January): 3–23.
Hebblethwaite, Benjamin. 2016. "Arabic Lexical Borrowings in German Rap Lyrics: Religious, Standard and Slang Lexical Semantic Fields." *Delos* 31: 113–25.
Hebblethwaite, Benjamin. 2017. "Sik salitasyon nan Rit Rada a: Patwon fondalnatal ak eleman patikilye nan salitasyon lwa Rada yo." *Revue Legs et Littérature* 9: 95–114.
Hebblethwaite, Benjamin. 2019a. "Rap and the Islamic Lexical Field in Parisian French: A Study of Arabic Religious Language Contact with Vernacular French." In *Le français dans les métropoles européennes*, edited by Françoise Gadet, 167–84. Paris: Classiques Garnier.
Hebblethwaite, Benjamin. 2019b. "Rastafari Resurgence in Reggae's Roots Revival Generation: Two Reggae Songs by Chronixx in Jamaican Patwa." *Delos* 34: 96–126.
Hebblethwaite, Benjamin, with Joanne Bartley, Chris Ballengee, Vanessa Brissault, Erika Felker-Kantor, Andrew Tarter, Quinn Hansen, and Kat Warwick. 2012. *Vodou Songs in Haitian Creole and English*. Philadelphia: Temple University Press.
Hebblethwaite, Benjamin, and Michel Weber. 2016. "Arabian Religion, Islam, and Haitian Vodou: The 'Recent African Single-Origin Hypothesis' and the Comparison of World Religions." In *Vodou in the Haitian Experience: A Black Atlantic Perspective*, edited by Celucien L. Joseph and Nixon S. Cleophat, 209–37. Lanham, MD: Lexington Books.
Herskovits, Melville J. 1937. *Life in a Haitian Valley*. New York: Alfred A. Knopf.
Herskovits, Melville J., and Frances S. Herskovits. 1938. *Dahomey: An Ancient West African Kingdom*. New York: J. J. Augustin.
Heusch, Luc de. 2000. *Le roi de Kongo et les monstres sacrés: Mythes et rites bantous III*. Paris: Éditions Gallimard.
Höftmann, Hildegard. 2003. *Dictionnaire fon-français, avec une esquisse grammaticale*. Cologne: Rüdiger Köppe Verlag.

Hornung, Erik. 1999. *The Ancient Egyptian Books of the Afterlife*. Translated by David Lorton. Ithaca, NY: Cornell University Press.

Houlberg, Marilyn. 2011. "Two Equals Three: Twins and the Trickster in Haitian Vodou." In *Twins in African and Diaspora Cultures: Double Trouble, Twice Blessed*, edited by Philip M. Peek, 271–90. Bloomington: Indiana University Press.

Howard, Keith. 2014. "Foreword: The Past Is No Longer a Foreign Country." In *Theory and Method in Historical Ethnomusicology*, edited by Jonathan McCollum and David G. Hebert, 8–12. Lanham, MD: Lexington Books.

Hurbon, Laënnec. 1993. *Les mystères du vaudou*. Paris: Éditions Gallimard.

Hurston, Zora Neale. (1938) 1990. *Tell My Horse: Voodoo and Life in Haiti and Jamaica*. New York: Harper Perennial.

Hurston, Zora Neale. 2018. *Barracoon: The Story of the Last "Black Cargo."* New York: Amistad Press.

Ifie, Egbe, and Dapọ Adelugba. 1998. *African Culture and Mythology*. Ibadan, Nigeria: End-Time Publishing House.

Imperato, Pascal James, and Gavin H. Imperato. 2011. "Twins and Double Beings among the Bamana and Maninka of Mali." In *Twins in African and Diaspora Cultures: Double Trouble, Twice Blessed*, edited by Philip M. Peek, 39–60. Bloomington: Indiana University Press.

Innocent, Antoine, and Duraciné Vaval. (1906) 1935. *Mimola, ou L'histoire d'une cassette; Petit tableau de mœurs locales*. Port-au-Prince: V. Valcin.

Institut Géographique National. 1951–1968. *Carte de l'Afrique de l'ouest au 1/50,000e (Type Outre-Mer): République du Dahomey*. Paris: L'Institut Géographique National, 1951; 1954; 1955; 1962; 1963; 1968.

Janzen, John M. 1982. *Lemba, 1650–1930: A Drum of Affliction in Africa and the New World*. New York: Garland Publishing.

Jil, Dyeri, and Ivwoz S. Jil [Gilles, Jerry M., and Yvrose S. Gilles]. 2009. *Sèvis Ginen: Rasin, rityèl, respè lan Vodou*. Davie, FL: Bookmanlit.

Joseph, Celucien L. 2016. "Vodouphobia and Afrophobic Discourse in Haitian Thought: An Analysis of Dantès Bellegarde's Religious Sensibility." In *Vodou in Haitian Memory: The Idea and Representation of Vodou in Haitian Imagination*, edited by Celucien L. Joseph and Nixon Cleophat, 79–100. Lanham, MD: Lexington Books.

Kadish, Doris Y., and Deborah Jenson, eds. 2015. *Poetry of Haitian Independence*. Translated by Norman R. Shapiro. New Haven, CT: Yale University Press.

Kangni, Atah-Ekoué. 1989. *La syntaxe du Gẽ: Étude syntaxique d'un parler Gbe; Le Gẽ du Sud-Togo*. Frankfurt: Peter Lang.

Kendi, Ibram X. 2016. *Stamped from the Beginning: The Definitive History of Racist Ideas in America*. New York: Nation Books.

Ladefoged, Peter, and Ian Maddieson. 1996. *The Sounds of the World's Languages*. Oxford: Blackwell.

Laguerre, Michel. 1980. *Voodoo Heritage*. Beverly Hills, CA: SAGE Publications.

Laman, Karl E. (1936) 1964. *Dictionnaire kikongo-français*. 2 vols. Ridgewood, NJ: Gregg Press.

LaMenfo, Bon Mambo Vye Zo Komande [Patricia D. Scheu]. 2011. *Serving the Spirits: The Religion of Vodou*. Philadelphia: Sosyete du Marche.

Lando, Paul. 2016. *Territoires du vodoun en milieu urbain: Le cas de Ouidah en République du Bénin*. Paris: L'Harmattan.

Larose, Serge. 1975. "The Meaning of Africa in Haitian Vodou." In *Symbols and Sentiments: Cross-Cultural Studies in Symbolism*, edited by Ioan Lewis, 85–116. London: Academic Press.

Law, Robin. 1997. *The Kingdom of Allada*. Leiden: Centrum voor Niet-Westerse Studies Publications.

Law, Robin. 2002. "An Alternative Text of King Agaja of Dahomey's Letter to King George I of England, 1726." *History in Africa* 29: 257–71.

Law, Robin. 2004. *Ouidah: The Social History of a West African Slaving "Port," 1727–1892*. Athens: Ohio University Press.

Lawal, Babatunde. 2011. "Sustaining the Oneness in Their Twoness: Poetics of Twin Figures (Ère Ìbejì) among the Yoruba." In *Twins in African and Diaspora Cultures: Double Trouble, Twice Blessed*, edited by Philip M. Peek, 81–98. Bloomington: Indiana University Press.

Laye, Camara. 1954. *The Dark Child*. Translated by James Kirkup. New York: Farrar, Straus and Giroux.

Le Hérissé, Auguste. 1911. *L'ancien royaume du Dahomey, mœurs, religion, histoire*. Paris: Émile Larose.

Leyburn, James G. (1941) 1998. *The Haitian People*. Lawrence: Institute of Haitian Studies, University of Kansas.

Lomax, Alan, Elizabeth Lyttleton, Révolie Polinice, Gage Averill, Ellen Harold, H. P. Davis, and Anna Lomax Wood. 2009. *Alan Lomax in Haiti*. Alan Lomax Collection. San Francisco: Harte Recordings.

Marcelin, Milo. 1949. *Mythologie vodou (rite arada I)*. Port-au-Prince: Éditions Haïtiennes.

Marcelin, Milo. 1950. *Mythologie vodou (rite arada II)*. Port-au-Prince: Éditions Haïtiennes.

Matsushita, Toshi, dir. 1997. *Voodoo Kingdom*. Brooklyn: Cinema Guild.

Mbembe, Achille. 2017. *Critique of Black Reason*. Translated by Laurent Dubois. Durham, NC: Duke University Press.

McAlister, Elizabeth. 2002. *Rara! Vodou, Power, and Performance in Haiti and Its Diaspora*. Berkeley: University of California Press.

McAlister, Elizabeth. 2012. "From Slave Revolt to a Blood Pact with Satan: The Evangelical Rewriting of Haitian History." *Studies in Religion/Sciences Religieuses* 41, no. 2 (April): 187–215.

Meehan, Kevin. 2009. *People Get Ready: African American and Caribbean Cultural Exchange*. Jackson: University Press of Mississippi.

Merlo, Christian. 1940. "Hiérarchie fétichiste de Ouidah." *Bulletin de l'Institut Français d'Afrique Noire* 2, nos. 1–2 (January–April): 1–85.

Merlo, Christian, and Pierre Vidaud. 1984. "Dangbé et le peuplement houéda." In *Peuples du golfe du Bénin (Aja-Éwé): Colloque de Cotonou*, edited by François de Madeiros, 269–306. Paris: Éditions Karthala.

Merriam, Alan P. 1964. *The Anthropology of Music*. Evanston, IL: Northwestern University Press.

Métral, Antoine, and Isaac Louverture. 1985. *Histoire de l'expédition des Français à Saint-Domingue: Sous le consulat de Napoléon Bonaparte (1802–1803)*. Paris: Éditions Karthala.

Métraux, Alfred. (1959) 1972. *Voodoo in Haiti*. New York: Schocken Books.
Michel, Claudine. 1995. *Aspects éducatifs et moraux du vodou haïtien*. Port-au-Prince: Presses de l'Imprimerie Le Natal.
Michel, Claudine. 2006. "Of Worlds Seen and Unseen: The Educational Character of Haitian Vodou." In *Haitian Vodou: Spirit, Myth, and Reality*, edited by Patrick Bellegarde-Smith and Claudine Michel, 32–45. Bloomington: Indiana University Press.
Michel, Claudine, and Patrick Bellegarde-Smith, eds. 2006. *Vodou in Haitian Life and Culture: Invisible Powers*. New York : Palgrave Macmillan.
Mobley, Christina Frances. 2015. "The Kongolese Atlantic: Central African Slavery and Culture from Mayombe to Haiti." PhD diss., Duke University.
Monroe, J. Cameron. 2011. "In the Belly of Dan: Space, History, and Power in Precolonial Dahomey." *Current Anthropology* 52, no. 6 (December): 769–98.
Monroe, J. Cameron. 2014. *The Precolonial State in West Africa: Building Power in Dahomey*. New York: Cambridge University Press.
Montilus, Guérin. 1985. *Les dieux en diaspora: Les loa haïtiens et les vandou du royaume d'Allada (Benin)*. Niamey: Organisation de l'Unité Africaine, Centre d'Études Linguistique et Historiques par Tradition Orale.
Moreau de Saint-Méry, Médéric Louis Élie. 1797. *Description topographique, physique, civile, politique et historique de la partie française de l'isle Saint-Domingue: Avec des observations générales sur la population, sur le caractère & les mœurs de ses divers habitans, sur son climat, sa culture, ses productions, son administration, &c. &c.* Philadelphia: self-published; Paris: Libraire Dupont.
Mosala, Itumeleng J. 1989. *Biblical Hermeneutics and Black Theology in South Africa*. Grand Rapids, MI: William B. Eerdmans.
Murray, Gerald. 1977. "The Evolution of Haitian Peasant Land Tenure." PhD diss., Columbia University.
Murray, Gerald. 1980. "Population Pressure, Land Tenure, and Voodoo: The Economics of Haitian Peasant Ritual." In *Beyond the Myths of Culture: Essays in Cultural Materialism*, edited by Eric B. Ross, 295–321. New York: Academic Press.
Nettl, Bruno. 1964. *Theory and Method in Ethnomusicology*. New York: Free Press of Glencoe.
New World Encyclopedia. n.d. "Kingdom of Dahomey." Available at https://www.newworldencyclopedia.org/entry/Kingdom_of_Dahomey.
Nicholls, David. (1979) 1996. *From Dessalines to Duvalier: Race, Colour and National Independence in Haiti*. New Brunswick, NJ: Rutgers University Press.
Norris, Robert. (1789) 1968. *Memoirs of the Reign of Bossa Ahádee, King of Dahomy: An Inland Country of Guiney, To Which Are Added the Author's Journey to Abomey, the Capital, and a Short Account of the African Slave Trade*. London: Frank Cass.
Olson, Mark J. "Angels." 1990. In *Mercer Dictionary of the Bible*, edited by Watson E. Mills and Roger A. Bullard, 29–30. Macon, GA: Mercer University Press.
Oriol, Michèle. 2002. *Histoire et dictionnaire de la révolution et de l'indépendance d'Haïti, 1789–1804*. Port-au-Prince: Fondation pour la Recherche Iconographique et Documentaire.
Palau Martí, Montserrat. 1993. *Société et religion au Bénin (les Ṣàbẹ̀-Ọpara): (République du Bénin)*. Paris: Maisonneuve et Larose.
Parsons, Elsie Clews. 1928. "Spirit Cult in Hayti." *Journal de la Société des Américanistes* 20: 157–79.

Paultre, Carrié, and Bryant C. Freeman. 2001. *Tonton Liben*. Lawrence: Institute of Haitian Studies, University of Kansas.

Peek, Philip M. 2011. "Introduction: Beginning to Rethink Twins." In *Twins in African and Diaspora Cultures: Double Trouble, Twice Blessed*, edited by Philip M. Peek, 1–36. Bloomington: Indiana University Press.

Pétrequin, Anne-Marie, and Pierre Pétrequin. 1984. *Habitat lacustre du Bénin: Une approche ethnoarchéologique*. Paris: Éditions Recherches sur les Civilisations.

Peukert, Werner. 1978. *Der atlantische Sklavenhandel von Dahomey, 1740–1797: Wirtschaftsanthropologie und Sozialgeschichte*. Wiesbaden: Franz Steiner Verlag.

Popkin, Jeremy D. 2012. *A Concise History of the Haitian Revolution*. Malden, MA: Wiley-Blackwell.

Price, Hannibal. 1900. *De la réhabilitation de la race noire par la république d'Haïti*. Port-au-Prince: Imprimerie J. Verrollot.

Price-Mars, Jean. (1928) 1954. *Ainsi parla l'oncle*. New York: Parapsychology Foundation.

Price-Mars, Jean. (1936) 1956. *Formation ethnique, folk-lore et culture du peuple haïtien*. Port-au-Prince: Imprimerie N. A. Théodore.

Quénum, Maximilien. (1936) 1999. *Au pays des Fons: Us et coutumes du Dahomey*. Paris: Maisonneuve et Larose.

Ramsey, Kate. 2011. *The Spirits and the Law: Vodou and Power in Haiti*. Chicago: University of Chicago Press.

Rey, Terry. 1998. "The Virgin Mary and Revolution in Saint-Domingue: The Charisma of Romaine-la-Prophétesse." *Journal of Historical Sociology* 11, no. 3 (September): 341–61.

Rey, Terry. 1999. *Our Lady of Class Struggle: The Cult of the Virgin Mary in Haiti*. Trenton, NJ: Africa World Press.

Rey, Terry. 2017. *The Priest and the Prophetess: Abbé Ouvière, Romaine Rivière, and the Revolutionary Atlantic World*. Oxford: Oxford University Press.

Richman, Karen E. 2005. *Migration and Vodou*. Gainesville: University Press of Florida.

Richman, Karen E. 2007. "Chante pwen sou kasèt." In *Mozayik: Yon konbit literè ann Ayisyen*, edited by Woje E. Saven and Drèksèl G. Woudsonn, 89–102. Plantation, FL: Language Experience.

Rodney, Walter. 1966. "African Slavery and Other Forms of Social Oppression on the Upper Guinea Coast in the Context of the Atlantic Slave-Trade." *Journal of African History* 7, no. 3: 431–43.

Rouch, Jean, dir. (1955) 2014. *Les maîtres fous*. Brooklyn: Icarus Films.

Rouget, Gilbert. (1980) 1990. *La musique et la transe: Esquisse d'une théorie générale des relations de la musique et de la possession*. Paris: Éditions Gallimard.

Rouget, Gilbert. 2001. *Initiatique vôdoun, images du rituel: Chants et danses initiatiques pour le culte des vôdoun au Bénin*. Saint-Maur-des-Fossés, France: Éditions Sépia.

Roumain, Jacques. 1943. *Le sacrifice du tambour-assoto(r)*. Port-au-Prince: Imprimerie de l'État.

Roumain, Jacques. 1947. *Masters of the Dew*. Translated by Langston Hughes and Mercer Cook. New York: Reynal and Hitchcock.

Saint-Lot, Marie-José Alcide. 2003. *Vodou, A Sacred Theatre: The African Heritage in Haiti*. Coconut Creek, FL: Educa Vision.

Savary, Claude. 1975. "Traditions du peuple fon." In *Dahomey: Traditions du peuple fon*, edited by Roger Brand and Claude Savary, 31–62. Geneva: Musée d'Ethnographie.

Seabrook, William. 1929. *The Magic Island*. New York: Harcourt, Brace and Company.
Segurola, Basilio, and Jean Rassinoux. 2000. *Dictionnaire fon-français*. Madrid: Société des Missions Africaines.
Smith, Katherine Marie. 2010. "Gede Rising: Haiti in the Age of *Vagabondaj*." PhD diss., University of California, Los Angeles.
Smith, Robert Sidney. 1989. *Warfare and Diplomacy in Pre-Colonial West Africa*. Madison: University of Wisconsin Press.
Snelgrave, William. (1734) 1971. *A New Account of Some Parts of Guinea and the Slave Trade*. London: Frank Cass.
St. John, Spenser. 1884. *Hayti; or, The Black Republic*. London: Smith, Elder.
Swartenbroeckx, Pierre. 1973. *Dictionnaire kikongo- et kituba-français: Vocabulaire comparé des langages kongo traditionnels et véhiculaires*. Bandundu, Democratic Republic of the Congo: Ceeba.
Tarter, Andrew. 2015. "Trees in Vodou: An Arbori-Cultural Exploration." *Journal for the Study of Religion, Nature, and Culture* 9, no. 1: 87–112.
Tarter, Andrew. 2016. "Haiti Is Covered with Trees." EnviroSociety, May 19. Available at www.envirosociety.org/2016/05/haiti-is-covered-with-trees/.
Thornton, John K. 1998. *Africa and Africans in the Making of the Atlantic World, 1400–1800*. 2nd ed. Cambridge: Cambridge University Press.
Thornton, John K. 1999. *Warfare in Atlantic Africa, 1500–1800*. London: UCL Press.
Tinsley, Omise'eke Natasha. 2018. *Ezili's Mirrors: Imagining Black Queer Genders*. Durham, NC: Duke University Press.
Tossounon, Alain. 2012. "L'île d'Agonvè dans la commune de Zagnanado: Un patrimoine naturel encore méconnu du monde." *Le Podcast Journal*, September 16. Available at http://www.podcastjournal.net/L-ile-d-Agonve-dans-la-commune-de-Zagnanado-Un-patrimoine-naturel-encore-meconnu-du-monde_a12511.html.
Trouillot, Duverneau. 1885. *Esquisse ethnographique: Le Vaudoun; Aperçu historique et évolutions*. Port-au-Prince: Imprimerie R. Ethéart.
Trouillot, Michel-Rolph, Mariana Past, and Benjamin Hebblethwaite. 2021. *Stirring the Pot of Haitian History* [*Ti difé boulé sou istoua Ayiti*]. Liverpool: Liverpool University Press.
US Office of Geography. 1965. *Dahomey: Official Standard Names*. Washington, DC: US Department of the Interior.
Valdman, Albert, Iskra Iskrova, Nick André, and Jacques Pierre. 2007. *Haitian Creole–English Bilingual Dictionary*. Bloomington: Creole Institute, Indiana University.
Verger, Pierre. 1957. *Notes sur le culte des Orisa et Vodun à Bahia: La baie de tous les saints au Brésil et à l'ancienne Côte des esclaves en Afrique*. Dakar: Institut Fondamental d'Afrique Noire.
Verger, Pierre. 1999. *Notas sobre o culto aos orixás e voduns na Bahia de Todos os Santos, no Brasil, e na antiga costa dos escravos, na África*. São Paulo: Editora da Universidade de São Paulo.
Vieux-Chauvet, Marie. 2009. *Love, Anger, Madness: A Haitian Trilogy*. Translated by Val Vinokur and Rose-Myriam Réjouis. New York: Modern Library.
Vilson, Georges. 2013. *Kandelab*. Vol. 1, *101 Notated Haitian Folk and Vodou Songs*. New York: Kandelab Foundation.
Vilson, Georges. 2015. *Kandelab*. Vol. 2, *102 Notated Haitian Folk and Vodou Songs*. New York: Kandelab Foundation.

Wartburg, Walther von. 1950. *Französisches Etymologisches Wörterbuch: Beiheft, Ortsnamenregister, Literaturverzeichnis, Übersichtskarte*. Tübingen, Germany: J. C. B. Mohr, 1950.

Wilcken, Lois. (1986) 2017. Liner notes, *Èzili*, La Troupe Makandal. Portland, OR: CD Baby.

Wilcken, Lois, and Frisner Augustin. 1992. *The Drums of Vodou*. Performance in World Music Series, no. 7. Tempe, AZ: White Cliffs Media Company.

INDEX

abolition, 12, 57; anti-abolitionists, 233; pamphlets of European, 63, 233

Abomey, 8, 50, 52, 57–59, 64–68, 75, 76, 78, 84, 87, 93, 95–97, 108, 109, 118, 122–24, 126, 129, 130, 133, 146, 236, 238; Gedevi settlements, 43, 54, 184, 186; plateau, 8, 50–55, 73, 187, 198; religion in, 70, 72, 74–75, 114, 118, 122

Adanloko, Adanlokovi, 126

Adjahouto, King, 52–53, 117, 243n15; as major vodun, 123–24. *See* Agasu (Aja-Fon spirit)

Adonon, 64

afagbadji (room of oracles), 113. *See also* sogbadji (Aja-Fon altar room)

Africa/Africans, 3–10, 13, 14, 17–23, 27, 30, 35–40, 43, 46–50, 54, 56, 57, 59, 60–61, 62–67, 74–76, 86, 89, 91–133, 138, 141, 149, 151, 153, 159, 165, 169, 174, 189, 198, 204, 218, 219, 230, 232–34, 236, 239; Central, 138, 241n8; coastal communities, 7, 88; East, 61; inter-African violence, 59, 237; memory and preservation, 15, 35; North, 58; pan-African, 152; South, 179, 238; theology and ceremonialism, 16

Agaja, King, 36–37, 56, 62, 65–69, 70–77, 80, 83–85, 112, 114, 118, 122, 130, 169, 171, 235, 243n15, 246n50; refugees under, 121; targeting Dutch traders, 55; *tohosu* protector of, 128

Agasou (Haitian spirit), 52, 146

Agasu (Aja-Fon spirit), 52, 84, 86, 94, 99, 108, 109, 123–24, 131. *See* Agasuvi (descendants of Agasu); Dahomey, kingdom of

Agasuvi (descendants of Agasu), 8, 52–54, 57, 78, 117, 124, 132, 146; conquered Allada, 70, 124, 126; royal cult, 60

Agbe, King, 59, 72, 116–17, 125, 237; *agbetawoyó*, 117

age, 64; initiation, 103–4; slave buyers' estimate, 63

Agwe (Haitian spirit of the sea), vii, 17, 43, 72, 117, 170–73, 237; epithets for, 167; Èzili's lover, 169; Lasirèn's husband, 169; *lwa mèt tèt*, 202; protector of fishermen, 216; Rada Rite spirit, 141, 143–45, 188. *See also* Agbe, King

ahe (beginner Vodunists), 95

Ahouandjigo (neighborhood of Hueda), 116

ahouansi (Vodun initiate), 102

Aida (Aja-Fon spirit), 51; forest of, 124. *See* Ayida Wèdo (Haitian spirit)

Aizan (Aja-Fon spirit), 59, 103, 125–26, 163; originates in Hueda, 71. *See also* Ayizan Velekete (Haitian spirit)

Aja, 3, 13, 16, 43, 46, 47, 49, 51, 52, 54, 55, 57, 58, 61, 65–67, 70, 76, 78, 89, 115–20, 124–26, 146, 159, 217, 237, 243n1; coast controlled by, 7; divination among, 80; as enslaved people, 81; in Haitian Creole, 50; kingdoms of, 39, 46, 50, 53; language, 52, 102; migration among, 115–22; referenced in song, 204; religion of, 68, 70, 79, 125–27; ruling classes, 109; spiritual lineages of, 86; Yoruba conquests of, 50–51; Yoruba region, 7, 152, 184. *See also* Allada, kingdom of; Arada; Ayizo (ethnic group and language); Hueda, Aja kingdom and town of

261

Aja-Fon (Dahomians), 5, 36, 39, 40, 44, 45, 91, 92, 94, 107–8, 131–33, 186, 187, 217, 234, 244n5, 245n16; captives, 7; founder ethnicities, 159; religious traditions of, 96, 99–107, 109; spirits of, 127

Ajoho (Dahomian administrator of religion), 75

Akaba, king of Dahomey, 36, 56, 65, 128

ako vodun (ancestors of nation), 16, 109

Akpè (village), 117

alcohol, 12, 25, 51, 82, 89, 95, 113, 152, 198; Ayizan's abhorrence of, 163; dissolved traditional alliances, 66; libations with, 97, 152; lives stolen for, 15

Aligbonon, Princess, 52, 123, 124, 146

Alisma, oungan Michelet, 32. *See also* Société Linto Roi Mystères

Allada, kingdom of, vii, 4–6, 8, 13, 21, 24, 37, 39, 40, 42, 51, 52, 54, 58–70, 75–77, 90, 108, 115–19, 120–26, 130, 137, 138, 141, 146, 163, 171, 233, 237, 238, 246n50; Aja kingdom, 50; Alladahonu, 52, 84; religion in, 43, 53, 86, 120, 133; slave trade of, 47, 56–57, 232, 235

alms songs, 103

altruism, 19, 23

ammunition, 51, 61, 76

amnesia, formal, 101, 104, 105

amulets, 21, 80, 84, 113–15, 132

ancestors, 5, 16–18, 30, 53, 58–60, 69, 86, 93, 97, 109, 123, 126, 128, 137, 172, 176, 185, 186, 191, 199, 201, 202, 204, 207, 209

Anigbézoun (temple in Porto-Novo), 117

Annual Customs (in Dahomey), 58–59, 60, 66, 75, 88, 108; epistemic violence, 233; redistribution at, 95; ritual murders at, 58–59, 96, 233, 236

Aristide, Jean-Bertrand, 179, 181

armée indigène (indigenous army), 88

ase (Aja-Fon and Haitian concept), 93, 174; vital force, 115

asen (metal altar for ancestors), 96, 119

assemblies, 12, 20, 22, 44, 99, 158

asymmetry, 6, 47, 218, 236

Ati, 241n11

atínmévódún (spirits that dwell in trees), 16

Ave-Dan (Aja-Fon spirit), 116

Ávila, Teresa of, 104

Avlékété (village), 72, 125. *See also* Ayizan Velekete (Haitian spirit)

ayi vodún (Aja-Fon spirits of the earth), 16

ayibobo (praise to the spirits), 141, 149, 150, 151, 164, 165, 167, 170

Ayida Wèdo (Haitian spirit), 92, 141, 145, 147, 165, 169, 246n42; Dan Ayida Wèdo, 70, 127, 143; Dan serpent spirit, 243n8; personal intervention of, 164; prominence of, 116; Rada spirit, 70, 141, 147; rainbow spirit, 165, 232; songs for, 162–68. *See* Aida (Aja-Fon spirit); Danbala Wèdo (Haitian spirit)

Ayida Wèdo, Dan (Haitian spirit), 43, 51, 70, 92, 114; rainbow spirit, 17, 115. *See also* Aida (Aja-Fon spirit); Dan (Aja-Fon spirit); Dan Ayida Wedo (Aja-Fon spirit); Danbala Wèdo (Haitian spirit); Dangbe (Aja-Fon spirit)

ayizan (braided palm staff), 163

Ayizan Velekete (Haitian spirit), 34, 43, 71, 92, 141, 143, 163, 246; epithets for, 145, 163; importance of, 126; possessions by Ayizan, 164; receives water, 142; royal palm leaves, 163, 243; songs for, 162–64; village of Avlékété, 125, 146; wife of Loko, 126. *See* Aizan (Aja-Fon spirit); Loko (Aja-Fon spirit)

Ayizo (ethnic group and language), 51, 100, 108, 119, 243

babaláwo (priest of Fa), consultations with, 112

badji (Haitian altar room), 16, 65, 71–74, 139; etymology of, 150. *See sogbadji* (Aja-Fon altar room); *sobagi* (Haitian altar room)

baobab (sacred tree), 126

Bawon Samdi (Haitian spirit), 136, 189–91, 193–94, 198–200, 204, 208, 215, 227; characteristics of, 189–91, 247n1; father of Gede spirits, 192; in Gede Rite, 196–97; Grann Brijit, 196; loves children, 208; multifarious functions of, 231; role in *desounen*, 195; songs for, 207–10. *See* Gede Rite

Bawon Simityè (Haitian spirit), 193, 208

Beauvoir, oungan Max, 39, 123, 142, 148, 171, 185, 242n11, 247n62

bell, 96, 122, 137, 139, 244n9. See *ogan* (Haitian Vodou cowbell)

Benin (modern state), 49, 50, 100, 103, 113, 126, 151, 157, 159, 161, 162, 163, 164, 165, 169, 243n1, 247n6. *See also* Abomey; Allada, kingdom of; Dahomey, kingdom of; Hueda, Aja kingdom and town of

bewilderment, 100, 105, 107

Bight of Benin, vii, 3, 4, 5, 13, 16, 17, 35–37, 41, 43, 46, 47, 49, 83, 88–90, 133, 138, 150, 233–37; map of, 45

bila (tent to honor spirits), 20–21, 242n14; *manman-bila*, 21

birth defects, 128

Bizoton, affaire de, 26

blood, 25, 55, 58, 97, 145, 180, 181, 209, 218, 224–25, 236; anointing with, 191; feeding spirits with, 93, 97; of humans, 97; leopard's blood, 84; meaning of imbibing, 94; pact, 23, 94, 218–19. *See* ritual murder; sacrifice (animal)

bo (amulet), 114. *See also* amulets; talisman/talismans

Bo (spirits), 94. *See* Bosou (Haitian spirits)

bokanto (Aja-Fon diviner), 5; father of amulets, 80. See *bòkò* (Haitian diviner)

bòkò (Haitian diviner), 24, 80, 112, 113, 114, 146, 191, 236, 247n64. *See* Bo (spirits); *bokanto* (Aja-Fon diviner); Fa, Ifa (vodun)

bokonon (Aja-Fon diviner), 112, 113, 114, 236

Bondye (God), 15, 92, 155, 160, 179, 258, 248n8, 249. *See also* God; Mawu (Mawou)

bosal (African-born enslaved people), 9, 10, 105, 149, 189, 245

Bosman, William, 117

Bosou (Haitian spirits), 37, 83–85, 146; dangerous, 78, 85; Rada Rite examples, 84, 143; Sèvis Ginen, 186. *See* Agaja, King; Bo (spirits)

Bosou Twa Kòn (Three Horned Bosou), 243n18

Bosouhon (*tohosu* spirit), 128

Bòsú/Bosu, 77, 83, 85, 146. *See* Bosou (Haitian spirits)

Boukman Dutty, 25, 94, 178, 187. *See also* Bwa Kayiman ceremony

Boukman Eksperyans, 187, 234

Boyer, Jean Pierre, 26

Brand, Roger, 40, 114

branding, 10, 64

Brazil, 4, 74, 78, 105, 108

Bwa Kayiman ceremony, 24–25, 94, 218–19

calabash bowl, 31, 49, 123; for Fa symbol, 112

call-and-response singing, 102, 150, 183, 209

Cana (town), 82, 117, 118, 120, 122; convent for Dangbe, 117

canon (body of sacred songs or texts), 127, 134, 152, 154, 163, 212, 230; animal sacrifice, 93; cycles of salutation, 147; expanding, 148; food offering, 98; libations as, 97

Cap-Français, 9, 11

capital (money), 12, 14, 199, 200; human, 48

Catholicism, 5, 6, 19, 103, 156; in Benin, 103, 117; European royal, 236; forced conversion to, 19; syncretism with Vodou, 22, 25, 32, 159, 185

Catholics, 7, 26–29; antagonists of Vodou, 230; chromolithographs, 160; Church, 27; churchmen, 29; extremist, 219; pro-Catholic president, 26, 149, 156, 194, 247n64

Central Africa, 13, 36, 38, 46, 49, 138, 159, 241n4

ceremonies of Vodou and Vodun, 15, 17, 18, 20, 23–25, 33, 34, 41, 44, 53, 60, 66, 72, 74, 85, 95, 96, 98, 110, 112, 114, 119, 128, 129, 140, 146, 147, 158, 159, 173, 242n23, 244n15, 245n6, 247n64; Dahomian administration of, 75, 79; as danced, 101; expense of, 35; familial, 109; Gede Rite, 184, 185, 189, 192, 193, 195, 201, 205, 225–27, 230, 231, 242, 244, 245; Hueda for ancestors, 71; possessions at, 105–6; public religion, 80, 99, 108; Rada Rite, 137, 145, 148, 150, 152, 155, 157, 162, 165, 167, 171; in Sèvis Ginen, 44 chameleon, 94, 129

chante pwen (song of criticism), 170, 178, 183, 218–20, 223, 228, 229; betrayal and unfairness, 222; confrontational style, 121; warning, 176

Christian myticism, 6, 99, 104, 230

Christianity, 3, 16, 27, 99, 156, 230, 242n20; forced conversion to, 27, 156, 242n20

Christians, 6, 104, 129, 189, 219; anti-Vodou campaign, 29; brutal side of, 236; consulting Fa, 111; Europe, 7; royalist, 232. *See* evangelical Christians

chromaticism, 102

circumcision (Aja-Fon), 103

clitoris, 213, 214, 216, 217, 219, 220, 221, 222, 228, 229

Code Noir (1685 French colonial law), 10, 19

coffee, 4, 10, 11, 12–50, 97, 234, 241n4

collaboration (in Vodou), 19, 35

colonialism, 3, 6, 7, 19, 35, 79

colony, 6–13, 20, 21, 24, 46, 57, 62, 89, 137, 138, 141, 156, 169, 198, 205, 232, 235, 236; slave colony, 6. *See* Saint-Domingue

comparative methodology, 37, 38, 40, 91, 132, 133, 197, 233, 237

compartmentalization, 231

congregations of Vodun, 30, 34, 35, 60, 70, 71, 78–80, 86, 96, 98, 109, 236; in Hueda, 71–75; leadership of, 109–10

Conseil Supérieur du Cap, 20, 21

convent, 95

cowries (currency), 51, 58, 72, 74, 75, 82, 89

Creole people, 3, 10, 13, 14, 22, 144, 196; alleged corruption of, 165; of color, 15

crisis, 104

crops, 13, 61

cross (*lakwa, kwa*), 43, 193, 194, 197, 201, 203–18, 222, 224–27, 246, 247, 251; for Bawon Samdi, 188–91, 200; Great Cross, 197; Susanne of the, 199; Trase Fouse Lakwa, 197

cross-dressing, 192. *See* Romaine-la-Prophétesse

crossroads, 113, 152, 199, 204

cycles of salutation, 15, 34, 35, 44, 106, 137, 140, 145, 155, 243n2

Dahomey, kingdom of, vii, 4–8, 35–37, 40, 43, 51–56, 58, 59, 62, 63, 65, 73, 75–80, 82, 83, 87, 89, 90, 92, 110, 114, 118, 121, 141, 169, 187, 233; Aja and Agasuvi founders, 50, 52; Benin region, vii; conquest of Hueda, 69–70; divination in, 80; female "amazon" fighters, 36; Fon-speaking, 74; food supply in, 59; imported vodun, 108; King Agaja, 66–69; *kpojito*, 79; motivations for founding, 124; relics in, 67–68; royal institutions of, 53; slave trade of, 3, 6–8, 43, 47–49, 53, 62–64, 68–69, 89, 232, 235. *See* Abomey

Dahomians, 56, 65, 74, 75, 186; army, 62, 64, 68, 73, 76, 78, 83, 87, 88, 108, 118, 120, 235; kings, 98, 110, 114; slave trade of, 54–55, 66–67. *See* Dahomey, kingdom of

Dako, King, 36, 54–56, 186, 235; strong names of, 84

Dan (Aja-Fon spirit), 21, 22, 97, 114–22, 165, 243n7, 243n8; Danwonmen Rite, 70; proliferation around Hueda, 72. *See* Dangbe (Aja-Fon spirit)

Dan ayida wedo (Aja-Fon spirit), 114, 127. *See also* Aida (Aja-Fon spirit); Ayida Wèdo (Haitian spirit)

Danbala Wèdo (Haitian spirit), vii, 22, 43, 115, 116, 136, 143, 145, 167, 169, 188, 198, 237, 243n8, 246n39; basin of, 168; initiation spirit, 22, 141; married to Ayida Wèdo, 92, 165; Master of the Water, 167; ordering in Rada Rite, 141; personal intervention of, 164; possessions by, 165; prominence of, 116; Rada spirit, 70; serpent spirit, 17; songs for, 162–68; terms used for, 165; universal features, 191. *See* Ayida Wèdo (Haitian spirit)

Dangbe (Aja-Fon spirit), 22, 69–70, 75, 94, 114–22. *See* Dan (Aja-Fon spirit)

Dangbe-klounon-toyi, 119

Dangbenon (Aja-Fon priest of Dangbe), 118

Danwonmen Rite, 36, 70, 79, 84, 130, 138, 142, 168, 186, 187, 243n9; Èzili Dantò in, 146–47

de Mézy, Lenormand, 20, 25

dead, 32, 191, 193, 199–201; channeling, 104–5; cleansing rites for, 192; communality with, 41; communicating with, 208; Day of the, 190; living and dead, 131; Lord of the, 189; national, 202; pass through to, 209; remember, 184, 231; rituals for, 195–96, 201; royal, 127, 236; souls, 200; unburying, 211; unconsecrated, 192. *See* Gede Rite

decolonization, 238; Haitian Creole for, 42, 238, 239

depersonalization, 104, 174

Dessalines, Jean-Jacques, 4, 25, 26, 88, 159, 174, 177, 178

dialectical methodology, 5, 40, 90, 133, 183. *See* Vodou hermeneutics

diet, 98, 107

divination, 16, 80, 99, 102, 113, 133; Fa for, 111–12, 128. See also *bòkò* (Haitian diviner); Fa, Ifa (vodun)

djab (Haitian antisocial spirits), 17, 100. *See* Vodou spirits (Haitian)

Djò (sacred breath of life), 143, 149, 245n2. See *Lapriyè Ginen* (liturgy before Rada Rite)

Djobolo Bosou, 84, 143, 244n2

Dogbagri, 53, 54, 117

dogwe/djògwe, 140, 151; etymology of, 245n4; Marasa Dogwe, 144, 245n4. See *ladogwesan* (community of African heritage)

Don Pèdre, 24

drapo (Haitian Vodou flags), 16, 85, 166–67, 245n6

drugs, 98; during scarification, 101

Dutch, 51, 55, 57, 61, 62

Duval-Carrié, Edouard, vii

Duvalier, François, 29; smashed tomb of, 209

Duvalier, Jean-Claude, 28, 29, 181

ecology, 13, 29, 30, 94, 129, 159, 165, 166. *See* nature

eisegesis, 219

enslaved people, vii, 3, 4, 6–9, 12–15, 35, 37, 39, 43, 46–49, 50–52, 54–56, 58, 62–63, 69, 73, 76, 77, 81–83, 86, 87, 133, 136, 156, 198, 232, 237, 241n7; African-born *bosal*, 189; baptizing as Catholic, 19; colony-born Creole, 189; Dahomian trade in, 66–67, 68–69, 80–82, 87, 236, 243n3; Dahomians sold as, 75; embarkation of, 64; enslaved in Africa, 49, 66; Europeans' demand for, 59; French traders buying, 57; infected with smallpox, 64; items traded for, 51, 65, 78; men versus women, 10; rebellion of, 24; religious prohibitions on, 19, 20; songs about traumas of, 172–73; treatment of, 10

enslavement, 7, 8, 48, 55, 59, 61, 67, 81, 233, 235, 236; of Dahomians, 75; of Gedevi-Yoruba people, 8, 132, 187; judicial, 48; zombification as, 211. *See* slavery; slave trade

epithets, 145, 174, 189, 197; as descriptors, 161, 166; as ethnonyms, 146; as mythological figures, 146; as place names, 174; transparency of, 198

ethnomusicological methodology, 38–39, 136, 233

ethnonym, 50, 68, 146, 151, 197

etymological linguistic methodology, 28, 129; comparative etymological analysis, 38

Europe/Europeans, 6, 10–12, 14, 19, 22, 27, 42, 47–49, 57, 61, 64, 70, 72, 73, 74, 86, 237; banning from Dahomey, 80; branding enslaved people, 64; buying slaves, 37; Christian, 7; intolerance of, 26; relations with Agaja, 66–67, 68, 69; slave traders, 3, 5, 8, 47–49, 54, 56, 76; slave trading with Africans, 47; terrorizing coastal communities, 51, 124; weapons trading, 51, 54, 76

evangelical Christians, 218, 219

exegesis, 38, 40

Èzili (album), 147

Èzili (Haitian spirit), 43, 73, 136, 141, 143, 144–46, 171, 243n1; as Haitian spirit, 169; navigators call upon, 216; in other rites, 246n48; as Petwo Rite tradition, 146; sleeping, 170

Èzili Dantò (Haitian spirit), 25, 146–47, 169, 199; stream near Savalou, 73

Èzili Freda (Haitian spirit), 35, 163, 168, 169; songs for, 168–70

Fa, Ifa (vodun), 80, 99, 111–13; daily offerings, 102; as personal vodun, 110. See *bokanto* (Aja-Fon diviner); *bokonon*; *bòkò* (Haitian diviner)

family, 17, 30–32, 41, 48, 55, 59, 60, 63, 71, 74, 81, 86, 93, 95, 96, 98, 101, 109, 126, 135, 142, 157, 160, 187, 191, 201, 202, 205, 207, 208, 210, 227; Agasuvi, 8, 52, 53, 70, 109, 123, 124, 146; altars of, 97, 164; chief spirit of, 174; Dangbe of the, 115–16; erosion of networks, 32; Fa of the, 112; feeding spirits of, 30; inalienable land, 30, 31; motivations for initiation, 103; paying for initiation, 95–96; possessed by deceased, 201; priest of, 96; redeeming enslaved people, 64; relics of, 67; separation from, 157, 185; of spirits, 16, 71, 73, 84, 138, 142–45, 165, 169, 174, 175, 192, 193, 195–97, 201, 208, 223, 225, 244n14; spiritual, 3, 30, 94, 160, 184
fast/fasting, 107, 151
feather/feathers, 132, 213, 219, 222, 247n1
fetish, 20, 27, 71, 84; leopard as, 132; in rural code, 28. See also *bo* (amulet); *lwa* (spirits); spirit/spirits; vodun (Aja-Fon spirits)
Fon people, 16, 18, 31, 37, 50, 54, 73, 74, 80, 84, 89, 102, 129, 131, 145, 146, 150–52, 154, 155, 157, 159, 165, 169, 171–72, 174–75, 187, 205, 234, 237, 239, 241n11, 245n4, 245n16, 247n63; citizens, vii; Gbe- language group, 62; Ouemenou Fon, 115; religion of, 79. *See* Agasuvi (descendants of Agasu); Aja-Fon; Dahomey, kingdom of; Gedevi/Gedevi-Yoruba
Fonsaramè (neighborhood of Hueda), 71, 72, 73, 116
France, 8, 11, 12, 57, 125, 238, 243n4
French people, 7, 19, 20, 61, 71, 72, 77, 103, 156, 172, 175, 185, 188, 238; alcoholism of, 89; attacking holdings of, 25; businessmen, 15; and Catholic colonialism, 6, 7; colonial army, 6, 12; colony of Saint-Domingue, 3, 9, 79, 237; enslavers, 94, 178; metropolitan citizens, 15; refugees from Samaná, 14; slave ships, 9; slave trade of, 4, 10, 49, 51, 56–57, 61–64, 81, 87, 88, 124, 232, 233; West India Company, 59

Gede (Haitian spirits), 44, 186, 189, 191–92, 194–96, 199–201, 202, 213–15, 223, 230, 231, 247n64; based on ethnonym, 197; and cemetery, 196, 198–99; concern with genitalia, 213–14, 224, 228, 229; deriding death, 205, 206; epithets for, 197–98; in Gede Rite, 196–97; as healers, 207, 208, 231; links to sexuality, 185, 192, 204; representation of, 212–13; theological function of, 184; as trickster, 186; venturing into public, 184
Gede Avadra, 200
Gede Feast (Fèt Gede), 226
Gede Masisi (Gay Gede), 192
Gede Nibo, 188, 191, 193, 194, 196–97, 204, 225, 227, 231, 247n1; songs for, 215–16, 224–27
Gede Nouvavou, 196, 203, 205
Gede Rite, 5, 13, 20, 32, 39, 43, 44–46, 50, 56, 97, 108, 132, 133, 135, 137, 183, 187, 196–98, 200–202, 210–11, 220, 231, 232, 247n1; early references to, 188–89; growth of importance, 202; and homosexuality, 217; as prominent tradition, 4; ritual formula of, 212, 214–15, 217–18, 222, 227; vulgarity in, 221, 224
Gedevi/Gedevi-Yoruba, 3, 5, 16, 36–38, 39, 40, 43, 44, 46, 47, 50–54, 57, 68, 79, 89, 91, 183, 184, 186, 198, 233, 234, 237; Dahomian enslavement of, 8, 55, 132, 133, 187, 204, 235; religion as systematic, 133. *See also* Gede (Haitian spirits); Gede Rite
gender, 37, 92, 103, 121, 192, 199; inclusivity versus exclusivity, 22, 33–35, 44; and initiation, 103
genitalia/genitals, 43, 64, 200, 213, 221; as Gede's domain, 229, 231; threat of mutilation, 214, 228
Geze, Na, 69
Ghana, 16, 49
Ginen (authentic ancestral tradition of Haitians), 17, 187, 188, 245n6; Africa in general, 157, 245n17; *Ginen*, 32, 141; Ginen order, 50; *Ginen yo*, 17, 31; Lapriyè Ginen, 17, 148, 149, 250; *lwa Ginen*, 138, 149, 186–87; *nèg Ginen*, 17, 241n9; *priyè Ginen*, 148–49; "21 Nanchon Ginen," 35, 43, 44, 75, 140. *See* Sèvis Ginen
girls, 83, 95, 103, 106, 118. *See* women
God, 17, 19, 22, 25, 92, 111–12, 116, 129, 150, 154, 155–58, 165, 170–72, 178–79, 188–89, 195,

207–8, 210, 212, 214–16, 218, 227–29; Haitian Vodou songs about, 149, 155, 170, 177, 179, 182, 203, 205, 206, 209, 214, 215, 218, 228, 229; imbued with mercy, 91; serving, 15, 18. *See also* Bondye (God); Mawu (Mawou)
god (spirit), vii, 41, 79, 85, 116, 123, 142, 178. *See* vodun (Aja-Fon spirits); *lwa* (spirits)
gold, 78, 89, 97
Gold Coast, 61, 74
Gou (Aja-Fon spirit), attributes of, 103. *See also* Ogou/Ogun (spirit)
govi (Haitian clay pot for channeling spirits), 28, 29, 31, 195
grands-blancs (wealthy whites in Saint-Domingue), 11
Guede (album), 4, 44, 134, 136, 184–231
gunpowder, 24, 51, 65, 69, 76, 77, 78, 89
guns, 29, 51, 65, 69, 76
Gwo Wòch (Haitian spirit), 215, 216

Haitian Creole, 6, 10, 20, 31, 35, 38, 80, 130, 133, 145, 146, 148–49, 150, 155, 156, 170, 171, 174, 178, 183, 198, 214, 232–34, 238, 242n27, 244n5, 245n3; documentation of, 42, 237; prejudice against, 238; songs and prayers in, 39, 41, 135, 140, 148, 185, 239
harvest ceremonies, 98
Hebrew, 159, 181
Hebyoso (Aja-Fon spirit), 92, 97, 100, 116, 123, 124–25, 243n13. *See also* Ogou/Ogun (spirit); Zo (Aja-Fon spirit)
hennou-vodun (family's founding spirit), 17, 109, 116, 124
hermaphrodite, 25, 237
hierarchy in Vodun and Vodou: among lwa, vii; in Vodun leadership, 109–10
historical methodology, 39–40
history of Saint-Domingue and Haiti, 47; historians of Haiti, 235; submerged African part, 42, 51
Hoho (spirit of twins), 94, 157. *See* Marasa (Haitian spirits)
homosexuals/homosexuality, 44, 112, 189; in Gede Rite, 217; serve Èzili, 168
Houéda-ho-mé-nou, 119–20
Houéta-nou, 102

Houffon, king of Hueda, 65, 69, 114, 119, 235
houmbônon (high priest), 96
houn (spiritual blood), 97, 110, 244n5, 245n6; Haitian *lwa* Adjehoun, 142
Hounon (priest of Hu), 72, 118, 122, 123; Daagbo Hounon Houna, 150; five scarifications of, 119; profiting from slavery, 75
hounso (carrier of the spirit), 109–10
Hu/Hou (Aja-Fon spirit), 72, 74; served in Hueda, 71. *See* Agbe, King; Agwe (Haitian spirit of the sea)
Hueda, Aja kingdom and town of, 5, 6, 8, 15, 21, 22, 24, 37, 39, 40, 42, 43, 47, 50, 51, 54, 56, 61–67, 69, 70, 71, 75, 76, 81–83, 87, 90, 96, 100, 108, 114, 117, 118, 122, 130, 133, 138, 141–42, 146, 163, 232–33, 235, 237, 243n11, 244n13; Igelefe fort, 80; refugees from, 79; religious traditions of, 53, 67, 69, 150; Vodun congregations of, 71–75, 114–21, 122–23
Huedan people, 39, 43, 53, 65, 66, 115–19; King Houffon, 68
hungán (chief of the vodun, priest) 15, 97, 247n63
hunsi/hunsì (Aja-Fon initiate spouse of the spirits), 95, 97; etymology of, 150. *See ounsi* (spouse of spirits, initiate)
Hwanjile, Nae, 78, 79, 80, 92, 129
Hwesi (Aja-Fon spirit), 71, 73, 74, 75, 120, 122, 130, 132

Jakin, kingdom of, 49, 50, 51, 67, 68, 81
Jan Simon Britis (Haitian spirit), 194, 198, 203, 204, 214, 215
Jesuits, 15. *See* Catholicism
Jupera (son of King Tegbesu), 82
Jupiter of the Cross, 226, 227
justice (in Vodou), 19

kanzo (initiation in Haitian Vodou), 31–33, 35, 73, 123, 149, 151, 154, 162; centrality of, 73, 141; oral pedagogy, 15; prestige of, 31–32, 155; in Saint-Domingue, 22; secrecy of, 242n17; ten days, 31, 244. *See ounsi kanzo* (initiate completed *kanzo* initiation)
Ketu, kingdom of, 87; army of, 88

Kikongo (language), 20, 130, 239, 247
kings (of the Bight of Benin), 6, 7, 8, 36, 37, 41, 42, 46–49, 55, 58–59, 60, 62–64, 65, 72, 77, 83–84, 85, 88, 89, 97, 98, 119, 122, 232, 233; ritual murders for, 53, 58, 59, 108, 235, 236; strong names of, 53, 84
Kongo Fran Rite, 36, 137, 142, 186
Kongo nation, 13, 48, 49, 132, 241n4
Kongo Rite, 13, 17, 24, 108, 140, 147, 161, 187, 188, 234, 239; formula of, 20–21; influences in Haitian, 4. See Petwo Rite (Petwo-Kongo Rite)
Kongo Savann Rite, 36, 142, 246n48
Konvèjans (political party), 180, 181, 182
Kossola, Oluale, 36, 64, 131, 132
Kpase, king of Saï, 121; founder of Hueda, 73, 244n12; neighborhood in Hueda, 72
Kpase-Loko (sacred silk-cotton tree), 244
Kpate, king of Hueda, 73; Houla monarch serving Zo, 123
Kpengla, King, 36, 53, 56, 58, 59, 63, 78, 86, 88, 128; reign of, 86–88; slave trading, 81
Kpétou (town), 117, 119
Kwa Bawon (large cross for Bawon Samdi), 188, 190, 199, 200

Labat, Jean-Baptiste (Catholic priest), 117–18, 244n11
ladogwesan (community of African heritage), 149, 150, 153, 154, 158, 161. See *dogwe/djògwe*; *langaj* (Haitian Vodou ritual language)
Lakou (extended family homestead in Haiti), 17, 18, 30, 31, 135, 171, 186, 187, 201, 202, 208, 210, 241; Souvenance, 34, 75, 92, 130, 171, 187, 241n5
land, 6, 48, 79, 201, 211, 232, 233; inalienable familial, 30; in *plasaj* partnership, 212; protecting ecology of, 94
langaj (Haitian Vodou ritual language), 148–49
language documentation methodology, 38
laplas (Haitian master of ceremonies), 167, 244n15, 245n6
Lapriyè Ginen (liturgy before Rada Rite), 17, 148, 149, 250

Lasirèn (Haitian spirit), 17, 141; Mermaid Priestess, 144, 146, 171; wife of Agwe, 169, 171
Lavalas (political party), 179, 180, 181, 182
Leclerc, General Charles, 88, 178
Legba (Aja-Fon spirit), 16, 71, 92, 97, 110–11, 126, 137; matched with dog, 94; as national vodun, 17; role in initiation, 96; wisdom of, 92
Legba (Haitian spirit), 34, 94, 140, 143–45, 152–54, 157, 162, 188, 191, 195, 200; building bonfire for, 85; epithets of, 145; Ginen spirit, 188; Rite spirit, 43; spirit migration of, 138
Legba Atibon (Atibon Legba) (Haitian spirit), 138, 140, 141, 152, 158
Lënsouhouè (divinized royalty), 127–28. See also tohosu (Aja-Fon spirits)
lesbians: lovers, 217; suicide and trauma, 189. See homosexuals/homosexuality
lexical fields, 38, 156, 253
libations, pouring of, 97
liberty (in Vodou), 18; spirit possession as, 19
linguistics/linguistic methodology, 37, 38, 46, 91, 133, 136, 196, 205, 233, 237, 238, 245n16; comparative, 197; documentation, 237; groups in Benin, 50; shared intelligibility, 45, 61; shifting dominance, 74; universal language, 10. See Vodou hermeneutics
Lisa (Aja-Fon spirit), 17, 73, 79, 92, 94, 100, 115, 123, 131, 250, 257; myths about, 129–30; variability, 92
literary critical methodologies, 38, 233, 237, 252
loko (African teak tree), 16, 73, 94, 126, 159. See also *pye repozwa* (spirit resting tree)
Loko (Aja-Fon spirit), 17, 34, 92, 93, 126–27, 143–45; links to Aizan, 125
Loko (Haitian spirit), 140, 158, 159–60, 188, 225, 227, 237; affection for, 164; daddy and brother, 160; healing spirit, 158; husband of Ayizan, 162, 163; and magical charms, 159; Master of the Water, 167; Rada spirit, 43, 126, 141, 163; resting tree, 160; songs for, 158–60

lwa (spirits), vii, 15, 17, 19, 23, 106, 146, 149, 156, 160, 169, 170, 171, 174, 175, 185, 186–87, 190, 208, 210, 237, 242n27, 245n4, 247n64; adaptability of, 33; altars for, 18; calling, 18, 31, 151, 245n8, 245n14; created by God, 18, 165, 248n8; elevated spirits, 191–92; failure to serve, 141; families of, 174, 225; feeding rituals for, 34, 151; *gwo lwa*, 152; healers, 197; *lwa batize*, 105; *lwa bosal*, 105; *lwa Ginen*, 138, 148; *lwa mèt tèt*, 195, 201; *lwa rasin*, 142; *oungan-lwa*, 204; protectors, 16; representing, 150; of sex workers, 223; songs about, 152, 155, 164, 166, 182, 183. *See also* vodun (Aja-Fon spirits)

magic, 21, 71, 84, 94, 113–14, 116, 130, 159, 162, 191, 193, 199–201; antisocial variety of, 209; fees for, 201; prohibitions on, 20; of spirit Olicha, 175; of twins, 130
magician/magicians, 84, 175, 186, 200–201; making zombies, 210–11; poisoner, 198
Mahi (Bight of Benin people), 16, 73, 81–82, 87, 128, 243n11; chiefdoms of, 118; service to Dangbe, 118; Sèvis Ginen, 186; spirits of, 108, 138
Makandal, François, 20
manbo (Haitian Vodou priestess), 15, 23, 26, 33, 35, 42, 141, 149, 151, 154, 160, 162–63, 195, 218, 226, 227, 236, 246n31; *ason*, 4, 15, 31, 33–34, 137, 139, 155, 163; Aunt Tansia, 50; Cécile Fatiman, 25; Èzili Freda as, 168, 169; freedom of, 44; initiators, 23, 31, 32, 242n19; Mama Lola, 142, 193, 199, 201; man Choune, 187; possessed by Gede, 191; prostrating for, 57, 244n15; refusing some spirits, 200; roles in ceremonies, 138–40, 154; -priest, 18; spirits who are, 144, 146; Téla, 188; vocalists, 135, 150, 209. *See oungan* (Haitian Vodou priest)
maps, 45, 134
Marasa (Haitian spirits), 34, 43, 126, 130–31, 140, 142, 155–56, 157–58, 167, 191, 244n17, 245n4; family of, 145; in Gede Rite, 203, 205, 214, 215, 216, 217; Marasa Twa, 158, 243n18; Rada Rite spirits, 143–44. *See* Hoho (spirit of twins)

maroon, 10; maroonage, 19, 20
Mass Konpa Records, ix, 136, 147, 202, 238, 244, 249
mawon. See maroon
Mawu (Mawou), 74, 79, 91–92, 94, 100, 111, 115, 131; couple Mawu-Lisa, 73, 79, 92, 94; diminished in Haiti, 130; extending of *ace*, 115; *jì vodún*, 17; myths about, 129–30; *tovodun*, 123. *See* Bondye (God); God; Lisa (Aja-Fon spirit)
mendicancy, ritual, 74, 107
menstruation, 111, 112, 163, 225
Middle Passage, 42, 173, 175, 181, 185, 205, 232
migration, 30, 115, 117, 118, 119, 159, 201, 205, 210, 242n24, 245, 257; Gede Rite and, 201–2, 205; legacy of, 153
mixed race, 4, 11, 55, 169
Moreau de Saint-Méry, Médéric Louis Élie, 21–24, 31, 44, 238, 242n15
multiculturalism, 8, 74; diverse religious traditions, 8, 18, 31, 91, 142, 155, 175, 239
multidisciplinary methodology, 38; diverse scholarly methods, 37
music, 32, 39, 42, 98, 106, 135–36, 147, 155, 185, 236, 237; boxes, 51; during initiation, 102–3; *rasin*, 234; sacred, 18, 183, 202
mystification, 84, 186
myth, 40–41, 116, 244n2; about Mawu, 92; of Ogou Badagri, 227; origins of life, 92, 93, 165
mythological methodology, 40–41, 198, 246n46
mythology, 31, 37, 39, 40, 99, 115, 117, 133, 157, 169, 174, 183, 219, 234, 237; of Fa, Ifa, 111; of family, 109; of Gede spirits, 186–95, 227; of major vodun, 123–31; of Rada spirits, 140–47; of royal Agasuvi, 52, 53, 77, 83, 86

National Endowment for the Humanities Collaborative Research Award, ix
naturalization, 107, 108
nature, 17, 18, 91–93, 128, 137, 152, 159, 165; spirits emanate from, 93–94
neocolonial order, 215, 217, 238

Nesuhwe (Aja-Fon royal cult of ancestors), 59, 60
normative Vodou, 199–201

ogan (Haitian Vodou cowbell), 137, 202, 203
Ogé, Vincent, 12
Ogou/Ogun (spirit), 16, 26, 27, 33, 35, 92–93, 103, 167, 174, 176, 178; Badagri, 87, 169, 188, 225, 227, 246n30; Balizay, 173–74; Chango, 73, 125, 197; cuts umbilical cord, 103, 115; Nago Rite spirit, 142, 173–74, 176; Yoruba spirit, 17. *See also* Gou (Aja-Fon spirit)
oppositional complementarity, 130–31
oracles, 78; of Fa, 112
orisha (spirit), 17. See *lwa* (spirits); vodun (Aja-Fon spirits); Vodou spirits
oungan (Haitain Vodou priest), 15, 35, 62, 80, 97, 141, 142, 147, 149, 151, 160, 161, 187, 188, 189, 200, 236, 242, 244n3, 245, 247n63, 247n64; accusations against, 218; *ason* and bell, 4, 15, 31, 33–34, 137, 139, 155, 163; Boukman Dutty, 25; channeling the dead, 32–33; Gede Nouvavou as, 204; initiators, 23, 31, 32, 242n19; magic of, 200–201; mediators of spirits, 18, 85, 164, 195; non-apostolic leader, 18, 44; possession of, 162; prostrating for, 57, 244n15; roles in ceremonies, 138–40, 154; vocalists, 135. See *bòkò* (Haitian diviner); manbo (Haitian Vodou priestess)
ounsi (spouse of spirits, initiate), 34–35, 106, 140, 150, 163–64, 167; choir of, 137, 162; initiated, 33, 244n5; meaning of, 15; possessed in ceremonies, 33, 34; ranking of ounsi, 149, 151, 245n6; songs about, 149, 151, 153, 154, 158, 161; wearing white clothing, 138. See *kanzo* (initiation in Haitian Vodou)
ounsi kanzo (initiate who completed *kanzo* initiation), 149, 151, 153, 154, 158, 161, 162
Ountò (Haitian spirit), 43, 126, 137, 139, 143, 145, 149, 244n5, 245n6
ountògi (Haitian Vodou drummer), 139, 149, 244n5, 245n6
Oyo, kingdom of, 43, 49, 50, 51, 58, 63, 65, 67, 75, 78, 80, 83, 86, 87, 89, 121, 131; slave raiders, 76. *See also* Yoruba people

pakèt (Haitian membership packets), 16, 23, 28, 242n19
palatalization, 171, 246n61
palm tree (Florida royal palm), 54, 97, 101, 102, 111–12, 163, 243n3; leaves, 123, 128, 163, 164; representing Haitians, vii; staff, 163
participant observation methodology, 39, 41, 141
penis, 214, 224; Gede and, 193; Legba's phallus, 111
people of color, free, 9, 11, 12, 14, 15. *See* mixed race
personal Vodun, 110
petits blancs (poor whites), 10
Petwo Rite (Petwo-Kongo Rite), 13, 36, 108, 140, 141, 142, 161, 242n20; distinct from "Ginen," 187; Don Pèdre, 24; Èzili Dantò, 25, 73, 146–47, 246n48; Gede Petwo, 186, 197; Petwo Fran Rite, 138, 141; Sèvis Ginen and, 108, 137, 239. *See also* Kongo Rite
plantation/plantations, vii, 9, 10–14, 21, 25, 44, 46, 233, 241n3, 241n7; coffee in mountains, 46; sugar cane on plains, 46
plasaj (common-law partnerships), 212, 213, 228
Port-au-Prince, ix, 9, 11, 20, 29, 33, 35, 44, 184, 188, 189; main cemetery of, 198, 209; Sèvis Ginen in, 13, 187
Porto-Novo, 64, 69, 83, 86, 88, 116, 117, 119, 120, 121; dominated by Agasuvi, 123
potomitan (centerpost), 15, 139, 151, 161, 185; association with Legba, 152; circumambulating, 164, 167. *See also* cycles of salutation; stations of salutation
priest (male or female) of Vodou or Vodun, 16, 32, 52, 58, 79, 82, 86, 96, 109–10, 116, 121–22, 138–40, 244n3, 245n6; gender roles of, 34–35; generating revenue for, 74, 101; in Hueda, 122–23; liberation movements and, 25; lineage of ancestor, 119; of the *tohosu*, 128; spirits who are, 92
priestess of Vodou or Vodun, 116, 131, 144; patronage of, 163. See *manbo* (Haitian Vodou priestess)
priesthood, 18, 35, 44, 79, 96, 120, 128, 133, 151, 155, 158, 247

prohibitions, 20, 131–32; imposed on Vodou, 28, 29, 156; in Vodun practice, 94, 96, 102

pye repozwa (spirit resting tree), 17, 29, 136, 159, 193, 198, 199, 227, 247n5; for Bawon Kriminèl, 209

python, 69, 70, 71, 94, 108, 114–21, 132, 164, 246n46

queen, 236; Hwanjile, 77, 79, 92, 129; as Vodou priestess, 22

racism, 8, 11, 238

Rada Rite (Haitian), 3, 4, 5, 13, 21, 36, 39, 43, 45, 46, 50, 51, 56, 66–67, 70, 73, 84, 89, 108, 116, 117, 125–27, 130–31, 132, 133, 134–83, 187–88, 205, 217, 231, 232, 233, 243n2; Agasou, 52; Arada, 242n15; prostration in, 244n15

Rada spirits, 50, 141, 145, 171, 174; classification questions, 146–47; creation myth involving, 192; epithets of, 145–46; as escorts, 149, 245n2; list of, 142–45; send mild punishments, 141–42; as sweet-tempered, 142

rainbow/rainbows, 42, 115, 119, 165, 232; Dan Ayida Wèdo's symbol, 17, 114, 115; Oloufa's symbol, 120. See also Ayida Wèdo (Haitian spirit); Dan ayida wèdo

rape, 58, 220; of Wanman Wèdo, 194

rasin (roots Vodou music), 4, 41, 136, 187, 233, 234, 237

Rasin Bwa Kayiman, ix, 4, 42, 44, 133, 135, 147, 184–231, 233, 238, 249; discography of, 249. See *Guede* (album)

Rasin Figuier, xi, 4, 42, 43, 136, 147, 234, 237, 238, 249; album cover, 135

refugees, 55, 116, 118–21, 132; French from Samaná, 14; from Gedevi communities, 132; from Hueda, 69, 79

règleman (ordering of spirits in ceremonies), 15, 141, 145, 189

revelation, 120–21

rites, 18, 32, 35, 44, 127, 175, 186, 236, 239, 242n23; annual, 102; and ethnicity, 231; of initiation, 244n7; mortuary, 20; of passage, 18, 29; priestly, 110–11; public, 60; seasonal, 126; systematic, 47; West African, 159. See Gede Rite; Rada Rite; Sèvis Ginen

ritual murder, 8, 19, 53, 59, 60, 108, 181, 233. See also blood; Dahomey, kingdom of; slave trade

ritual/rituals, 16, 18, 30, 58, 86, 98–102, 104, 122, 151, 185, 189, 201; dramatic, 103; for family members, 126; Gede Rite, 195; mortuary, 17; Rada ritual rigidity, 141; of vaporizing rum, 106

roi (king in *rara* groups), 22, 23

Romaine-la-Prophétesse, 24–26

rosary, 113

royal/royals, 5, 36, 40, 60, 89, 99, 108–10, 116, 124, 127, 129, 130, 154, 160, 172, 232–33; family of Dahomey, 60; family's ancestor cult, 60; Legba as, 152; patronizing Vodun congregations, 86; prohibitions of, 132; *tohosu*, 128; Vodun, 5, 116, 123, 146, 235, 236

sacrifice (animal), 25, 26, 70, 71, 75, 85, 86, 93, 94, 97, 100, 101, 110–13, 120, 122, 123, 126, 139, 157, 174, 187, 190, 195, 242n23; sacrificer, 60; under trees, 227. See ritual murder (humans)

Saint-Domingue, 3–5, 7–9, 10–14, 19, 21–24, 36, 47, 56, 57, 66–67, 88, 133, 159, 165, 232, 234, 237; African founders of, 3, 15; ethnic composition of, 9, 77; Kongo connections to, 132; map of, 134; violent culture of, 141; Vodouists transformation of, 6. See Catholicism; colonialism; essentialism; France; French people; racism; slavery

Sakpata (Aja-Fon spirit), 16, 73, 77, 79, 92, 93, 94, 115, 116, 125, 130, 243n12, 243n15, 244n9; initiates learn Yoruba, 100; major *tovodun*, 123; princess's initiation to, 99; protector, 97. See Hwesi (Aja-Fon spirit)

scarification in Vodun initiation, 100, 101, 104, 107, 119

secret societies, 211

Senbo, 203, 205, 206, 211, 212, 215, 216, 217, 222, 227

serpent, 17, 21–24, 53, 92, 114–21, 132, 141, 145, 154; in Haitian Vodou, 164–68; origin of veneration, 70; python veneration, 114. *See also* Ayida Wèdo (Haitian spirit); Dan (Aja-Fon spirit); Danbala Wèdo (Haitian spirit); Dangbe (Aja-Fon spirit)

servant of the spirits, 128, 168, 192, 198, 199, 210, 218, 237, 242n11, 245n6

Sèvis Ginen, 4, 13, 18, 31, 32, 35, 44, 46, 51, 75, 86, 108, 135, 137, 140, 142, 147, 155–56, 159, 183, 186–88, 192, 198, 202, 230–31, 236, 239, 246n39; ceremonies of, 34, 148, 149; gender parity in, 34–35; historical evidence of, 188–89; *kanzo* initiation, 31, 32, 73, 151, 154; rites of, 43; in Ti Rivyè, 33

sèvitè (initiate or priest in Lakou Vodou), 15, 32, 33, 34, 185, 186, 187, 242n27, 245n6

sex, 11, 12, 32, 92, 111, 189, 192, 199, 204, 213–14, 217, 225, 229, 231; diversity, 35; during menstruation, 112; and Gede Rite, 43, 183, 184, 185, 191, 217, 223; independence, 220–21; oral, 221, 224; organs, 221; proclivities of spirits, 171; in representation, 168; tickling, 222; transmitted diseases, 220; violence and predation, 194, 220; work, 32, 200, 220, 222, 223, 224, 228. *See also* homosexuals/homosexuality; lesbians

skulls, 43, 53, 67, 68, 69, 125, 132, 188, 190

slave market, 75; European, 40

slave trade, 5, 36, 42, 46, 63, 68, 69, 80, 82, 83, 88–89, 232; Dahomey's opposition to, 68; foundation of Dahomey, 51, 52; Hueda's dominance of, 65; producing demographic diversity, 74

slave traders, vii, 5, 6, 7, 8, 42, 47, 49, 51, 56, 60–61, 62–64, 68, 71, 75, 80, 83, 86, 87, 235, 242n21; Dutch, 51, 55; European slave traders, 39, 62–63, 77, 186, 204; Portuguese, 78; Robert Norris, 55, 58, 78, 83, 84; William Snelgrave, 58, 68, 69, 131

slavery, 3, 6, 7, 12, 18, 19, 20, 24, 26, 35, 37, 40, 46–51, 55, 56, 59, 63, 66, 68, 70, 76, 78, 79, 83, 85, 88, 89, 178, 186, 187, 238, 242n20; defenders of, 21, 59

smallpox, 64, 71, 73, 88, 92, 122, 130

Smith, Katherine, 192, 201

Snelgrave, William, 39, 58, 131

sobagi (Haitian altar room), 149, 150, 151. *See badji* (Haitian altar room); *sogbadji* (Aja-Fon altar room)

Société Halouba, 22, 34

Société Jenndantor des Gonaïves, 22, 33

Société Linto Roi Trois Mystères, ix, 22, 31, 32, 135, 139, 147, 159, 161, 195, 246n42; assistant priests at, 244n3; *kanzo* initiations at, 151; *pakèt inisyasyon* at, 242n19

Société Makaya, 22, 33, 34, 35, 205

Société Tipa Tipa, 22

sogbadji (Aja-Fon altar room), 113; etymology of, 150. *See badji* (Haitian altar room); *sobagi* (Haitian altar room)

Sogbadji (neighborhood of Hueda), 71, 72, 73, 74, 116, 122, 150, 244n13; shrine for Hu, 74

songs, 4, 15, 18, 20, 32, 35, 37–44, 58, 90, 95, 98, 101, 103, 106, 107, 121, 133, 134–231; collected for Vodou, 147; crystallization of centuries, 239; hermeneutics of Vodou, 189, 233–34; linguistic documentation of, 237; monotonic, 105; transitions between, 151

Souvenance (Lakou in Haiti), 34, 75, 92, 130, 171, 186, 187

spirit/spirits, 17–19, 20, 31, 33–35, 41, 46, 71, 92, 97–102, 108, 167, 231, 242n18; ancestors, 67; Bight of Benin, 91–133; categories of, 109; chosen by, 50; dangerous, 211; ecology of, 94, 129; epithets of, 198; fundamental traits of, 93–94; Gede Rite, 184–231; glass-eating, 205; hierarchy of, 79, 122; inherited, 200; and linguistic methodologies, 38; love of music, 106; migration, 138, 159; politics of, 108; and possession trance, 104–6; protector and guide, 70, 119, 207; public and familial, 97, 108; Rada Rite, 134–83; religions, 39; as sacred beings, 91–93; servants of, 168; spirit family, 71, 73, 84, 138, 145, 165, 169, 174, 175, 192, 193, 195–97, 201, 208, 223, 225, 244n14; spirit-centric, 106. *See also houn* (spiritual blood); *lwa* (spirits); Vodou spirits (Haitian); *vodun* (Aja-Fon spirits)

stations of salutation, 34, 44, 81, 139, 150, 154, 155, 163. *See* cycles of salutation

strong names, 53, 65, 84, 85, 174, 246n50
sugar, 10, 11, 12–15, 46, 241n3
superstition, 19, 20, 29
syncretism, 13, 22, 74, 108
systematic theology, 22, 44, 47, 76, 133

Tado (place in Togo), 52, 108, 116, 120, 123, 124, 126, 138, 146; fleeing from, 117, 121, 124; Huedan migration to, 115
talisman/talismans, 25, 114, 115, 125, 146
tattoos in Vodun initiation, 100–101
tax, 57, 58, 60, 63, 66, 81
Te-Agbalin, prince, 53, 55, 117, 120, 121
Temple of the Pythons, 60, 61, 69, 114–21
Titanyen, 200
tobacco, 10, 15, 61, 89
Togo, 49, 52
tohosu (Aja-Fon spirits), 93
tohwiyo (animal totem), 71, 115; python, 116
tovodun (spirits of countryside and places), 109, 123
trance, 97, 101, 217, 236; possession trance, 104–6
transatlantic studies, vii, 3–5, 8, 56, 65, 235, 239; commodities traded, 89; as empirical orientation, 38; etymological relationships, 40; features of religion, 4, 68, 70, 131, 162, 174; as historical period, 5, 51, 96, 217, 231, 234; research methodology, 91, 133, 237, 239; slave trade, 12, 46, 48, 59, 75, 89, 96; survival, 83; triangular trade, 88
transformation, 100, 107, 184, 197
Treaty of Rijswijk of 1697, 65, 243n4
trees (sacred), 18, 19, 41, 73, 92, 93, 94, 105, 117, 126, 241n11; boabab, 186; extraction of hardwood, 137; lemon, 227; Loko and, 158–59; mango, 204, 247n1; oak, 198; possessed climbing, 165. *See* palm tree (Florida royal palm); *pye repozwa* (spirit resting tree)

unconsciousness, 5, 38

vèvè (traced diagrams for Vodou spirits), 16, 23, 84, 85, 137, 167, 171, 189, 195, 204, 242; Fon etymology, 242n18

Vodou (Haitian religion), 3–7, 16, 18–24, 32; colonial traces in, 15; as community, 15; core features of, 15–16; as initiatory religion, 31; oral pedagogy of, 15, 16; pan-African syncretism in, 13; relation to power and politics, 7, 15; spirits of, vii
Vodou hermeneutics, 3, 37–42, 91, 102, 131, 133, 189, 217, 238; comparative methodology, 40, 237; dialectics of, 133; multidisciplinary, 183, 238; as theory and practice, 233
Vodou spirits (Haitian), 17, 142–45, 196–97. *See lwa* (spirits); vodun (Aja-Fon spirits)
Vodouists (Haitian), 6, 15, 16, 31, 33, 35, 37, 38, 42, 43, 50, 85, 89, 133, 148, 159, 178, 185, 204, 227, 230, 237, 238; advance spiritual family, 3; enslavers trampled, 4; live in cycles, 17; siege of, 210; subconscious of, 17; US Marines massacre, 28; values of, 19
Vodun (Aja-Fon religion), 5, 6, 18–19, 31, 35, 46, 49, 53, 74, 78–79, 89, 92–94, 95–97, 99; congregations of, 78; connections to Vodou, 3; fundamental practices, 97–98; as multipolar, 3; theology of, 16–18. *See* Vodou (Haitian religion)
vodun (Aja-Fon spirits), 5, 8, 22, 46, 84, 92, 94, 108; calling initiates, 98; categories of, 93–94; harassment of, 99; incorporating after conquest, 70; as national protector, 70; resting in nature, 93; revenge of, 97; as royal ancestors, 93; temple of, 95; Vodunist/Vodunists, 5, 6, 46, 93, 236
vodunon (Vodun priests), 5, 75, 79, 82, 86, 96, 109, 110; generating revenue, 74
vodunsi (spouse of spirit, initiate, Vodunist), 60, 102, 110

war, 4, 6, 7, 9, 18, 24, 26, 28, 49, 51, 56, 58, 63, 70, 76, 78, 94, 96, 116, 117, 120, 233, 236, 237; fratricidal, 116; King Agaja's, 66–67; King Tegbesu's, 87–89; Ogou and, 92, 103, 167, 174; refugees of, 118, 120, 121
Wawè (Gedevi and Haitian spirit), 124, 196, 198
weapons, 7, 37, 49, 61, 69, 76, 77, 87
Wegbadja, king of Dahomey, 36, 56–59, 61, 235
wives, 48, 55, 63, 64, 66, 68, 81, 83, 97, 111, 128, 250

women, 9, 11, 12, 14, 34, 35, 37, 52, 55, 58, 64–66, 78, 81, 82, 89, 92, 96, 106, 111, 132, 169, 171, 184, 199, 201, 214, 224, 241n3; capturing and selling, 10, 62, 63; Gede possessions of, 217; initiates in Ti Rivyè, 33; initiates mostly women, 103, 118, 150, 185; as priestesses, 22; songs about, 162–63; warriors in Dahomey, 36–37, 66, 76. *See* gender; girls

yanvalou (*manyanvalou*), 152, 154, 245n12; honoring Loko with, 159; songs about, 153–54, 158–60

Yoruba people, 5, 7, 8, 13, 16, 17, 21, 36, 38, 40, 43–46, 49–52, 61, 62, 65, 67, 73–75, 78, 80, 81, 91, 108, 112, 120, 121, 125, 129–31, 133, 152, 159, 174, 175, 183–84, 186, 217, 233–35, 237, 239, 247; Ogou, 17, 87; Sakpata initiates learn, 100. *See also* Gedevi/Gedevi-Yoruba; Oyo, kingdom of

Zandò Rite, 138, 142, 186, 246n48
zombie/zombies, 191, 192, 198, 211; *Jan Zonbi*, 198; songs about, 210; *zonbi*, 200–201

ABOUT THE AUTHOR

Benjamin Hebblethwaite is associate professor in the Department of Languages, Literatures, and Cultures at the University of Florida, where he teaches courses on Haiti, Jamaica, and France. His books include *Vodou Songs in Haitian Creole and English* and, with Mariana Past, *Stirring the Pot of Haitian History*, a translation of Michel-Rolph Trouillot's *Ti dife boule sou istwa Ayiti*. Born in South Africa, he lives in Gainesville, Florida, with his wife and two daughters.

Printed in Great Britain
by Amazon